The Biblical Seminar
35

TEXT &

EXPERIENCE

TEXT &
EXPERIENCE
TOWARDS A CULTURAL
EXEGESIS OF THE BIBLE

Edited by Daniel Smith-Christopher

Sheffield Academic Press

Copyright © 1995 Sheffield Academic Press

Published by
Sheffield Academic Press Ltd
Mansion House
19 Kingfield Road
Sheffield, S11 9AS
England

Typeset by Sheffield Academic Press
and
Printed on acid-free paper in Great Britain
by Cromwell Press
Melksham, Wiltshire

British Library Cataloguing in Publication Data

A catalogue record for this book is available
from the British Library

ISBN 1-85075-740-2

CONTENTS

ACKNOWLEDGMENTS

A collection like this, as other editors know, is often fraught with difficulties, delays and general administrative difficulties. In spite of all of this, and because of the patient assistance of a number of people, this book was made possible. I wish to thank the members of the administration of Loyola Marymount University, especially those who carried the vision of the Casassa Conferences, Fr Anthony Brzoska, SJ, who was Dean of Liberal Arts at the time of this gathering, and Carole Keese, the co-administrator of the conference, and my LMU colleagues who assisted with the actual running of the conference, Drs Jeffrey Siker, Elizabeth Morelli, Charles Rosenthal and Christopher Chapple.

I wish to thank Sheffield Academic Press for their patient persistence in pursuing this project, particularly Webb Mealy and Eric Christianson. I had strong encouragement in this project from two other scholars whose work in the field of cultural exegesis and cultural issues in biblical interpretation came to my attention only after this event, but who nonetheless became very interested and supportive of the results, Dr R. Sugirtharajah of Selly Oak Colleges in Birmingham, UK, and Dr Archie Lee of the Chinese University of Hong Kong.

Finally, I want to express my appreciation to all those who have patiently waited for this collection, namely the participants themselves, who put up with so many delays caused by my own difficulties in balancing various administrative and teaching responsibilities, and endured a number of unfortunate misunderstandings along the way with regard to the status of this project. Publishing the proceedings of such an important gathering a full three years after the event is regrettable and my own responsibility entirely, but I hope that your patience is now richly rewarded.

Dr Daniel L. Smith-Christopher
Los Angeles and Hong Kong, 1995

ABBREVIATIONS

ABD	Anchor Bible Dictionary
ANRW	Aufstieg und Niedergang der römischen Welt
BJS	Brown Judaic Studies
BR	*Biblical Research*
BSac	*Bibliotheca Sacra*
BZ	*Biblische Zeitschrift*
BZAW	Beihefte zur *ZAW*
CTA	A. Herdner, *Corpus des tablettes en cunéiformes alphabétiques*
EB	*Encyclopaedia Britannica*
EstBíb	*Estudios bíblicos*
FOTL	The Forms of the Old Testament Literature
HibJ	*Hibbert Journal*
HR	*History of Religions*
ICC	International Critical Commentary
IDB	G.A. Buttrick (ed.), *Interpreter's Dictionary of the Bible*
IDBSup	*IDB*, Supplementary Volume
JA	*Journal asiatique*
JBL	*Journal of Biblical Literature*
JSOT	*Journal for the Study of the Old Testament*
JSOTSup	*Journal for the Study of the Old Testament* Supplement Series
LCL	Loeb Classical Library
LTJ	*Lutheran Theological Journal*
NTD	Das Neue Testament Deutsch
NTS	*New Testament Studies*
RSV	*Revised Standard Version*
SBL	Society of Biblical Literature
SBLDS	SBL Dissertation Series
SJOT	*Scandinavian Journal of the Old Testament*
SJT	*Scottish Journal of Theology*
Str–B	[H. Strack and] P. Billerbeck, *Kommentar zum Neuen Testament aus Talmud and Midrasch*
TDNT	G. Kittel and G. Friedrich (eds.), *Theological Dictionary of the New Testament*
VT	*Vetus Testamentun*
WBC	Word Biblical Commentary
ZAW	*Zeitschrift für die alttestamentliche Wissenschaft*
ZTK	*Zeitschrift für Theologie und Kirche*

MARIE THERESE ARCHAMBAULT
  Regis University
  Denver, Colorado, USA

JOHN BARTON
  Oriel College, Oxford University
  Oxford, England

TAMARA C. ESKENAZI
  Hebrew Union College—Jewish Institute of Religion
  Los Angeles, California, USA

JOHN KAMPEN
  Payne Theological Seminary
  Wilberforce, Ohio, USA

HISAO KAYAMA
  Meiji Gakuin University
  Yokohama-shi, Japan

TEMBA L.J. MAFICO
  Interdenominational Theological Center
  Altanta, Georgia, USA

MARY MILLIGAN RSHM
  Loyola Marymount University
  Los Angeles, California, USA

ITUMELENG J. MOSALA
  National Department of Education
  South Africa

THOMAS W. OVERHOLT
  University of Wisconsin—Stevens Point
  Stevens Point, Wisconsin, USA

ANNE PATTEL-GRAY
        National Council of Churches in Australia
        Sydney, Australia

STEPHEN BRECK REID
        Austin Presbyterian Theological Seminary
        Austin, Texas, USA

PABLO RICHARD
        Dept. Ecumenico De Investigaciones
        San José, Costa Rica

FERNANDO F. SEGOVIA
        Vanderbilt University
        Nashville, Tennessee, USA

ROGER SYREN
        Institute of Exegetics
        Åbo, Finland

GEORGE E. TINKER
        Iliff School of Theology
        Denver, Colorado, USA

MATTHEW VELLANICKAL
        Pontifical Oriental Institute
        Kerala, India

SZE-KAR WAN
        Andover Newton Theological School
        Newton Center, Massachusetts, USA

HAROLD C. WASHINGTON
        Saint Paul School of Theology
        Kansas City, Missouri, USA

JOHN Y.H. YIEH
        Protestant Episcopal Theological Seminary in Virginia
        Alexandria, Virginia, USA

INTRODUCTION

Dr Daniel L. Smith-Christopher

In the report of a gathering held some years ago between native American spiritual leaders and Christian theologians, a native leader made the following comment during a discussion of Old Testament themes: 'I now understand that the Ancient Hebrews were *also* a tribal people...'[1] Hidden in that small word 'also' is a potential revolution in the modern study of the Bible. The use of a term like 'also' suggests a kinship—a kind of empathy—that allowed this native American elder to create the basis for a dialogue with the writers of the Hebrew Bible. Furthermore, it was a statement that *most* modern biblical commentators would never make, because it would not be a true description of their own self-perceived identity, as it was a true description of the self-identity of the native American elder. Finally, it was an empathy that was premised on bases that are *not* common within the academic study of the Bible. Does this mean, however, that such insights based on cultural empathies (or presumed empathies) do not have value for academic study of the Bible?

Many of us engaged in biblical studies in the last quarter of the twentieth century are aware that there is a growing (and welcome) involvement in biblical scholarship on the part of non-Europeans (or their progeny in the Americas and Australia). But we are also aware that it is only recently that some of these non-European scholars have stopped sounding like Europeans as a result of dominant European-styled educational processes, and have suggested that it may be possible to interpret texts drawing on their own unique cultural identities as points of reference for an 'African' or 'Asian' reading of the Bible. The recent collection of essays edited by my friend, Dr R. Sugitharajah

---

1. Howard Anderson, *Recalling, Reliving, and Reviewing: Creation Theology in Native and Christian Theologies* (Minneapolis: Native American Theological Association, 1980).

entitled, *Voices from the Margin: Interpreting the Bible in the Third World*[2] and also the work on Asian exegetical patterns that he is himself currently involved in, are important examples of this, although African-Americans have also already built up a significant library of works addressing these questions (one of the best and most recent examples being the collection edited by Dr Cain Hope Felder, *Stony the Road we Trod: African American Biblical Interpretation.*[3] What is the implication of this 'multiculturalism' in the approach to the study of the Bible on an academic level?

In a very important sense, the Casassa Conference of 1992, held on the campus of Loyola Marymount University in Los Angeles, California, was a gathering based on an investigation of these sorts of questions. It was a rare opportunity to issue invitations to biblical scholars from around the world to gather and consider a common question. As the director of that gathering, I hope to address (somewhat informally) some of the issues raised by this gathering, and introduce the papers that follow.

'Cultural exegesis' was a term that the conference participants accepted for this gathering. I am not aware of a previous existence of the phrase, but would not be entirely surprised if others had used it in other contexts. I certainly wouldn't want to claim exclusive rights to a term. However, lest there be any confusion on this matter, I would like to clarify in this opening essay what I mean by this phrase, and therefore, what we believed our task was when we gathered as a group of biblical scholars for discussion.

First, let us clarify what we think 'cultural exegesis' is *not*. It is not a form of using sociological or anthropological material to compare to biblical texts. Robert Wilson, for example, has contributed work on a method of sociological analysis of the Bible,[4] and has even enumerated 'guidelines' for the use of sociological and anthropological data in biblical studies. Prominent among these guidelines is the call to avoid cultural bias and the ideological formulations of the sociologists and anthropologists whose work is being cited. Wilson's impressive book, *Prophecy and Society in Ancient Israel*[5] attempts to illustrate his guidelines at

2. Maryknoll, NY: Orbis Books, 1991.
3. Minneapolis: Fortress Press, 1991.
4. *Sociological Approaches to the Old Testament* (Philadelphia: Fortress Press, 1984).
5. Philadelphia: Fortress Press, 1980.

work. Wilson compares Biblical prophets to prophet-like figures (such as shamans and witch-doctors) by drawing on ethnographic literature in an attempt to understand more about the function of the prophets in ancient Israelite society. More recently, Thomas Overholt has advanced the comparative discussion even more systematically in his work, *Channels of Prophecy*,[6] this time referring to native American prophetic figures. I would suggest that it is helpful to see the work of both Overholt and Wilson as important contributions to comparative socio-logical or anthropological exegesis (in addition to the work of John Rogerson, Norman Gottwald, and many others), but that 'cultural exegesis' is something different.

Wilson used ethnographic data on, for example, Siberian shamans in his comparative analysis of the Hebrew prophets. Cultural exegesis, however, asks another question—cultural exegetes would want to know what Siberian shamans would *themselves* say upon reading some pas-sages from Jeremiah or Amos. Would a shaman see something that Wilson (or any other European-American biblical scholar) has missed? This is an example of the sorts of questions raised by a 'cultural exege-sis'. Clearly, Wilson and Overholt's work is closely *related* to questions of cultural exegesis, but I would suggest (as I have in my dialogue with Thomas Overholt, whose important contribution to these papers is included here) that Wilson and Overholt are doing a kind of 'second hand' cultural exegesis. They are allowing ethnographic data to influence their own formulations of questions for the biblical text, but these cultural influences come from published data and not from first hand experience. I have myself found this use of ethnographic and socio-logical material extremely helpful in my own work. But how is this, then, different from what we tried to define as 'cultural exegesis'?

My own methodological struggles may perhaps be relevant at this point. In my own studies of the Babylonian exile, I also used ethno-graphic and sociological data about exiled peoples in order to be alert to sociologically significant themes in the biblical texts dealing with exile. I read about Japanese-American internees, forced removal of native Americans to reservations, African-American slavery, and other cases of conquest, uprooting and forced resettlement. At no point did I make the simplistic equation, 'this is like that', but a familiarity with social and

6. Minneapolis: Fortress Press, 1990. See also Overholt's edited collection, *Prophecy in Cross-Cultural Perspective* (SBLSBS, 17; Atlanta: Scholars Press, 1986).

historical experiences forced me to ask new questions of the biblical texts.

What began to persistently intrigue me, even after this work was completed, was the limitations of my second hand acquaintance with exile. I began to be fascinated with the possibilities inherent in sitting down with former internees in the Japanese-American camps, and reading, for example, Daniel, Ezra-Nehemiah, or Esther and then listening to what they said. In other words, in the absence of Japanese-American biblical scholars who could speak out of their own experiences of the camps, could one create such a dialogue? In the years since the Casassa Conference in 1992, I have been experimenting with this methodology by interviewing members of the Lakota tribe on chapters in the book of Daniel, and am currently working with Chinese biblical scholars and students on related questions. I recently discovered that the experiments I was engaging in were closely related to the experiments of certain reader/audience-response literary theorists who are working on reading as a social phenomenon, or more precisely, a 'sociology of literature'.

In their essays in the collection, *The Reader in the Text*, Pierre Maranda and Jacques Leenhardt make very provocative suggestions for the social experience of 'reading'. Jacques Leenhardt has actually engaged in interview experiments intended to elicit interpretive responses to two different novels among French and Hungarian populations of readers. While he was more interested in comparing views across different socio-economic levels of French and Hungarian society, his conclusions clearly support the formulation of a *cultural* exegesis:

> By establishing the reality of national patterns of literary perception, our research points to the predominant unifying cultural schemes whose efficiency is felt even in the most general attitudes of readers toward the text. These patterns are brought into play according to the place of the individual in the systems of hierarchization and the division of labour in society. It is therefore not surprising to discover the importance of particular types of schooling, both as regards the use of language (and consequently the activity of reading), and as regards familiarity with a certain literary tradition, which always comes into play in the reading process. All these factors have their place in a sociology of knowledge, and in a sociology of the transformations that the structures of knowledge undergo once they are put into practice.

Liberation Theology and Moral Imperatives in Exegesis

There are similar questions being raised by liberation theologians. Latin American liberation theologians have long talked about an 'exegesis of the poor'. What they normally mean to suggest is that the poor have a unique insight into the Bible (typically the Exodus or the Gospels are discussed) because their socio-economic circumstances are in some ways similar to the circumstances of those who drafted the Bible, or those spoken about in large sections of the Bible. Similar ideas have recently been argued by Fr Carlos Mesters in his new book, *Defenseless Flower*.[7] But Mesters, like most liberation theologians who use this phrase, actually turns out to be talking about the use of the Bible for contemporary life and faith—applied theology or *applications* of the biblical message. Mesters is not primarily interested in asking whether a biblical scholar would be forced to rethink a passage's historical meaning and context in the light of the comments of Brazilian peasants. For Mesters, it appears that accurate interpretation arises out of prior personal commitments, but there are others who place such a 'prerequisite commitment' in more Marxist terms:

> ...attempts at a non-idealist approach to the Bible do not originate in the academic world of university theology, but rather in the commitment of the leftist Christians who opt for the oppressed in the class struggles of our time and join them in the fight for liberation...[8]

But while phrases like 'the poor understand the Bible better than the rich...' (and other phrases often associated with liberation theology themes) are certainly catchy, is it true? Perhaps just as important, can we be permitted to even ask if it is true? Liberation theologians deny that present events and interpretive strategies can be separated. Boff, for example, writes about the inescapable hermeneutical circle:

> Thus, although in a first moment, a basic one, to be sure, sense or meaning is obtained under sign, word under writing, spirit under letter—now, in another moment, sense is obtained in the present, word in time, spirit in history. But all of this comes through the meaning of scripture. The hermeneutic circle is not broken.[9]

---

7. Maryknoll, NY: Orbis Books, 1989.
8. Kuno Füssel, 'The Materialist Reading of the Bible', in N. Gottwald (ed.), *The Bible and Liberation* (Maryknoll, NY: Orbis Books, 1983), p. 138.
9. Clodovis Boff, 'Hermeneutics: Constitution of Theological Pertinency', in

But does Matthew 5 (for example) actually mean something different in New York City than in Medillin? Or does it depend on whether the words are read in a Manhattan office building, or outside its doors on a steaming street-grate among the homeless? Of course, the words will be *understood* differently, but can we escape asking questions of accuracy of understanding? Thus, what we would like to know from the liberation theologians is whether the poor Brazilian peasants who read the Bible can give any insights into what the text means *for others besides themselves*, let alone whether their observations can actually guide a process of rethinking historical-critical reconstructions of past events. *That* is the question of cultural exegesis of the Bible. Can the native American elder, the Indian or African student or scholar, give all of us new ideas about what the text *historically meant*? If this question cannot be separated from contemporary application, as Boff and others would argue, we are still left with historical questions about texts such as the Bible—questions that are not thereby removed. Even the liberation theologians want to argue against some interpretations in favour of others (e.g. was a pro-slavery/pro-imperialist interpretation of the Hebrew texts *ever* correct, and for whom?)

Secondly, however, does cultural exegesis eliminate, or make impossible, the entire discussion of standards of credibility in reading texts? One of my friends in the 'guild' of biblical studies recently accused me of engaging in 'noble savage exegesis', assuming that my only criteria of acceptance of alternative readings (suggested by, for example, those that I have been interviewing) is simply a kind of political or moral sympathy with the source. The implied dilemma of criteria for evaluation is certainly an important debate, and is frequently alluded to in the papers that follow.

One of the continued controversies in many discussions of 'postmodern' readings of biblical texts is whether some versions of postmodernism come out, in the end, as a sophisticated form of relativism. Jonathan Culler seems to share such a concern when he states:

> Interpretation cannot take place unless one assumes that a reading can constitute an advance in knowledge and that there are standards of adequacy which will enable others to see why the reading one proposes is superior to others.[10]

R.S. Sugirtharajah (ed.), *Voices From the Margin* (Maryknoll, NY: Orbis Books, 1991), p. 16.
10. 'Prolegomena to a Theory of Reading', in S. Suleiman and I. Crossman (eds.),

The suggestion of any historical, literary or critical criteria for determining better or worse readings is often met with angry denunciations of 'Western imperialism' and attempts to 'control' by means of subtle use of criteria for intellectual acceptability. Indeed, it raises the spector of authoritarianism in another form; e.g. *religious* authoritarianism.[11] In his spirited attack on E.D. Hirsch's insistence on a belief in a 'correct' reading of texts, R. Crosman herds together theism, authoritarianism and the assumption about a correct reading of texts:

> The idea that Truth is One—unambiguous, self-consistent and knowable—has a long and venerable history in the West. The intellectual equivalent of aggressiveness and a wish to dominate, it has been an important part of the ideology of Hebrew, Athenian, Roman, Christian, European, and finally American and Russian imperialism. Such a successful idea cannot have been all bad, but it may have not outlived its usefullness... In order to serve the various needs and desires of various readers, texts *ought* to have plural meanings.[12]

The problem is, of course, that unless we have a basis for discussion, then there is little point to meeting and talking. In Los Angeles in 1992, critical methodologies such as form, redaction and other historical-critical tools were often accepted as a kind of 'lingua franca' that helped to assess not the question of 'acceptability', but what was new and challenging in suggested 'new' readings of texts. Thus, if it *is* possible that cultural perspectives can suggest new possibilities for *historical* meaning of biblical texts, then once such a new interpretive idea is suggested, it should hold up to critical scrutiny. There are two good reasons why this is so. First, because we are not suggesting a total abandonment of the scientific/literary critical method of biblical analysis—but merely an openness to new suggestions and hypotheses. But second, even though there may be those who would suggest that such a critical scrutiny is simply a way in, through which Western academic biases can sneak back to discredit 'indigenous' readings, critical scrutiny is nevertheless the way in which insights are 'translated' into the language familiar to the Western academic mind. It would seem a self-evidently positive goal that

The Reader in the Text: Essays on Audience and Interpretation (Princeton: Princeton University Press, 1980), p. 47.

11. I was impressed at the SBL meeting in Kansas City when Dr David Jobling quipped, 'those who are too convinced they are right, risk becoming the right...'

12. R. Crossman, 'Do Readers Make Meaning?', in Suleiman and Crossman (eds.), *The Reader in the Text*, p. 162.

dialogue should continue in the world-wide community of scholarship. It is therefore a necessary step in the process that new readings be examined critically, and not simply accepted on the basis of a moral sympathy with the source. In our attempts to be mindful of this set of problems, however, we did invite European scholars (Roger Syren and John Barton) to reflect on the possibilities of reading Scandinavian scholars (or Wellhausen) within their own cultural setting. We were quite aware, therefore, that *all* readings are cultural (contrary to some of our critics who suggested that we ignored the cultural bias of European-American scholarship).

There are other fields of study, however, that further contribute ideas to the development of 'cultural exegesis'. The psychological study of cross-cultural perception helps us to formulate some 'thought experiments' that helpfully begin to clarify some of what we mean by cultural exegesis. Studies of the differences in the perception of standard pictorial or optical illusions between children in Scotland and children in Ghana,[13] for example, have clearly revealed different 'ways of seeing' which seem based largely on experiential and cultural differences. In his survey of such studies, Deregowski notes that 'there are cross-cultural differences...in the manner in which the perceptual mechanisms operate among cultures'.[14] If there are cultural differences in perception, is it then possible for a member of a tribal society, for example, to read Old Testament texts (particularly those associated with ancient tribal practices) with fresh perspectives and insights even apart from a critical education in biblical studies? For our purposes, these studies are significant for one main purpose: they empirically prove the supposition that different cultures can have different perceptions and interpretations of the

---

13. There have been some interesting attempts to explain this phenomenon, such as the thesis that certain illusions may involve familiarity with a 'carpentered environment' and thus familiarity with certain aspects of perspective and depth perception. If one is not from a context that is daily familiar with squared corners and buildings built in 'box shapes', then the illusion may not have the same impact. See Jahoda and Stacey, 'Susceptibility to Geometrical Illusions according to Culture and Professional Training', *Perception and Psychophysics* 7 (1970), pp. 179-85; see also J.B. Deregowski, *Illusions, Patterns, and Pictures: A Cross-Cultural Perspective* (New York: Academic Press, 1980); A. James Gregor and D. Angus McPherson, 'A Study of Susceptibility to Geometric Illusion among Cultural Subgroups of Australian Aborigines', *Psychologia Africana* 11 (1965), pp. 1-13.

14. Deregowski, *Illusions*, p. 50.

same physical phenomenon. It is, of course, quite a jump from a simple optical illusion to the interpretation of texts, but it is the hypothesis of this study that it is not an impossible jump, particularly when one considers Dorothy Lee's argument:

> If that which different codes refer to is ultimately the same, a careful study and analysis of a different code and of the culture to which it belongs, should lead us to concepts which are ultimately comprehensible, when translated into our own code. *It may even, eventually, lead us to aspects of reality from which our own code excludes us.*[15]

On a philosophical level, the work of Paul Feyerabend and Thomas Kuhn questions the social, and indeed cultural, context of the scientific method itself. In his controversial work, *Against Method*, Feyerabend called for scientific inquiry that breaks old rules, and causes what Kuhn called a 'paradigm shift'.[16] Feyerabend, for example, points out that recent discussions in the history of scientific thought reveal that many of the most significant theoretical advances—for example, the Copernicus Revolution, quantum theory, the wave theory of light—occurred only because certain scientists '...decided not to be bound by certain "obvious" methodological rules, or because they unwittingly broke them'.[17] The importance of these issues of the 'sociology of knowledge' is illustrated by Cahnman and Boskoff when they point out that, 'the selection of facts for descriptive purposes always presupposes some criteria of relevance which in turn are grounded in an explanatory system'.[18] Simply the interpretation of data may not escape cultural and experiential bias. Is it possible that textual analysis can never be objective, because a reader cannot step outside his or her identity? If this is the case, then the future of biblical analysis must include the encouragement and training of as many different cultural representatives as

15. Dorothy Lee, 'Lineal and Nonlineal Codifications of Reality', *Psychosomatic Medicine* 12 (1950), pp. 89-97 (emphasis mine).

16. Paul Feyerabend, *Against Method: Outline of an Anarchistic Theory of Knowledge* (New Jersey: Atlantic Highlands, 1988); Thomas Kuhn, *The Structure of Scientific Revolutions* (Chicago: Chicago University, 1962).

17. Feyerabend, *Against Method*, p. 23.

18. W.J. Cahnman and A. Boskoff, *Sociology and History* (Chicago: Chicago University, 1964), p. 3. Further interesting discussions can be found in M. Somers and T. Skocpal, 'The Uses of Comparative History in Macro-Social Inquiry', *Comparative Studies in Society and History* 22 (1980); and V. Bonnell, 'The Uses of Theory, Concepts, and Comparison in Historical Sociology', *Comparative Studies in Society and History* 22 (1980).

possible, and the encouragement of these new students and scholars to work within the context of their cultural identity, and not outside of it in the name of a misguided 'objectivity'. Only a chorus of perspectives will prevent false unanimity and actually ensure the progress of the discipline of biblical studies.

In the somewhat puckish view of Feyerabend, it is the persistence of *alternative world-views* that provide new insights and methodologies in order to challenge our assumptions even when existing theories appear to account for much of the data before us. Feyerabend himself calls for an 'anarchist theory of knowledge' (that is, one that is not under the dictatorship of any theoretical orthodoxy). In the language of biblical studies, this is tantamount to a call for textual critics to abandon their 'objective' guidelines and take the problem of 'bias' seriously.

One way that such 'alternative world-views' can be brought to bear on biblical analysis, is the diverse cultural perspectives of biblical scholars from a variety of cultural, national and traditional backgrounds, as well as the attempt to incorporate alternative views in the work of European and American scholars. This was part of the premise of a gathering in Los Angeles in 1992.

Dilthey suggested that

> the first condition for the possibility of a science of history consists in the fact that I myself am not an historical being, that he who researches into history is the same as he who makes it... [19]

But in the postmodern era, such a view evokes a storm of protest, not the least of which deals with the impossibility of crossing historical boundaries that separate the world of the reader from the world of the author of a text. But Dilthey presumed the ability to have a dialogue with these two people. The problems with such a dialogue, interestingly, is similar to all the problems raised by a dialogue between contemporaries from different cultural and experiential backgrounds. These thorny methodological issues were addressed in 1992 by papers such as Fernando Segovia's 'The Text as Other: Towards a Hispanic American Hermeneutic', Stephen Breck Reid's 'The Role of Reading in Multicultural Exegesis'. Further methodological issues that combined case studies were explored in Harold Washington's work, '"And your

---

19. Wilhelm Dilthey (1833–1911), cited in Josef Bleicher, *Contemporary Hermeneutics: Hermeneutics as Method, Philosophy, and Critique* (London: Routledge and Kegan Paul, 1980), p. 23.

Daughters shall Prophesy?'": Gender and Culture in Early Quaker Biblical Interpretation' and Sze-Kar Wan's 'Allegorical Interpretation East and West: A Methodological Enquiry into Comparative Hermeneutics'.

It would seem that cultural bias is not only unavoidable, but can possibly also be a *positive* element in interpretation. In short, is there such a thing as a 'culturally specific' exegesis that is *more accurate* on some aspects of interpretation than other culturally specific orientations? Temba Mafico's paper, 'Were the "Judges" of Israel like African Spirit Mediums?', tries to suggest an 'African' reading of biblical phenomena that actually succeeds in helping us understand historical texts. Similar 'case studies' were offered by Dr Matthew Vellanickal from India ('A Dhvani Interpretation of the Bible: According to Indian Tradition'); Tamara Eskenazi ('Perspectives from Jewish Exegesis'); Archambault and Tinker ('A Native American Interpretation of *Basileia tou Theou*'); Dr Hisao Kayama ('The Cornelius Story in the Japanese Cultural Context'); Mary Milligan ('The Bible as Formative in a Basic Christian Community of Brazil').

Yet other papers approached the issue of cultural exegesis in ways that combined methodological discussions with examples. Among an entire program of superb papers, some will surely become classic statements; such as John Yieh's masterful collation of a century or more of Chinese approaches to the Bible ('Cultural Reading of the Bible: Some Chinese Christian Cases'), and John Kampen's study of Apocalyptic themes ('The Genre and Function of Apocalyptic Literature in the African American Experience').

Some of the papers pushed the importance of political actions and commitments in the exegesis of Scripture; such as Anne Pattel-Grey's 'Dreamtime: An Aboriginal Interpretation of the Bible', and Pablo Richard's 'Indigenous Biblical Hermeneutics: God's Revelation in Native Religions and the Bible'.

I cannot speak for others who attended the Casassa Conference on Cultural Exegesis of the Bible. I can, however, report that my own suspicions (and they were, in the beginning, only suspicions) about the importance of intentionally listening across cultures for one's own clarity of thought and analysis have become convictions.

Let me summarize by saying that previous academic discussions of 'multiculturalism' (the term most prominent in the USA) have, unfortunately, been limited to discussions dominated by the *morality* of multicultural agendas in academic studies. It is therefore suggested that it is 'good' that we be 'aware' of other cultural perspectives and that we 'affirm diversity'. As sympathetic as I might be to such perspectives, this context of morality has severely handicapped the debate by making it prey to the accusation of ulterior motives, hidden agendas or 'political correctness'. The point, however, is more critically expressed as a question of knowledge.

Multiculturalist approaches to textual interpretation, by intentionally seeking and encouraging readings that are consciously influenced by the cultural identities and experiences of the persons involved in the exegetical process, will result in improved readings. If they do not, then they operate under severe limitations as an academic exercise. In short, cultural exegesis is an attempt to practice a more accurate method of understanding texts more than it is an attempt to be 'good' according to some form of Christian or Marxist ethical ideal.

Cultural exegesis is also by definition communal and cross-disciplinary because it forces a biblical scholar to listen to (indeed, not merely to listen, but actively seek out) alternative perspectives influenced by cultural contexts of readers. The proper insistence that a scholar 'know the literature' must now include attempts to listen across cultures.

Dr Daniel L. Smith-Christopher
Los Angeles and Hong Kong, 1995

'AND YOUR DAUGHTERS SHALL PROPHESY': GENDER AND CULTURE IN EARLY QUAKER BIBLICAL INTERPRETATION

Harold C. Washington

Introduction

Around 1670 the 'ancient and eminent' Quaker Elizabeth Hooton addressed the king of England in the tone of an admonishing parent: 'How often have I come to thee in my old age, both for thy reformation and safety, for the good of thy soul, for justice and equity'.[1] What, we may ask, possessed this frail member of an illegal religious group, herself about seventy years old, of low social standing and with no claim to worldly authority, to presume to approach the sovereign with words directed toward his 'reformation and safety'? Hooton may be compared to the young Quaker, Mary Fell of Swarthmore, who in 1656 addressed to the local Anglican priest, William Lampitt, the following blistering stream of biblical invective: 'Lampitt, the plagues of god shall fall upon thee and the seven viols shall be poured upon thee, and the millstone shall fall upon thee and crush thee as dust under the Lord's feet. How can thou escape the damnation of hell?' The intrepid Mary Fell was eight years of age at the time and, no doubt, the apple of her mother's eye.

Elizabeth Hooton and Mary Fell are but two examples of hundreds of seventeenth-century female Quakers who prophesied openly in a culture which prohibited public expression by women. Early Quaker women were likewise prolific authors, engaging the religious and social debates

---

1. The anecdotes of Elizabeth Hooton and Mary Fell given here are recounted by Phyllis Mack, 'Gender and Spirituality in Early English Quakerism, 1650–1665', in E.P. Brown and S.M. Stuart (eds.), *Witnesses for Change: Quaker Women over Three Centuries* (New Brunswick: Rutgers University Press, 1989), p. 33. For additional detail on Elizabeth Hooton, including her appeals to Charles II, see A. Fraser, *The Weaker Vessel: Woman's Lot in Seventeenth-Century England* (London: Weidenfeld & Nicolson, 1984), pp. 358-65.

of the day in their writings.[2] In a society which limited religious leadership to male clergy, Quaker women participated fully in the religious life
of their community. The social activities of these early Quaker women
have been recognized as the prototypes of women's involvement in the
American anti-slavery movement, the campaigns for women's suffrage,
modern pacifist activism, and the broader women's movements of the
nineteenth and twentieth centuries.[3] Yet in the eyes of their contemporaries, these Quaker women violated the biblical requirement that
women should submit to male authority. In the debate over the religious
and social roles of women in seventeenth-century England, the Bible
was a common point of reference among all parties. Thus as early
Friends defended their dissent from the prevailing gender norms, their
arguments were necessarily exegetical.

The aim of this essay is to place this early Quaker biblical interpretation in its social-historical context and to consider its relevance to the
contemporary hermeneutical situation. First I will describe the cultural
conditions which accompanied the enfranchisement of women in the
seventeenth-century Religious Society of Friends. Then I will examine
how early Friends, resisting a culture in which the Bible sanctioned the
subordination of women, read the Bible in support of the empowerment
of women. Among clerics who tirelessly cited 1 Timothy, 'I suffer not a
woman to teach, nor to usurp authority over the man, but to be in
silence' (2.12), how did these people claim the prophetic word of Joel, 'I
will pour out my spirit upon all flesh; and your sons *and your daughters
shall prophesy*' (2.28)? I will suggest that despite the largely uneducated
background and 'pre-critical' posture of early Friends, the 'folk
exegesis' of first-generation Quakers anticipated the hermeneutical

2.   Phyllis Mack counts 253 documented Quaker women preachers and writers
from the first decade of the movement, 1650 to 1660 ('Gender and Spirituality in
Early English Quakerism', p. 58 n. 6). Cf. Hugh Barbour: 'At a period when books
by women were rare and few women intended to be known as authors, Quaker
women wrote 220 tracts of the 3853 which Friends are known to have published
before 1700. Eighty-two of the 650 early Quaker authors were women, though 48 of
them published only one tract each' ('Quaker Prophetesses and Mothers in Israel', in
J.W. Frost and J.M. Moore (eds.), *Seeking the Light: Essays in Quaker History in
Honor of Edwin B. Bronner* (Wallingford and Haverford, Pennsylvania: Pendle Hill
Publications and Friends Historical Association, 1986), p. 46.
3.   See M.M. Dunn, 'Latest Light on Women of Light', in Brown and Stuard
(eds.), *Witnesses for Change*, p. 71; and M.H. Bacon, *Mothers of Feminism: The
Story of Quaker Women in America* (San Francisco: Harper & Row, 1986).

strategies of contemporary feminist biblical critics. Early Quakers, like contemporary feminists, rejected the subordination of women; thus it is not surprising that they pursued like-minded approaches to interpretation.

The Social-Historical Context of Early Quakerism

The chaotic events of the English Civil War in the seventeenth century dominated the social-historical context of the emergence of the Quaker movement. Witnessing the ghastly destruction of the European Continent in the Thirty Years War (1618–1648), Puritan England watched with dismay as its own country descended into civil war. The Thirty Years War and the English Civil War (1642–1648) were fought among nominally religious factions, but economic and political causes were inextricably linked to the religious parties in each conflict. Social historians find that the parties in the English Civil War were aligned. according to socio-economic class. The upper-class royalists comprised a landed gentry. Puritan conservatives, a swing faction in the conflicts, constituted a middle class whose position was ultimately strengthened by the outcome of the war. Among the lower classes of English society the experience of economic exploitation inspired a range of radical parties with far-reaching social demands. These included the egalitarian Levellers, who advocated extension of the franchise to all male heads of household (rich and poor), and a group known as the Diggers, who attacked the private ownership of land.[4] From a social-historical perspective, the early Quakers may be likened to these working-class protest movements. Although the Friends drew converts from all classes (excluding the royalty), most early Quakers were either tenant farmers from the economically depressed northern district of England or urban hand workers.[5] The Society of Friends had a higher proportion of

4.   Illuminating accounts of religious radicalism and proletarian protest groups during the English Civil War period include C. Hill, *The World Turned Upside Down: Radical Ideas during the English Revolution* (New York: 1984); A.L. Morton, *World of the Ranters: Religious Radicalism in the English Revolution* (London: Lawrence & Wishart, 1970); B.S. Capp, *The Fifth Monarchy Men: A Study in Seventeenth-Century English Millenarianism* (London: Faber, 1972); and K. Thomas, *Religion and the Decline of Magic: Studies in Popular Beliefs in Sixteenth and Seventeenth-Century England* (London: Weidenfeld & Nicolson, 1971).
5.   See H. Barbour, 'The Quaker Galilee: Regional and Personal Backgrounds',

working-class leaders than other religious groups of the period.[6]

In the social turmoil of the 1640s, culminating in the execution of King Charles I in 1649 and the inauguration of Cromwell's Commonwealth, radical groups like the Levellers, Diggers and Quakers were increasingly disenfranchised. The Quakers fared even worse under the Restoration monarchy of 1660, which outlawed dissent under pain of debilitating fines, imprisonment, often eventual death. The Quaker peace testimony, denying 'all bloody principles and practices', forgoing 'all outward wars and strife and fightings with outward weapons, for any end and under any pretence whatsoever',[7] was inspired by the futile spectacle of English internecine bloodshed in the 1640s. Quakers' commitment to non-violence was then hardened by their experience of deadly persecution under the succeeding government.

Historians have often designated the earliest Quakers, like other radical Puritan groups, as a religious 'sect'.[8] The Friends, however, are better viewed as a seventeenth-century English subculture, for unlike the classic model of sectarianism, in Troeltsch's sense, which self-consciously withdraws from society, the early Quakers were fully engaged with society.[9] They nurtured an apocalyptic hope that divine purposes were being worked out in history, and like the Puritan movement as a whole, looked toward the reformation of all society. It was only later generations of Quakers who deemed themselves a 'peculiar people', removed from the world in order to preserve their unique witness. Far from being a withdrawn sect, early Quakerism should be seen as a subculture with larger designs, perhaps even a 'counter-culture', as Quaker historian Margaret Hope Bacon has suggested by comparing the first-generation Quakers to the American counter-culture movement of the 1960s.[10]

ch. 3 in *The Quakers in Puritan England* (Yale Publications in Religion, 7; New Haven: Yale University Press, 1964), pp. 72-93.

6. H. Barbour and J.W. Frost, *The Quakers* (Denominations in America, 3; New York: Greenwood Press, 1988), p. 30.

7. *The Journal of George Fox* (ed. J.L. Nickalls; Philadelphia: Religious Society of Friends, rev. edn, 1985), p. 399.

8. E.g. K.V. Thomas, 'Women and the Civil War Sects', *Past and Present* 13 (1958), p. 44.

9. Barbour, *The Quakers in Puritan England*, p. 254.

10. *The Quiet Rebels: The Story of Quakers in America* (New York: Basic Books, 1969), p. 10. Cf. C. Hill's description of the Ranter ethic preached by A. Coppe and L. Clarkson as the basis of a seventeenth-century 'counter-culture' (*The World Turned Upside Down*, p. 273).

Bacon's comparison is apt: both cultural movements emerged from periods of deep social turmoil, both witnessed the horrors of war and reacted against it, both cultivated, at least in their better moments, lifestyles of simplicity and gentleness, and both trusted that expressions of love have the power to transform a hardened and cruel society.

Original Quakerism, occupying the margins of Puritan society, developed a stubbornly egalitarian ideology. While their political goals did not go so far as those of the Levellers, and their economic ideas were not as radical as those of the Diggers, the Friends shared much in outlook with such groups. A cardinal belief of early Quakerism was that the hierarchical quality of all social relationships was a product of human sin, a consequence of the original Fall from grace. All the unnatural forms of social hierarchy were to be overcome by the faithful.[11] The social practices of Friends which so exasperated their contemporaries—the refusal, for example, deferentially to remove their hats in the presence of social superiors, even when appearing before a magistrate, a practice which senselessly enraged many a judge and harshened the penalties meted out to Quakers from the courts, or the use of the familiar thee and thou to address people of all social ranks—these were emblematic of a Friendly commitment to overcome social distinctions which subjugate one group of humanity to another.

The first-generation Quakers had an exceptional ability to include gender distinctions among the sinful social conventions which they sought to overcome.[12] Puritan social values had brought some degree of increased gender equity into the arrangement of the household. Contemporary witnesses suggest that 'on the farm or in the workshop, Puritan husbands and wives shared spinning, weaving, and tilling' to an unprecedented extent.[13] Women preachers were not unknown among other groups of the English radical reformation.[14] But only the Quakers

11. P. Mack, 'Gender and Spirituality in Early English Quakerism', p. 39.

12. The Quakers were not unique in this. On the inclination toward gender egalitarianism, for example, in the writings of the Digger agitator Gerard Winstanley, see C. Hill, 'Gerard Winstanley and Freedom', in *A Nation of Change and Novelty: Radical Politics, Religion, and Literature in Seventeenth-Century England* (London: Routledge, 1990), p. 123.

13. Barbour, 'Quaker Prophetesses and Mothers in Israel', p. 42.

14. K. Thomas notes that preaching by women was known among other English separatist groups from the 1640s on, but 'it was of course among the Quakers that the spiritual rights of women attained their apogee' ('Women and the Civil War Sects', p. 47). Cf. Barbour, 'Quaker Prophetesses and Mothers in Israel', p. 43. For

developed an express value of gender equity in participation in their religious society. The first convert and adjutant preacher of George Fox, originator of the Friends movement, was Elizabeth Hooton, whose address to the king was cited at the beginning of this essay. The first Friends to 'publish the truth' at the academic bastions of Oxford and Cambridge and the first Quaker preachers in the cities of London and Dublin were women.[15] Women were prominent among the early Quaker missionaries, usually travelling for safety's sake in pairs to such remote places as Turkey, Norway, Barbados, Bermuda, Holland and New England.[16]

Early in the development of Quakerism there emerged independent women's meetings, notably free of male control. Some collected and disbursed their own financial resources without accountability to any other body, an uncustomary prerogative for a group of women at the time.[17] As the sufferings of Quakers under the persecutions of the Conventicle Act of the 1660s grew more severe, much of the most important work of the Society of Friends, caring for the sick, elderly and imprisoned, for example, was carried out by the women's meetings. Independent women's meetings also made it possible for members to be self-sufficient in providing for concerns particular to women. Quaker historian Isabel Ross observes, 'Centuries before nursing, midwifery, social welfare and widow's pensions were thought of as national services, we find these women discussing and arranging for help of this sort among their own members'.[18]

Controversial among Friends was the provision that any proposed marriage had to be approved not only by a committee of the plenary meeting, but also by the women's meeting. This veto power over marriages gave the women's meetings an unparalleled ability to look after the concerns of their members, and it was bitterly—although

---

examples of women preachers among seventeenth-century English Baptists, Brownists, and Fifth Monarchy groups, see Fraser, *The Weaker Vessel*, pp. 244-64.

15. Thomas, 'Women and the Civil War Sects', p. 47.

16. See e.g. E.C. Huber, ' "A Woman Must not Speak": Quaker Women in the English Left Wing', in R. Ruether and E. McLaughlin (eds.), *Women of Spirit* (New York: Simon & Schuster, 1979), pp. 163-64.

17. On the women's meetings, see A. Lloyd, *Quaker Social History: 1669–1738* (London: Longmans Green, 1950), pp. 107-20; I. Ross, *Margaret Fell: Mother of Quakerism* (York: William Sessions, 1984, 2nd edn), pp. 283-302.

18. *Margaret Fell: Mother of Quakerism*, p. 291.

unsuccessfully—opposed by men separatists within the Society of Friends.[19] Many examples of seventeenth-century Quaker marriage vows survive in extant records. Typically these spare vows are symmetrical—women and men alike pledge simply 'to be loving and faithful'.[20]

Since Quakers had no clergy, ordination of women was not an issue in the Society. In plenary meetings, however, Quaker women were just as free to speak as male Friends. It was this license to speak, which Quaker women claimed both in meeting for worship and in public criticism of religious and civil authorities, that drew the constant opposition of contemporary Church leaders, who invoked Paul's admonition that women are to remain silent. Thus while the question of women's ordination was lost in the larger debate over the validity of ordination *per se*, the biblical defense of women's ministry was an important topic among early Friends. The Quakers' opponents found the Bible unequivocally negative on this question; we may now examine the perspective of the Friends. Before addressing the particular question of the roles of women, however, it is helpful to consider the general view of the authority of Scripture among Quakers.

The Early Quaker View of Scripture

If the early Friends can be viewed socially and politically as the radical left wing of the Puritan revolution, the same is true of their religious beliefs, including their understanding of Scripture. Biblically based popular religious movements like the seventeenth-century Quakers could not have arisen without the Reformation heritage of lay access to a vernacular Bible. Norman Sykes finds the epitome of 'the refusal of non-Roman Christians to accept the equation of Scripture and oral tradition required by the Council of Trent' in the formulation of William Chillingworth: 'The BIBLE, I say, the BIBLE only, is the religion of Protestants'.[21]

---

19. R.T. Vann, *The Social Development of English Quakerism: 1655–1755* (Cambridge, MA: Harvard University Press, 1969), p. 103.

20. Huber, '"A Woman Must not Speak"', p. 159; P.H. Michaelson, 'Religious Bases of Eighteenth-Century Feminism: Mary Wollstonecraft and the Quakers', *Women's Studies* 22 (1993), pp. 283-84.

21. Chillingworth's *The Religion of Protestants: A Safe Way to Salvation* (Oxford, 1638) is quoted by N. Sykes, 'The Religion of Protestants', in S.L. Greenslade (ed.), *The Cambridge History of the Bible. III. The West from the*

Chillingworth's manifesto was issued less than a decade before the emergence of the Quaker movement in England. It is in the wake of Luther's insistence that the Bible alone is authoritative alongside the principle of justification by faith alone, and Calvin's 'sure axiom—that nothing ought to be admitted in the Church as the Word of God save that which is contained, first in the Law and the Prophets, and secondly in the writings of the Apostles', that the early Quakers took pains to defend their faith and practice in biblical terms. The typical seventeenth-century Quaker tract is densely packed with biblical quotations and allusions in support of the author's Quaker views.[22]

Quaker interpretation of the Bible, however, entailed the radicalizing of another Calvinist doctrine, that of the internal testimony of the Holy Spirit. 'Scripture', as Calvin put it, 'is self-authenticated, carrying its own evidence along with it, and ought not to submit to proofs and arguments, but obtains the conviction which it merits with us by the testimony of the Spirit'. As Sykes aptly demonstrates, however, in the seventeenth century this appeal to the Spirit did not unify. The intractable hermeneutical problem of the era came to be whether the Word would be tried by the Spirit or the Spirit by the Word.[23] Early Friends settled on the former alternative.

This Quaker disavowal of the written text as final authority, however, is not a mere doctrinal idiosyncrasy; rather it is a response to the social-historical setting of early Quakerism. Seventeenth-century Quakers were acutely aware that the ecclesiastical, educational and economic establishments of the day colluded against the rights of the poor and excluded.[24] Such charges are a frequent theme in the extemporaneous invective which Quaker prophets hurled against local magistrates and priests. Most of the early Quakers had little education. George Fox had only elementary schooling. Although Fox seems to have known the

Reformation to the Present Day (Cambridge: Cambridge University Press, 1963), p. 175. In this and the following paragraph I rely on Sykes's account of the period.

22. For details of the immediacy with which early Quakers identified with the biblical text, see T.V. Palmer, Jr. 'Early Friends and the Bible: Some Observations', *Quaker Religious Thought* 26.2 (March, 1993), pp. 41-55.

23. 'The Religion of Protestants', p. 179. For the quotations from Calvin, see Sykes, 'The Religion of Protestants', pp. 176, 179.

24. On the collusion of interests among the English church, state and universities in the seventeenth century, see C. Hill, 'The Radical Critics of Oxford and Cambridge in the 1650s', in C. Hill, *Change and Continuity in Seventeenth-Century England* (London: Weidenfeld & Nicolson, 1974), pp. 127-48.

King James Bible virtually by heart,[25] the Bible is probably the only work of enduring literature which he knew closely. As Hugh Barbour points out, the northern region of England as a whole had fewer and poorer schools than any in England. Although the Bible and a few other books were likely to have been read at home, a survey of 89 wills from the region in the period of 1650–1662 shows only 12 men who owned any books. In Barbour's estimation, 'the Quaker attitude to learning and to universities was again a reaction to their own futile experience'.[26] Susan Mosher Stuard observes that 'for men, joining the Quaker sect meant being banned from Anglican Oxford and Cambridge Universities on grounds of heterodoxy. Sons born to Quaker families could not attend these universities because of their religious affiliation'.[27] Given the literacy rates among the lower classes, the question of attending university was moot for most early Quakers in any event. At the time of the English Civil Wars approximately 30 percent of English men and 10 percent of English women could sign their names.[28] Thus Quaker exegesis is chiefly a folk interpretation of the Bible, developed in self-conscious opposition to the authoritative learned exegesis of the period.[29]

Fox's first public confrontation with a preacher in a 'steeplehouse', as

25. The prison writings of Fox usually quote the King James Version verbatim even when he is known to have had access only to a Geneva Bible or a Cranmer–Coverdale translation (T.C. Jones, 'The Bible: Its Authority and Dynamic in George Fox and Contemporary Quakerism', *Quaker Religious Thought* 4 [1962], p. 21).

26. H. Barbour, *The Quakers in Puritan England* (Yale Publications in Religion, 7; New Haven: Yale University, 1964), p. 83.

27. 'Women's Witnessing: A New Departure', in Brown and Stuard (eds.), *Witnesses for Change*, p. 24 n. 22.

28. B. Reay, 'Introduction', in B. Reay (ed.), *Popular Culture in Seventeenth-Century England* (London: Croom Helm, 1985), p. 4; cf. D. Cressy, *Literacy and the Social Order: Reading and Writing in Tudor and Stuart England* (Cambridge: Cambridge University Press, 1980).

29. Early Quakers' lack of education also inclined them toward what some would deem a 'naive' or 'pre-critical' reading of the Scriptures: they read as literally as possible, taking the Bible stories as realistic narrative. Although they were contemporary to pioneers of biblical criticism like Hobbes and Spinoza, the first Quakers were, apart from a few notable exceptions such as the Oxford-educated former Baptist Samuel Fisher, innocent of the growing influence of rationalism and the declining authority of Scripture and the Church among contemporary intellectuals. On Samuel Fisher, see C. Hill, 'Samuel Fisher and the Bible', in *The World Turned Upside Down*, pp. 208-15.

he derisively referred to the established churches, occurred when the priest referred a text from 2 Peter 1 ('we have also a more sure word of prophecy'), to Scripture as the final authority by which all doctrines and religions should be judged. 'Oh, no', Fox cried out, 'it is not the Scriptures...but...the Holy Spirit, by which the holy men of God gave forth Scriptures, whereby opinions, religions, and judgements were to be tried; for it led into all Truth, and so gave the knowledge of all Truth'.[30] In this instance Fox continued speaking until he was arrested and jailed, 'so the very first Quaker imprisonment had to do with the issue of biblical authority'.[31] The view of the Bible which George Fox impulsively expressed on this occasion was later articulated more rigorously by Fox himself and by Robert Barclay, and it became one of the major breaches between Quakerism and the majority Protestant communion. Fox insisted that the Bible must be read in the power of that same Spirit which gave it forth. But as Martha P. Grundy asks, what could these words mean when other seventeenth-century Protestants used similar formulas, asserting that the reader is dependent upon the spirit of Christ to explain the Bible's meaning?[32] The early Quakers might appear inconsistent in refusing to recognize the Bible as a final authority while they adduce it assiduously as justification in their polemics against other religious groups.[33]

A key to understanding the Quaker position is their confidence that the Spirit will lead them not only into unity with the Scripture, but also into unity with each other. For the early Quakers, the individual must always rely on the check of the community, otherwise one risks the contemporary error of 'Ranterism', mistaking a private whim for the guidance of the Spirit. Friends maintained that only in the larger community could one be sure that the Spirit guided one's appropriation of Scripture.[34] Thus in subordinating the written word to the authority of the Spirit in interpretation, Quakers were recognizing the role of their community's values and larger social aims in appropriating the Scripture. What distinguished the Quakers from other groups was not

---

30. *The Journal of George Fox*, p. 40.

31. M.P. Grundy, 'How Early Friends Understood the Bible', in C. Fager (ed.), *Reclaiming a Resource: Papers from the Friends Bible Conference* (Falls Church, Virginia: Kimo Press, 1990), p. 66.

32. 'How Early Friends Understood the Bible', p. 67.

33. Cf. Jones, 'The Bible: Its Authority and Dynamic', p. 28.

34. Cf. Grundy, 'How Early Friends Understood the Bible', p. 72.

the fact that their scriptural interpretation was ideologically motivated, but that they came closer than their contemporaries to acknowledging the role of a community's interests in its biblical interpretation. Despite the assertions of any religious community about the role of its authoritative texts, interpretation always involves a dialogue between the community's contingent interests and the received tradition of the text. A group's reading of the Bible is always part of a larger text, comprehending the entire network of the community's social structure and commitments.[35] Early Friends were no different from their contemporaries in this; they were simply nearer the recognition that their biblical exegesis arose out of their praxis.

The Quakers thus realized that the normative reading of the Bible in the contemporary culture served the interests of the dominant classes of society. One way to subvert this domination was to refuse the final authority of any reading of the text. The founder of the movement acknowledged this option clearly. George Fox presented ample biblical support for the ministry of women, but in an early tract, after citing scores of passages from both Testaments he concludes, 'And if there was no Scripture for our men and women's meetings, Christ is sufficient, who restores man and woman up into the image of God, to be helps—meet in righteousness and holiness, as they were in before they fell'.[36] The Society of Friends was so compelled by the historical moment to reject the subordination of women that it would do so without biblical warrant. Now we may examine the way in which early Quakers found in the Bible extensive justification for their view.

Biblical Support for Women's Preaching and Ministry

George Fox wrote two notable treatments of the question of women's vocal ministry: *The Woman learning in Silence, or, the Mysterie of the womans Subjection to her husband, as also, the Daughter prophesying, wherein the Lord hath, and is fulfilling that he spake by the prophet*

35. For incisive illustration of these matters, see R. Carroll, *The Bible as a Problem for Christianity* (Philadelphia: Trinity International Press, 1991).

36. G. Fox, 'An Encouragement to All the Faithful Women's Meetings in the World', in *A Collection of Many Select and Christian Epistles, Letters and Testimonies*, II (Philadelphia: Marcus Gould; New York: Isaac Hopper, 1831), p. 115; cf. Thomas, 'Women in the Civil War Sects', p. 59 n. 34; and Jones, 'The Bible: Its Authority and Dynamic', p. 22.

Joel, I will pour out my Spirit unto all Flesh (1656); and *Concerning Sons and Daughters, and Prophetesses speaking and Prophesying in the Law and the Gospel* (1661); along with other tracts and epistles, especially 'An Encouragement to All the Faithful Women's Meetings in the World'.[37] In these writings Fox takes three steps which exemplify the early Quaker approach to the question. First, he emphasizes that the good creation recounted in Genesis, before the appearance of sin, entails no sexual hierarchy. Eve, created as Adam's 'helpmeet', is his equal. Thus Adam and Eve become the model for Quaker men and women, prophesying and 'labouring together in the gospel' with equal authority.

Secondly, Fox qualifies, and thereby discounts, the Pauline strictures against women's speaking in worship. He argues that Paul addresses in each case a specific group of women in a particular church. These women, Fox maintains, are not yet reborn in Christ, so not yet restored to the level of helpmeet as in Genesis 1. Paul's restrictions therefore do not apply to Quaker women who prophesy in the spirit of Christ. Thus, although Fox has no access to the techniques of modern historical criticism, he attempts to relativize Paul's injunctions by demonstrating the contingent nature of the historical circumstances they address.

Thirdly, Fox inventories female characters in the Old and New Testaments and at every opportunity affirms the agency of biblical women, taking them as models for women's activity in the Church. By virtue of their sheer volume these catalogues of female role models are persuasive, although Fox's effort to read the texts affirmatively is often a stretch. In the controversy over the women's meetings, for example, Fox adduces the passage in Judges which recounts how 'the daughters of Israel went yearly to lament the daughter of Jeptha' (Judg. 11.40). This, he argues, is proof that 'they had a yearly meeting upon this occasion'.[38]

Among the first generation of Quakers the greatest achievement in the promotion of women's interests through biblical interpretation belongs to the work of Margaret Fell published in 1666: *Women's Speaking Justified, Proved, and Allowed of by the Scriptures, All such as speak by the Spirit and Power of the Lord Jesus. And how WOMEN*

---

37. See especially G. Fox, *The Works of George Fox*, I (Philadelphia: Marcus Gould; New York: Isaac Hopper, 1831), pp. 104-10; and *A Collection of Many Select and Christian Epistles, Letters and Testimonies*, II (Philadelphia: Marcus Gould; New York: Isaac Hopper, 1831), pp. 92-116.

38. Fox, *Epistles*, p. 377; quoted by Lloyd, *Quaker Social History*, p. 108.

*were the first that preached the Tidings of the Resurrection of Jesus,
and were sent by Christ's Own Command, before he ascended to the
Father, John 20.17.*[39] Before looking in more detail at this treatise, an
account of the author will be of value. Margaret Fell, 'Mother of
Quakerism', was the important co-worker and eventually the spouse of
George Fox, although extensive travels and repeated imprisonments prevented the two from living together most of the time. Fox, moreover,
declined to pursue his legal entitlement to Margaret Fell's extensive pro-
perties. Margaret Fell's estate, Swarthmore Hall, became the center of
Quaker activity in the north of England. Fell was imprisoned twice; her
landmark treatise *Women's Speaking Justified*, the first book written by
a woman on this topic since the Reformation, was one of four books she
wrote during her first period of incarceration (1665–1668) in Lancaster
Castle in a room open year-round to the snow, wind and rain.[40]

In *Women's Speaking Justified*, Fell pursues vigorously the direction
set in George Fox's writings. She introduces the treatise as follows:

> Whereas it hath been an objection in the minds of many, and several times
> by the clergy or ministers and others, against womens speaking in the
> Church. And so consequently [it] may be taken that they are condemned
> for meddling in the things of God; the ground of which objection is taken
> from the Apostle's words which he writ in his first epistle to the
> Corinthians, chap. 14. vers. 34, 35 ['Let your women keep silence in the
> churches...']. And also what he writ to Timothy in the first epistle, chap.
> 2. vers. 11, 12 ['Let the woman learn in silence...'] (p. 4).

Fell thus begins by facing squarely the problematic passages of Paul, but
before treating them she will return, like Fox, to the point of creation:

> But how far they wrong the Apostle's intentions in these Scriptures we
> shall show clearly when we come to them in their course and order. But
> first let me lay down how God himself hath manifested his will and mind
> concerning women, and unto women (p. 4).

Fell begins by citing Gen. 1.27:

> God created man in his own image, in the image of God created he them,
> male and female; and God blessed them.

---

39. Quotations from Fell's work are from the edition of Christine Trevett,
*Womens Speaking Justified and other Seventeenth-Century Quaker Writings about
Women* (London: Quaker Home Service, 1989), pp. 4-17.
40. Ross, *Margaret Fell: Mother of Quakerism*, pp. 191-201; cf. Fraser, *The
Weaker Vessel*, pp. 369-76.

Like George Fox, Margaret Fell insists that no sexual hierarchy is ordained by this text. She bases her view on the text's specification that the divine image in humanity includes both male and female:

> Here God joins them together in his own image and makes no such distinctions and differences as men do; for though they be weak, he is strong... And God hath put no such difference between the male and female as men would make (pp. 4-5).

Through the ages most interpreters have found in the Genesis creation account sanction for the subordination of women. The early Friends, however, are an important example of dissent from this interpretative tradition. They anticipate the exegetical strategies of contemporary feminist critics such as Phyllis Trible. In her book *God and the Rhetoric of Sexuality*, Trible emphasizes the same feature of the text as George Fox and Margaret Fell: humanity is created in the divine image as *male and female*. Trible goes on in a careful rhetorical analysis to maintain that the completeness of the divine image as male and female is reflected in feminine aspects of the conception of God in the Hebrew Bible, and that woman, far from being an afterthought in the order of creation, is the crowning achievement.[41]

'It is true', Margaret Fell continues, 'the serpent that was more subtle than any other beast of the field came unto the woman with his temptations', whereupon she recounts the sad story of Genesis 3 (p. 5). Beginning with the author of 2 Timothy, interpreters have used the story to blame Eve: 'and Adam was not deceived, but the woman was deceived and became a transgressor' (2 Tim. 2.14). The Quakers, however, have a different emphasis. Fox and his followers stress that the outcome of the story in the subordination of woman to man (Gen. 3.16), must be recognized as a curse. As such, the sentence upon woman reflects not the divine will for humanity but the broken goodness of God's creation. Friends look toward the healing of this fracture in the new creation through Christ.[42] This seventeenth-century reading also anticipates contemporary feminist critics such as Trible in *God and the Rhetoric of Sexuality*, where the sentence of Gen. 3.16 is viewed not as a divine sanction for the oppression of women, but as a lamentable curse that calls for remedy.

41. P. Trible, *God and the Rhetoric of Sexuality* (Overtures to Biblical Theology; Philadelphia: Fortress Press, 1978).

42. Cf. T.C. Jones, 'The Bible: Its Authority and Dynamic in George Fox and Contemporary Quakerism', *Quaker Religious Thought* 4 (1962), p. 24.

Quaker exegesis converts the curse of Gen. 3.14-19 into a promise of redemption through an explicitly Christological reading, concentrating on the sentence pronounced upon the serpent:

> And I will put enmity between thee and the woman, and between thy seed and her seed, it shall bruise thy head and thou shall bruise his heel (Gen. 3.15).

Overlooking the declaration to the serpent that 'thou shall bruise his heel', early Friends, like most Puritan readers, celebrate the promise that the seed of the woman, which is Christ, will tread down all evil, symbolized by the serpent. This metaphor of the seed becomes definitive for Quaker religious discourse, and it is held to be of great consequence that since the beginning of the world the promise of redemption had been located in the 'Seed of Woman'.

Margaret Fell follows this Christological interpretation, reveling in the fact that it is the seed of woman, as Christ, who will ultimately defeat the evil of the serpent. But she also astutely converts the curse upon the serpent into an argument for her side of the conflict over women's vocal ministry:

> See what the Lord saith after he had pronounced sentence on the serpent: 'I will put enmity between thee and woman, thy seed and her seed. It shall bruise thy head and thou shalt bruise his heel'. Let this word of the Lord which was from the beginning stop the mouths of all that oppose womens speaking in the power of the Lord. For he hath put enmity between the woman and the serpent; and if the seed of the woman speak not, the seed of the serpent speaks; for God hath put enmity between the two seeds. And it is manifest that those that speak against the woman and her seed's speaking speak out of the enmity of the old serpent's seed (p. 5).

To the critical exegete Fell's application of the text may seem strained, but rhetorically her argument is effective: she places the dispute over women's ministry back into the context of the primeval marring of creation, aligning the opponents of women with the serpent. Thus, although she has no recourse to contemporary critical techniques, Fell directs her own 'hermeneutic of suspicion' toward the dominant reading of the text.[43] Those who denounce women, Fell argues, 'speak out of

---

43. For a contemporary feminist formulation of the hermeneutic of suspicion, see E. Schüssler Fiorenza, 'Women-Church: The Hermeneutical Center of Feminist Biblical Interpretation', in *Bread Not Stone: The Challenge of Feminist Biblical Interpretation* (Boston: Beacon Press, 1984), pp. 15-18.

the enmity of the serpent's seed'. Who could argue further? Of course, Fell does argue further, but it will take some time to get to Paul.

Next Fell addresses the theme of the Church represented as a woman:

> Moreover the Lord is pleased when he mentions his Church to call her by the name of woman by his prophets, saying, 'I have called thee as a woman forsaken and grieved in spirit, and as a wife of youth' [Jer. 54.6]... And David, when he was speaking of Christ and his Church, he saith 'The king's daughter is all glorious within...' [Ps. 45.15] And also King Solomon in his Song, where he speaks of Christ and his Church...he saith, 'If thou knowest not, O thou fairest among women, go thy way by the footsteps of the flock' [Song 1.8]. And John, when he saw the wonder that was in heaven, he saw 'A woman clothed with the sun, and the moon under her feet and upon her head a crown of twelve stars' (pp. 5-6).

Today it is common to assert that the representation of Christ and the Church in the figure of the husband and his bride inscribes an oppressive hierarchy, placing 'God' over 'man' as 'man' is over 'woman'.[44] Fell's strategy is different, but nonetheless subversive: she simply claims an affirmation of the feminine in the identification of the Church with woman. Since the Church *is* a woman, she argues, it is illegitimate to suppress women *in* the Church. After presenting a series of biblical citations illustrating feminine characterizations of the Church, Fell concludes,

> Thus much may prove that the Church of Christ is a woman. And those that speak against the woman's speaking, speak against the Church of Christ and the seed of the woman, which seed is Christ (p. 6).

Fell turns next to the example of Jesus, showing from the gospel accounts how carefully Jesus attended to women. She recounts the story of the woman at the well in John 4 to whom Jesus intimated that he was the Christ. It was to Martha, she observes, that Jesus pronounced 'I am the Resurrection and the Life'. She tells the story of the woman who broke the precious jar of ointment to anoint Jesus, how this would be recounted wherever the Gospel is told, 'in memory of her'. She describes the women who followed Jesus from Galilee and who watched as he was crucified; women who were healed by Jesus and who ministered to him, Mary Magdalene, Joanna the wife of Chuza, Herod's steward's wife, and others; and the women who came to anoint Jesus'

---

44. E.g. R.R. Ruether, *Sexism and God-Talk: Toward a Feminist Theology* (Boston: Beacon Press, 1983), pp. 139-152.

body and discovered him risen, Magdalene, Mary the mother of James, and Salome. 'Thus we see', Fell concludes, 'that Jesus owned the love and grace that appeared in women and did not despise it' (pp. 6-7).

Next Fell takes up the example of women teachers in the New Testament. It was women who brought back word of the Resurrection from the empty tomb. She observes,

> Mark this, you that despise and oppose the message of the Lord God that he sends by women; what had become of the redemption of the whole body of man-kind if they had not believed the message that the Lord Jesus sent by these women, of and concerning his resurrection? (p. 8).

Next she cites Acts 18, where Aquila and Priscilla instruct Apollos:

> Yet we do not read that he despised what Priscilla said, because she was a woman—as many now do (p. 8).

Given the contributions of feminist biblical interpreters in recent decades, such a recital of important women in the gospels is a familiar litany. It must be recalled, however, that the dominant tradition of biblical interpretation has resolutely overlooked the significance of these figures. Margaret Fell's review of women in the gospels seems familiar today only because exegetes like Elisabeth Schüssler Fiorenza have taken seriously the role of women in the gospel narratives and have suggested that this must indicate something of the role of women in the early Christian community.[45] Schüssler Fiorenza and others have balanced Paul's strictures against women with his greetings in Romans 16 to all women of prominence and his co-workers in the early Church, Phoebe (a deacon), Prisca, Mary, Junia, Persis, Julia. Margaret Fell works in a similar fashion—for her time it is a remarkable innovation.

With all the foregoing in view, Fell returns to Paul's strictures against women: 'And now to the Apostle's words, which is the ground of the great objection against women's speaking' (p. 8). Fell's approach, like that of George Fox, is to attempt to qualify the applicability of these texts by discerning the particular situations they address:

45. E. Schüssler Fiorenza, *In Memory of Her: A Feminist Theological Reconstruction of Christian Origins* (New York: Crossroad, 1989). Even in the title of her work Margaret Fell exhibits an affinity with Schüssler Fiorenza, recognizing the important role of female characters: 'And how WOMEN were the first that preached the Tidings of the Resurrection of Jesus, and were sent by Christ's Own Command, before he ascended to the Father'.

> And first 1 Corinthians 14. Let the reader seriously read that chapter, and
> see the end and drift of the Apostle in speaking these words (p. 9).

Paul, she argues, is teaching Christian charity and spiritual maturity. God,
he would have us understand, is the author not of confusion but of peace:

> And then he saith, 'Let you women keep silence in the Church' etc.
> Where it doth plainly appear that women, *as well as others* were in con-
> fusion.

If a man speaks unintelligibly, in the absence of an interpreter he is
commanded to be silent (1 Cor. 14.27-28). Fell comments:

> Here the *man* is commanded to keep silence as well as the woman, when
> they are in confusion and out of order.

1 Cor. 14.35 stipulates that the women should remain silent 'as saith the
Law'. Fell responds: 'Here the Apostle clearly mentions his intent; for
he speaks of women that were under the Law', that is, not yet living in
Christian grace. Of course, Fell allows, such women should remain silent
and not speak publicly, as should men who are unredeemed. 'And what
is all this to women's speaking that have the everlasting gospel to
preach?' (p. 9). Nothing, of course, is Fell's answer. Fell deftly invokes
Joel 2.28-32 and Acts 2.16-18 ('and your daughters shall prophesy') and
asks how the Apostle could have meant to stop that which the Spirit of
the Lord had poured upon the people. She maintains that 1 Cor. 11, the
tortured passage about veils and women's speaking, does not forbid
women prophesying but rather stipulates the conditions under which it is
seemly for them to do so.

Finally Fell addresses 1 Timothy 2. Here she suggests that Paul is
simply invoking the conventions of his day for appropriate relations
between wife and husband, accepting the norm that the woman should
defer to her spouse. She continues,

> But let it be strained to the utmost, as the opposers of women's speaking
> would have it: that is that they should not preach or speak in the Church,
> *of which there is nothing here* (p. 10).

Fell later implies that if Paul in 1 Timothy 2 is addressing women in
relation to their husbands, then he cannot be forbidding all women to
speak. There were many widows among the early Christians, and other
women with no husbands. Philip had four daughters who were prophets.
If all women were to be prevented from speaking, Fell suggests, then
Paul would have contradicted himself (p. 16).

The appearance of Fell's treatise naturally provoked great consternation. In 1667, while still in prison, Fell published a second edition with a postscript to answer her critics in the official Church. Here she ridicules the churchmen for taking the words of women into their Book of Common Prayer, while proscribing the words of women in their own day. Miriam and Hannah, she observes, prophesied in the time of the Law. She cites the prophetess Huldah in 1 Kings 22 and says,

> Now let us see if any of you blind priests can speak after this manner, and let us see if it be not a better sermon than any of you can make, who are against women's speaking (p. 14).

Fell quotes Elizabeth speaking to Mary, 'Blessed art thou amongst women, blessed is the fruit of thy womb', and Mary, 'my soul doth magnify the Lord', and continues,

> Are you not here beholden to the woman for her sermon, to use her words to put into your Common Prayer? And yet you forbid women's speaking (p. 14).

Fell quotes the 'sermons' of Ruth, Hannah, the queen of Sheba and Judith. Read the prayer of Judith, she says, and see how the

> elders of Israel did not forbid her speaking, as you blind priests do. Yet you will make a trade of women's words to get money by, and take texts, and preach sermons upon women's words, and still cry out, 'Women must not speak. Women must be silent'. So you are far from the minds of the elders of Israel, who praised God for a woman's speaking (p. 16).

Conclusion

At the 1992 Casassa Conference on 'Text and Experience: Toward a Cultural Exegesis of the Bible', where this paper was first presented, there was lively discussion of the problem of validity in interpretation. This remains a compelling question, but in my view the contemporary hermeneutical discussion has made abundantly clear that interpretative communities need not consider validity, or 'accurate' appropriation of the text, as their ultimate aim.[46] It is appropriate to strive rather for adequacy in interpretation. This must of course entail scrupulous

46. See the discussion of S. Fish, *Is There a Text in This Class? The Authority of Interpretive Communities* (Cambridge, MA: Harvard University Press, 1980), pp. 303-71.

attention to the text, but also and just as indispensably, adequacy to the situation of the interpreting community.

Biblical interpretation is currently undergoing a paradigm shift as profound as that which attended the nineteenth-century triumph of historical-critical methods and the consequential relativizing of the authority of traditional readings. Compared to the earlier hegemony of conventional historical criticism, the present methodological landscape looks anarchic, but I suspect that this is a salutary anarchy. The recognition that vested interests are always at work in interpretation now undermines the authority of every method which heretofore had pretended to objectivity. Thus is it incumbent upon interpretative communities (scholarly and popular, religious and secular) not just to apply their hermeneutical procedures faithfully, but also to examine the interests, implicit and explicit, that motivate their readings.[47]

It is no surprise that seventeenth-century Quakers and twentieth-century feminists are drawn to the same texts and propose similar solutions in the face of the disenfranchisement of women in the Church and society. Despite the distance in time between these interpretative communities, given common interests, the biblical tradition yields itself to similar approaches. In subcultural contexts which are 'Friendly' to women, it becomes possible to recover biblical resources for resisting the oppression of women. Thus prototypes for the readings of contemporary feminist critics appear in a seventeenth-century Quaker like Margaret Fell.

Readings of the Bible will always be conducted amidst the competition of contending ideologies and cultural perspectives, but if reading would have a redemptive function for confessional communities, then interpretations that reinforce social relations of domination and exploitation must be deemed inadequate. I think it is clear that Margaret Fell's reading of the Bible is both adequate to the text and to her historical moment, and that her example can instruct the hermeneutical discussion today.[48]

47. Cf. E. Schüssler Fiorenza, 'The Ethics of Biblical Interpretation: Decentering Biblical Scholarship', *JBL* 107 (1988), pp. 3-17.

48. For help and inspiration in writing this essay I would like to thank my research assistants Pamela Hadsall and Katharine Simmons, and the Quakers of Oread Monthly Meeting of the Religious Society of Friends, Lawrence, Kansas. For a summer research grant which supported its completion I am grateful to the E. Lilly Endowment.

THE GENRE AND FUNCTION OF APOCALYPTIC LITERATURE IN THE AFRICAN AMERICAN EXPERIENCE

John Kampen

In 1932 Paul Laubenstein published in the *Journal of Biblical Literature* an enthusiastic article entitled 'An Apocalyptic Reincarnation' in which he advanced the claim:

> One of the most striking religious and literary parallels in all history is that between this Jewish-Christian apocalyptic... and the Aframerican apocalyptic psalmody, born some two thousand years later in a land undreamed of by the early Jewish-Christian authors.[1]

After an extensive evaluation of the similarities between the two forms of expression as well as an accounting for some of the departures of the latter from the former, he concludes, 'The Aframerican apocalyptic psalmody is no mere imitation or borrowing of the real thing. The Negro slave actually gave to the world a new and distinctive body of apocalyptic literature'.[2] Thus was established for the scholarly world what the Black preacher already knew—that one could find important aspects of the African American reality described in the biblical accounts concerning the figure of Daniel.

While there are of course other figures such as Moses and Joshua who also were utilized regularly by these African American interpreters I focus on Daniel as a way of bringing some control to my study of this early African American literature. Within the biblical material, of course, Daniel is associated more clearly with apocalyptic literature, hence his importance for this investigation. While figures such as Moses and Joshua often are used in a manner similar to Daniel in the data investigated herein, this is not true in the biblical literature. Were I, of course, to include from antiquity other apocalyptic materials from that

---

1. P.F. Laubenstein, 'An Apocalyptic Reincarnation', *JBL* 51 (1932), pp. 238-52, 238.
2. Laubenstein, 'Apocalyptic', p. 252.

amorphous literature known as the Pseudepigrapha, Moses and Joshua
would be associated much more closely with apocalyptic literature.
There is no evidence, however, to suggest that those early African
American slaves had any access to these other compositions. Accepting
the importance of apocalyptic imagery and of the figure of Daniel for
African American religion is merely a beginning point in our study,
however, since there is a scholarly consensus neither on the description
of the nature of Black religion nor on the definition and nature of
apocalyptic literature. In this paper I will first of all describe the nature
and use of apocalyptic literature in the ante-bellum period of the Black
experience in America. I then will summarize the recent discussion
concerning the definition of the genre of literature known as
apocalypses. Finally I will evaluate those definitions from the standpoint
of its manifestations in the African American experience.

African American Use of Apocalyptic Literature

In one of the classic studies of black thinking about God Benjamin Mays
highlighted the compensatory view of God, giving examples such as the
use of the story about Daniel in the lion's den and the Hebrew children
in the fiery furnace, which was

> to show that God in due time would take things in hand. Almost invari-
> ably after assuring them that God would fix things up, he [i.e. the
> preacher] ended his sermon by assuring them further that God would
> reward them in Heaven for their patience and longsuffering on earth...
> Being socially proscribed, economically impotent, and politically brow-
> beaten, they sang, prayed, and shouted their troubles away. This idea of
> God had telling effects upon the Negroes in my home community. It kept
> them submissive, humble, and obedient.[3]

He goes on to assert that this was the nature of the majority of the
spirituals. Franklin Frazier dismissed the attempts 'to invest most of the
Spirituals with a revolutionary meaning or to claim that they represented
disguised plans for escape from slavery. It is our position that the sacred
folk songs or Spirituals were essentially religious in sentient and...
otherworldly in outlook'.[4] In Mays's elaboration of the compensatory

---

3. B.E. Mays, *The Negro's God: As Reflected in His Literature* (Boston:
Chapman & Grimes, 1938), p. 26.
4. E.F. Frazier, *The Negro Church in America* (New York: Schocken Books,
1964), p. 12.

worldview he relies in part on the work of the Harlem Renaisance writer and interpreter of the African American experience, James Weldon Johnson. Johnson provides one of the most moving descriptions available of the use of the spirituals, as viewed from this other-worldly perspective:

> At the psychic moment there was at hand the precise religion for the conditions in which he [the African-American slave] found himself thrust. Far from his native land and customs, despised by those among whom he lived, experiencing the pang of the separation of loved ones on the auction block, knowing the hard task master, feeling the lash, the Negro seized Christianity, the religion of compensations in the life to come for the ills suffered in the present existence, the religion which implied the hope that in the next world there would be a reversal of conditions, of rich man and poor man, of proud and meek, of master and slave. The result was a body of songs voicing all the cardinal virtues of Christianity—patience—forbearance—love—faith and hope—through a necessarily modified form of primitive African music. The Negro took complete refuge in Chistianity, and the Spirituals were literally forged of sorrow in the heat of religious fervor. They exhibited, moreover, a reversion to the simple principles of primitive, communal Christianity.[5]

What we find here represented is an attempt to capture the genius of the spirituals beginning with the presupposition that a future other-worldly orientation was the essence of an apocalyptic worldview.[6]

Mays did suggest that some of these songs, admittedly a limited number, such as 'Go down, Moses' and 'Oh, Freedom', were not of this other-worldly character.[7] He maintained that there was present in black literature a constructive development of the idea of God which supported the need of the society for social adjustment.[8] It is this latter element which was developed by some African American leaders in the Reconstruction era and has now been advanced by the black liberation theologians.

---

5.   J.W. Johnson and J.R. Johnson, *The Book of American Negro Spirituals*; repr. in *The Books of American Negro Spirituals* (New York: De Capo Press, 1977 [1925]), p. 20.

6.   Note the critique of J. Lovell, Jr, 'The Social Implications of the Negro Spiritual', *Journal of Negro Education* October (1939), pp. 634-43; repr. in, B. Katz (ed.), *The Social Implications of Early Negro Music in the United States* (New York: Arno, 1969), pp. 127-137, see pp. 132-33.

7.   Mays, *Negro's God*, pp. 28-30.

8.   Mays, *Negro's God*, p. 15.

When James Cone speaks of the use of the Bible by African Americans, the so-called compensatory element retreats into the background:

> The hermeneutical principle for an exegesis of the Scriptures is the revelation of God in Christ as the Liberator of the oppressed from social oppression and to political struggle, wherein the poor recognize that their fight against poverty and injustice is not only consistent with the gospel but is the gospel of Jesus Christ.[9]

Evidence for this tradition within the history of African American religion is found in some notable leaders such as Sojourner Truth, Harriet Tubman and Henry MacNeal Turner, as well as more controversial figures such as Nat Turner, Denmark Vesey and David Walker (collected and analyzed in the detailed work by Gayraud Wilmore, *Black Religion and Black Radicalism*).[10] This observation compels a further examination of the apocalyptic phenomenon in the experience of the African American slave. What is immediately apparent to researchers of the music which has its origin in 'The Invisible Institution', the slave meeting,[11] is that the future orientation of the spirituals need not be other-worldly.[12]

In collections of these songs, one quickly sees that the tale about Daniel in the lions' den is one of the stories that captured the interest and the imagination of the slave.[13] Some of these songs were analyzed by Miles Mark Fisher, a researcher who argued that a number of spirituals such as 'Deep River' are a reference to the desire of slaves to return to Africa:

9. J.H. Cone, *God of the Oppressed* (Minneapolis: Seabury/Winston, 1975), p. 81. While elsewhere in his work we do find an attempt to provide a more comprehensive view (e.g. pp. 13-14 and 32-33) this quote captures the essence of his work with regard to the appropriation and use of the Scriptures.

10. G.S. Wilmore, *Black Religion and Black Radicalism: An Examination of the Black Experience in Religion* (Garden City, NY: Doubleday, 1973).

11. M.M. Fisher, *Negro Slave Songs in the United States* (Secaucus: Citadel 1978 [1953]), pp. 66-87; A.J. Raboteau, *Slave Religion: The Invisible Institution in the Antebellum South* (New York: Oxford University Press, 1978), pp. x-xi, concerning the term.

12. Note the article by John Lovell, Jr, 'The Social Implications of the Negro Spiritual', pp. 127-37.

13. Daniel 6.

Deep River, my home is over Jordan, Deep River,
Lord, I want to cross over into camp ground;
Lord, I want to cross over into camp ground.[14]

In the early 1800s some slaves, because of the work of the American Colonization Society, did return to found the state of Liberia. Fisher locates the setting for the song 'O my Lord delivered Daniel' in the context of the difficulty the slaves encountered securing manumissions for expatriation.[15] He goes on to assert that blacks on the Port Royal Islands were understood to sing that Daniel locked the lion's jaw, the implication being that they could wait until the end of the Civil War to go home to Africa. This element of time also appears in a spiritual encompassing Daniel in the collection of the jubilee Singers from Fisk University:

Go, chain the lion down,
Go, chain the lion down,
Go, chain the lion down,
Before the heav'n doors close.
Do you see that grand old sister,
Come a wagging up the hill so slow,
She wants to get to heav'n in due time,
Before the heav'n doors close.[16]

Subsequent verses include the good old Christians and the good old preachers. The lion has to be held in check until the time at last arrives. Elsewhere Daniel while waiting seems to replace Samsom:

Wai', poor Daniel
He lean on de Lord's side; (Say) Daniel rock de lion j'oy,
    Lean on de Lord's side.[17]

Waiting for the opportune time is a theme which runs through a good number of these songs. Waiting for the opportune time is not seen in many of these songs as waiting for the release from this world that comes through death. This is evidence of waiting for God to do some kind of activity in human history. We are reminded, of course, of the periodization of apocalyptic literature, the number of days which make up the three and one-half years in Daniel 12, the ten weeks of Enoch 93

14. Fisher, *Slave Songs*, pp. 41-65.
15. Fisher, *Slave Songs*, p. 52.
16. B.T. Marsh, *The Story of the Jubilee Singers: With Their Songs* (New York: S.W. Green's Son, rev. edn, 1883), p. 174.
17. Fisher, *Slave Songs*, p. 52.

and 91, or the dream vision of Enoch 85–90 concerning the history of the world which results in the sheep being avenged and restored in a new house in which they assemble as the Lord of the sheep rejoices. How long will it be until the deliverance of the Lord comes?

In order to penetrate the ideology of some of these spirituals concerning Daniel we need to examine in detail a song already mentioned as it is found in the collection of the Jubilee singers:

> Didn't my Lord deliver Daniel,
> D'liver Daniel, d'liver Daniel,
> Didn't my Lord deliver Daniel,
> And why not every man?[18]

Some of the verses following that chorus include the following lines:

> He delivered Daniel from the lion's den,
> Jonah from the belly of the whale,
> And the Hebrew Children from the fiery furnace, And why not every man?

> The moon run down in a purple stream,
> The sun forbear to shine,
> And every star disappear,
> King Jesus shall be mine.

> The wind blows East,
> and the wind blows West,
> It blows like the judgment day,
> And every soul that never did pray, 'll be glad to pray that day.

> I set my foot on the Gospel ship,
> And the ship it began to sail,
> It landed me over on Canaan's shore,
> And I'll never come back any more.

Unpacking the imagery of this song, we find that at its root it raises the issue of theodicy. In the refrain slaves ask the question: Why does the Lord not deliver us victimized and brutalized slaves in this desperate situation in the same way that he delivered Daniel from the lion's den? In the first verse we already find part of the answer to that question; the Bible includes stories that the Lord delivered others besides Daniel such as Jonah in the whale and the three Hebrew children, Shadrach, Meshach and Abednego, thereby reminding the singers of a history of God's liberating activity. God delivered these others as well as Daniel. If

---

18. Marsh, *Jubilee Singers*, pp. 134-35.

that is true, can God not deliver others as well? Remembering that, the slaves would go on to a second response to the same issue of theodicy. There will be a day in the future so spectacular that nature will be overturned, the sun and the moon will not behave in the manner we expect. Winds will be blowing from every direction on that great and terrible day—judgment day. It is this fantastic language which is usually seen as the basis of this view labelled by Mays as compensatory and by other researchers as other-worldly. That is not the only interpretation for this imagery that is available. In fact, we find the same imagery used in a different manner in the same period by African Americans.

Evidence for this tradition within the history of African American religion in the ante-bellum period can be found with regard to some notable leaders such as Nat Turner, Denmark Vesey and David Walker. A glance at the viewpoints of some of these leaders will take us one step further in our examination of the use of apocalypticism.

Denmark Vesey, the leader of the famous slave insurrection in South Carolina in 1822, had purchased his freedom from a slave trader, Joseph Vesey, in 1800.[19] Through his own efforts Denmark became a cultured, educated leader among the blacks in that state. His education made him an important personage among the emerging independent black churches of the era, receiving a good deal of support in the years leading up to the revolt from the black Methodists of the area. In 1816 they had been organized as the African Methodist Episcopal Church following the walk-out of Richard Allen and his companions from St. George Methodist Episcopal Church of Philadelphia in 1787. Morris Brown, a leading AME minister in the area and later a bishop in the church, was a secret counselor to Vesey and his group.[20] Even Bishop Daniel Alexander Payne makes clear the support of the A.M.E. church for the Vesey plot.[21] Betrayed by a household servant, Vesey had between three and nine thousand blacks ready to move in the Charleston area. What is of interest for our purposes here is his use of the biblical texts, Zechariah 14 and Josh. 6.20-21.[22] In the latter passage we read about the fall of the walls of Jericho. What we forget about that text is the second verse: 'Then they devoted to destruction by the edge of the sword all in the

19. See Wilmore, *Black Religion*, pp. 79-87.
20. Wilmore, *Black Religion*, p. 83.
21. D.A. Payne, *History of the African Methodist Episcopal Church* (Nashville: A.M.E. Book Concern, 1891), pp. 45, 50.
22. Fisher, *Slave Songs*, p. 68; Wilmore, *Black Religion*, pp. 80-81.

city, both men and women, young and old, oxen, sheep, and donkeys' (NRSV). Vesey's interpretive context for that verse is made clear from the Zechariah passage, which emphasizes the day of the Lord:

> See, a day is coming for the Lord, when the plunder taxed from you will be divided in your midst. For I will gather all the nations against Jerusalem to battle, and the city shall be taken and the houses looted and the women raped; half the city shall go into exile, but the rest of the people shall not be cut off from the city. Then the Lord will go forth and fight against those nations as when he fights on a day of battle. On that day his feet shall stand on the Mount of Olives, which lies before Jerusalem on the east; and the Mount of Olives shall be split in two from east, to west by a very wide valley; so that one half of the Mount shall withdraw northward, and the other half southward.[23]

The destruction mentioned in Joshua is to take place on *that day*, which in apocalyptic imagery designates the day of the Lord. The latter portion of the book of Zechariah is one of the sections of the Hebrew Scriptures which is distinguished by its similarity to the more fully developed apocalyptic literature of Daniel and postbiblical Judaism. These chapters 'stem from visionaries whose dreams were increasingly frustrated by realities'.[24] Denmark Vesey's use of biblical literature is rooted in apocalyptic imagery.

The best known of the black leaders who fomented insurrection is Nat Turner.[25] In this case we have the first person account of Turner himself concerning the development and execution of this 1831 revolt, which involved approximately, seventy slaves and resulted in the deaths of some fifty-five whites.[26] We do of course have to remember while dealing with this text that it recorded by a white lawyer. For our purposes, we are again interested in the biblical texts which motivated

---

23. Zech. 14.14 (NRSV).

24. P.D. Hanson, 'Zechariah, Book of', *IDBSup*, p. 983. Note also his articles on 'Apocalypse, Genre', pp. 27-28 and 'Apocalypticism', pp. 28-34. Hanson's thesis concerning the historical development of apocalyptic literature is contested by J.J. Collins, *The Apocalyptic Imagination: An Introduction to the Jewish Matrix of Christianity* (New York: Crossroad, 1987), pp. 19-20.

25. Wilmore, *Black Religion*, pp. 87-100.

26. 'The Confessions of Nat Turner, the Leader of the Late Insurrection in Southampton, VA; As Fully and Voluntarily Made to Thomas R. Gray... Baltimore, 1831', in T.R. Frazier (ed.), *Afro-American History: Primary Sources* (New York: Harcourt, Brace & World, 1970), pp. 64-75; see p. 64.

Turner, a bright and gifted child who learned to read at a young age.[27] The text which Nat Turner emphasizes in his confession is Lk. 12.31 he, following the King James Version, reads, 'Seek ye the kingdom of Heaven and all things shall be added unto you'.[28] In his discussion of Turner, Wilmore rightly points to the wider context of this passage.[29] Towards the end of a chapter which points to the element of waiting and preparedness, we read what the followers of Jesus are waiting for:

> I came (KJV—have come) to bring fire on the earth, and how I wish it were already kindled! I have a baptism with which to be baptized, and what stress I am under until it is completed! Do you think that I have come to bring peace to the earth? No, I tell you, but rather division! From now on five in one household will be divided, three against two and two against three...[30]

Turner claims it is the spirit of the prophets who revealed this to him.[31] Following this we find Turner's statement that has occasioned lively debate, explaining the reason for his return to the plantation after he had run away, as his father had before him:

> But the reason of my return was, that the Spirit appeared to me and said I had my wishes directed to the things of this world, and not to the kingdom of Heaven, and that I should return to the service of my earthly master—'For he who knoweth his Master's will, and doeth it not, shall be beaten with many stripes, and thus have I chastened you'.[32]

Wilmore again correctly points out the context of Luke 12, arguing that Turner is citing the conclusion of the parable of the faithful and wise steward waiting for the Lord's coming. While probably playing on the dual meaning of the word 'master' in the situation of slavery, Turner is indicating that he returned to the plantation at the word of the master Jesus Christ in order to wait for the day of the Lord.[33] This was much more important than any personal freedom he may have relished.

Upon his return Nat now has visions of white spirits and black spirits engaged in battle, where 'the blood rolled in streams'.[34] The spirit now

27. Frazier, *Afro-American History*, p. 65.
28. Frazier, *Afro-American History*, p. 66.
29. Wilmore, *Black Religion*, p. 91.
30. Lk. 12.49-52.
31. Wilmore, *Black Religion*, p. 66.
32. Frazier, *Afro-American History*, p. 66.
33. Wilmore, *Black Religion*, pp. 92-94.
34. Frazier, *Afro-American History*, pp. 66-68.

reveals to him 'the knowledge of the elements, the revolution of the planets, the operation of tides, and changes of the seasons'. While Lk. 12.54 makes a reference to clouds and wind, we see here the kind of apocalyptic speculation which finds development in works such as Enoch.[35] Following this he works harder than ever to obtain 'true holiness' and begins to receive 'true knowledge' with the result that 'I was made perfect'. Then we read of lights in the sky whose names the 'children of darkness' distort. This apocalyptic imagery demonstrates the setting in which he interpreted Luke 12 and points to the similarities between his appropriation of the biblical materials to that of Denmark Vesey.[36] A third figure also warrants our attention.

In 1829 David Walker published what was probably the most powerful anti-slavery document written, an 'Appeal to the Colored Citizens of the World'.[37] He must have published hundreds, perhaps a few thousand copies, of the three editions of this text which was distributed quite broadly, including throughout the south.[38] The theological issue of theodicy again lies at the centre of this work.[39] The first and major issue, far beyond the scope of this essay, is to maintain the premise that God is just in spite of the presence of such unremitting evil within God's creation. Important for our subject is the subsequent query; If God is just, can and will God permit the savagery and dehumanization known as slavery to continue? Walker's answer to this question comes in language informed by apocalyptic conceptions. Speaking about those who derive economic benefit from the utilization of slave labor, which he dubbed 'avaricious usurpers', Walker declared that they

> forget that God rules in the armies of heaven and among the inhabitants of the earth, having his ears continually open to the cries, tears and groans of his oppressed people; and being a just and holy Being will at one day

35. Note Enoch 72–82 and elsewhere.

36. For other examples of this phenomenon see Raboteau, *Slave Religion*, pp. 124, 312.

37. For a recent edition of the text see: H. Aptheker, *'One Continual Cry': David Walker's Appeal to the Colored citizens of the World (1829–1830); Its Setting and Its Meaning. Together with the Full Text of the Third—and Last—Edition of the Appeal* (New York: Humanities Press, 1965).

38. Aptheker, *Continual Cry*, pp. 45-53.

39. J.C. Diamond, 'David Walker's "Appeal": A Theological Interpretation', *Journal of the International Theological Center* 3, 1 (Fall, 1975), pp. 32-39.

appear fully in behalf of the oppressed, and arrest the progress of the avaricious oppressors.[40]

A God who rules the armies in heaven as well as on earth is the God of Daniel and is portrayed in some of the works from the Dead Sea scrolls collection. Further in this document Walker again relates,

> Know this, my dear sirs, that although you treat us and our children now, as you do your domestic beast—yet the final result of all future events are known but to God Almighty alone, who rules in the armies of heaven and among the inhabitants of the earth, and who dethrones one earthly king and sits [*sic*] up another, as it seemeth good in his holy sight. We may attribute these vicissitudes to what we please, but the God of armies and of justice rules in heaven and in earth, and the whole American people shall see and know it yet, to their satisfaction.[41]

It is with regard to Nebuchadnezzar in the book of Daniel that we learn about the power of the Most High to set up and depose kings,[42] thereby laying the literary groundwork for the kingship and dominion to be given to the people of the most high for an everlasting kingdom later in the work.[43]

Other relevant themes in Walker's work would include the absurdity of the calls for peace by the oppressors in this situation,[44] reminiscent of Mt. 10.34, 'I have not come to bring peace but a sword'.[45] This call should be interpreted in an apocalyptic context, as well as Walker's insistence on the inevitability of a total destruction, only to be averted by a highly unlikely repentance on the part of the white population.[46] These examples are sufficient to point out a few of the ways in which antebellum African Americans used apocalyptic literature and imagery to form a basis for their religious worldview. Of greatest importance for the subject of this lecture is the apparent fact that the imagery used in some

40. Aptheker, *Continual Cry*, pp. 65-66.

41. Aptheker, *Continual Cry*, p. 102.

42. Dan. 7.27.

43. Dan. 4.17, 32; 5.21.

44. Aptheker, *Continual Cry*, p. 67.

45. We are reminded of the spiritual, 'Singin' wid a sword in mahan', found in J.W. Johnson and J.R. Johnson, *The Book of American Spirituals*, pp. 86-87. See also: J.M. Spencer, *Protest and Praise: Sacred Music of Black Religion* (Minneapolis: Fortress, 1990), pp. 6-7.

46. Aptheker, *Continual Cry*, pp. 65-66, 108.

of the spirituals often labelled compensatory is remarkably similar to that
cited by Denmark Vesey, Nat Turner and David Walker.[47]

Defining the Genre

The vast difference in the interpretations of the same phenomenon (that
is, African American religion) is one example of the problem which
apocalyptic literature has posed for scholars of religion in the twentieth
century as they have attempted to define it as well as to assess its role
and function within religious communities. It seems to me, for example,
that the problem concerning the nature of the God behind the spirituals
discussed by Mays and Frazier noted above is not that different from the
perceptions of apocalyptic literature which lay behind the issues concerning the historical Jesus articulated by Johannes Weiss at the end of the
last century and Albert Schweitzer a short time later.[48] Apocalyptic
imagery and literature was assumed to be lacking any connection with
real historical experience. This assumption pervaded all attempts to study
the literature. In the wake of the discoveries in the Judean Desert in
1947 a new interest in apocalyptic literature again has forced us to deal
with the question of comprehension, and hence definition, of this strange
body of literature. The problem has received in recent years considerable
attention in the field of Biblical Studies.

There has not been any agreement, to put it mildly, among biblical
scholars in this century concerning the nature of apocalyptic literature,
its definition and form. Most of the disagreements have focused on
issues of definition of terms, description of the relevant literary genre, as
well as the relationship of the pertinent literature to social function and
identity. I will abbreviate some of this discussion because major aspects
of it have been adequately rehearsed in recent literature.[49] A watershed

47. This is also noted by C.H. Marybury, 'The Ethos of Transcendence: Crisis
and Hope in Black Spirituals', *A Journal of Theology* 4 (1978), pp. 39-57; see p. 55.
    48. J. Weiss and D.L. Holland (eds.), *Jesus' Proclamation of the Kingdom of
God* (trans. R. Hiers; Philadelphia: Fortress, 1971 [1892]); A. Schweitzer, *The
Quest of the Historical Jesus: A Critical Study of its Progress from Reimarus to
Wrede* (trans. A.W. Montgomery; New York: Macmillan, 1961 [1906]).
    49. A recent review of the history of the use of the term can be found in the
article, R.E. Sturm, 'Defining the Word "Apocalyptic": A Problem in Biblical
Criticism', in J. Marcus and M.L. Soards (eds.), *Apocalyptic and the New
Testament: Essays in Honor of J. Louis Martyn* (JSNTSup, 24; Sheffield: JSOT
Press), pp. 17-48.

year in these deliberations was 1979, when the issue of genre, its definition and function, advanced to center stage.[50] During that year the volume on the apocalpytic genre edited by John Collins appeared[51] and the international colloquium on apocalypticism was convened at Uppsala.[52] These events marked a new stage in the study of this literature and the movements associated with it. The apparent focus on the issue of genre represented an emerging consensus concerning the terms employed in the discussion as well as the point of departure for bringing some clarity to an area of study which up to that time had been rather chaotic. There is a new consensus on some elementary terminology, which rejects the use of the term 'apocalyptic' as a noun: (1) 'apocalypse' refers to a literary genre; (2) 'apocalypticism' suggests a social ideology; and (3) 'apocalyptic eschatology' points to a set of ideas and motifs.[53] As already mentioned, most attention has centred on the question of genre, the subject of primary concern in this paper. The landmark definition of the apocalyptic genre published by John Collins in the Semeia volume mentioned above reads as follows:

> 'Apocalypse' is a genre of revelatory literature with a narrative framework, in which a revelation is mediated by an otherworldly being to a human recipient, disclosing a transcendent reality which is both temporal, insofar as it envisages eschatological salvation, and spatial insofar as it involves another, supernatural world.[54]

50. The history of the recent discussion is presented in the introductory article to the volume on early Christian apocalypticism: A.Y. Collins, 'Introduction', *Semeia* 36 (1986), pp. 1-11.

51. J.J. Collins (ed.), *Apocalypse: The Morphology of a Genre*, *Semeia* 14 (1979).

52. D. Hellholm (ed.), *Apocalypticism in the Mediterranean World and the Near East* (Tubingen: J.C.B. Mohr [Paul Siebeck], 1983).

53. J.J. Collins, 'Introduction: Towards the Morphology of a Genre', *Semeia* 14 (1979), pp. 3-4; *idem*, *The Apocalyptic Imagination: An Introduction to the Jewish Matrix of Christianity* (New York: Crossroad, 1983), p. 2; P.D. Hanson, 'Apocalypse, Genre' and 'Apocalypticism', *IDBSup*, pp. 27-34; K. Koch, *The Rediscovery of Apocalyptic* (trans. M. Kohl; Naperville: Allen R. Allenson, 1972), pp. 18-35; M.E. Stone, 'Lists of Revealed Things in the Apocalyptic Literature', in F.M. Cross, W.E. Lemke and P.D. Miller, Jr (eds.), *Magnalia Dei: The Mighty Acts of God* (Garden City: Doubleday, 1976), pp. 439-44.

54. J.J. Collins, 'Introduction', *Semeia* 14 (1979), p. 9; Also found in Collins, *Imagination*, p. 4.

As far as Collins is concerned, 'the key word in the definition is transcendence'.[55] Of particular significance in this definition was the attempt to encompass with equal weight two of the dominant elements found in works broadly accepted as apocalyptic literature; that is, 'historical' apocalypses and those which contain otherworldly journeys. In both cases salvation involves 'a radically different type of human existence, in which all the constraints of the human condition, including death, are transcended'.[56] This description of the literary genre provided the centerpiece for subsequent controversy concerning the nature of this literature.

Challenges to the definition advanced above have come from a number of quarters. Martha Himmelfarb raised questions about any attempt to encompass the otherworldly and historical elements within one genre, suggesting that we have here two independent genres which come together somewhere in the first century CE.[57] Her response is based in two observations, shared by a number of other researchers, that (1) the eschatological dimension of apocalyptic literature has received undue emphasis, and/or (2) this literature is so diverse that any attempt to find common elements is doomed to failure.

Christopher Rowland contends that the underlying religious conviction behind the collection of apocalyptic writings is the direct revelation of divine mysteries.[58] This is the basis for the several elements found to be common to the literary genre; that is, a three-fold structure of legends, visions and admonitions.[59] The apocalyptic visions can communicate truths about earthly realities in symbolic form or the actual contents of the heavenly world.[60] As opposed to Collins the basic feature of apocalyptic literature is identified as the revelation of divine mysteries through visions or some other form of immediate disclosure of heavenly truths.[61] While arguing for the phenomenological similarity of the prophetic figures of the Hebrew Scriptures to the authors of apocalyptic literature, John Barton accepts the thesis that 'Apocalypses were

55. Collins, *Imagination*, p. 10.
56. Collins, *Imagination*, p. 10.
57. M. Himmelfarb, *Tours of Hell: An Apocalyptic Form in Jewish and Christian Literature* (Philadelphia: Fortress Press, 1985), pp. 60-61.
58. C. Rowland, *The Open Heaven: A Study of Apocalyptic in Judaism and Early Christianity* (New York: Crossroad, 1982), p. 49.
59. Rowland, *Open Heaven*, pp. 50-61.
60. Rowland, *Open Heaven*, pp. 52-61.
61. Rowland, *Open Heaven*, p. 70.

certainly all written to describe the disclosure of secrets', but quickly qualifies his viewpoint by adding that 'what the secrets had as their subject matter varies widely'.[62] As far as he is concerned, 'the attempt to find any unifying theme among all the apocalypses is doomed to failure'.[63] Similar viewpoints are also presented by Jean Carmignac[64] and Hartmut Stegemann.[65] Neither Rowland nor Barton begin, however, as Collins did, from the perspective of genre. Rowland begins by attempting to identify the religious perspective in Judaism and Christianity known as apocalyptic,[66] while Barton is interested in tracing the phenomenon of prophecy in the post-exilic era. According to Collins, their attempts to downplay the role of eschatology in apocalyptic litera- ture derives from too narrow a definition of eschatology and misses, in particular, the role of personal eschatology, belonging to this genre of literature.[67] Adela Yarbro Collins suggests in response that eschatological content seems to be the primary distinguishing mark of apocalypses over against other revelatory texts such as those dealing with revelatory magic or ritual prescriptions for creating revelatory experiences.[68] The two primary issues are (1) whether such a description adequately describes material found within apocalyptic literature, and (2) whether it permits sufficient differentiation from related literatures of the era.[69] Critiques of the definition however, did not come only from this quarter.

In his paper at the Uppsala conference E.P. Sanders advanced a dif- ferent case: 'What is peculiar to the works which have traditionally been considered Jewish apocalypses is the combination of revelation with the promise of restoration and reversal'.[70] In his advocacy of what he calls

---

62. J. Barton, *Oracles of God: Perceptions of Ancient Prophecy in Israel after the Exile* (London: Darton, Longman and Todd, 1986), p. 201.

63. Barton, *Oracles*, p. 201.

64. J. Carmignac, 'Qu'est-ce que l'Apocalyptique? Son emploi a Qumran', *RevQ* 10 (1979), pp. 3-33.

65. H. Stegemann, 'Die Bedeutung der Qumranfunde für die Erforschung der Apokalyptik', in D. Hellholm (ed.), *Apocalypticism in the Mediterranean World and the Near East* (Tübingen: J.C.B. Mohr [Paul Siebeck], 1983), pp. 495-530.

66. Rowland, *Open Heaven*, p. 49.

67. J.J. Collins, 'Genre, Ideology and Social Movements in Jewish Apocalypticism' (unpublished paper read at the Society of Biblical Literature Meeting, 1989).

68. J.J. Collins, 'Introduction', *Semeia* 36 (1986), p. 5.

69. Collins, *Imagination*, p. 8.

70. E.P. Sanders, 'The Genre of Palestinian Jewish Apocalypses', in Hellholm

an 'essentialist' definition, he has moved eschatology to the centre of the definition and lays the groundwork for a clearer identification of the social function of the literature, a subject initially avoided in the definition advanced above. Since

> the revelation of a coming restoration seems generative of these particular works... we have probably identified something about *authorial intent* and *audience expectancy*: the authors intended to promise restoration by God from present oppression, and the audience understood the devices being used to make that promise impressive: it was revealed, accompanied by visions, and the like.[71]

The major question concerning Sanders's proposal is whether it adequately accounts for the diversity of material found in works commonly called apocalypses.[72]

We find in the studies of David Hellholm and David Aune essential agreement with the elements of Collins's definition given above,[73] but note that they raise the consideration of function. Hellholm proposed that the definition given above be expanded to include, 'intended for a group in crisis with the purpose of exhortation and/or consolation by means of divine authority'.[74] While Adela Yarbro Collins accepts the argument that such a criterion need not be based on a study of the actual functions of all apocalypses in their original and subsequent social settings and can rather be established from the implied function in the text itself, she observes that the proposed expansion seems to take the perspective of the implied author as an accurate representation of reality and questions whether the world created in the text necessarily reflects the external reality.[75] In an extended addendum to the definition, David Aune stresses the functions of legitimating the transcendant authorization of the message and encouraging its recipients to modify their cognitive and behavioral stance in conformity with the transcendant

(ed.), *Apocalypticism*, pp. 447-59; see especially p. 456.

71. Sanders, 'Genre', pp. 458-59 (italics are those of the author).

72. See Collins, *Imagination*, p. 8.

73. D.E. Aune, 'The Apocalypse of John and the Problem of Genre', *Semeia* 36 (1986), pp. 65-96. He records a few differences concerning the question of form on pp. 87-88.

74. D. Hellholm, 'The Problem of Apocalyptic Genre and the Apocalypse of John', *Semeia* 36 (1986), pp. 13-64. See p. 27 for this proposal.

75. Collins, 'Introduction', p. 6.

perspective.[76] These critiques led Adela Yarbro Collins to propose the following addition to the original definition:

> intended to interpret present, earthly circumstances in light of the supernatural world and of the future, and to influence both the understanding and the behavior of the audience by means of divine authority.[77]

This addendum has subsequently been accepted by John Collins.[78] While having taken into account the matter of content, this proposal does not presuppose any particular social setting for the genre as a whole.

Testing the Definitions

I have previously indicated some acknowledgment of the relationship between the apocalyptic literature from Jewish and Christian antiquity and portions of the African American experience.[79] Those scholars who advanced such a thesis did so, however, more on the basis of what they perceived to be a shared worldview than on similarities in the literary genre.[80] The purpose of this excercise in cultural exegesis is to test these definitions in the light of a different but related experience. Having identified what I consider a representative sample of the use of apocalyptic images and viewpoints in ante-bellum African American religion I now turn briefly to that task.

This examination must begin with the definition given above. The first portion reads, '"Apocalypse" is a genre of revelatory literature with a narrative framework, in which a revelation is mediated by an otherworldly being to a human recipient'.[81] The process of revelation and mediation in the African American experience is somewhat different for the most part from the Jewish and Christian apocalypses of antiquity. The vision experience of Nat Turner comes closer to this definition, where the upcoming apocalyptic battle is mediated in the vision by the spirit. The use of biblical figures such as Daniel, Joshua and Moses as persons who received deliverance from the Lord would also seem to

76. Aune, 'Apocalypse of John', pp. 87, 89-90.
77. Collins, 'Introduction', p. 7.
78. Collins, 'Genre, Ideology and Social Movements', p. 12.
79. See the introductory paragraph to this essay above. Note also the study by Marybury, 'Ethos of Transcendence', pp. 39-57.
80. Laubenstein, 'Apocalyptic', pp. 242-44. This is less true of Marybury's work, 'Ethos of Transcendence', pp. 39-57.
81. See above, p. 55.

carry some authority. It must be noted, however, that one of the purposes served by the otherworldly interpreter is to provide an authoritative aspect for the revelation being received. Since the slaves would have seen the Bible as authoritative, regardless of whether they could read it or not, the need for such justification of the vision would have been less necessary. The revelatory aspect, at least in part, would have been encompassed within the biblical message which lies behind the spirituals and some of the other uses of apocalyptic materials.

The second portion of this definition gets to the heart of what we also find in the material discussed above: 'disclosing a transcendent reality which is both temporal, insofar as it envisages eschatological salvation, and spatial insofar as it involves another, supernatural world'. Both the temporal and spatial elements are found in the sources we have used for the description of African American religion. When David Walker, for example, says, 'I call God—I call angels—I call men, to witness that your DESTRUCTION *is at hand*, and will be speedily consummated unless you REPENT',[82] we understand the temporal dimension of that worldview. A similar sentiment is found in the prayer sung by the slave:

> O, rocks, don't fall on me,
> Rocks and mountains don't fall on me,
> I look ovah yondah on Jericho's walls,
> Rocks and mountains don't fall on me,
> An' see dem sinners tremble an' fall,
> Rocks and mountains don't fall on me,
> 0, ina dat great judgment day,
> Rocks and mountains don't fall on me,
> De sinners will run to the rocks and say,
> Rocks and mountains don't fall on me.[83]

Regardless of what we think the heaven is which the grand old sister is trying to reach, we find in that song another expression of the temporal dimension.[84] We already mentioned the manner in which this seems to evoke thoughts similar to those expressed in the periodization schemes of early Jewish and Christian apocalypses. But we also find in the spirituals the expression of a desire for Jesus to be with the slaves in their earthly experiences or spatial dimensions:

82. Aptheker, *Continual Cry*, p. 108 (capitals and italics are Walker's).
83. J.W. Johnson and J.R. Johnson, *The Book of American Negro Spirituals*, pp. 164-65.
84. See above.

When I'm in trouble, Be with me!
When I'm on my lonesome journey,
I want Jesus, Be with me.[85]

Or:

Jesus is our friend,
He'll keep us to the en'
And a little talk with Jesus,
Makes it right.[86]

As Jim Cone says, 'Jesus was their "rock in a weary lan"', their "shelter in a time of storm"'.[87] Is it not the spatial dimension of apocalyptic expression which is alluded to in the well-known spiritual, 'Ev'ry time I feel de spirit?'

Ev'ry time I feel de spirit, movin' in my heart, I will pray.
Upon de mountain, my Lord spoke,
Out o' his mouth came fire and smoke.
An' all aroun' me, look so shine,
Aska my Lord, if all was mine.
Jordan river, chilly, cold,
Chilla de body, but not de soul.[88]

What about those songs which speak of the appearance of Jesus to a human being?

One day when I was walkin' alone, Oh yes Lord,
De element opened, an' de Love came down, Oh yes, Lord,
I never shall forget dat day, Oh yes, Lord,
When Jesus washed my sins away, Oh yes, Lord.[89]

It is not only the future that the slave encountered in these songs, there was also a present reality. It is this same apocalyptic reality to which the numerous conversion stories point.[90] While less obvious, the spatial dimension certainly would be present in some of the spirituals of the heavenly land.

85. J. Cone, *The Spirituals and the Blues: An Interpretation* (Maryknoll, NY: Orbis Books, 1991 [1972]), p. 46.
86. Cone, *The Spirituals and the Blues*, p. 50.
87. Cone, *The Spirituals and the Blues*, p. 50.
88. J.W. Johnson and J.R. Johnson, *The Book of American Negro Spirituals*, pp. 142-43.
89. Cone, *The Spirituals and the Blues*, p. 84.
90. G.P. Rawick, *The American Slave: A Composite Autobiography*, XIX (Westport: Greenwood, 1972).

Even Nat Turner's vision of white spirits and black spirits engaged in battle is not temporal but spatial; this battle is a present reality in another dimension. The temporal and spatial dimensions of this definition are adequately reflected in and account for the material found in the African American spirituals.

We must at this point recall that in his comments on this definition Collins related that 'the key word in the definition is transcendence'.[91] In his research on the African American spirituals, Carl Marybury finds this element within the very music itself: 'Rhythm and black intonation most likely constituted the first survival techniques of the slaves, not just as a matter of physical survival, but in creating an ethos of human transcendence in an otherwise destroyed personality'.[92] He goes on to connect it with another feature frequently identified as constituting the center of this literature: 'Imagination as an act of human transcendence is characteristic of both ancient apocalyptic and the more recent Spiritual'.[93] We are reminded of the title of Collins's book, *The Apocalyptic Imagination*. The significance of the elements of imagination and transcendance in the African American spiritual, however, cannot be understood without an examination of the context in which they were used, the slave meeting, 'The Invisible Institution'.[94]

In the extensive publication of the interviews of ex-slaves conducted by the Federal Writers Project of the Works Progress Administration, and edited by George Rawick, we find continual references to the fact that many slaves had two kinds of religious meetings. I cite, for example, Lewis Faber, born a slave in Georgia in 1855:

> On Sunday all were required to attend the white church in town. They sat in the back of the church as the white minister preached and directed the following text at them: 'don't steal your master's chickens or his eggs and your backs won't get whipped'. In the afternoon of this same day when the colored minister was allowed to preach the slaves heard this text:

91. Collins, *Imagination*, p. 10. See the discussion above.

92. C.H. Marybury, 'Ethos of Transcendence', p. 42.

93. C.H. Marybury, 'Ethos of Transcendence', p. 42. On the role of imagination among the Ante-bellum African-Americans see also, V.L. Wimbush, 'The Bible and African-Americans: An Outline of an Interpretive history', in C.H. Felder (ed.), *Stony the Road we Trod: African-American Biblical Interpretation* (Minneapolis: Fortress Press, 1991), pp. 87-88; D.T. Shannon, '"An Ante-bellum Sermon": A Resource for an African-American Hermeneutic', in C.H. Felder (ed.), *Stony the Road we Trod*, p. 103.

94. See above.

'Obey your masters and your mistresses and your backs won't get whipped'.[95]

This refrain is continuously repeated throughout the volumes of this collection. The other meeting, however, is also described:

> Massa never 'lowed us slaves go to church but they have big holes in the field they gits down in and prays. They done that way 'cause the white folks didn't want them to pray. They used to pray for freedom.[96]

Or:

> No suh, we never goes to church. Times we sneak in de woods and prays de Lawd to make us free and times one of the de slaves got happy and made a noise dat dey heerd at de big house and den de overseer come and whip us 'cause we prayed de Lawd to set us free.[97]

What was frequently involved in this 'getting happy' was a release from their real world of toil, pain and drudgery and an experience of a world that was not like that, a world of freedom. The frequency of the prayer for freedom is a good corrective to those who would emphasize the other-worldy nature of this religious expression. It is in this experience that we find the element of transcendance mentioned above. It does appear that the power of the invisible institution, the 'hush arbor' meetings, was grounded in the fact that this was where the slave experienced the presence of God and an affirmation of identity absent from the preaching of those appointed by and in service to the plantation owners.[98] The transcendance experienced in these meetings was the true religion.

We are reminded of Collins's statement that salvation involves 'a radically different type of human existence, in which all the constraints of the human condition, including death, are transcended'.[99]

When we refer to the previous discussion of definitions, we quickly see that support in the Antebellum appropriation of apocalyptic literature for this emphasis on the transcendant which encompasses both a spatial and a temporal dimension does not permit primary consideration of a number of the other definitions which have been proposed. No

95. G.P. Rawick, *The American Slave: A Composite Autobiography* (Westport: Greenwood, 1972), p. 12.1.1.323.

96. Rawick, *American Slave*, p. 177.

97. Rawick, *American Slave*, p. 4.1.266-67.

98. Raboteau, *Slave Religion*, pp. 213-18.

99. Raboteau, *Slave Religion*, p. 10.

justification is to be found for Himmelfarb's attempt to separate the genre into two, one emphasizing the otherworldly and the other the historical.[100] This would only lead to a misunderstanding of the phenomenon in African American religion. Similarly, any attempt to describe the apocalyptic elements in the slave experience which omits any emphasis on the eschatological, such as Carmignac, Rowland and Barton would only resuit in distortion.[101] The African American utilization of apocalyptic imagery provides more support for the thesis advanced by E.P. Sanders which emphasizes that the revelation is accompanied by a promise of restoration and reversal.[102] We certainly have found evidence for the interpretation of apocalyptic elements which refer to a return to Africa, to travels north out of the slave states and to emancipation. But to see all of the spirituals as code songs would be to eliminate some of the genius of their function within the life of the slave. Highlighting restoration and reversal does not adequately account for the multi-faceted functions which apocalyptic imagery apparently served. The element of transcendence combined with some attempt to address the question of function is more productive.

When an apocalypse reveals a transcendant reality which, according to the addendum to the original definition of Collins, is 'intended to interpret present, earthly circumstances in light of the supernatural world and of the future',[103] we come closer to the experience described in this essay. This transcendance is not merely a future reality, it encompasses the basis for a reorientation of the understanding of present circumstances. This reorientation in the slave experience was a source of empowerment and resistance, for what it provides is a foundation for saying that reality is not what it appears to be. Just as in the book of Daniel Nebuchadnezzar is only a blip on the screen of world history, so is the slave owner. Just as Enoch ascends through the seven heavens to approach the throne of the Ancient of Days, so the slave in singing and prayer can experience both freedom and heaven. That freedom, that heaven, is reality. The present experience is a mere aberration. This type of transcendent reality empowered Nat Turner, Denmark Vesey and David Walker no less than it did the individual slave who resisted attempts to denigrate the native culture and religion, as well as efforts

100. See above.
101. See above.
102. See above.
103. See above.

which should have resulted in total dehumanization. The validity of their humanity could be asserted because of a reappropriation of reality based on transcendence.

We can conclude that the basic use and purpose of this apocalyptic imagery was the maintenance of identity and community in the midst of a system which attempted to deny there was such a possibility. The communal purpose of apocalyptic literature is entailed in the latter portion of the addendum to Collins's original definition: 'to influence both the understanding and the behavior of the audience by means of divine authority'.[104] Peter Paris in his work has referred to the black churches as having their origin in a religion of exile.[105] I have here argued that the religious imagery of that community of exile had its roots in the African American appropriation of apocalyptic imagery and perspectives. Apocalyptic language permitted the slave communities to live from some reference point other than the ones simultaneously denied and forced upon them by their masters and that of the North American world to which they were so violently introduced.

A footnote on another problem in Daniel from the viewpoint of cultural exegesis: The evidence discussed in this essay may provide a clue for the continued discussion of the perplexing problem of the unity of the book of Daniel. Scholars continue to debate the question of the relationship between the narratives of chapters 1–6 and the visions of chapters 7–12. The oppressed slaves who sang the song, 'Didn't my Lord deliver Daniel', did not know the difference. While they could sing about Daniel, Jonah and the three Hebrew children in the furnace, they could in a later verse relate that 'the moon run down in a purple stream, the sun forbear to shine, and every star disappear',[106] imagery much more closely related to the latter half of the book. From their standpoint the stories of Daniel's resistance and faithfulness were part of the experience of the transcendent reality they encountered in the visions of that book. My suspicion is that the case was similar for the Jews at the time of the persecution of Antiochus IV.

104. Collins, 'Introduction', p. 7.
105. P. Paris, *The Social Teachings of the Black Churches* (Philadelphia: Fortress Press, 1985), pp. 57-59.
106. See above.

THE BIBLE AS FORMATIVE IN A BASIC
CHRISTIAN COMMUNITY OF BRAZIL

Mary Milligan RSHM

Since the Second Vatican Council, the Word of God has been 'support and energy' for many Christians, the strength of their faith, the 'pure and perennial source' of their spiritual life.[1] Recognizing the formative power of God present in the biblical word, the Council called for 'easy access to sacred Scripture' to be provided for all the Christian faithful. More than 25 years later, the Scriptures, as proclaimed in the liturgy or read and meditated 'in secret', have come to be part of Christian life in a way unknown to previous generations.

Within the church of Latin America, the Bible has played a role in the church which might be termed unique. Indeed, one biblical scholar has stated that the Brazilian church provides 'what may well be the most impressive example of the use of the Bible on a large scale in the post-conciliar church'.[2] This article will look at several ways in which the Scriptures have formed persons and communities within Brazil. It will look at the 'accessibility' of the Bible through various materials, examine the most common methodology used for Bible reflection, and explore some approaches to biblical interpretation. My development of the question is based particularly on biblical reflection groups in Bairro Goiá, a populated area on the outskirts of the city of Goiânia in the center-west of Brazil, where I spent the month of June 1991.

Bairro Goiá, part of the Archdiocese of Goiânia, is mainly composed of the working poor, many of whom have come from the interior of the country looking for better living conditions. Like the neighborhoods on the outskirts of so many big cities, it has few of what we in the First World would call necessities: a good transportation system, a post-office,

---

1. Cf. *Dei Verbum*, par. 21.
2. J. Swetnam, 'Brazilian Catholics and the Bible', *The Bible Today* 22 (1984), p. 376.

adequate health facilities, solid educational institutions, a supermarket or a bank. Many of its residents are unemployed; all experience the effects of a national inflation which, though it is perhaps 'galloping' less rapidly, is 'galloping' nonetheless. Salaries do not increase while each day brings significant rises in the price of basic commodities and services. In June of 1991, many who work in federal employments (including government schools) had not received their salary for several months. The church in Bairro Goiá, however, is alive and well.

The Basic Christian Community in Brazil and the Bible

Someone has said that if the church in Brazil has made an effective and evident option for the poor, the poor had in the 1960s made their option for the church as a space of freedom and a place of resistance to an oppressive government. Throughout the past 25 years, church leadership in Brazil has consistently denounced injustice, supported workers, the poor and the landless in their struggles and has offered solid and continuous opportunities for the education of the faith of the catholic community.[3] Perhaps more importantly, it has nourished the poor with the Word of God.

One of the most significant options of the Brazilian church was a structural one: the formation of what have been called basic Christian communities (or 'grassroots' Christian communities, in an attempt to capture the full meaning of the word 'basic', from the 'base'). In Brazil these grassroots communities arose and took shape at the historical conjunction of a national situation of oppression with the ecclesial reality of Vatican II. According to Marcello Azevedo, SJ, the soil into which the challenge of the Council fell was well prepared by pastoral work especially of priests and religious.[4]

The basic Christian communities (BCCs) have flourished especially in rural areas and on the outskirts of the major population centers. While in each diocese they have their own particular characteristics, generally they are composed of about 20 or so families living in the same area. The basic community is not a particular group of people who belong to a committee or an association within the larger parish. Rather, the basic

3. P. de Andrade, 'Le choix de l'église du Brésil', *Lumière et Vie* 35 (1986), pp. 61-73.

4. M. Azevedo, *Comunidades eclesiais de base e inculturação da fé* (São Paulo: Ediçoes Loyola, 1986), pp. 50-57.

community is just that—a community. The perimeter of the community is fluid with new persons and families arriving and others moving to other areas. The basic community is made up of persons who want to pray, share and celebrate life, who are committed to caring for one another and to struggling together for human rights and dignity. Newcomers are always welcome and once a new group is 'able to stand on its own two feet', that is, once it has within it the necessary leadership, commitment and resources to continue, it is recognized by the larger ecclesial community—parish or diocese—as a basic Christian community.

There is no doubt that the Bible is the backbone of these communities. They are the places where faith meets life in an explicit way, where the light of God's word is brought to bear on human reality. At Puebla in 1979, the bishops of Latin America renewed their determination to 'give priority to the proclamation of the Good News, to biblical catechesis, and to the celebration of the liturgy as a response to the growing thirst for the Word of God' which they recognized on the continent.[5]

Bible Reflection in Bairro Goiá

In Bairro Goiá, the basic Christian community understands itself as part of a larger group—a parish, a region. It is related as well to a number of smaller Bible reflection groups which meet weekly. These latter groups, usually composed of people who live on the same block or within two or three blocks of one another, are not themselves, strictly speaking, basic Christian communities, but the members of the larger basic community are most often the animators of these neighborhood reflection groups.

There are, then, several levels at which Bible reflection is done in Bairro Goiá: the 'parish' or regional level, the level of the BCC, and that of the small neighborhood group. Not included in these groupings are various commissions and committees based within the community and which meet on a regular basis: youth ministry; health services; vocation ministry; liturgical committee. All of these groups build Scripture reading and reflection into their meetings; the liturgical committee in

---

5. J. Eagleson and P. Scharper (eds.), 'Evangelization in Latin America's Present and Future: Final Document of the Third General Conference of the Latin American Episcopate', in *Puebla and Beyond* (Maryknoll, NY: Orbis Books, 1979), p. 141 n. 150.

particular structures its gatherings around the Bible readings for the following Sunday.

My reflections here begin where most things begin in the Brazilian church—at the base, that is, with the small neighborhood groups. These groups meet once a week, each time in the home of a different person. If the house is too small to receive the group of 8 to 12 who come, the meeting can easily be moved outside and often is. Several characteristics of these small groups are pertinent here. First of all, those groups in which I participated always included persons who were attending for the first time. In two cases, the group met in the house of someone who had not previously attended but who had been approached by a neighbor or, knowing about the Bible meetings, had taken the initiative to invite the group. There was as well a 'core group', so to speak, of those actively involved in the BCC. The fluidity of membership reflected the 'missionary' concern of the members of the community.

If 'grace builds on nature', this concern for bringing others into the community has its substratum in the warm and welcoming temperament of the Brazilian people. Indeed, doors are always open and guests are always welcome. But the concern to extend the perimeter of the community springs also, no doubt, from concern about the great popularity of fundamentalist religious groups in Brazil. While walking to the various meetings, we always passed other Christian churches where people were gathered to sing, to witness and often to 'shout in the Spirit'. I think of one particular meeting where our entire biblical conversation took place against the background of various hymns issuing from what sounded like very healthy lungs!

Secondly, the groups in which I participated included persons of all ages—children were always welcome. Often parents brought babies with them. Women outnumbered men, a common characteristic in the basic communities as well. While all came from the same neighborhood, there was a diversity of backgrounds in the group. Some were not able to read; others both read and spoke with great ease. Some had been in the area for a number of years; others had arrived relatively recently. While BCCs in rural areas might evidence greater homogeneity, the diversity of the groups in Bairro Goiá reflects the general pattern of the BCCs on the outskirts of the cities.

Thirdly, the leadership of the small groups is shared according to the capacity of the group. The leader is responsible for seeing that the meeting and the meeting place are properly prepared and for moving the group through the different moments of the reflection process. Each group that I attended was led by a woman, though most often one or several men were also in attendance. Since 1985 there has been a group of women religious in Bairro Goiá. Each of the sisters participates in a different Bible reflection group and the role they play there varies. Sometimes the sister has been a catalyst for getting a neighborhood group together; at other times she participates in the reflection led by another member of the group. The sisters share in the life of the community in a very simple way, each one according to her own gifts. The larger Christian community of Bairro Goiá is led by a laywoman, Geralda Bento, elected by the other leaders of the community.

The way in which Scripture is used in these Christian communities is influenced both by the biblical materials and resources available to the people and also by the methodology of reflection common in the Brazilian church. In both these cases, the community in Bairro Goiá is typical of BCCs throughout the country.

Biblical Materials

From the earliest days of the formation of BCC, church leaders were concerned to make available a variety of resources for use in these groups. The rediscovery of the Bible in the church after Vatican II coincided with the formation of these communities, so that the Bible truly became the 'book of the people'. The Word of God guided the renewal of the church 'from within', so to speak, and became an integral part of the spirituality of the people.

As of the mid-sixties, the Brazilian Bishops' Conference (CNBB) took several initiatives designed to make the Bible accessible to the common people, especially the poor. First of all, it established what is called the *Campanha da Fraternidade* (Solidarity Campaign). This annual campaign which takes place during Lent is a formative instrument affecting the entire country. Each year a pertinent theme is chosen, most often related to a situation of injustice within the country. In 1986, for example, the theme was land reform and in 1990 it was the fundamental dignity and equality of women and men. A variety of materials are produced on this theme, materials appropriate for diverse audiences: theological reflections destined for those 'pastoral agents' trained in theology; simplified materials for those with less training but who will have a role in leading the implementation of the campaign. For children in schools there are materials, often illustrated, adapted to their age, and for those many adults unable to read, a visual presentation is prepared.

In addition to the written materials, appropriate liturgical readings are suggested for each of the Sundays in Lent, and special songs and hymns are written and recorded for the occasion. Assemblies learn these songs which are often based on biblical themes. Music and dance run in the Brazilian blood and this music becomes a kind of mantra educating for social justice!

The Solidarity Campaign has a unifying impact on the entire Brazilian church; its materials are used in all kinds of communities: parishes, basic communities, schools, families, religious communities, prayer groups, ministerial groups. Its formative effects on the Brazilian church are incalculable. I remember visiting Brazil several years ago and being surprised at hearing so much exclusive language and so little reference to women. There seemed to be a rather generalized feminist 'unconsciousness'. That is certainly not the case today. Not only are there a growing number of recognized women theologians in the country, but language and consciousness have changed. In one meeting of the liturgical committee of Bairro Goiá in which I participated, the first reading for the following Sunday was Gen. 3.9-15. When, after listening attentively to the reading, the group was asked for its response, the first person to speak said spontaneously, 'It's discriminatory!' What role did the Solidarity Campaign on 'Women and Men as Images of God' have to play in this awareness? It would be hard to give any kind of scientific answer to that question, but I suspect that it has played a significant role in forming a new consciousness in the country.

Another initiative has been the celebration of Bible Month. Starting in 1946, Bible Weeks began to appear, but it was only in 1971 that the entire month of September was proposed as Bible Month. During that time, the various local churches throughout the country are urged to reflect on a particular book of the Bible. In recent years, the texts have been chosen in relationship to the Solidarity Campaign, in order to avoid duplication of efforts and to strengthen the effectiveness of both events. Next year, when the situation of the worker will be the theme of the Solidarity Campaign, Bible Month will focus on 'Saint Paul: Worker and Preacher of the Gospel'. One of the booklets already available, written by Carlos Mesters, O. Carm.,[6] presents Paul as an itinerant missionary,

---

6. Carlos Mesters, a Carmelite priest from Holland, has been in Brazil for 41 years. He is responsible for much of the biblical material which has been used in the Brazilian church over the past 25 years. His recent book on the letters of St Paul is

as a worker who preached the gospel, as coordinator of the early church communities, and as one who had to face a variety of conflicts. The place of women in the Pauline communities is also addressed, following up on last year's Solidarity Campaign theme. This booklet is complemented by another one which contains suggestions for four meetings and a celebration on the letters of St Paul. Materials for Bible Month follow the same guidelines as for the Solidarity Campaign, that is, they begin with today's questions and are adapted to a variety of levels and audiences.

In the category of materials, a recent initiative also deserves mention. In preparation for the commemoration of 500 years of evangelization in Latin America, the Latin American Religious Conference (CLAR) proposed that all women and men religious on the continent undertake an intensive five-year period of prayer and study of the Bible. While this project met with serious obstacles, the church in Brazil made some modifications in the original proposal and has already published materials to begin the five-year reflection. A methodological volume, 'A Prayerful Reading of the Bible', introduced the series. Volume 2 on the formation of the people of God will be followed by volumes on the prophetic and wisdom books, the Gospels, Acts and the letters of St Paul. The final volume on apocalyptic literature is scheduled for publication in 1995. These materials destined for religious have been adapted for use in other communities as well.

One of the groups responsible for producing biblical materials is the Bible Study Center for People's Pastoral Action. This group was formed in 1977 by 'concerned Catholics and Protestants who shared the new vision of a church which was being recreated through the spontaneous formation of an estimated 80,000 basic ecclesial communities'.[7] The Bible Study Center has as its objective not only to 'collect and organize

typical of his ability to express in language accessible to the common people the results of contemporary biblical scholarship. One of the recent initiatives in which he has participated is the language preparation of a number of lay leaders from the Christian communities. This study of Greek and Hebrew is meant to help the communities experience that all translations are made from a certain perspective, most often from the perspective of the dominating class. Language study is therefore a tool to help the communities free themselves in one more area from dependence.

7.   C. Mesters, 'The Use of the Bible among the Common People', in R. Kinsler (ed.), *Ministry by the People* (Geneva: WCC; Maryknoll, NY: Orbis, 1983), pp. 78-92.

material relevant for popular study of the Bible...' but also to 'provide biblical training...and to stimulate the study of the Bible at the level of the people...'[8]

Methodology of Biblical Reflection
This vast array of biblical material is generally unified by a basic methodology. The proposed methods of reflection in small groups always take the people's reality as their starting point. Each meeting begins by articulating the situation of the community and/or its members as the human reality to be illuminated by the Word of God. Only when the group has reflected on its own reality is the Bible brought to bear on it. The 'see, judge and act' model used so widely by Catholic Action groups in the past is common practice in biblical reflection groups. The situation which is *seen* is then *judged* by God's Word.

Reflection on God's word is always completed by action. That action can take a variety of forms. At times, it might merely involve a preparation for the next meeting. At other times, it might require a political action to denounce a particular injustice. In the final section of any document published at a national or regional level is found a list of concrete and practical suggestions. The documents always include questions to be discussed in small groups—not theoretical questions but questions meant to provoke reflection on the group's experience.

In 1986, for example, when the theme of the Solidarity Campaign was 'God's Land: Land of Brothers and Sisters', the official text gave extensive documentation regarding the situation in Brazil where ownership of the land is in the hands of very few people. In the context of this overview, individuals reflected on their own experience of possession or non-possession of the land. In a similar reflection on the land in June, I remember Dona Natália's remarks on the parcel of land her family had owned but lost when they moved to Bairro Goiá. 'The land', she said, 'is like a mother. We live from her, we live on our own piece of land. We find water under the land. Here in the city I feel like a prisoner. We can't go out without worrying about violence and when our children go out, we worry about them'.

I have referred here to the materials and the processes used in Bible reflection groups today. It is important to state as well the importance of symbols and celebration in the biblical formation of the Brazilian church.

8. Mesters, 'The Use of the Bible', p. 92.

Whether in the small groups of 10 or 12 people or regional gatherings of 300,000 such as that which took place in Trindade (Goiânia) in honor of the 'Divino Pai Eterno' at the end of June, signs and symbols are an expression of the people's reverence for and response to the word. In Bairro Goiá, a group reflection on Mark 4, the seed which grows by itself, for example, took place around some soil, seeds, a candle and the Bible. At another meeting focussing on work and human dignity, each member brought a symbol of his or her work. Geraldo, a bus conductor who leaves for his work at 3 a.m. each day, presented his ID card; Marilia, a seamstress, brought her scissors, which, she told the group, are as essential to her life as is the Bible. Maria da Graça brought an empty pot, saying that although it was the pot she used to cook food for her many children, it had often been empty. Two of the men in the group—Elio, a construction worker, and Jaime, a rubber worker—brought nothing and spoke of their anguish and humiliation at being unemployed.

In these small group meetings as in the Sunday eucharistic celebration, the book of the Bible is given a central place. In one meeting of pastoral workers in the region, one of the participants danced down the aisle holding the Bible high above her head. The symbolism which is never absent from meetings of the community touches people on the unconscious level, creating and supporting a common veneration for the Word of God and a conviction of the presence of that Word in life.

Biblical Interpretation

The Objective of Interpretation

What is most striking about biblical interpretation within the small communities of Brazil is its ultimate purpose. Carlos Mesters, who for years has been reflecting on Scripture from his position among the poor of Brazil, prefers to speak not of biblical interpretation but of interpretation of *life* in the light of the Bible. Very much in the line of liberation theology, he sees theological and biblical study as incomplete if they do not lead to liberation of people in their real everyday lives. There is no doubt from the methodology followed that *life* is the starting point, the substance and the objective of biblical reflection.

Within this context, biblical scholarship has its role to play. Brazilian biblical scholars are actively involved in writing the materials which serve as a basis for reflection in the base communities. They, as so many others, recognize the limitations of the historical-critical method, that is, the limitation of seeing the biblical text primarily as historically informative. They acknowledge the importance of discovering the meaning of the text for its original audience but are unwilling to end the investigative process there. If today's questions are the starting point of biblical interpretation, so also its goal is to discover the meaning of the text for life here and now.

Brazilian exegetes use the tools of historical-critical methods: textual, source, form and redaction criticism, as well as the history of tradition.[9] Referring to hermeneutical method, theologian Clodovis Boff has presented a model which he terms 'a correspondence of relationships'.[10] This model stresses the relationship between the text and its original context as illuminative of the present hearers in their context. Boff calls the attitude of the early community in which the Gospels were first written one of 'creative fidelity', that is, 'they attributed to Jesus even later developments undergone by his message and work, based on the identity of the Christ of glory with the historical Jesus'.[11] This same attitude of creative fidelity does not look to the text for formulas or techniques merely to be applied to a very different historical context. Rather than pass directly from the text to ourselves, this method of interpretation necessarily passes through the context of the original text. The necessary work of exegesis serves as a guarantee of objectivity. This model of the 'correspondence of relationships' avoids both the direct application of the words of the Bible to the contemporary situation and a simplistic identification between the original and the contemporary contexts.

In the exploration of the original context, Brazilian exegetes pay special attention not only to the composition and faith-situation of the community to which the writings were first addressed, but they explore the political, social and economic factors influencing that community. They avoid, however, equating the context of present-day hearers with

---

9.   A.J. da Silva, 'Notas sobre alguns aspectos da leitura da Bíblia no Brasil hoje', *Revista Eclesiástica Brasileira* 50/197 (1990), p. 124. Da Silva bases his analysis on C. Boff, *Theology and Praxis: Epistemological Foundations* (Maryknoll, NY: Orbis Books, 1987), pp. 132-53. C. Boff calls for the formation of a 'hermeneutic *habitus*' which will always consider the Bible as a 'complex hermeneutic totality', thus avoiding facile, simplistic and manipulative one-to-one applications.

10.   Boff, *Theology and Praxis*, pp. 132-53.

11.   Boff, *Theology and Praxis*, pp. 147-48.

that of the first Christian audience, a method which would not respect the complex hermeneutical process and which would lead to funda-mentalistic interpretations.

The contemporary understanding that all interpreters have their own viewpoint (as did the biblical writers) is lived in a particular way in Brazil. The theologians' 'preunderstanding' of the text is explicit: an option for the poor and oppressed.[12] There is no doubt that *liberation* is the prism through which the people read and interpret the Bible. A people who are oppressed hear special echoes in God's voice to the people of Israel. How do the unemployed, the underpaid, and the unjustly treated of Bairro Goiá, for example, hear the passage from James:

> Come now, you rich, weep and howl for the miseries that are coming upon you. Your riches have rotted and your garments are moth-eaten. Your gold and silver have rusted... Behold, the wages of the labourers who mowed your fields, which you kept back by fraud, cry out; and the cries of the harvesters have reached the ears of the Lord of hosts. You have lived on the earth in luxury and in pleasure; you have fattened your hearts in a day of slaughter. You have condemned, you have killed the righteous ones; they do not resist you.[13]

The prism through which the history of Israel and of Jesus is read, then, is always one of oppression/liberation. While most often this libera-tion is a communal one (freedom from poverty, from political and social injustice), it is a personal one also. I remember well how Mark's story of the seed growing by itself inspired Dona Felisarda's joyful cry: 'I've dis-covered the seed within'. That 'seed within' was courage and serenity to face a family situation in which two of her sons were in prison for drug-related crimes. Dona Felisarda is unable to worship with the community because her Sundays are spent walking to the two prisons where her sons are kept and then standing in a long line to see them.

Interpretation as a Community Task
Vatican II emphasized that the Bible is the book of the church, of the community. The Scriptures were formed and written within a commu-nity; the task of their interpretation depends on a community. Whether this 'community' is one of bishops or of common people in Bairro Goiá,

---

12. E. Schüssler Fiorenza, 'The Function of Scripture in the Liberation Struggle', in *Bread Not Stone* (Boston: Beacon Press, 1985), pp. 43-63.
13. Jas 5.1-6 (RSV).

it is likewise related to the generations that have preceded. The presence of the risen Jesus in the church has enlightened sincere Christians throughout the ages. Indeed, Jesus' promise that the Spirit 'will teach you everything and remind you of all I have said to you' (Jn 14.26) is realized in a particular way in ecclesial communities standing in continuity with tradition.

Boff's interpretative model of 'correspondence of relationships' can, it seems to me, create a relationship of solidarity between the contemporary Christian community and its predecessors in the faith. Through emphasis on the relationship between the text and its original hearers, that original community becomes somehow present to today's hearers. There were times in my stay in Bairro Goiá when that sense of solidarity was almost palpable. The community's comments on the letter of James did not reflect a simplistic identification with a former context but rather a sense of being part of a long Christian struggle for justice and freedom, a struggle motivated and illuminated by the life and word of Jesus.

Once again, it is important to state the relationship that exists between the theologians or exegetes of Brazil and the Brazilian people. Those who articulate theology in academic circles do so from a position 'within' the people, within the community of faith of the poor. They maintain ongoing contact with the 'commonfolk', with the 'base', with the religious expressions and experience of oppression of their people. Indeed, personal experience within the community is the starting point of their theology. It is the reflection of these theologians which is presented in materials used for biblical reflection in the BCCs.

Belief in the Spirit present in individuals and in the community is a faith presupposition of the biblical movement in Brazil. As Carlos Mesters says, those responsible for animating reflection in the small communities are not so much concerned to bring new knowledge (*conhecer*) to the group as to help them to recognize the Word within (*reconhecer*).[14] The conviction of the Spirit's presence in each person and in the community, prompting individuals to see links and similarities between their own personal and communal experience and that of Jesus, is the foundation of the communitarian nature of interpretation.

In Brazil as throughout Latin America, a strong cultural sense of community forms the substratum of church. The community dimension

14. Conversation with Carlos Mesters, June 3, 1991 in Cachoeiro do Campo, Brazil.

of sin and salvation are strongly emphasized in liberation theology. This communitarian way of being is operative in biblical interpretation as well. Individuals experience themselves as being part of a people, a pilgrim people. This people is situated in a history meant to be transformed by Christian love and action.

It is not difficult to see the connections between the 'little ones' of the Hebrew Scriptures and the exploited of Bairro Goiá. It is clear that the people of Bairro Goiá identify in a special way with Jesus' preference for the outcast, the sinner and the marginalized. Throughout these postconciliar years, the Bible has been a powerful means for helping the oppressed discover their own dignity and power. It has been in the center of the struggle for justice, accompanying masses of 'invaders' as they take over tracts of land unjustly held; it has been light on the path of those uprooted from their land by drought or flood, by exploitation or famine. It has sustained the many who have lost life or limb in the struggle for justice, as it has sustained those communities affected by these losses. Very much like the ark of the covenant for the Israelites, the biblical text, truly a presence of God, has accompanied the Brazilian church on its long, perilous, festive journey these past 25 years.

Interpretation by the Poor
Some would claim that the poor and the oppressed can better understand the gospel message because it is addressed to them.[15] Is it true that only the poor can grasp the gospel message in its purity? That the poor have a special insight into the Scriptures? It seems to me that to claim that the gospel message can only be grasped by the poor is to profess a sort of gnosticism, a hidden knowledge to which only certain persons have access—and that because of their socio-economic situation.

On the other hand, there is no doubt that throughout the Bible the poor and marginalized are God's preferred. The divine choice of Israel because it was the least of all peoples (cf. Deut. 7.7); God's constant concern for the widow, the stranger and the orphan, the unprotected ones of Israel; the prophetic message that God will come to the aid of those unjustly treated—all these form the backbone of the Hebrew Scriptures. The poor and unjustly treated of Brazil, in reading these passages, surely identify with their Israelite ancestors and feel themselves to be loved and championed by God: 'The poor and needy ask for water

15. J. W. Roffey, 'On Doing Reflection Theology: Poverty and Revelation 13.16-17', *Colloquium* 14.2 (1982), pp. 51-58.

and there is none, their tongue is parched with thirst. I, Yahweh, will answer them, I the God of Israel, will not abandon them' (Isa. 41.17).

In the New Testament, Jesus manifests in his own person this choice of God for the little ones. His words and his actions give evidence of this choice. Whether through the parable of the good shepherd or through his association with women, children, sinners and lepers, Jesus' preference for the outcast is clear. He, as his prophetic predecessors, had come not only to give sight to the blind and hearing to the deaf, but especially to proclaim good news to the poor and to set the downtrodden free (cf. Lk 4.16-22). Certainly these texts can be interpreted and understood by anyone sincerely seeking their meaning. But to hear them proclaimed in a community of the outcast, the powerless and the oppressed is to gain strength, courage and consolation, if not a particular insight.

The place in which we stand, our own perspective, surely influences the way we hear the message. Feminist biblical scholarship today is evidence of this fact. Those whose sensitivities have been sharpened by exclusion and whose faith has been enlightened by the proclamation and contemplation of the word surely help the whole community to discover dimensions of the text which might not otherwise find a hearing. In this sense, the poor and oppressed do in fact help the entire community to understand the depth of the biblical message at a particular time in history.

In another sense as well, the poor help the entire church hear and interpret the word of God. The Bible's consistent message is that the poor and the unprotected are to be the concern of the whole community. They are to be cared for within the total society. It was when Israel failed in this responsibility that the prophets expressed God's concern and will. Because the leaders of Israel have not cared for the weak, the sick and the wounded sheep, God will come to be Israel's shepherd (cf. Ezek. 34.4); because the poor are neglected within a relatively affluent society, God will come in judgment on those 'who are not made sick by the ruin of Joseph', that is, who are more concerned with their own advancement and comfort than they are with those vulnerable people neglected and overlooked by society (cf. Amos 6.6).

The presence of the poor is a symptom, a proof that something is wrong in society. Their very existence is a 'biblical word' against which all of life is to be interpreted.[16] In this sense, the poor once again call the

---

16. Conversation with Carlos Mesters.

entire ecclesial community to an interpretation of the biblical texts from their perspective.

Conclusion

There is no doubt that millions of catholics in Brazil have been formed by the Bible which has become part of their lives. So accustomed have they become to bringing God's word to bear on their daily lives that the process has become second nature to them. The biblical conviction that God is with them on their long journey toward liberation sustains the community throughout very difficult moments.

At the present time, there are several difficulties facing the church of Brazil. First of all, there seems to be a general fatigue, a sense of discouragement among the 'pastoral agents' and the people in general. No doubt disillusionment with the present government which promised much for the poor and yet has failed to realize those promises is a strong factor in this discouragement. That 'the rich grow richer and the poor poorer' is all too evident in the country, where a middle class is quickly disappearing. The church continues to support the dispossessed who 'invade' idle land, and yet land reform is not seriously undertaken. In the workplace, individuals and groups continue to protest for more just wages and conditions, and yet overall social reform for the worker is not undertaken. Rising prices and stagnant wages make hunger an ever more widespread reality. Massive migration from the countryside to the outskirts of the big cities continues, and yet little is done to bring the basic educational, health and economic services to the interior regions. The failure of the enormous Transamazonia project is not admitted and so Indian populations continue to be displaced. In short, hopes for a better society are frequently dashed. And yet the communities continue their struggle, taking courage from one another and being sustained by their common reading of the Bible.

It is no secret that fundamentalism has a great appeal in Latin America today, and Brazil is no exception. Whether this appeal is related to the communities' discouragement or not is hard to know. The individualistic spirituality of these fundamentalistic groups easily evades social issues and seems to offer a respite to those weary of fighting the battle of social justice. The method of interpreting the Bible has been and will continue to be a key issue in the way in which the basic Christian communities face the fundamentalist challenge. If the life of the people and the perspective of their liberation continue to be the starting point and the goal of interpretation, there is little chance of confusing the way Scripture is used in the BCCs and in the fundamentalist sects.

The way the Bible is read, heard, contemplated, interpreted and celebrated in Brazil today is a source of great hope for the whole church. Because of its option for the poor, the Brazilian church can echo the words of Diedrich Bonhoffer:

> We have...learnt to see the great events of world history from below, from the perspective of the outcast, the suspect, the maltreated, the powerless, the oppressed, the reviled—in short, from the perspective of those who suffer.[17]

This identification with the poor has been concretized in the basic Christian communities where God's word has truly been a source of life and liberation.

17. Cited in R. Shaull, 'The Latin Phoenix', *Colloquium* 14.2 (1982), pp. 5-12.

PERSPECTIVES FROM JEWISH EXEGESIS

Tamara C. Eskenazi

> In Judaism, unending commentary and commentary upon commentary are
> elemental. Talmudic exegesis exfoliates into uninterrupted study of the
> commentary on the Talmud... Hermeneutic unendingness and survival in
> exile are, I believe, kindred. The text of the Torah, of the biblical canon,
> and the concentric spheres of texts about these texts, replace the destroyed
> Temple... In dispersion, the text is homeland.[1]

In reflecting upon the process of exegesis in Judaism, I speak out of my
own social location as a traditional Jew, a woman and an Israeli. I will,
therefore, sketch three different, sometimes conflicting, Jewish exe
getical perspectives: (1) rabbinic exegesis, (2) women's interpretations,
and (3) cultural secular approaches to the Bible in Israel.

1. First Perspective: Rabbinic Exegesis

'Studying the Torah—interpretation—is the dominant cultural practice
of rabbinic Judaism.'[2] For centuries, as a result, the greatest talents of
the community were encouraged to pore over texts. Rabbinic Judaism,
in theory, has been Judaism led by a community of sages, a meritocracy
of the learned.[3] From its earliest days, Rabbinic Judaism valued study
not only as a prerequisite for piety but also as a form of devotion.

---

1.   George Steiner, *Real Presences* (Chicago: The University of Chicago Press,
1989), p. 40.
2.   Daniel Boyarin, *Intertextuality and the Reading of Midrash* (Bloomington:
Indiana University Press, 1990), p. 22. Rabbinic Judaism conventionally refers to a
dominant form of Judaism from the third century CE to the modern era.
3.   It is probably the case that wealth in ancient Jewish communities exercised as
much power as it did and does in other communities. But communal values
considered the most learned man as the best husband for the wealthiest girl in town.
As a result, learning and money were more often in cahoots with each other than in
conflict.

The importance of study can be gathered from the rabbinic claim that God also studies Torah and that indeed the Torah was created before all else. God even consulted the Torah in order to create a world.

But what is Torah? Torah, most commonly translated as 'Law' (NRSV) or 'Teaching' (JPS), usually refers to the Pentateuch. But in Rabbinic Judaism it also refers to the whole Hebrew Bible and to the totality of rabbinic literature: the Targums,[4] Talmud,[5] midrash collections, and the mediaeval commentaries and their heirs. These writings span over two thousand years of continuous interpretation.

We will organize our quick journey through this vast body of teachings by examining three basic characteristics which, I believe, typify Jewish interpretative tradition and help distinguish it from other exegetical patterns.

a. The role of the Hebrew language
b. Pluralism as an interpretative stance.
c. A distinctive emphasis on community.

The map for our journey will be a standard page from the text of Torah as it has been studied in traditional Jewish circles for the last few hundred years. And so, in typical rabbinic fashion, I place a text before you—a page from *Miqraot Gedolot*, also known as the Rabbinic Bible.[6]

Miqraot Gedolot represents the most common, basic form of the Bible that traditional Jews study. This glossed text became a standard form of the Bible in the sixteenth century. A page of *Miqraot Gedolot* contains the biblical text (often in boldface), literally surrounded by targumic expositions, a number of mediaeval commentaries, cross references to the Talmud, and textual information, encompassing over a thousand of years of Jewish interpretation.

With this map we will trace one verse through centuries of rabbinic interpretation in order to discover the content and processes of rabbinic exegesis. The verse before us is Gen. 2.18: 'It is not good for the human

---

4. The Aramaic translations of the Bible, rendered in the first centuries of the common era.

5. The authoritative record of rabbinic discussions on matters of law and lore. There are two editions of the Talmud: the Jerusalemite and the Babylonian. The Babylonian Talmud, the more definitive collection, comprises (in English translation) 37 volumes. It had been compiled by the sixth century CE.

6. The terms *Miqraot Gedolot* could be translated as 'Great Readings' or 'Big Scriptures', which is a most appropriate description of the work.

to be alone. I will make him a helper opposite him'. The verse expresses
divine purpose in creating a partner for the first human.

a. *The Role of the Hebrew Language*
On a page of *Miqraot Gedolot,* the Targum section, of course, is in
Aramaic. All the rest, like most rabbinic exegesis over the centuries, is in
Hebrew. In Jewish exegesis, the Hebrew language is the *medium* of exegesis, not merely its subject. Intimacy with the language helps access
linguistic possibilities encoded within the language of the Bible. The continuity of the biblical language transcends time and space and enables
exegetes living hundreds of years apart and thousands of miles apart to
continue to speak (as it were) with the text and with each other, literally
(not only metaphorically) in the same language.

'Language is country', Fernando F. Segovia has said.[7] For about two
thousand years, for Jews who had lost their homeland, language was the
only secure country and text was the only sure home. A student of
Torah was required to gain facility with Hebrew. For most of Jewish
history this meant the study of a second language, for Jews did not lead
an autonomous life in their own country and therefore spoke primarily
the language of the host country. Hebrew was reserved for study and
liturgy. It remained alive through the intense linguistic activities of the
rabbis. In Jewish society, education was a prerequisite for status and
Hebrew literacy was presumed.

b. *Pluralism as an Interpretative Stance*
A second characteristic of rabbinic exegesis is a commitment to diversity
in interpretation. I do not mean simply to state the obvious, that rabbinic
exegesis includes diverse interpretations, but rather to emphasize that
such diversity is valued and encouraged.

From the earliest stages, Jewish exegesis celebrated the polyvalence of
the biblical text and its interpretation in a manner that seems decidedly
modern, even postmodern.[8] The Bible itself provides obvious examples

7.   See his 'The Text as Other: Towards a Hispanic American Hermeneutic' in
this volume. The observation was made during the discussion of the paper in the
Casassa Conference.
8.   Indeed, there has been a growing interest in recent years in certain forms of
rabbinic exegesis, especially midrash, among modern literary critics who saw
parallels with deconstruction and other new literary approaches. See, for example,
G.H. Hartman and S. Budick, *Midrash and Literature* (New Haven: Yale University

of pluralism (with its multiple perspectives on many important events, such as creation in Genesis 1 and 2). During the early centuries of the common era, a major expression of multiple interpretations took the form of midrash.[9]

A page in *Miqraot Gedolot* does not contain a separate section for the midrash. Midrashic traditions are presupposed and appear embedded in the passages of individual commentators. Let me therefore quote some comments from the midrashic work on Genesis known as *Genesis Rabba*, a collection compiled around 400 CE.[10] Discussing our passage, 'It is not good for the human to be alone...' (Gen. 2.18), the sages of the midrash elaborate on what a man misses by living alone:

> It has been taught...: Whoever has no wife lives without good, without help, without joy, without blessing, without atonement... [there follow verses from Genesis and Leviticus to support these assertions]
> Rabbi Simon in the name of Rabbi Joshua son of Levi [said] 'Also without peace, as it is said, "And peace be to your house [meaning wife]"' [1 Sam. 25.6].
> Rabbi Joshua of Kikhnin in the name of Rabbi Levi [said], 'Also without life, as it is written, "Enjoy life with the wife whom you love"' [Eccl. 9.9].
> Rabbi Hiyya... said, 'Also he is not a complete man: "And he blessed *them* and called *their* name Adam"'... [Gen. 5.2].
> And some say, 'Such a person also diminishes the image of God...'[11]

As for the creation of a partner for the first human, some sages develop a polarity betwen the two Hebrew words used: *'ezer* ('help/helper') and *k^eneg^eddô* ('opposite him'), concluding 'If a man has merit, his wife will be like the wife of Hananiah son of Hakhinai, and if not, she will be like the wife of Rabbi Yose the Galilean'. The good wife of Hanaiah is never mentioned again but we do get a full report about poor Rabbi Yose and his mean-spirited wife.[12]

Press, 1986). Note, however, Boyarin's caution against too facile an equation of the two (see *Intertextuality*, esp. pp. 1-26).

9.   'Midrash' refers both to the rabbinic processes of interpretation that will be described and to collections of these interpretations (such as *Genesis Rabbah*).

10.   See Jacob Neusner, *Confronting Creation: Judaism Reads Genesis. An Anthology of Genesis Rabbah* (Columbia, NC: University of South Carolina, 1991) p. 3.

11.   Slightly revised from the translation in Neusner, *Confronting Creation*, p. 73.

12.   Neusner, *Confronting Creation*, pp. 74-75.

To begin with, we learn from this midrashic passage about the emphasis on marriage and family in Rabbinic Judaism—an emphasis that persists throughout the literature. Next, we also discern something of the style and method of midrashic discourse: its use of quotations and its intertextuality. Each rabbi quotes from the rest of the Bible to elucidate this verse. All parts of the canon are presumed to be equally relevant and at home in any context.

The rabbis 'did not write *about* scripture, they wrote *with* scripture, for scripture supplied the syntax and grammar of their thought...'[13] They recognized 'no single and original meaning that dictates for all time to come what scripture is permitted to say. To the contrary, they exercised a freedom of interpretation, by insisting that God speaks through the Torah to Israel and continually.'[14]

'The verses of the Bible function for the rabbis much as do words in ordinary speech. They are a repertoire of semiotic elements that can be recombined into new discourse'.[15] Just as words of any language can be placed into new relations, to generate new meanings, so can the verses of the Bible.[16] And so they combine verses from Leviticus, Second Samuel, Ecclesiastes and elsewhere in Genesis to fill in the gap in the biblical text with meaningful explications.

We also discover the polyphony of midrash. Rabbis quote and name other rabbis quoting Scripture or transmitting traditions. Various opinions stand side by side and, here at least, there is no attempt to unify interpretation.

The sages of late antiquity seemed to revel in the infinite possibilities within a text and to exercise their imagination and energy to interrogate and coax the text to yield as many interpretations as possible. The

13. Neusner, *Confronting Creation*, pp. vii-viii.

14. Neusner, *Confronting Creation*, pp. 10-11. Neusner continues: 'So they exemplify for us how to read scripture, and they also teach us some lessons that scripture has to offer them and us. The power of Genesis Rabbah is not only its messsge, therefore, but also its method. What is the method? To take up scriptures, bring to the written Torah the deepest anguish of the age. Allow the Torah to speak to us here and now' (ibid., p. 11).

15. Boyarin, *Intertextuality*, p. 28.

16. 'Just as in a lexicon words are placed into juxtaposition revealing semantic similarities and differences, so in the midrashic text, semantic similarities and differences between texts are revealed via new juxtapositions. Just as the words of any language can be placed into new syntagmatic relations, so can the verses of the Bible', Neusner, *Confronting Creation*, p. 28.

impression is of an ever unfolding (even overflowing) totality, brimming with multiplicity of meanings.

The master image comes from Jeremiah. The midrash takes Jer. 23.19 ('Behold, my word is like fire—declares YHWH—and like a hammer shattering a rock') to mean, 'Just as the hammer splinters a rock into several sparks, so does one verse have several meanings'.[17] The goal of students of Torah is to gather as many of these sparks as possible.[18]

As Boyarin shows, the key to midrashic hermeneutic is a specific kind of intertextuality.[19] Midrash is a hermeneutic that resists a bipolar division of object/subject. It keeps alive a dialectic in which the interaction between texts, or between texts and interpreters, is persistently mutual. Midrashic intertextuality neither privileges one biblical corpus over another, nor one context (i.e. original meaning) over another. Instead, Boyarin writes, 'We have rather the establishment of intertextual connection between two signifiers which mutually read each other'.[20] Texts are re-situated to release meanings through intensification and confrontation so that both are mutually illuminated.[21] Let us take our

17. *b. Sanh.* 34a.

18. Edward L. Greenstein adds: 'Jeremiah had been speaking of prophetic revelation, which he likened to fire and the blow of a hammer. The rabbis transfer the verse's contextual reference from the experience of revelation to the substance of revelation. That which is revealed, the sacred text, has many meanings...' ('Medieval Bible Commentaries', in *Back to the Sources: Reading the Classic Jewish Texts* [ed. B. Holtz; New York: Summit Books, 1984], pp. 215-16). Greenstein also writes, 'In the Medieval period it was acknowledged that multiplicity in the Bible's signification not only inheres in the nature of the text, but also results from divergent methods or dimensions of reading it' (ibid., pp. 216).

19. According to Boyarin, 'The sovereign notion informing the present reading of midrash is "intertextuality". This concept has several different accepted senses, three of which are important in my account of midrash. The first is that the text is always made up of a mosaic of conscious and unconscious citations of earlier discourse. The second is that texts may be dialogical in nature—contesting their own assertions as an essential part of the structure of their discourse—and that the Bible is a prominent example of such a text. The third is that there are cultural codes, again either conscious or unconscious, which both constrain and allow the production (not creation) of new texts within the culture; these codes may be identified with the ideology of the culture, which is made up of the assumptions that people in the culture automatically make about what may or may not be true and possible, about what is natural in nature and in history' (Boyarin, *Intertextuality*, p. 12).

20. Boyarin, *Intertextuality*, p. 112.

21. Boyarin, *Intertextuality*, p. 31.

midrashic reading of Gen. 2.18. Here the pairing of Ecclesiastes' 'Enjoy life with the wife whom you love' (Eccl. 9.9) as an exposition on what is not good about being alone illumines both passages. Ecclesiastes' recommendation of marriage now makes marriage partake of Eden and all its connotations, whereas the creation of human partners is now, through Ecclesiastes' mention of a partner 'whom you love', introduces love into the creation of the first pair, something otherwise lacking in Gen. 2.18.

Although Boyarin does not quite formulate it this way, it seems to me that midrash, as he describes it, is a hermeneutic of dialogue in the full Buberian sense of I and Thou. It models an exegetical dialogue that is both committed and open to the other, with the 'other' not as an objectified 'it' but rather as a 'you' to be encountered.

Midrash responds to contradictions; thrives on them, in fact. Far from smoothing over tension, midrash exposes and magnifies it in the service of multiple meanings, increasing interpretative options. Multiplicity of interpretations is not itself unique to rabbinic exegesis, nor is the presence of contradictions. What may be distinctive, however, is the position that the rabbis take towards this multiplicity. They credit a heavenly voice with declaring, during a rabbinic debate between opposing views, that opponents on both sides speak the words of the living God.[22]

These seemingly free exercises of the imagination in infinite possibilities nevertheless conform to rigorous methodological contraints and express certain precise overriding visions, necessarily rooted in a particular place and time. The most important one may be what Neusner has termed the shift to meta history as a result of the loss of political autonomy. The text is a response to catastrophe and attempts to reconstruct a cosmos independent of the vicissitudes of history and foreign powers. Neusner links, for example, the midrash on Genesis with the triumph of Christianity in the fourth or fifth centuries CE and the repressive policies that followed.[23]

---

22. *b. B. Meṣ.* 59b.

23. According to Neusner, 'the fourth century in fact presented the West, including Israel, with its first Christian century. While the Jewish people had managed on the whole to ignore the Christian slow but steady rise to power, they no longer could pretend Christianity constituted a temporary setback in the journey to the end time... Genesis Rabbah in its final form emerges from that momentous first century in the history of the West as Christian, the century in which the Rome empire [*sic*] passed from pagan to Christian rule, and, in which, in the aftermath of the Emperor Julian's abortive reversion to paganism in 360, Christianity adopted that

A different cultural context, that of Islam, gave rise to another approach. 'This approach, that of peshat, sought to understand the biblical text within the parameters of its historical, literary, and linguistic context. Historical context requires that interpretation must read the text in terms of the world of ancient Israel and the biblical story as a whole'.[24]

Peshat is not 'plain', 'simple' or 'literal' interpretation (as is often supposed) but rather what Greenstein prefers to call 'context approach'.[25] The ascendency of *peshat* is itself an expression of a three-way cross-cultural encounter between Judaism, Islam and Christianity, as well as a result of certain inner Jewish developments (emerging first under Islam and spreading to Christian areas).[26] The rabbis on the page of *Miqraot Gedolot* first make their appearance during this era. Greenstein writes:

> Jewish scholars in Arabic-speaking lands devoted more and more attention to contextual, or *peshat*, method of interpretation. This approach required historical perspective, rationalism, and linguistic and literary sophistication. By dint of its fairly secular orientation, this method allowed Jewish interpreters to argue the meaning of Scripture on common ground with partisans of other faiths... The peshat approach emerged in the Orient and spread to Spain, where grammarians, such as Ibn Janah, and synthetic commentators, like Ibn Ezra, defined its decisive applications to biblical studies. Simultaneous with Ibn Ezra, *peshat* surfaced as a major force in Bible commentary in France, where style and plain sense guided interpretation more than ever before.[27]

With *peshat*, historical issues came more vividly to the fore, leading to probing of historical questions about authorship, date, canonicity and sources. As F.E. Greenspahn observes, 'the earlier rabbis had already recognized the Psalter's diverse authorship'.[28] They also acknowledged

policy of repression of paganism that rapidly engulfed Judaism as well' (Neusner, *Confronting Creation*, p. 8).

24. Greenstein, 'Medieval Bible Commentaries', p. 217. For examples and reasons for these developments, see pp. 217-23 in his essay.

25. Greenstein, 'Medieval Bible Commentaries', p. 217.

26. Internal dynamics include the completion of the Talmud and the challenge of the Karaites, which required defenders of Rabbinic Judaism to muster linguistic tools for their defense (see Greenstein, 'Medieval Bible Commentaries', p. 224)

27. Greenstein, 'Medieval Bible Commentaries', p. 255.

28. F.E. Greenspahn, 'How Modern Are Modern Biblical Studies?', in M. Brettler and M. Fishbane (eds.), *Minha le-Nahum: Biblical and Other Studies*

the heterogeneity of other books such as Isaiah, Jeremiah and Nahum.[29]
Greenspahn further comments:

> Even sections of the Pentateuch were recognized as unlikely to be Mosaic,
> not just by Spinoza or his acknowledged source, Ibn Ezra, but by the
> Talmud, which points out that Moses could not have written
> Deuteronomy's description of his own death, nor Joshua or Samuel
> about their deaths...[30]

But it is during the mediaeval period that such questions grow in importance, moving to the foreground, without becoming heretical. The rabbinic presupposition of 'Torah from heaven' did not 'relegate questions
of authorship to irrelevance, but instead freed Jewish exegetes from fear
of heresy since it entailed no commitment to the date of the human
intermediary through whom the biblical writings has been given'.[31]

The Spanish Jewish exegete Abraham Ibn Ezra (1089-1164) is a recognized master of *peshat*. Like so many mediaeval Jewish commentators he was many things: poet, philologist, mathematician. In the case of
our passage, his entry in *Miqraot Gedolot* is terse, elucidating the syntax
of the verse. Ibn Ezra simply says, '''not good'', meaning for the
human'. What Ibn Ezra's brief comment accomplishes is a confinement
of the reference to goodness and an exclusion of certain other
interpretations as to the nature of humanity.

His contribution gains significance when we realize that the Hebrew
of this verse, לא טוב היות האדם, could be otherwise read 'the human is not
good' or 'the being of the human is not good'. Ibn Ezra, with a single
brush stroke, eliminates this possibility.

Elsewhere, Ibn Ezra proves deft at identifying literary as well as
philological matters (word play, chiasmus, parallelism) and at developing
some theories about how the texts work. But he also demonstrates a

Presented to Nahum M. Sarna in Honor of his 70th Birthday (JSOTSup, 154;
Sheffield: JSOT Press, 1993), pp. 164-82 (174). For numerous examples from the
Midrash and Talmud, see ibid., p. 174 n. 3.

29. Greenspahn, 'How Modern Are Modern Biblical Studies?', p. 174. For
rabbinic examples, see p. 174 n. 4.

30. Greenspahn, 'How Modern Are Modern Biblical Studies?', p. 174. For
rabbinic references, see pp. 174-75 n. 5.

31. Greenspahn, 'How Modern Are Modern Biblical Studies?', p. 173. For a
fuller discussion of this issue, see ibid., p. 173 n. 2, which includes a reference to
J. Petuchowski (among others), 'The Supposed Dogma of the Mosaic Authorship of
the Pentateuch', *HibJ* 57 (1958–59), pp. 356-60.

sophisticated sense of history and social context and gives, on occasion, what we might call an anthropological interpretation.

Peshat and midrash combined in the mediaeval synthesis is best represented by Rashi (1040–1105) of France, the most widely revered commentator.[32] Rashi's commentary on the Torah is a distillation of rabbinic midrash on select texts with a dose of *peshat* (so Greenstein).[33] Rashi's hermeneutics displays

> sensitivity to the nuances, even the spelling, of the text's wording; midrashic analysis of words into their possible components and permutations; drawing out the lessons of the text for pious living; expanding the story by filling in background and dialogue; a constant consideration of rabbinic exegesis that is both deferential and critical; and above all, a pedagogical desire to make clear.[34]

Rashi, writes concerning our passage:

> 'I shall make a help opposite him' in order that people may not say that there are two deities, the Holy One Blessed Be He, the only One among the celestial Beings without a mate, and this one (adam) the only one among the terrestial beings without a mate (Pirke de R. Eliezer; my translation).

Rashi's concern is theological, affirming the oneness of God. We cannot help but detect controversies with Christians lurking in the background. Like many of the other biblical exegetes, he is also concerned with transmitting earlier traditions. He thus continues by reiterating the midrashic teaching about 'help' and 'opposite', stating that if one is worthy, the partner shall be a help; if one is unworthy, the partner shall be an opponent.

Ramban,[35] also known as Nachmanides (1194–1274), of Spain, brought together Spanish and French influences. His interpretations included mystical and legal material as well as specific references to 'The Philosopher' (Aristotle), whose writing had become part of contemporary intellectual discourse. Ramban was charged by Christian authorities with defending Judaism in a public debate and had apparently done so with courage as well as humour. However, even though he had been promised immunity, he was consequently tried for blasphemy and

---

32. Rashi is an acronym of Rabbi Solomon son of Isaac.
33. Greenstein, 'Medieval Bible Commentaries', p. 228.
34. Greenstein, 'Medieval Bible Commentaries', p. 242.
35. That is, Rabbi Moses son of Nachman.

forced to leave. He went to Israel where he later died. Commenting on our passage, Ramban writes:

> Adam wasn't created to be alone in the world and not give birth. All who were created, male and female, were created to propagate seed. Even grass and trees have their seeds in them. But it is possible to say that things were as someone had said [a reference to a sage, Jeremiah son of Elazar]: that they [i.e. humanity as adam] were created two-faced/double-faced (my translation).

Ramban then explores the kind of reproduction mechanisms possible for this two-faced human (with male and female reproductive organs), making reference to some controversies, to physicians and Greek philosophers, incorporating science.[36] He then continues, 'The second face helped the first in giving birth. The Holy One Blessed Be He saw that it will be good that the helper will stand over against him and he will see him, and separate from him and join him as he wishes' (my translation. I have retained the confusing 3rd person masc. of the Hebrew original).

Sforno (approximately1470–1550) of Italy lived in Rome where he studied medicine, philosophy, philology and mathematics. He met the humanist Reuchlin and helped him with his Hebrew. Sforno typically used *peshat* but wove in sayings from the sages to illustrate ethical teachings. Commenting on Gen. 2.18 he writes, '"Helper". That there be an equal to him in image and form; for that is necessary for knowing his wants and meeting them as needed. "Opposite him"—a counter weight in the balance'. However, Sforno concludes that it is not worthwhile that the helper be completely equal, for then it would not be appropriate that one will serve and work for his friend (the masculine language is Sforno's).

In *Miqraot Gedolot* all of these commentators appear on a single page, representing an array of mediaeval Jewish views from different decades and countries. As even this brief sampling shows, mediaeval Jewish exegesis did not signal a retreat from the earlier polyvalence/polysemy. As the examples before us demonstrate, even a simple passage elicited multiple possible explanations, a range of them reproduced for the reader. The issue of final meaning remains unsettled.

36. Clearly, the first human here is considered to be androgynous, a view already proposed by the rabbis in *Genesis Rabbah*, and more recently invoked by some modern scholars (see esp. Phyllis Trible, *God and the Rhetoric of Sexuality* [Philadelphia: Fortress Press, 1978], pp. 73-105).

Emblematic of this era and subsequent Jewish interpretation is the view concerning the four-fold nature of interpretation—*peshat, remez* (allusion) *derash* (midrashic) and *sod* (secret meaning)—which enters Jewish discourse in the thirteenth century. There is little doubt that the formulation is derived from an earlier Christian four-fold interpretation (even though the Christian categories somewhat differ; see, for example, Fishbane[37]). Nevertheless, the Jewish appropriation of the four modes of interpretation has its own nuances, the most striking of which is the meaning ascribed to the quartet as a whole. The four methods add up to the acronym *PRDS*, or *par^e dēs*, meaning in Hebrew 'pleasure garden' or 'park'.[38] Already in the early rabbinic period, *par^e dēs* came to refer to the garden of Eden, to paradise. This new expression for interpretation not only preserves multiplicities but also helps us to understand the meaning of the exegetical process for the rabbis. For them paradise is directly and intimately related to the processes of interpretation: to grasp all the levels of the text is to have *par^e dēs*, to have, to create or to be in paradise.

c. *Community*

Jewish exegesis persistently emphasizes community, not only in its content but through the exegetical process itself. Early rabbinic literature is, above all, the compilation of the teachings of hundreds of voices. At least 600 named individuals appear in the Mishnah, and over 1800 in the Talmud. As we have seen, the midrashic literature is yet another vast collection of voices.

Rabbinic literature reproduces communal, public discourse that had transpired presumably in academies, rather than the work of private individuals working in isolation. As we have seen, rabbis speak in their own names or quote their teachers. The result is not only polyvalence but also polyphony (either a cacophony or symphony, depending on how well trained one's ear is).

Only in the mediaeval period do individuals begin to write their own,

---

37. M. Fishbane, 'The Teacher and the Hermeneutical Task: A Reinterpretation of Medieval Exegesis', in *The Garments of Torah: Essays in Biblical Hermeneutics* (Bloomington: Indiana University Press, 1989), pp. 112-20. See also the several essays on biblical exegesis under 'Tanach, Parshanut', in *Encyclopaedia Biblica*, VIII (Jerusalem: Bialik Institute, 1982), pp. 641-749 (Hebrew).

38. The word is a Persian loan word.

continuing commentaries on biblical books.[39] Rashi, Ibn Ezra and Ramban, for example, wrote such commentaries. Nevertheless, *Miqraot Gedolot,* as we saw, organizes them piecemeal around the biblical text. Consequently, traditional Judaism reads them as a community of sages. Community triumphs.[40]

This glossed text, explicitly creating or recreating community around individual biblical verses, became normative. Individual voices are heard distinctly but never alone. The dialogue of text with text, commentator with commentator, takes place on every single page.

2. *Second Perspective: Women*

Having looked at what is literally on the page in rabbinic exegesis, let us look at what is not there: the words of women. Bearing in mind that the search for and creation of paradise continued and continues among the learned rabbis and their communities to the present time, we now shift perspectives to focus on women and their roles in Jewish exegesis.

For most of its history, Jewish exegesis, like Christian or Islamic exegesis, did not represent the interpretative concerns of women. Post-biblical exegesis in Judaism has been typically the domain of men.[41] The propriety of educating women in Torah had been the subject of heated talmudic debates, debates that continue presently in some circles. Yet several women (often wives or daughters of eminent sages) do seem to have had a role, albeit marginal.

Talmudic literature acknowledges Ima Shalom and Bruriah as two formidable exegetes.[42] Later stories about Bruriah's tragic death,

39. These commentators often preface their work with introductions where they explain their hermeneutical methods (and debunk others').

40. The formal features of *Miqraot Gedolot* do not necessarily reflect the conscious decision by the Jewish community to subsume individual voices to communal dialogue. As far as we know, this was purely the decision of some fifteenth or sixteenth-century publisher, presumably for economic reasons. Nor did this arrangement necessarily originate in Judaism. Peter of Lombard's text is already a glossed text. But it is in Judaism that this format becomes normative for reading the Bible.

41. The Bible itself occasionally grants women an important voice in interpretation, as the role of the prophetess Huldah demonstrates (2 Kgs 22).

42. On Ima Shalom, wife of Eleazer ben Hyrcanus (c. 50 CE), see *Written Out of History: Our Jewish Foremothers* (Sondra Henry and Emily Taitz [eds.]; New York: Biblio Press, 1983), pp. 48-53. On Bruriah, see ibid., pp. 54-58 and Rachel Adler, 'The Virgin in the Brothel: The Legend of Beruriah', *Tikkun* 3/6 (1988), pp. 28-32 and 102-105.

however, may have been a polemic intended to discourage such learning among women. Some reports about women as exegetes have been preserved in travellers' diaries that mention women teachers of Scripture in mediaeval Baghdad and elsewhere.[43] In addition, we learn that Rashi's daughters and granddaughters were well-educated. One of them had written Responsa in Rashi's behalf when he was sick and unable to do so. But none of their writings have been preserved. Their voices have been lost.

In the sixteenth century, roughly paralleling the emergence of *Miqraot Gedolot* as a more widely available text of the Bible, the book *Tzenah Urenah* appeared and quickly became the most influential popular source of Bible stories for the next two centuries.[44] The title, which exhorts women to 'go out and see' (a quotation from Song of Songs), indicates that the intended audience was women. The book is a selective retelling of biblical tales through rabbinic eyes. It was written in Yiddish, the mother tongue of European Jews since the Middle Ages. Although the book frequently highlights stories concerning women, its aim is to transmit traditional, rabbinic teachings to women. The book was compiled by a man, Rabbi Yaakov son of Isaac Ashkenazi.

We begin to have sources for women's interpretation of the Bible in Jewish women's prayers. Chavah Weissler has collected and analyzed prayers that had been used since the early eighteenth century. Realizing

---

43. Bat Halevi (literally, 'daughter of the Levite'; apparently her name has not been preserved), a daughter of the head of the academy, had been an 'expert in Scripture and Talmud'. She (so a traveller wrote in his memoirs) 'gives instruction in Scripture to young men through a window. She herself is within the building, whilst her disciples are below outside and do not see her' (Henry and Taitz, *Written Out of History*, p. 87). Bat Halevi was the daughter of Rabbi Samuel son of Ali, a rival of Rambam, who, unlike the latter, believed in educating women and incorporating them in public roles (see ibid., pp. 86-87). The report concerning Bat Halevi comes from the travel diary of Rabbi Petachiach of Regensburg. For further information concerning Bat Halevi, see ibid., p. 266 nn. 3 and 4.

44. Modern editions of the book include an English version of Exodus published as *Tzenah U-Reenah: A Jewish Commentary on the Book of Exodus* (trans. N. Gore; New York: Vintage Press, 1965), a more recent one by Art Scrolls Judaica Series as *Tz'enah ur'enah: The Classic Anthology of Torah Lore and Midrashic Comment* (trans. M.S. Zakon; New York: Mesorah Publications, 1983), and a Hebrew edition of Genesis known as *Tze'enah U-re'enah* (trans. M. Kozak; Jerusalem: Machon haMa'or, 1974).

that prayers written for women could have been, like the book *Tzenah Urenah*, composed by men, she nevertheless succeeds in identifying many that clearly were authored by women.[45]

These individual and private prayers in Yiddish, called *Tekhines* (meaning 'petitions') focus on issues specific to the lives of traditional women as wives, mothers and homemakers: asking for easy childbirth, for health for a child or spouse, safe journey for one's husband, even success in cooking.

Biblical Hannah figures prominently in these prayers, not only because of her role in the Bible but because her name forms the acronym for the three *miṣôt*, commandments, special to women: *ḥālāh*, *niddāh* and *hadlākat nerôt* (the baking and dividing of the Challah bread for the Shabbat, the observance of menstruation laws for family purity, and the lighting of the Sabbath candles; hence Ḥ-N-H, that is, Chanah, Hebrew for Hannah).

The 'women's devotional literature picks out well-known (and obscure) biblical women and selectively uses their midrashic characteristics to make them a focus for identification'.[46] Many of the roles express lives centred around the family and home, and thus focus on Sarah, Rebekah, Rachel and Leah as enablers.

An important author of such women's prayers is Sarah bat Tovim (1700s). In her collection, entitled *Shloyshe She'orim* (Three Gates), Sarah bat Tovim invokes the matriarchs Sarah, Rebekah, Rachel and Leah whose merit, she hopes, will also benefit her, or any other praying woman (a close parallel to the invocation of the merits of the fathers in the liturgy that both men and women use). She concludes with the following, telling petition: 'And may God forgive me for the fact that in my youth I talked in the Synagogue when they were conducting the service and reading the dear Torah'.[47]

Sarah bat Tovim introduces each prayer with the pertinent biblical verse that underlies the commandment, followed by an exposition of context and of the larger system of tithes and commandments in ancient

45. Chava Weissler, 'The Traditional Piety of Ashkenazic Women', in Arthur Green (ed.), *Jewish Spirituality from the Sixteenth-Century Revival to the Present* (New York: Crossroad, 1987), pp. 245-75. See also her 'Prayers in Yiddish and the Religious World of Ashkenazic Women', in Judith R. Baskin (ed.), *Jewish Women in Historical Perspective* (Detroit: Wayne University Press, 1991), pp. 159-81.

46. Weissler, 'The Traditional Piety', p. 268.

47. Weissler, 'The Traditional Piety', p. 254.

Israel. She supplements these with an exposition about the new significance of these commandments in light of the destruction of the Temple in 70 CE and in the wake of subsequent events in Jewish history.

Her prayers, the themes of which resemble many other extant prayers from that era, empower women to link their seemingly humble, private domestic activities with the whole of Jewish history. According to these prayers, the laws of the Challah bread parallel sacrifices of atonement for all of Israel. And the lighting of the candles is analogous to the activities of the High priest, the highest religious functionary in ancient Israel. 'I also pray over the candles that the dear God may accept my *mizwah* of the lights as if my candles were the olive oil lamps which burned in the temple and were never extinguished'.[48]

A more audible voice of women emerges in the nineteenth century in Grace Aguilar's works. Her magisterial book on women in the Bible has 576 pages and was published in 1845, preceding the celebrated *Woman's Bible* of Elizabeth Cady Stanton by some 50 years. The full title amply describes Aguilar's book: *The Women of Israel or Characters and Sketches from the Holy Scriptures and Jewish History Illustrative of the Past History, Present Duty, and Future Destiny of the Hebrew Females, as Based on the Word of God.*[49]

Aguilar (1816–1847) was an English Jew, of Marranos descent,[50] who considered it her special task to encourage Jews, especially women, to go back to the Bible for sources of Jewish identity (and bypass rabbinic commentaries).[51] Her own exploration, she tells us, seeks to counter two troublesome issues: (1) the view expressed in her time that 'Christianity is the sole source of female excellence';[52] and (2) the allegations that the Hebrew Bible shows how 'the law of Moses sunk the Hebrew female to the lowest state of degradation'.[53]

---

48. Cited by Weissler, 'The Traditional Piety', p. 256.

49. The citations here are from the edition published by London: George Routledge and Sons, no date.

50. I.e., her Spanish or Portugese ancestors had forcefully been converted to Chritianity during the period around the expulsion from Spain but retained secret Jewish identity.

51. According to Aguilar, 'To desert the Bible for its commentators, never to peruse its pages without notes of explanation; to regard it as a work which of itself is incomprehensible, is, indeed, a practice as hurtful as injudicious' (*The Women of Israel*, p. 9).

52. *The Women of Israel*, p. 10.

53. *The Women of Israel*, pp. 9-10.

Her exegesis thus has a double agenda defined by her time and place. First, it is to defend the Hebrew Bible and Jewish interpretations of it in the face of Christian readings that devalue Judaism vis à vis Christianity. Secondly, it is to demonstrate to Jews that the Bible reflects a high regard for woman in both public and private life and teaches, thereby, the importance of equal Jewish education for women.

Aguilar wrote essays, novels and poetry. In her treatment of the Bible, she not only examines all the major women but also lingers on minor characters and obscure references to women. She hardly misses a note. She discusses the female workers of the Tabernacle (Exod. 38.8), Achsa, Caleb's daughter (Judg. 1.10-15) and laws concerning wives, widows and female servants.

Not forgetting the Israelite maid who had directed the foreigner Naaman to the prophet Elisha in 2 Kings 4, Aguilar uses this story to urge the training of Jewish women of all classes. After all, she points out, even lower-class women, such as an Israelite maid, were obviously educated religiously in ancient Israel![54]

Aguilar's attention to issues of class, religion and gender is startling for its modern ring. Her reading of the story of Samson's mother (Judg. 13) anticipates most of what feminists have said in recent years and more. Having highlighted the story's subtleties, Aguilar writes (in florid nineteenth-century English),

> Regarding this narrative and its bearings on our history as Women of Israel, it is confirmation strong of our always attested declaration, that neither Written nor Oral Law interfered with the perfect equality of man and wife. The chapter before us displays a simple and natural picture of conjugal confidence and equality, and of the respective peculiarities of man and woman. It is impossible to read this chapter, without perceiving that Manoah's wife was a perfectly free agent, only bound by the links of love and confidence which marriage laws enjoin. As the mother of the child selected to deliver Israel in part from the Philistines, she was even of more importance in the sight of God than her husband, a fact inferred from the angel appearing both times to *her*, and only addressing Manoah when addressed by him.[55]

> Still more clearly demonstrative that the Hebrew wife really occupied the free and equal position which the laws of God Himself assigned her, is the fact that it was her ready wit, and quickness of intellect, which reassured her husband. She had been awe-struck like himself, but yet,

54. *The Women of Israel*, pp. 319-22.
55. *The Women of Israel*, p. 226.

perfectly in accordance with woman's nature, was the first to comprehend the real intention of the revelation...[56]

Elaborating on the range of faculties that Manoah's wife wisely employs, Aguilar observes,

> But that Manoah's wife could thus comprehend, and thus correctly judge, implies a domestic and social position which not only permitted, but exercised these peculiar faculties. In an enslaved and degraded position, their possession was practically and theoretically impossible.[57]

Though she demonstrates that women, like Manoah's wife, can often be superior to men, Aquilar nevertheless urges them *not* to press their superiority: 'It is a woman's province to influence, never to dictate; to conceal rather than assume superiority...never let her permit her husband to feel his inferiority...for if she does, she may rest assured that from that instant her influence is at an end for ever'.[58] (I prefer not to comment on this observation!)

Aguilar was 31 years old when she died.

Only recently have Jewish women become truly visible in both the acedmic arena of biblical scholarship and in specifically Jewish circles. One needs only mention Nehema Leibowitz and Sara Japhet, two Israeli biblical scholars of unrivaled international reputation, to realize the great contribution that Jewish women have began to make to biblical studies.

When Jewish feminism emerged, its earliest agenda included entering the exegetical process because of the power that exegesis holds in Jewish life. It is difficult to be a subject in Judaism without entering the exegetical debate.[59] Like Aguilar, Jewish feminists first found themselves battling two fronts, when some Christian feminists sought to redeem Christianity for feminism by relegating unpalatable aspects of Scripture to Judaism. Jewish feminists, struggling with their own relation to unacceptable aspects of Scripture, responded thus to the attitude of non Jews towards Judaism and to attitudes in Jewish traditions towards women's role.[60] Eventually the range of interests and concerns broadened.[61]

56. *The Women of Israel*, p. 227.
57. *The Women of Israel*, p. 227.
58. *The Women of Israel*, pp. 227-28.
59. See Rachel Adler, 'The Jew Who Wasn't There: Halakhah and the Jewish Woman' (originally 1973), reprinted in Susannah Heschel (ed.), *On Being A Jewish Feminist: A Reader* (New York: Schocken Books, 1983), pp. 3-12.
60. Key works on Jewish feminism are Susannah Heschel (ed.), *On Being a Jewish Feminist*, and Judith Plaskow, *Standing Again at Sinai: Judaism from a*

Not all women biblical scholars identify themselves explicitly as Jewish and/or feminist. Nehama Leibowitz, widely recognized as one of the foremost Bible teachers in Israel, for example, does not represent a feminist perspective but rather a traditional rabbinic one.[62] Athalia Brenner[63] and Ilana Pardes,[64] on the other hand, speak as feminists but do not explicitly identify a Jewish agenda. Tikvah Frymer-Kensky, however, does express concern for both feminist and Jewish issues.[65]

Rachel Adler exemplifies, perhaps, one of the clearest explicit attempts to face the challenge of both feminism and tradition. She reads Genesis 1–3, for instance, with an eye towards transforming the Jewish tradition from a specific Jewish feminist perspective.[66] Adler highlights the tension between Genesis 1 and Genesis 2: Genesis 1 depicts gendered humanity created as two varieties of a single species. 'The creation precedes not by polarization but by differentiation within wholeness'. Male and female, the two varieties of *adam*, 'embody diversity within similarity'. Genesis 2, however, reflects a process of opposition and partialization. 'Adam in this story is a male individual and bears a curious resemblance to the motherless asocial resident of the state of nature posited by liberal political theory'. Woman has no independent being. She is derivative (Gen. 2.23). Together they are the human and his woman (Gen. 2.25). Genesis 2 is best understood as the creation of patriarchy, depicting 'the patriarchs' inner experience—loneliness, and a sense of mutilation—and its attempt to recover the banished other

Feminist Perspective (San Francisco: Harper & Row, 1990).

61. Note the several Jewish contributers to the new *Women's Bible Commentary* (Westminster/John Knox Press, 1992); see also the work of Athalia Brenner: esp. *The Israelite Woman: Social Role and Literary Type in Biblical Narrative* (Sheffield: JSOT Press, 1985); Tamar Frankiel. *The Voice of Sarah: Feminine Spirituality and Traditional Judaism* (San Francisco: Harper & Row, 1990); and Carol Meyers, *Discovering Eve: Ancient Israelite Women in Context* (Oxford: Oxford University Press, 1988).

62. See, e.g., her *Studies in Bereshit/Genesis* (Jerusalem: World Zionist Organisation: Department for Torah Education and Culture in the Diaspora. 1972).

63. See, e.g., *A Feminist Companion to Genesis* (Sheffield: JSOT Press, 1993) which she edited.

64. See her *Countertraditions in the Bible: A Feminist Approach* (Cambridge. MA: Harvard University Press, 1992).

65. See *In the Wake of the Goddess: Women, Culture, and the Biblical Transformation of Pagan Myth* (New York: Macmillan. 1992).

66. 'A Question of Boundaries: Toward a Jewish Feminist Theology of Self and Others', *Tikkun* 3/6 (May/June, 1991) pp. 43-46 and 87.

through fusion... An Eden founded upon a fantasy of obliterating the other is bound to be unstable'.[67] She proceeds to enquire about the implications of these stories for Jewish theology and offers biblical support for a more inclusive vision of self and other.

3. *Third Perspective: Israel and a Secular Appropriation of the Bible*

If the midrashic rabbis wrote with Scripture, modern Israeli Jews speak and sing with Scripture, sometimes unknowingly so. With the return to the land of Israel in the twentieth century, the Hebrew language became the language of everyday speech, not simply of study and worship. And the Bible became a basis for a different kind of Jewish culture. Prior to this era the text was the map, but, to recontextualize Jonathan Z. Smith, map is not territory. And territory opened new ways to live and interpret the Bible as a document of national identiy that is not focused on religion.[68] For those Israelis who are secular Jews, the Bible tells the stories of ancestors connected to places and seasons much like their own.

In Israeli public education, starting with elementary school, the Bible is taught as the greatest national heritage. Courses on literature, grammar and history all teach the Bible. The vocabulary, images and teachings are absorbed in a secular mode for their human values and their specific applications to life in the land.

For modern Israelis, biblical proclamations about Israel's relations to Syria, Lebanon or Egypt are not simply names from the past; they are the stuff of daily news. The promised land is not a metaphor for some unknown space. It is *this* place. 'Place,' writes Walter Brueggemann (building on Jonathan Z. Smith) 'is space which has historical meanings, where some things have happened and which provide [sic] continuity and identity across generations. Place is space in which important words have been spoken which have established identity, defined vocation and

---

67. All quotations in this paragraph from Adler, 'A Question of Boundaries', p. 46.

68. As is well known, many Israeli Jews are religious and the Bible continues to be their source of spiritual and practical guidance, along with other aspects of Jewish teachings and traditions. What I want to stress in this portion of the paper is the fact that the Bible can also engender a rich and complex secular culture, as it does in Israel.

envisioned destiny'.[69] Place is also the declaration that our humanness is nurtured by attachment and commitment. 'A yearning for place is a decision to enter history'.[70]

For a people who had been homeless for 2000 years, the passion for the land, for roots, finds strong conformation in the Bible itself. Many biblical teachings pertain to and presume a life in Israel. Furthermore, according to Rabbinic Judaism, there are many commandments that can be fulfilled only in Israel, therefore life in exile necessarily diminishes one's ability to do God's will. Israelis look around them and the stories they read in the Bible live before their eyes. Defeat at Megiddo or victory at the Jordan are part of the landscape. Beer Sheba where Abraham dwelled is where one lives or visits; Schechem is over there to the left. Street signs are a lesson in who's who in the Bible. Just ask for directions and biblical history unfolds before you as you are instructed to take Kings' street to the intersection with Prophets' street, and so on. Everywhere you go you know whose footsteps you follow.

These are the Gilboa mountains commanded by David to mourn over Jonathan and Saul; those are the hills that must shout with joy when Israel returns from exile. To paraphrase a well known song, the hills are alive with the sounds of Scriptures.

'Land and language!' exclaims Halkin (a former American, now an Israeli), 'They are the ground beneath a people's feet and the air it breathes in and out'.[71] Writing to an American Jewish friend he says,

> The almond tree is already in bloom, a white blaze on the hillside... Everything is sprouting now, shooting, racing madly to gorge itself on the soused earth and grow while there's time... 'And I will give the rain for your land in its season, the early rain and the later rain, that you may gather in your grain and your wine and your oil. And I will give you grass in your fields for your cattle, and you shall eat and be full' [Deut. 11.14-15]. How many times did I say those words as a boy without knowing what a first or later rain was or how the world looked when one fell? I can tell you exactly: three times a day, because they belong to the Shema, which is recited as part of the morning, evening, and bedtime Prayers. My

69. *The Land* (Overtures to Biblical Theology; Philadelphia: Fortress Press, 1977), p. 5. See also Jonathan Z. Smith, 'Earth and Gods', *JA* 49 (1969), pp. 108-27; *idem, To Take Place: Toward Theory in Ritual* (Chicago: Chicago University Press, 1987).

70. Brueggemann, *The Land*, p. 6.

71. Hillel Halkin, *Letters to an American Jewish Friend* (Philadelphia: JPS, 1977), p. 153.

children will not know it by heart like their father, but they will speak the
language in which it is written and know about this land...[72]

They may not have the prayer, but they will have inherited the
experience itself.

4. *Conclusions*

I have sketched three different ways that the Bible lives in the Jewish
community. Some of these echo the experiences and patterns of other
interpretative communities. Some are distinctive to Judaism.

The dominant cultural context for Jewish exegesis since the first
century CE has been exile, where Jews usually felt powerless and at the
mercy of the host culture. To these landless people, language and text
were home. Through them the rabbis constructed, not unlike God, a
world. The women's movement and the emergence of the State of Israel
brought new challenges to this understanding of text and interpretative
communities. Like all healthy challenges, they illumine new possibilities
and limits not only in Jewish exegesis but in the Bible itself. I hope that
they contribute to our discussions of the Bible and cultural exegesis.
John Barton observed during the Casassa Conference that what has
emerged in the conference is a double notion of what is cultural
exegesis. This reminds me of what the rabbis had said about the passage
with which I began. They spoke, as you recall, about the partner created
for *adam,* the first human, a partner who could be either a help or a hin-
drance. I think that their interpretation may apply to cultural exegesis. If
we are worthy, it will be of help; if we are not it will be against us.
Either way it is better than speaking only to ourselves for, after all, it is
not good for the human—or the Bible—to be alone.[73]

72. Halkin, *Letters to an American Jewish Friend*, pp. 150-51.

73. I thank my colleagues and friends Rachel Adler, Lewis Barth, Lisa Edwards
and J. William Whedbee, who thoughtfully responded to an early draft of this paper
and made many excellent suggestions.

FEEDING THE WIDOW, RAISING THE DEAD:
WHAT COUNTS AS CULTURAL EXEGESIS?

Thomas W. Overholt

Before I began corresponding with Daniel Smith-Christopher, I had
never heard the term 'cultural exegesis'. In the intervening months my
task has therefore been to arrive at a definition, as well as to sort out the
kind of claims being made for 'cultural exegesis' and the validity of
those claims. This has involved me in some reflections on methodology.
While I have no particular interest in studying methodology for its own
sake, I have considerable interest in enhancing the self-awareness and
clarity of my own interpretative work, and that has also been on my
mind.

I. *Definition and Claims*

The Principle
In one of his early letters to me (7-23-90), Daniel Smith-Christopher
noted that cultural bias is 'usually considered a negative reality to be
scrupulously avoided by the "scientific critic"'. He went on to a
counter-proposal that such bias is 'not only unavoidable, but can possibly also be a positive element in interpretation'. So, for example, a
sheep-herder might be able to see things in Jesus' people-acting-like-
sheep stories that would be lost on someone with urban upbringing. This
example, along with the fact that Smith-Christopher is involved in
research projects involving Lakota (Sioux) Indians and Aboriginal
Australians, and has had students working in ethnic communities around
Los Angeles, suggests that he views 'cultural exegesis' as a kind of
'folk' interpretation.
    So for Smith-Christopher the question is, Can there be 'such a thing
as a "culturally specific" exegesis that is *more* accurate on some aspects
of interpretation than other culturally specific orientations' (e.g. our

'scientific' form criticism, which had its birth in the study of Germanic folklore)? This is an interesting query, though there are obviously some prior questions, to which I will later return, such as: How does one read and interpret texts? How does one decide what a given text means?

Some Distinctions

In his letters, Smith-Christopher distinguished 'cultural exegesis' from two other enterprises that may appear to be very similar to it. The first of these is comparative studies utilizing sociological and anthropological materials. Since Smith's book on the exilic community, *The Religion of the Landless*, is such a comparative study, and since he seems to have gotten the idea of 'culture exegesis' while working on that project, some remarks about the book are appropriate.

In *The Religion of the Landless* Smith-Christopher argues that we will understand the Babylonian Exile 'better if we understand the phenomenon of mass deportation itself'. Toward this end, he surveys 'the experience of exile, deportation, forced migration, refugee camps, and ethnic identity preservation among minorities', and on the basis of this survey constructs a model comprised of 'four social and socio-psychological behavior patterns that recur in these situations' (1989: 10)—structural adaptation, the rise of new leadership, ritual and folklore (hero stories). This model, which he illustrates with case studies on Zulu religious responses to apartheid, African-American slavery, Japanese-American internment during World War II, and the displacement of Bikini Islanders to make way for atmospheric testing of atomic bombs, presents us with a picture of the dynamics of exiled communities. The claim is not that any of these groups are 'exactly like' the Babylonian exile (1989: 69), but rather that the model derived from their experience will help us to study the biblical exile from 'the perspective of the exiled themselves' (1989: 9). This is the kind of enterprise in which I myself have frequently engaged, and I appreciate its value.[1]

But such an enterprise is not 'cultural exegesis', for, Smith-Christopher writes, it seems likely that people who *actually experienced* deportation (e.g. the Japanese-Americans who were interned during WW II) will see things in the texts that would never occur to persons who had only *read about* such experience (7-23-90). This suggests that scholarly comparative studies are at best a kind of 'secondhand' cultural

---

1.   Overholt 1989; see section III below.

exegesis, an attempt to '"appropriat[e]" cultural perspectives through research' (1-30-91). The implication that interpretation is influenced by the reader's experiences, and that the experiences of scholars are not likely to produce the same meanings as those of native peoples is, we will see, to be taken seriously. But it raises a further question, namely, whether cultural exegesis assumes a hierarchy of experience. Are folk understandings likely to be 'more accurate' than alternatives?

The second enterprise from which Smith-Christopher distinguishes cultural exegesis is liberation theology. Smith-Christopher raised this issue in a letter in which he noted that some liberation theologians speak of the 'exegesis of the poor', and went on to criticize Carlos Mesters, who he says 'does not really deal with the methodological problems suggested by this notion that the "poor" might actually *understand* the Bible more accurately' (7-23-90).

This distinction is perhaps less obvious than the first, since liberation theology postulates 'the poor' reading Scripture in light of their own real world experiences. Such readings are above all 'culturally specific'. Furthermore, it is the poor who are actually *doing* the interpretation, rather than scholars investigating the sociology of poverty *in preparation for* doing it.

In thinking about this issue I have profited from a recent book by Christopher Rowland and Mark Corner, *Liberating Exegesis*. That study suggests to me that there are at least four principles which underlie liberation readings of Scripture. The first is that the biblical texts are not homogeneous, but reflect the social discord of the context in which they were produced (1989: 191-92). Important here is a modern notion about 'ideology' to which I will return shortly. The second principle is that the appropriate context in which to interpret a biblical text includes both the social situation in which it was written and that in which it is read. Drawing on the work Clodovis Boff, Rowland and Corner argue that between then and now there is a 'correspondence of relationships'. The Bible, that is to say, was never intended to be a historical record; it is 'a development of church tradition...represent[ing] the response of the early Christian communities to the challenges of their day' (1989: 60-61), and liberation theology's emphasis on commitment to the present rather than researching the past is part of that church tradition. Furthermore, to renew old traditions in light of new situations is to copy the biblical writers themselves, as von Rad has shown. It must be observed, however, that Rowland and Corner do not consider all 'reinterpretation[s] in the present context' equally valid. Narrowly individualistic, Evangelical readings focusing on the 'inner life of the individual Christian', for example, are rejected in favor of community-oriented readings focusing on 'a world of poverty, disease and death in which good news comes to offer hope and a path to life' (1989: 14). The liberation reading does, it seems, represent a privileged point of view.

The third principle underlying liberation readings is that since readers of biblical texts operate within an interpretative community, 'we should accept the inevitable eisegesis...which is an unavoidable part of the complex process of finding meaning in texts' (1989: 5). Rowland and Corner observe that in the 'emphatically communitarian' context of Basic Christian Communities, 'a new way of reading the text has arisen, not among the exegetical elite of the seminaries and universities but at the grassroots' (1989: 38). This method, for which the poor are uniquely qualified, involves a dialogue with the text in which one's own experience is related to the biblical story of deliverance from oppression, and the meanings discovered lead to action. (It seems fair to ask whether there is not some confusion here between 'method' and 'point of view'.) The fourth principle that seems to underlie liberation exegesis is the idea that the criterion for judging the adequacy of exegesis is the assumption 'that the vantage-point of the poor is particularly and especially the vantage-point of God' (1989: 49).

Liberation readings of Scripture are clearly 'culturally specific' exegesis, and at the level of actual practice (say, in Basic Christian Communities) they seem quite similar to 'cultural exegesis'—a fundamental human experience (poverty, internment) shapes the result of a precritical reading of the texts. Do such readings represent a 'more accurate', or even an accurate, reading of the texts? If they are held to be either, to what extent is such an assessment dependent upon historical-critical judgments about the texts' 'original' content and intention?[2] Is the primary goal of 'cultural exegesis' after all to understand the text in its 'original' context (e.g. modern experiences of exile/detention will help us to unpack biblical references to the Babylonian exile)? Such questions propel us into more theoretical considerations of methodology.

---

2. See, for example, Willy Schottroff's study on Amos in *God of the Lowly* (1989).

II. *Methodological Reflections*

Literary Theory and the Interdeterminancy of Texts

In the everyday world, bringing culturally-specific experiences to bear on the understanding of texts and other forms of communication is standard practice. To give but one example, I remember and frequently cite a farm-boy and seminary classmate who 'deconstructed' selected stories in the Gospels with accounts from his own experience of the stupidity of sheep.

Nevertheless, there is a serious theoretical problem here: what is the status of such interpretations vis-à-vis the 'reality' of the text? It is a commonplace of contemporary literary criticism that there is a plurality of valid readings of a given text, but what would constitute a 'more accurate' reading? And there is a complicating practical problem as well: interpreters of a text may be hampered by insufficient awareness of the differences between their own understanding of literature and that of persons in other cultures and times. John Barton has pointed out, for example, that both biblical and medieval European literature seem to have been produced by 'authors who understood themselves to be pro- ducing for public performance texts that were primarily a compilation and re-ordering of older texts'. 'To ask about the detailed intentions of (such) authors...is to ask an anachronistic question' (1987: 143, citing Burrow 1982).

Contemporary literary criticism insists that for any given text there is a plurality of meanings, challenging the notion so dear to practitioners of the historical-critical method that exegesis brings out the meanings that are inherent in a text.[3]

This insistence rests on at least two assumptions. The first, labelled 'intertextuality', is the notion that 'the ground of any text is always another text' and that, therefore, even 'if all of the data were accessible', the original intention of a text 'would still be irretrievable' (Burnett 1990: 61). The second assumption concerns the process by which meaning is apprehended: texts are not objects, but are always products of the play between text and reader (Burnett 1990: 62). What keeps both text and reader from being dissolved 'into the infinite play of

---

3.   Many have stressed the need for, or at the very least the usefulness of, a multiplicity of methods; cf. Barton 1987: 153; Long 1991: 83-84; Phillips 1990: 13;
Suleiman 1980: 7, 35.

language' is that 'language itself is inscribed socially', its meanings 'produced within (public) discourse... [and] ultimately determined by ideologies' (Burnett 1990: 64-65; cf. Phillips 1990: 19-25).

To put the latter point in another way, language is a social fact, an arbitrary system of signs, and 'meaning is conventional, a matter of familiarity rather than intuition' (Belsey 1980: 26). Since 'language changes, meaning must be subject to change' (Belsey 1980: 19). Furthermore, since language 'is a way of articulating experience', it therefore 'necessarily participates in *ideology*, the sum of the ways in which people both live and represent to themselves their relationship to the conditions of their existence'. That the ideology inscribed in the language often functions to suppress the tensions and contradictions inherent in any society makes it difficult to see beyond the 'natural' meaning of a text (Belsey 1980: 42-46).

Thus the social nature of the production and the reading of texts requires us to speak of a plurality of meanings. This certainly makes 'cultural exegesis' permissible, even inevitable. But it also warns us that differences—and preferences—in interpretation can be explained at least in part as the result of prior commitments. I hope I am not being unfair to suggest that Smith-Christopher's dismissal of liberation theology as having little meaning for 'Fourth World peoples' (1989: 214) bears the stamp of his Quaker-Mennonite pacifism and may overlook some possibilities that liberation readings take for granted. Perhaps 'a theology of Exodus' does have a 'promised land' to offer to people of the Fourth World, the name for which is 'land reform'. In a sense, *all* exegesis is 'cultural exegesis', and 'eisegesis' is inevitable, but viewed in the context of contemporary literary theory this insight undercuts our confidence that 'folk' interpretations of texts might be 'more accurate' than academic ones.[4]

4.   An instructive example comes from H.C. Spykerboer's account of how some of his students, who were Australian aborigines, reacted to the Genesis stories of the creation of animals and 'the notion that the earth is blessed and cursed' with great 'enthusiasm' and apparent 'understanding'. He then says, 'The important observation to be made here is that aborigines find their own feelings and understandings confirmed by biblical notions of the land' (1987: 234). Their reading of these texts is apparently to some extent idiosyncratic for their group; the issue here does not seem to be whether this reading is 'more accurate'.

Modes of Reading Scripture

Continuing with the theme of the interplay of reader and text, I would like to explore the idea that there are different 'modes' of reading Scripture. I take as my point of departure John Barton's argument, in *Oracles of God*, that in New Testament times all books of the Hebrew Bible outside the Torah were considered 'prophets'. Even though people in the ancient world were aware of genre distinctions (cf. Aristotle's *Poetics*), that awareness was 'inhibited' in readers of the Bible 'by the overriding interest in the source of biblical books... The Scriptures were not the words of men, but the oracles of God. As such they were not subject to the same constraints of literary form and genre as human books' (1986: 142). Thus, the only way to discover what these books meant to readers in New Testament times is to observe 'what kinds of information people in fact turned to them to discover, and what content they poured into their own imitations of these books' (1986: 151). The information they sought, he says, was of four kinds: moral instruction, eschatological prediction, predictions illustrative of 'the shape and consistency of God's plan for human history', and 'truths about the eternal being and character of God'.

If we turn to more contemporary encounters with the text, it seems possible to identify several context-specific styles (or modes) of reading Scripture. With no attempt to exhaust the possibilities, let me suggest three:

1. Acculturative readings. One would expect to find these among native peoples who had come under the influence of Christianity. Regardless of the extent to which specific individuals or groups identify with an older tradition over against the influences of European culture, centuries of contact will have left their mark. The interpretation of Wovoka and the Ghost Dance of 1890 in terms of Christian messianism and the presence of the Bible and other Christian symbols in some peyote ceremonies would seem to be examples of this mode of reading Scripture.[5]

5. Texts on the Ghost Dance are reprinted in Overholt 1986: 122-42; Porcupine's account of his visit to Wovoka and the Cheyenne–Arapaho 'messiah letter' (125-31) are particularly relevant. On peyotism, cf. Christopher Vecsey 1988: 150-205.

2. Committed readings. By this I mean readings with a social agenda, which can run the gamut from preserving the status quo (synagogue, church or political order) to advocating reform or revolution (liberation theology).
3. Historical readings. Here the context is usually that of the 'academy'.

But given what has already been said about the indeterminacy of texts, what would a historical reading look like? What, indeed, is 'history'? A simple definition would be, 'a documented narrative about the past', but, of course, it is not as simple as that. As the historian Hayden White points out, 'historians emplot their narratives in the same ways as do writers of realistic fiction', that is, through a 'poetic...a purely discursive' act (quoted by Burnett 1990: 63).

Texts are the products of discourses which take place within the context of 'social practices and institutions', and we know that there can be a variety of discourses 'within the same language system' (e.g. gay, feminist and black power interpretations of Jesus). Furthermore, no discourse is neutral, since within these contexts 'power is distributed hierarchically', so that depending on the specific social location some discourses are favored, others are marginal, and still others are suppressed (Burnett 1990: 65-66). Such is the social reality lurking behind labels like 'dead white males' and 'politically correct'. This suggests that the role of historical critics is less to discover meaning in texts than to unpack the socio-cultural process of their production, or, as one writer puts it, 'to demystify what seems natural (hence ideological) in our discourse and to reveal its material, institutional effects' (Burnett 1990: 70).

According to this view, historical interpretation should not focus on either of two extremes: the text *itself*, or actualizations of the text by a contemporary reader or interpretative community. It should, rather, focus on the process by which the text was produced.

III. *Theory and Practice*

These comments on methodology lead me to some reflections based on my own work as an interpreter of biblical texts. First, I what to point out what I think is a fundamental similarity between Smith-Christopher's treatment of the exile and mine of prophecy. In *The Religion of the Landless*, Smith-Christopher proposes what might be described as a model of the social dynamics of exiled communities. In doing so he aspires to faithfully represent the experience of such communities in the same way that my model of the prophetic process (Overholt 1989) aspires to represent actual experiences of persons living in societies in which prophet-like figures are believed to function as intermediaries between the people and their god(s). Both try to unpack the experience that gave rise to the textual accounts. This apparently is not 'cultural' or 'folk' exegesis, but it yields useful results, nonetheless. Second, I offer a case study.

Raising the Dead: The Elijah and Elisha Narratives

Among the prophetic stories in Kings are accounts of how both Elijah and Elisha resuscitated a young boy who had become ill and died. I turn to these stories as a way of illustrating some of the points I have been discussing.

I do not know who told these stories first, or who first wrote them down. Some have argued that the narratives were not originally independent—one grew out of the other, and each has its own tendency (Schmitt 1977; Rofé 1988: 132-35). In any case, I am not so interested in trying to search into and behind the text for the intentions of an original author as I am in discovering what the language itself might tell me about the way in which the text was produced. Language, as we have seen, is a socially-constructed symbol system which provides us with 'a way of articulating (our) experience' that seems utterly natural. But this apparent naturalness masks the fact that language 'necessarily participates in *ideology*, the sum of the ways in which people both live and represent to themselves their relationship to their existence' (Belsey 1980: 42).

The language of the Elijah and Elisha narratives displays three assumptions which I take to form the core of their ideology. First, Yahweh has control over nature and history (he sends rain, 1 Kgs 18.1, and famine, 2 Kgs 8.1; he selects kings, 2 Kgs 9.3). Secondly, when things go wrong, this represents a punishment for human behavior (drought, 1 Kgs 18.17-8; illness, 2 Kgs 1.3-4). Thirdly, the prophets are Yahweh's spokesmen, confronting kings and announcing his intentions (1 Kgs 18.1; 19.15-18; 2 Kgs 1.16; 3.16-9; 7.1). This is not a very surprising list, agreeing as it does with the Deuteronomistic ideology which is so dominant in the historical books.

But on closer examination, we see that the very language which presents us with a world so seemingly natural (at least from the standpoint of pre-exilic Israel, as we perceive it) masks some underlying tensions or contradictions. It is 'the role of ideology...to suppress these contradictions in the interests of' preserving the socially agreed-upon view of reality. However, it does not always succeed in this, and when they can be found contradictions provide us the opportunity of 'transforming (the ideology) by producing new meanings' (Belsey 1980: 45-46). The resuscitation stories contain four important tensions, and I am going to suggest that implicit in them is another ideology altogether, one associated with the world view of shamanism.

Since Old Testament stories of the dead brought back to life are unique to the Elijah and Elisha narratives, the first and most obvious tension arises from the need to account for the very idea that resuscitation was a live possibility. The narratives leave us totally in the dark about what Elijah and Elisha thought they were doing in the ritual itself. Apparently, they had some hopes of reviving their patients, but how did they understand what they hoped would take place?

Our approach to this problem begins with the observation that though the two stories in Kings differ in length and some details, they are remarkably similar in both structure and content. The narratives display a definite pattern with the following elements: 1., introduction (1 Kgs 17.8-16, whose account of how the prophet came to take up residence in Zarephath in the house of a widow provides the introduction to the Elijah story; 2 Kgs 4.8-17), 2., the illness is reported (17.17; 4.20), 3., help is sought from the prophet (17.18-19a; 4.21-28), 4., the prophet performs a healing ritual (17.19b-21; 4.29-35), 5., report of the ritual's success (17.22-23; 4.36), and 6., a response to the cure (17.24; 4.37). Furthermore, the healing rituals themselves are identical in structure: the patient was laid out on a bed in the prophet's chamber (17.19, 4.21); when he was alone with the corpse, the prophet cried out (prayed) to Yahweh (17.20; 4.33), then mounted the bed and laid himself upon the body (Elijah did this three times, Elisha twice; 17.21, 4.34-35).

The striking thing about this pattern is that it is duplicated exactly in ethnographic reports of shamanic curing among tribal peoples. In one account, a Northern Ojibwa shaman was summoned to cure a sick girl, but she died soon after his arrival. At once the shaman 'tied a piece of red yarn around the girl's wrist', laid her body out, and lay down beside her. He lay very still, then after a while 'began to move ever so little. The girl began to move a little also...(he) moved a little more. So did the girl. Finally...(he) raised himself into a sitting posture and at the same time the girl' did likewise (Hallowell 1967: 154-55).

Unlike the Elijah and Elisha narratives, in this case a native explanation of the dynamics of resuscitation is available. From the Ojibwa point
of view the doctor had followed the girl's soul to the land of the dead,
captured it, and brought it back before it was too late. The red yarn tied
around the patient's wrist was to make his task of identification easier.
A.I. Hallowell assures us that according to the Northern Ojibwa 'theory
of the nature of things' such feats were possible, though only the most
powerful doctors could perform them.

Another parallel to the Elijah and Elisha narratives comes from south-
eastern Siberia. The patient was a young boy, and although he was not
dead, the healing ritual displays the pattern I have been discussing. On
this occasion the shaman sat at the boy's bedside 'singing a plaintive,
monotonous song' which first emphasized how poor and defenseless the
boy's family and he himself were and then went on to extol the power
of his spirit protector ('All the spirits tremble before my master...
Certainly he will help us'.). To the accompaniment of drums, he danced
around the fire, then stood beside the boy's bed and sang an invocation,
expressing confidence that the spirit would come to help 'these poor
people'. Again, he danced around the fire, and then leapt to the front
door, where he sang an invocation to his spirit protector. Suddenly, the
shaman shuddered, stopped singing, and in a changed voice, which sig-
naled the coming of the spirit, shouted, '"I am here; I have come to help
these poor people. I will look at the child."' 'In a state of ecstasy', he
approached the boy's bed and 'crouched over him' until their faces
almost touched. He then ran around the room beating his drum and and
crying out, 'I am flying... I will catch you'. From time to time he spoke
in different voices, apparently representing a dialogue between spirits,
and finally he cried, 'I have it; I have it!', cupping his hands 'as though
he held something in them'. At this point the parents rushed to the bed
and pulled the blanket off the boy. The shaman jumped in beside him,
and the parents covered them both with the blanket. 'After a few
minutes', the shaman got out and began again to dance and sing. When
he was completely exhausted, the parents placed him an a bed opposite
the boy's, and he slept.

Speaking later with the researcher, Ivan Lopatin, the shaman
'explained that the boy was sick because his soul had been stolen by a
spirit'. The running and leaping around the room represented the
shaman's flight 'into the spirit realm', where he found the offending

spirit and recaptured the boy's soul and brought it back 'in the shape of a sparrow'. Lopatin confessed that he hadn't seen this sparrow, but both his interpreter and the boy's parents 'assured' him that they had seen it 'quite plainly'. The shaman also said 'that while lying beside the boy he had restored the soul to the body' (Lopatin 1946–1949).

While the Elisha account does not clearly explain the boy's coming back to life, saying only that his body warmed and then he winked (or sneezed) and opened his eyes (4.34-5), the Elijah story links the resuscitation to the return of the *nepeš* ('soul', or 'breath'): the prophet called upon Yahweh to let the boy's *nepeš* return to his 'inward parts'; Yahweh listened, the *nepeš* returned, and the boy lived (17.21-2). The similarity in physical activities, together with the native explanations of resuscitation and healing we have just examined, suggests the possibility that the Elijah (and by inference the Elisha) narrative assumes a soul-loss theory of illness and death.

This idea would seem to go against the conventional wisdom that 'the distinction between soul and body is something foreign to the Hebrew mentality, and death, therefore, is not regarded as the separation of these two elements' (de Vaux 1961:56; cf. Porteous 1962: 428). Gen. 2.7 is often considered a key text in this discussion. Michael Knibb says it 'epitomises the Old Testament view of the constitution of man'. In this view there is no dichotomy between body and soul: 'the "breath of life" is not conceived of as having an existence somehow separate from the body, and it is man as an entity who becomes a "living being"' (1989: 398). The individual human being is understood to be 'a centre of consciousness and unit of vital power' (Johnson 1964: 19).

But matters do not appear to be that simple. The word *nepeš* has a great many connotations, running from physical (throat, neck, breath, body, blood) and emotional (hunger, thirst, grieving, desire, agreement) associations to 'life' in the abstract and even 'corpse' (Num. 19.11-3; cf. Johnson 1964: 3-22; Brotzman 1988). It is especially important to note that *nepeš* can be distinguished from 'flesh' (*bāśār*; Deut. 12.23; Isa. 10.18) and that it departs from the dying person (Gen. 35.18; the same idea, but utilizing the term *rûaḥ*, appears in Pss. 104.29, 146.4; Job 34.14-5; Eccl. 12.7). The *nepeš* is said to be poured out when one is sick (Job 30.16) or starving (Lam. 2.12). Recovery from illness can be described as Yahweh bringing up the *nepeš* from Sheol (Ps. 30.2-3). The term *ruâh* (spirit, wind) has a similar range of connotations (Johnson 1964: 23-37).[6]

Furthermore, the Hebrew Bible contains clear evidence that at least in some circles survival of the dead was assumed. One finds, for example, references to grave offerings (Deut. 26.14; Sir. 30.18), and to diviners who employed 'ghosts' and 'familiar spirits' (Lev. 19.31; 20.6, 27; Deut. 18.11; Isa. 8.19; 19.3). Saul's consultation at Endor with 'a woman who is master of a ghost' (*'ēšeh baʿlat-'ôb*; 1 Sam. 28.7) is particularly striking, since she divined by the ghost of a known historical figure, Samuel. Disembodied spirits (*rᵉpa'îm*, 'shades') were thought to reside in Sheol (Job 26.5; Isa. 14.9-10; cf. Ezek. 32.21).[7]

What this evidence suggests is that at least some persons in the society in which the Elijah and Elisha narratives were produced would have been prepared to believe that sickness and death were the result of the loss of the soul and that curing these conditions involved recovering the errant soul and reintroducing it into the body. Such a notion lies outside of the ideology of the narratives. It does, however, offer an explanation of our first tension.[8]

The narratives have other puzzling features. For one thing, it appears the prophets are held responsible for the boys' deaths. Thus, the mother confronts Elijah with an accusation that he has caused the death of her son (1 Kgs 17.18), while Elisha is accused of 'deceit' (2 Kgs 4.28; cf. v. 16). There are other texts, of course, where prophets are treated as

---

6.   L.R. Bailey writes that 'Greek culture introduced a new view of humans', namely, the notion of a soul that was 'detachable from the corpse' (1985: 213). The apparent contrast with Hellenistic conceptions seems to be a major reason for the consensus regarding unity of soul and body in the Hebrew Bible. But there has been another factor at work—a failure to be sufficiently sensitive to the folk background of ancient Israelite culture.

7.   On this general point, cf. T.J. Lewis (1989), and the review of this book by Bloch-Smith (1991, esp. 329-30).

8.   In light of this interpretation, it is interesting to note that Rofé (1988: 125) considers 2 Kgs 4.33b ('. . . and prayed to Yahweh') to be a later editorial addition 'from the perspective of the more profound and theologically more advanced strata of biblical thought' displeased with the 'primitive religious outlook' that saw miracles 'as magical acts that were a manifestation of the prophet's supernatural prowess'. In terms of genre, Rofé considers the Elisha narrative to be a 'literary elaboration' of the *legenda* and the Elijah story to be an 'ethical *legenda* (1988: 27-33, 132-35). His interest is in classifying the 'prophetical stories' as they appear in the completed Hebrew Bible, not in recovering the details of an anterior ideology.

adversaries, but these inhabit the sphere of the macro-political (Jer. 26.7-11) or the theological-political (Jer. 28.1-11; 29.24-28). The mothers' accusations are, by contrast, quite personal in nature. Another puzzle is that the prophets pass the blame on to Yahweh. Elijah's rhetorical question has the effect of explicitly accusing Yahweh of killing the boy (17.20), and Elisha's comment to Gehazi ('...she is in bitter distress; Yahweh has hidden it from me and has not told me', 4.27) hints at a similar sentiment. I identify these as the second and third tensions, and they may be dealt with together.

Among the common characteristics of the relatively diverse and 'fluid' religious phenomenon known as shamanism are the putative power of shamans 'to control the spirits, usually by incarnating them', and 'to engage in mystical flight and other "out of body experiences"' (Lewis 1981: 32-33). They were recognized as powerful individuals whose role was to uphold the welfare of the local community. The way of conceiving the shaman's defense of the community differs, of course, from group to group. A. Anisimov provides a particularly striking account of Siberian cosmology in which the shaman's task is to set spirit guards around the perimeter of the clan's territory to ward off hostile spirits that might enter and create havoc, as well as to cure those who have fallen victim to such an attack (cf. Overholt 1986: 158-65). When disaster strikes, people might blame the shaman, who might in turn accuse his spirit familiar.

It is worth noting that Elijah and Elisha are pictured as familiar figures in the communities within which they operate, known to be capable of powerful acts. In Elijah's case the immediate community is, admittedly, of quite limited scope. On the run from the Israelite king and hiding in territory controlled by Sidon, his reputation is nevertheless established in the mind of the widow in whose house he has taken refuge by the previous episode of multiplying her meager supply of oil and flour (17.8-16).[9] In the case of Elisha, the narrative suggests that he made regular rounds and performed specific functions on the people's behalf (4.8-10, 23). Though these stories do not specifically suggest that Elijah and Elisha controlled the deity who effected the resuscitations (acceptance of the ideology of the narratives renders such an idea unthinkable), the

9.   This interesting episode, alluded to in the title of my paper, has parallels in the Elisha narratives (2 Kgs 4.1-7, 42-44). Space does not permit an elaboration of the point here, but it is worth mentioning that the motif, 'inexhaustible food supply', is wide-spread in folklore.

diviner of Endor's 'mastery' of Samuel's ghost suggests there may have been some for whom that would have been the 'natural' explanation. And if their patrons believed these prophets to have such powers, it would have been natural to blame the arrival of misfortune on their lack of diligence, their duplicity, or the like.

These tensions, then, turn out to be very great. The shamanic world view presupposes the existence of multiple powerful spirits which can potentially be pressed into service by powerful humans. Such a view is submerged by the ideology of the resuscitation narratives in Kings. But it is well to remember that in 1 Kings 17–2 Kings 13 Yahweh is not the sole spirit inhabitant of even his own heaven (1 Kgs 22.19-23), and his supremacy is not assured, but a matter of dispute (1 Kgs 18.21; 2 Kgs 1.2-4).

The Elijah and Elisha narratives assume that a prophet is able to help in cases of serious illness (2 Kgs 4.22-27; 5.3). How are we to understand prophets that were sought out for help with essentially personal problems rather than the problems of the larger community or nation? This is the fourth point of tension, and given what has already been said, our discussion of it can be brief. Shamans are mainly healers, the doctors and protectors of their local residence groupings. When one is ill, these are the professionals to whom one turns.

Conclusion

In this interpretation of the resuscitation stories I have tried to let the language of the narratives lead me behind its own ideology. The result has been a historical reconstruction which suggests that the production of these texts involved the masking of an earlier ideology by a later one. The question of the 'origin' of these ideologies is left unresolved. The interpretation has, I think, some claim to accuracy, though not to exclusive validity.[10]

This interpretation of the resuscitation stories is clearly not 'cultural exegesis', for it derives from my own penchant for cross-cultural studies and not from any real life experiences of shamanism. Is it a kind of

---

10. In a study of 2 Kgs 4.8-37, B.O. Long comments that the story's 'contrary tendencies, Elisha-centered or Shunammite centered, both [of] which rest on one's response to items in the work, mitigate against any simplistic interpretation of the narrative' (1988: 174). The reading that I have proposed accounts for both of these tendencies.

'second hand' cultural exegesis? I doubt it, though an interesting idea does occur to me. I wonder if members of a group which still held the shamanic world view would see the same thing in these stories that I saw, and whether my interpertation—minus the jargon—would make any sense to them. What is the possibility that 'folk' readings of texts, in addition to having their own validity, might help us to assess the plausibility of readings produced on the basis of quite different assumptions?[11]

Bibliography

Bailey, L.R.
  1985   'Death', in P.J. Achtemeimer (ed.), *Harper's Bible Dictionary* (San Francisco: Harper & Row): 213-14.

Barton, J.
  1986   *Oracles of God: Perceptions of Ancient Prophecy in Israel after the Exile* (London: Darton, Longman & Todd).
  1987   'Reading the Bible As Literature: Two Questions for Biblical Critics', *Journal of Literature and Theology* 1: 135-53.

Belsey, C.
  1980   *Critical Practice* (London: Routledge).

Bloch Smith
  1991   'Review of T.J. Lewis 1989', *JBL* 110: 327-30.

Brotzman, E.R.
  1988   'Man and the Meaning of *nepes*', *BSac* 145: 400-409.

Burnett, F.W.
  1990   'Postmodern Biblical Exegesis: The Eve of Historical Criticism', *Semeia* 51: 51-80.

Burrow, J.A.
  1982   *Medieval Writers and their Work* (Oxford: Oxford University Press).

Hallowell, A.I.
  1967   'Spirits of the Dead in Saulteaux Life and Thought', in *Culture and Experience* (New York: Schocken): 151-71.

Johnson, A.R.
  1964   *The Vitality of the Individual in the Thought of Ancient Israel* (Cardiff: University of Wales Press, 2nd edn).

11. Spykerboer gives an example of something like this process when he comments that 'aboriginal students are not as concerned as some of the more conservative white students are when they discover that the Old Testament is of a composite nature and the result of the bringing together of various traditions'. He speculates that because their cultural background has accustomed them to oral tradition, they 'have a natural aptitude for the understanding of the processes which led to the formation of Scripture' (1987: 236). Conversely, their assent to the plausibility of such theories might serve to encourage the critical scholars who developed them.

Knibb, M.A.
 1989 'Life and Death in the Old Testament', in R.E. Clements (ed.), *The World of Ancient Israel* (Cambridge: Cambridge University Press): 395-415.

Lewis, I.M.
 1981 'What is a Shaman?', *Folk* 23: 25-35.

Lewis, T.J.
 1989 *Cults of the Dead in Ancient Israel and Ugarit* (Atlanta: Scholars Press).

Long, B.O.
 1988 'A Figure at the Gate: Readers, Reading, and Biblical Theologians', in G.M. Tucker *et al.* (eds.), *Canon, Theology, and Old Testament Interpretation* (Minneapolis: Fortress Press): 166-86.
 1991 'The "New" Poetics of Alter and Sternberg', *JSOT* 51: 71-84.

Lopatin, I.A.
 1946–49 'A Shamanistic Performance for a Sick Boy', *Anthropos* 41-44: 365-68.

Overholt, T.W.
 1986 *Prophecy in Cross-Cultural Perspective: A Sourcebook for Biblical Researchers* (Atlanta: Scholars Press).
 1989 *Channels of Prophecy: The Social Dynamics of Prophetic Activity* (Minneapolis: Fortress Press).

Phillips, G.A.
 1990 'Exegesis as Critical Praxis: Reclaiming History and Text from a Postmodern Perspective', *Semeia* 51: 7-49.

Porteous, N.W.
 1961 'Soul', *IDB*, 428-29.

Rofé, A.
 1988 *The Prophetical Stories* (Jerusalem: Magnes Press).

Rowland, C., and M. Corner
 1989 *Liberating Exegesis: The Challenge of Liberation Theology to Biblical Studies* (Louisville, KY: Westminster/John Knox Press).

Schmitt, A.
 1977 'Die Totenerweckung in 1 Kön. XVII 17-24: Eine form- und gattungskritische Untersuchung', *VT* 27: 454-74.

Schottroff, W.
 1984 'The Prophet Amos: A Sociohistorical Assessment of his Ministry', in W. Schottroff and W. Steggemann (eds.), *God of the Lowly: Socio-Historical Interpretations of the Bible* (Maryknoll, NY: Orbis): 27-46.

Smith, D.L.
 1989 *The Religion of the Landless* (Bloomington, IN: Meyer Stone Books).

Spykerboer, H.C.
 1987 'The Australian Aborigines and the Old Testament', in E.W. Conrad and E.G. Newing (eds.), *Perspectives on Language and Text* (Winona Lake, IN: Eisenbrauns): 229-38.

Suleiman, S.R.
1980   'Introduction: Varieties of Audience-Oriented Criticism', in
            S.R. Suleiman and I. Crosman (eds.), *The Reader in the Text*
            (Princeton: Princeton University Press): 3-45.
Vaux, R. de
1961   *Ancient Israel* (New York: McGraw–Hill).
Vecsey, C.
1988   *Imagine Ourselves Richly: Mythic Narratives of North American
            Indians* (New York: Crossroad).

CULTURAL READING OF THE BIBLE:
SOME CHINESE CHRISTIAN CASES*

John Y.H. Yieh

Interpretation, Exegesis, Culture

In his famous program of *Demythologizing* (1941),[1] R. Bultmann had attempted to solve a fundamental problem in biblical interpretation, namely, the enormous gap of incomprehensibility that lies between the cultural language of the Bible and the minds of modern readers. A preacher, he proposed, should bridge the two by first retrieving the intended kerygma from the mythological language of the Bible and then re-presenting it in compatible concepts which are sensible to modern minds. In his judgment, M. Heidegger's existentialist analysis of human reality provided the most appropriate conceptual categories for his generation to comprehend the messages of the Bible.[2] A similar effort to make the Bible understandable to people outside of its culture, in this case to Chinese, had also been launched by Chinese Christian scholars in the 1920s with the so-called *Indigenizing* movement.[3] In an article

    *   My sincere thanks go to George Hunsinger and Ann Johnston, my former colleagues at Bangor Theological Seminary, who read the manuscript and graciously offered their suggestions. Deep gratitude is also due to my good friends in the *Seminar on Chinese Culture, Judaism and Christianity* in Boston.
    1.   'New Testament and Theology' (1941), and 'On the Problem of Demythologizing' (1952 and 1961), in S.M. Ogden (ed.), *Rudolf Bultmann: New Testament and Mythology and the other Basic Writings* (Philadelphia: Fortress Press, 1984), pp. 1-44, 95-130, 155-164.
    2.   See Bultmann, 'New Testament and Theology', p. 23.
    3.   For its historical background, see C.H. Wang, 'Non-Christian Alliance and the Indigenizing Movement', in ch. 21 of *Chung-kuo chi-du-chiao shih-kang (History of Christianity in China)* (Hong Kong: Chinese Christian Literature Council, 1959), pp. 267-76. Representative essays that advocate Indigenizing movement are collected in W.H. Lam (ed.), *Chin-dai hwa-jen shen-hsueh wun-sien (A Source Book of Modern Chinese Theology)* (Hong Kong: China Graduate School

entitled 'Studying Chinese Religious Experience for the Indigenized Church' (1926), Liu Tingfang summarized its goal in this way:

> Having received the imported gift [i.e. Western Christianity brought in by missionaries], we Chinese Christians should extract the essentials from that configuration, and with God's guidance rematch it with the history and experience of our people and nation. A Christian doctrine needs to be Sinosized before it can become our own; so do the discipline, liturgy, ritual, and organization of the Church.[4]

From both *Demythologizing* and *Indigenizing* programs, we have indeed learned much about the challenging task of interpreting the Bible for readers in times and cultures different from those of the Bible. Now we appreciate the fact that the messages of the Bible are contained in and conditioned by a cultural language which is very different from the one we use for our conceptualization and communication in modern times, so much so that now we realize that we cannot effectively convey those biblical messages to modern readers without tailoring and matching the two cultural languages.

Analytically speaking, however, an intelligible interpretation is only the second half of a communication process which begins with an accurate exegesis of biblical texts.[5] In order to achieve 'accuracy', German-speaking scholars, since the mid nineteenth-century, have developed a historical-critical approach to the Bible which has become a protocol for modern theological reflections.[6] Their *wissenschaftlich* methods,

of Theology, 1986), pp. 623-700; Y.M. Shaw, *Erh-shih shih-chi chung-kuo chi-du-chiao wun-ti (Issues of Chinese Christianity in the Twentieth Century)* (Taipei: Chen Chung, 1980), pp. 229-65.

4.   T. Liu, 'Studying Chinese Religious Experience for the Indigenized Church', in *Chen-li yu sheng-min (Truth and Life Weekly)* (1926), pp. 1-7. English translation from Chinese is my own, here and after, unless noted otherwise. Liu Tingfang (= Timothy Liu, 1892–1947) earned a PhD from Columbia University (1920) and taught at Union Theological Seminary in New York (1918–20). Returning to China, he taught at Peking and Yenching Universities.

5.   'Exegesis' is the effort to reconstruct the original meaning of biblical text; 'interpretation' seeks to make that meaning understandable to readers; and the study of various methods of exegesis and interpretation is 'hermeneutics'. Nida and Reyburn also see a distinction between 'understanding the text' and 'making it understandable'. See E.A. Nida and W.D. Reyburn, *Meaning across Cultures* (Maryknoll: Orbis Books, 1981), p. 30.

6.   R.M. Grant and D. Tracy, *A Short History of the Interpretation of the Bible* (Philadelphia: Fortress Press, 2nd edn, 1984), p. 153.

however, cannot always guarantee an accurate reconstruction of the original meaning of the biblical text, because no exegete is completely objective or free from his or her own cultural presuppositions and personal prejudgments. It is truly a 'naive objectivism',[7] therefore, to believe that historical-critical methods can fully recover the unbiased meaning of the biblical text. F. Schleiermacher already saw the operation of the 'hermeneutical circle' closely connected to the interpreter and his or her 'cognitive community'.[8] Since W. Dilthey, ever-increasing attention has also been given to the nature and role of exegetes themselves. Bultmann, for instance, alerted us to the preunderstanding that we all carry to the text.[9] E. Fuchs, too, contended that a reader's pre-understanding will be transformed in the process of reading because biblical texts constitute a 'language event'.[10] Evidently, then, it is imperative for an exegete to discern and take into account his or her own cultural assumptions as well as those of the Bible.

Interestingly, inasmuch as we biblical scholars have strived to master the ancient cultures of the Bible such as that of the Near East and Greco-Roman societies, we remain very naive about our own cultural assumptions which evidently dictate the way we examine and explain biblical texts. Some of our colleagues, Bible translators and cross-cultural missionaries, on the other hand, have demonstrated an impressive ability to distinguish the cultural particularities of their own from those of the Bible and of the countries they serve.[11] E. Nida of the United Bible Societies, for example, has promoted the principle of 'dynamic/

---

7. A.C. Thiselton, *The Two Horizons: New Testament Hermeneutics and Philosophical Description* (Grand Rapids: W.B. Eerdmans, 1980), p. 315. See also G. Turner, 'Pre-Understanding and New Testament Interpretation', *SJT* 28 (1975), pp. 227-42.

8. W. Hamacher, 'Hermeneutic Ellipses: Writing the Hermeneutical Circle in Schleiermacher', in Gayle L. Ormiston and Alan D. Schrift (eds.), *Transforming the Hermeneutic Context: From Nietzsche to Nancy* (Albany, NY: SUNY Press, 1990), pp. 177-210, esp. 200.

9. R. Bultmann, 'Is Exegesis without Presuppositions Possible?', in Ogden (ed.), *Rudolf Bultmann: New Testament and Mythology*, pp. 145-54.

10. E. Fuchs, *Studies of the Historical Jesus* (London: SCM Press, 1964), pp. 65-83 and 207-212.

11. For a discussion on how modern missionary movements contributed to our understanding of cultures, see: C.R. Taber, *The World is Too Much with us: 'Culture' in Modern Protestant Missions* (Macon, GA: Mercer University Press, 1991).

functional equivalence'[12] for Bible translations in order to do justice to the forms and means of communication in both the Bible's and the receptor's cultures. The fact that Chinese Classics were translated into Western languages by missionaries like James Legge of the London Missionary Society[13] also shows how ably they have appreciated the culture of their mission field, and in this case the most condensed form of Chinese culture. It is therefore encouraging to see that now some biblical scholars in the Society of Biblical Literature have organized a group in the annual meeting called 'The Bible in Africa, Asia, and Latin America' which is devoted to learning how the Bible is being studied in other cultures. The Casassa Conference on 'Text and Experience: Toward a Cultural Exegesis of the Bible' has also provided a critically important occasion for us to discuss how a culturally-informed reading, if carefully discerned, can facilitate instead of handicap the exegetical study of the Bible.

As a contribution to the discussion of 'cultural exegesis', I will survey six Chinese Christian scholars in three distinct periods of time to see how their readings of the Bible have been informed by Chinese culture. In each case I will also compare their readings to historical-critical readings from Western Scholars to see how their culturally-informed readings have shed light or darkness on the original meanings of the biblical texts. Finally I will summarize the implications this survey may yield for our attempt to construct an approach or method of cultural exegesis.

But what is culture? Before the survey, I should like to make explicit

---

12. E.A. Nida, *Toward a Science of Translating* (Leiden: Brill, 1964), pp. 156-92; E.A. Nida and C.R. Taber, *The Theory and Practice of Translation* (Leiden: Brill, 1969), *passim*.

13. J. Legge, *Confucius: Confucian Analects, The Great Learning and The Doctrine of the Mean: Translation and Exegetical Notes* (Oxford: Clarendon Press, 2nd rev. edn; repr. as vol. I of *The Chinese Classics* [New York: Dover, 1971]); J. Legge, *The Works of Mencius* (Oxford: Clarendon Press, 2nd rev. edn; repr. as vol. II of *The Chinese Classics* [New York: Dover, 1970]); J. Legge, *The Texts of Taoism*. I. *The Tao Te Ching of Lao Tzu & the Writings of Chuang Tzu, Part I*. II. *The T'ai Shang Tractate & The Writings of Chuang Tsu, Part II* (Oxford: Oxford University Press; repr. New York: Dover, 1962); J. Legge, *I Ching: The Book of Changes* (Oxford: Clarendon Press, 2nd edn; repr. as vol. XVI of *The Sacred Books of the East* [New York: Dover, 1963]). Recently there has been increasing recognition of James Legge's contribution in East–West cultural exchange. Norman Girardot and Louis Pfister are co-authoring a multi-volume book intended to re-evaluate the importance of James Legge in introducing Chinese culture into the West.

my definition of culture so that my assumptions of what constitute a culture are clear in the following discussions. Among many others, Chinese and Western alike,[14] C. Geertz's symbolic-anthropological definition of culture as a 'pattern of meanings' is most relevant to our concern about the conceptual framework shaped by Chinese culture in which Chinese Christian scholars reconstruct the original meanings of the Bible. He states that culture

> denotes an historically transmitted pattern of meanings embodied in symbols, a system of inherited conceptions expressed in symbolic forms by means of which men communicate, perpetuate, and develop their knowledge about and attitudes toward life.[15]

In other words, culture is (1) a pattern of meanings and system of conceptions, (2) historically transmitted and inherited, (3) embodied in verbal and non-verbal symbols, and (4) the vehicle to shape a people's knowledge about and attitude toward life. According to this definition, Chinese culture can be perceived as a system of common knowledge or a philosophy of life[16] which is informed by Confucianism, Taoism and Buddhism as developed in the history of China, is studied in Chinese educational system, and has been shaping Chinese ways of thinking and judgment of values. Geertz is also right to contend that culture constantly changes, though often 'like an octopus'[17] moving one part of its body at a time and gradually cumulating to a directional change. Because culture changes, it is only realistic to perceive modern Western

14. For an excellent survey of anthropologists' definitions of culture, see L.J. Luzbetak, SVD, *The Church and Cultures: New Perspectives in Missiological Anthropology* (Maryknoll: Orbis Books, 1988), pp. 133-56. For a list of definitions by Chinese scholars, see L.C. Wu, *Chi-du-chiao yu chung-kuo wunhwa* (*Christianity and Chinese Culture*) (Shanghai: Youth Association, 1936), pp. 13-18.

15. C. Geertz, *The Interpretation of Cultures* (New York: Basic Books, 1973), p. 89.

16. For two excellent collections of essays concerning the patterns of thought of Chinese people, see C.A. Moore (ed.), *The Chinese Mind: Essentials of Chinese Philosophy and Culture* (Honolulu: University of Hawaii Press, 1967); R.E. Allinson (ed.), *Understanding the Chinese Mind: The Philosophical Roots* (Hong Kong: Oxford University Press, 1989). See also W.T. Chang, *A Source Book in Chinese Philosophy* (Princeton: Princeton University Press, 1963). For a history of Chinese philosophy, see: Y.L. Fung, *A History of Chinese Philosophy* (Princeton: Princeton University Press, 1952).

17. Geertz, *Interpretation of Cultures*, p. 408.

culture as having outgrown its Judaeo-Christian traditions, especially after the time of the Renaissance and the rise of science; even though it still shares some bases with them. In fact, their distance is no shorter than that between Chinese readers and the Bible. Again, because culture changes, our analysis of it will always be an incomplete guessing at meanings.[18]

Sampling the Approaches of Chinese Christian Scholars

Christian faith had been heard by Chinese,[19] if not earlier, by the time the Nestorians came to China in Tang dynasty (c. 635 CE).[20] Very prominent also were the Jesuit missionaries in the late sixteenth century.[21] However, it was the most recent wave of missionaries since the nineteenth century that successfully converted a number of Chinese people, established churches and participated in many aspects—educational, social and even political—of the life of modern China.[22] Christian

18. Geertz, *Interpretation of Cultures*, p. 20.

19. For the history of Christianity in China, see K.A. Latourette, *The History of Christian Mission in China* (London: SPCK, 1929); C.H. Wang, *Chung-kuo chi-du-chiao shih-kang* (*History of Christianity in China*) (Hong Kong: Chinese Christian Literature Council, 1986); R.R. Covell, *Confucius, The Buddha, and Christ: A History of the Gospel in Chinese* (Maryknoll: Orbis Books, 1986).

20. A.C. Moule, *Christians in China Before the Year 1500* (London, 1930); S.L. Lo, *Tang yuen erh-dai chih ching-chiao* (*Nestorian Christianity in Tang and Yuen Dynasties*) (Hong Kong: China Studies Press, 1966).

21. C.E. Ronan and B.B.C. Oh (eds.), *East Meets West: The Jesuits in China, 1582–1773* (Chicago: Loyola University Press, 1988). This book includes a selected bibliography (pp. 283-306) and a supplementary bibliography (pp. 307-309). An excellent study on the way Chinese responded to the Jesuits, see J. Gernet, *China and the Christian Impact: A Conflict of Cultures* (trans. J. Lloyd; Cambridge: Cambridge University Press, and Paris: Editions de la Maison des Sciences de l'Homme, 1985).

22. For the various works and impact of these missionaries, see P.A. Varg, *Missionaries, Chinese, and Diplomats: The American Protestant Missionary Movement in China, 1890–1952* (Princeton: Princeton University Press, 1958); P.A. Cohen, *China and Christianity: The Missionary Movement and the Growth of Chinese Antiforeignism 1860–1870* (Cambridge, MA: Harvard University Press, 1963); P.A. Cohen, 'Christian Missions and their Impact to 1900', in *The Cambridge History of China*, X (Cambridge: Cambridge University Press, 1978); J.K. Fairbank, *The Missionary Enterprise in China and America* (Cambridge, MA: Harvard University Press, 1974); J.G. Lutz, *China and the Christian Colleges,*

faith began to take root in the soil of China. The following survey
includes only Chinese Christian scholars who were converted by the
most recent missionaries since nineteenth century, and it will be divided
into three periods of time, each with distinctive political, social and intellectual characteristics which formed the *Sitz im Leben* in which the
selected scholars published their readings of the Bible. These scholars are
selected because (1) they are leaders of the church or Christian universities, with a large group of followers, (2) they represent liberal and conservative theological positions and thus reflect the broad diversity of
Chinese Christianity, and (3) they have published extensively on the
exegesis or interpretation of the Bible.[23] For each of them, I will briefly
introduce his educational and theological background, which may help
us understand his particular point of view. Then I will summarize and
analyze two examples of his Bible reading from his publications which
deal with the Bible for the purpose of either *explicatio, meditatio* or
applicatio,[24] though my analysis will be focused on his *explicatio*. I will
also examine the way in which Chinese culture informed his exposition
of the biblical passages or themes under discussion, and then compare
his exposition to what a historical-critical exegesis can reveal in the same

---

1850–1950 (Ithaca, NY: Cornell University Press, 1971); C.P. Lin (ed.), *Chi-du-
chiao ju-hwa pai-ch'i-shih-nien chih-nien-chi* (*Christianity Coming to China One
Hundred and Seventieth Anniversary Anthology*) (Taipei: Cosmic Light, 1977). For
a very good collection of essays on the cultural dimension of the encounter between
missionaries and China, see J.D. Whitehead, Y.M. Shaw and N.J. Girardot (eds.),
China and Christianity: Historical and Future Encounters (Notre Dame: Notre Dame
University Press, 1979). For missionaries' view on the encounter, see: S.W. Barnett
and J.K. Fairbank (eds.), *Christianity in China: Early Protestant Missionary
Writings* (Cambridge, MA: Harvard University Press, 1985).

23. For this reason, other prominent scholars such as Chao Tzu-ch'en, Wu Yau-
tsung and Hsu Pau-chien who wrote mostly on church and society are not included.
For a chapter-long introduction to each of them, see L.M. Wu, *Chi-du-chiao yu
chung-kuo she-hueh pien-chien* (*Christianity and Social Change in China*) (Hong
Kong: Chinese Christian Literature Council, 1981), chs. 1, 2 and 4.

24. One can read the Bible or other scholars for three purposes: to explicate and
clarify their ideas for them, to meditate and appropriate their ideas for one's own
view, and to apply and use their ideas directly in some situations. These selected
Chinese Christian scholars read the Bible indeed for such purposes. I owe these categories to George Hunsinger, who has applied them to analyze Karl Barth in his
book: G. Hunsinger, *How to Read Karl Barth: The Shape of his Theology* (New
York: Oxford University Press, 1991).

passages or themes to see whether or not his cultural reading yields any new exegetical insight.

First Period: 1911–1945

This period began with the establishment of the Republic of China and ended with the success of the Communists' revolution. Scholars who wrote in this period lived through three major historical events: (1) the Boxer Uprising (1900), which induced a united attack by eight Western countries on China,[25] (2) the exciting success of Sun Yat-sen's revolution (1911), which overturned the corrupted monarchy of the Ching dynasty, established the new Republic, and abolished many unequal treaties,[26] and (3) the long years of suffering under Japanese aggression since 1931.[27] During these years of humiliation and oppression by imperialist countries, the minds of Chinese leaders were preoccupied by the question of the survival of the young Republic. Patriotic nationalism rose to new heights in Chinese society.

Several anti-Christian movements rose as part of a popular outrage[28] against Western imperialism. (1) The Boxer Uprising (1900) turned into vicious assaults on foreign missionaries and Chinese Christians. According to Wang Chih-hsin, 23,241 Christians were martyred.[29] (2) The New Culture Movement (1917) led by Hu Shih,[30] a student of Dewey, sought

25. C.C. T'an, *The Boxer Catastrophe* (New York: W.W. Norton, 1955).

26. C.Y. Hsu, *The Rise of Modern China* (New York: Oxford University Press, 2nd edn, 1975).

27. Before its full-scale invasion in 1937, Japanese army had found excuses to occupy three provinces in the northeast of China. See J.W. Israel, *Student Nationalism in China, 1927–1937* (Stanford: Stanford University Press, 1966).

28. S.C. Lu, *Chung-kuo kuan-shen fan-chiao chih yuan-yin (The Origin and Cause of Anti-Christian Movement Officials and Gentry, 1860–1874)* (Taipei: Institute of Modern History, Academia Sinica, 1966).

29. Wang, *History of Christianity in China*, pp. 231-48, esp. 231. See also: I.T. Headland, *Chinese Heroes: Being a Record of Persecutions Endured by Native Christians in the Boxer Uprising* (New York: Eaton & Mains, 1902).

30. For a succinct introduction to Hu Shih and his relation to Christianity, see Y.M. Shaw, 'The Reaction of Chinese Intellectuals toward Religion and Christianity in the Early Twentieth Century', in Whitehead, Shaw and Girardot (eds.), *China and Christianity: Historical and Future Encounters* (Notre Dame: Notre Dame University Press, 1979), pp. 160-62. For the New Culture Movement, see: T. Chow, *The May Fourth Movement* (Cambridge, MA: Harvard University Press, 1960).

to transplant the idea of logic and modern science into China and so it denounced both traditional culture and Christian religion as obstacles to modern progress. (3) The Non-Christian Alliance (1922)[31] also launched a fierce propaganda war condemning Chinese Christians as traitors of Chinese people. Evidently these social upheavals resulted from a violent 'culture clash' between the weak China and the strong West, old traditions and modern science. At a time of resentment against foreign countries, the importation of Christianity was regarded as a cultural invasion by many Chinese. As a consequence, the majority of intellectual leaders of the time held an attitude of indifference, if not hostility, toward Christianity.[32] It was under such unfavorable circumstances that Wu Lei-ch'uan and Chia Yu-ming interpreted the Bible for both non-believers and believers.

Wu Lei-ch'uan (1870–1944)
Wu Lei-ch'uan[33] was a scholar of Chinese classics. He passed the *Civil Service Examination*, a 1300-year-old system for electing government officials,[34] in 1898 when it was held for the last time before it was abolished. He was also chosen as a *hanlin* (scholar of the highest distinction) in the Royal Academy of Ching dynasty. His opportunity for a promising government career was, however, shattered by the Reform Movement (1898) and the Boxer Uprising (1900), so he turned to the profession of education. Although he was converted to Christianity late in his life at 44 years of age (1914), he quickly became a vigorous advocate for the marriage of Christian faith and Chinese culture, both of which, in his view, could complement each other in fostering the moral character of Chinese people. He began teaching at Yenching University in 1922 and was appointed vice president in 1926 and Chinese chancellor of the University from 1928 till his retirement in 1934.

Wu's reading of the Bible was naturally shaped by his Confucian

31. K. Yip, 'The Anti-Christian Movement in China, 1922–1927, with Special Reference to the Experience of Protestant Missions' (PhD dissertation, Columbia University, 1971).

32. Shaw, 'The Reaction of Chinese Intellectuals', pp. 154-83.

33. For a short biography, see P. West, 'Christianity and Nationalism: the Career of Wu Lei-Chuan at Yenching University', in J.K. Fairbank (ed.), *The Missionary Enterprise in China and America* (Cambridge, MA: Harvard University Press, 1974), pp. 226-48.

34. P.T. Ho, *The Ladder of Success in Imperial China* (New York: Columbia University Press, 1962).

background,[35] but it was also directed by the challenges of anti-Christian movements. He was forced to confront the 'foreignness' of Christianity and thus decided to write an indigenous Christian philosophy.[36] As a gesture of sincerity, he began to dissociate himself from the *Life Fellowship*, a bi-cultural group organized by Christian members of the Yenching faculty, to form the *Truth Society* whose membership was offered exclusively to Chinese. After some 40 articles, he also published the well-known book, *Chi-du-chiao yu chung-kuo wun-hwa* (*Christianity and Chinese Culture*) in 1936,[37] in which he used Confucian categories to interpret Christian messages. How, then, did Chinese culture inform his exegesis? We will look at two excerpts from this book.

1. *On the Holy Spirit (pp. 56-59).* Framed by two purposes, exegetical (p. 56) and apologetic (p. 59), Wu compared the Holy Spirit to *jen*, the fundamental concept and highest virtue of Confucianism. He found six striking similarities between the two. (1) As the Holy Spirit is given to every one who asks (Lk. 11.13), so is *jen*: 'I wish to have *jen*, and lo *jen* is at hand' (*Analects, Shuh Urh* 29).[38] (2) As blasphemy against the Holy Spirit is unforgivable (Mt. 12.31), so is it against *jen*. He who does not cultivate *jen* 'will be worried and ashamed for all his life until death' (*Mencius, Le Low*, Part I). (3) As the Holy Spirit is related to forgiveness (cf. Mt. 6.14-15; 7.12), so is *jen*: 'If one acts with a vigorous effort

35. For a good introduction to the basic ideas of Confucianism in comparison to Christianity, see: J. Ching, *Confucianism and Christianity* (Tokyo: Kodansha International and The Institute of Oriental Religions, 1977).

36. For his own account about the challenge of anti-Christian publications, see: L.C. Wu, *Chi-du-chiao yu chung-kuo wun-hwa* (*Christianity and Chinese Culture*) (Shanghai: Youth Association Press, 1936), p. 10. See also: P. West, *Yenching University and Sino-Western Relations, 1916–1952* (Cambridge, MA: Harvard University Press, 1976), p. 65. For his intention to write an indigenized Christian philosophy, see C. Wu, 'Lun chung-kuo chi tu chio hui ti chien tu' ('On the Future of the Chinese Christian Church'), *Chen-li chou-kan* (*Truth Weekly*, 11 [1923], pp. 1-2; C. Wu, 'Tsai lun chung-kuo chi tu chio hui ti chien tu' ('On the Future of the Chinese Christian Church Again'), *Chen-li chou-kan* (*Truth Weekly*, 22 [1923], pp. 1-2.

37. Pub. by Youth Association (printed in Shanghai). For a complete list of his publications, see J.S.C. Cha, *Chung-kuo chi-du-chiao jen-wu siao-chuan* (*Concise Bibliographies of Chinese Christians*, vol. 1) (Taipei: China Evangelical Seminary Press, 1982), pp. 76-78.

38. Confucian quotations in English are cited from Legge, *Confucius* and *The Works of Mencius*.

to forgive, nothing is closer to the realization of *jen* than this' (*Mencius, Tsin Sin*, Part I). (4) As the Holy Spirit is prerequisite to the kingdom of God (Mt. 12.28; Jn 2.3) which is in our hearts (Lk. 17.2), *jen* is the 'human heart' itself (*Mencius, Kao Tsze*, Part I) and the condition for a better world, as Confucius said, 'To subdue oneself and return to propriety is *jen*. If a man can for one day practice *jen*, to subdue himself and return to propriety, all people under heaven will return to *jen*' (*Analects, Yen Yuen* I). In other words, the kingdom of God will be realized in all human hearts. (5) As Jesus' disciples with the Holy Spirit can judge the world (Mt. 16.17-19; Jn 20.19-23), so can people with *jen* 'alone can love or hate others' (*Analects, Le Jin* III), that is, judge people. (6) Why was the Holy Spirit given to the disciples only after Jesus had died (Jn 16.7)? This can be understood by Confucius' idea of *sha shen ch'en jen* (to kill oneself to fulfil *jen*; see *Analects, Wei Lin Kuon*). The Holy Spirit did not descend upon the disciples until after Jesus' death, because it was not until Jesus the righteous man had died for the sinful that his great virtue of *jen* moved and inspired their hearts. It was by way of emotional touch that the Holy Spirit came to them, Wu explained.

Instead of looking for references in Judaic or Greco-Roman cultures as historical critics would do, Wu searched for conceptual analogies in Confucianism in order to explain the Bible. He also adopted a 'social gospel' interpretation of the kingdom of God.[39] As a result, some similarities that he pointed out are questionable. For instance, in point (3) he cited Mt. 6.14-15 and 7.12 to suggest that the Holy Spirit is related to forgiveness, but neither the texts nor their contexts in the Sermon on the Mount indicate any role of the Holy Spirit in those two sayings on mutual forgiveness and human kindness. Besides, several sayings of Jesus regarding the power of the Holy Spirit (e.g. to defend, Mt. 10.20; to exorcise, Mt. 12.28; and to teach, Jn 16.23) are unwittingly overlooked. Important differences between the Christian idea of the Holy Spirit and the Confucian notion of *jen* were not discussed either. For example, the Holy Spirit is a person of the Trinitarian God for most Christians, but *jen* is a personification of the highest virtue in Confucianism. Christians believe that the Holy Spirit is their Lord and life-giver (the Nicene Creed), but Confucianists believe that human beings are their own masters and they can and should practice *jen*.

---

39. Wu, *Christianity and Chinese Culture*, p. 6.

Nevertheless, Wu's comparison highlights the Holy Spirit's relationship to people: readily available ('at hand' [1]; 'in heart' [4]), stunningly awesome ('blasphemy is unforgivable' [2]), and powerfully inspiring ('emotional touch' [6]). It also underlines the connection between the vicarious death of Jesus and the distribution of the Holy Spirit, a unique and important motif in the Gospel of John rarely noticed by historical-critical scholars.[40] Again, it accentuates the Holy Spirit's function to enable believers to judge the world ('love or hate' [5]), and to serve as the ultimate guidance for truth and their life (Jn 16.13; cf. Gal. 5.16). Hence, if a historical-critical study pursues and reveals the sources of Jesus' view on the Holy Spirit,[41] Wu's reading of the Holy Spirit by way of *jen* calls our attention to the Holy Spirit's relationship with people, its connection with Jesus' death, and its function for believers.

2. *On Jesus as Christ (pp. 82-98).* Wu began this chapter by explaining that Christ (the anointed one for Jewish people) was someone like *Tien-tzu* (Son of Heaven) in ancient China who was, at the same time, the king who ruled over his people, the prophet who taught them the heavenly will, and the priest who offered sacrifices for them. If Christ was also anointed in the heart, he became *Sheng Tien-tzu* (the Holy Son of Heaven) who had heavenly wisdom to serve as a 'sage-king'. Since Jesus began his public ministry at a time when Jewish people were hoping for such a political Christ, four questions regarding him as Christ could be asked. (1) Why did Jesus want to be a Christ? What was his plan? Wu contended that we know Jesus wanted to serve as a political Christ,[42] because as a twelve-year old boy in Jerusalem he already said

40. See Jn 3.5, 14-15; 7.39; 14.25-26; 16.7; 19.34. This important motif was not picked up by J.D.G. Dunn, *Jesus and the Spirit: A Study of the Religious and Charismatic Experience of Jesus and the First Christians as Reflected in the New Testament* (London: SCM Press, 1975), though he discussed 'Jesus and Spirit' on pp. 350-57. One of the few recent scholars who made a few remarks on this motif in John, see G.M. Burge, *The Anointed Community: The Holy Spirit in the Johannine Tradition* (Grand Rapids: Eerdmans, 1987), pp. 93-95.

41. See e.g. 'πνεῦμα', *TDNT*, VI, pp. 332-451.

42. For scholarly discussion in the West on Jesus as a political leader, see: S.G.F. Brandon, *Jesus and the Zealots: A Study of the Political Factor in Primitive Christianity* (Manchester: Manchester University Press, 1967); P. Winter, *On the Trial of Jesus* (Berlin: de Gruyter, 1961); O. Cullmann, *Jesus and the Revolutionaries* (New York: Harper & Row, 1970); M. Hengel, *Was Jesus a Revolutionist?* (Philadelphia: Fortress Press, 1971); E. Bammel and C.F.D. Moule (eds.), *Jesus*

in earnest that he must be concerned about his Father's affairs
(Lk. 2.49),[43] which, Wu assumed, were a political revolution to liberate
his people from the Roman rule and a social revolution to reconstruct a
moral society. In order to carry out these two revolutions, Jesus' original
plan was to have his cousin John the Baptist campaign in Galilee among
peasants while he himself would do so in Jerusalem among city elites.
That was why they both had the same message: 'Repent, for the kingdom of God is near' (Mt. 3.2; 4.17). Jesus also taught his people the
principles of a new society in his missionary discourse (Mt. 10) and the
Lord's prayer (Mt. 6; Lk. 11). (2) Did Jesus change his plan? Wu argued
that Jesus was forced to abandon his revolutionary plan when he found
very little support from religious leaders, and because of this change,
John the Baptist in jail had to send his disciples to ask Jesus whether he
wanted to continue their original plan. Wu also believed that Jesus' disciples were first attracted by his political revolution to restore Jewish
sovereignty, for which they were sent nowhere but to the cities of Israel
(Mt. 10.5-10) and they were promised to have the throne over the
twelve tribes of Israel in the new world (Mt. 19.28). It is little wonder
that on the way to Jerusalem they would be arguing with one another
for higher positions (Mt. 20.17-23; Lk. 9.34-48). Furthermore, it makes
better sense as to why Judas, a capable disciple trusted with the money
of the group, would feel betrayed when Jesus changed his plan, and
would decide to sell him out. (3) Why did Jesus retain the title of Christ
after he had already abandoned his political plan? Wu proposed that
Jesus realized later on in his ministry that his role as Christ could not be
political but social, as indicated in his answer to Pilate, 'You say that I
am a king. For this I was born, and for this I have come into the world,
to bear witness to the truth. Every one who is of the truth hears my
voice' (Jn 18.37). (4) Why did Jesus' disciples change their attitude so

---

and the Politics of his Day (Cambridge: Cambridge University Press, 1984);
R.A. Horsley, *Jesus and the Spiral of Violence: Popular Jewish Resistance in
Roman Palestine* (New York: Harper & Row, 1987). For an opposite view, see
M. de Jonge, *Jesus: Inspiring and Disturbing Presence* (trans. J.E. Steely;
Nashville: Abingdon Press, 1974), pp. 128-47.

43. Lk 2.49 reads, 'Did you not know that I must be in my Father's house?' in
RSV and NRSV, but the Union version of Chinese Bible renders it as 'Did you not
know that I must be concerned about my Father's affairs?' Both are correct render-
ings; see J. Fitzmyer, *The Gospel according to Luke, I–IX* (Garden City, NY:
Doubleday, 1981), p. 443.

dramatically after his death? Wu explained that they were inspired by Jesus' fearless martyrdom for the ideal of a new society. Finally, Wu lamented the fact that the disciples preached only Jesus' redemptive death but not his teachings on social reconstruction. They were therefore responsible for turning Christianity from a social gospel into an individualistic religion.

Clearly Wu's purpose was to show Chinese leaders that Jesus' religion was aimed at constructing a moral society (p. 291), so it can play a crucial part in shaping the future of China (p. 292). Like most Confucianists, he believed that only a moral people can build up a strong nation. Seemingly consistent, his account of Jesus' psychological journey is, however, based on an arbitrary interpretation of gospel traditions. As Chao Tzu-ch'en pointed out, Wu often proved his assumptions with other assumptions.[44] For instance, he assumed that the boy Jesus 'must' have meant a political revolution when he said that he must be concerned about God's affairs, without considering the possibility that Jesus could have meant a spiritual reform as did the leader of the Qumran community. Based on that, he then argued that John the Baptist 'must' have referred to a political Christ when he asked Jesus whether he was the coming one, without entertaining the possibility that he could have meant a spiritual Christ. Again, Wu assumed that Jesus was planning for a political revolution, so the disciples' mission to the cities of Israel 'must' have been a political campaign, without checking the possibility that it might be motivated by an eschatological concern. The same kind of logic can be found in his reading of Jesus' promise to the disciples that they will sit on the throne of judgment in the new world. Evidently Wu was not familiar with A. Schweitzer's work on the apocalyptic thought of Jesus and his contemporaries.[45] As such, Wu's view of Jesus as a political Christ is as shaky as a high tower with little ground under its base. However, his theory that Jesus changed his mind from a political revolution to a spiritual reform is an insight worthy of consideration in the scholarly pursuit of the historical Jesus. The painful experience of China as a nation, overwhelmed by the rapid social changes and plagued

44. T.C. Chao, '"Jesus as Christ"—A Review of Wu Lei-ch'uan's "Christianity and Chinese Culture"', in Y.M. Shaw (ed.), *Issues of Chinese Christianity in the Twentieth Century* (Taipei: Chen Chung, 1980), pp. 666-71.

45. A. Schweitzer, *The Quest of the Historical Jesus: A Critical Study of its Progress from Reimarus to Wrede* (trans. W. Montgomery; New York: MacMillan, 1968 [1957]).

by the deterioration of morality, resembles so much the social predicament of Jesus' time that Wu was sympathetic to Jesus' desire to rebuild
a sovereign and moral society among his people. Moreover, since a sage
in China is always expected to cultivate himself and take Confucius'
example in teaching the masses to improve social propriety, it is natural
for Wu, coming out of Chinese scholastic tradition, to find Jesus a
respectable reformer of social morality.

Chia Yu-ming (1880–1964)

Chia Yu-ming was one of the most prolific writers among Chinese
Christian scholars. He published commentaries for every book of the
Bible. His career can be divided into three stages: a Presbyterian pastor
(1904–26), a seminary professor (1915–36), and a spiritual director
(1936–56). He baptized more than one thousand people in the 12 years
of pastoral work in Santong. He taught at Nanking Union Theological
Seminary, Santong Hwa-pei Theological Seminary, and presided over
Nanking Union Women's Theological Seminary. The most well-known,
however, was his leadership in China Christian Retreat Center for
Spirituality which was established in 1936 and was closed in 1956 when
he was jailed by the Communists.

Chia's reading of the Bible was opposite to Wu Lei-ch'uan's in almost
every conceivable way. Wu wrote mostly in response to the anti-
Christian *literati*; Chia wrote exclusively for Christians in the form of
commentary and sermons. Wu intended to show Chinese the relevance
of Christianity to the social reconstruction of China; Chia sought only to
nurture the spirituality of individual believers. Wu used Chinese culture
to interpret the Bible; Chia adopted the principle of *scriptura scripturae
interpres*. Finally, Wu's style was scholastic and argumentative; Chia's
was poetic and reflective. Let's look at two excerpts from his book:
Shen-dao-shueh (*The Way of God*, 1921).[46]

1. *On the Incarnated Jesus (pp. 17-24)*. Beginning with a confession
that incarnation is the very mystery of all mysteries, Chia states that,
with the help of the Holy Spirit, he will discuss it in three ways. (1) Jesus
Christ is God-and-man, and man-and-God. It is hard to understand
but one needs to accept it humbly, he says. (2) Jesus Christ is the

---

46. Y.M. Chia, *Shen-dao-shueh* (*The Way of God*) (Youth for the Lord Press
[1921]).

personification of divinity, and the divinization of personality. The fusion of the two is the greatest wonder of God, he says. (3) Jesus Christ is in heaven as well as on earth, and on earth as well as in heaven. He is everywhere at all times for all saints. This is the unmeasurable mystery, he says.

Besides the frequent citations from the Bible, Chia's interpretation of Jesus is characterized by a 'binary-composite'[47] mode of thought, an all-embracing propensity to work out contradictory parts of the Scripture, indeed, a tendency commonly found among Chinese commentators of the Classics, Chinese Buddhist commentators of scriptures, and orthodox commentators of Western traditions.[48] Such a both–and inclusiveness is in obvious contrast to the either–or exclusiveness of many historical-critical scholars. It could be argued that both–and inclusiveness is very crucial, however, for biblical exegesis. The idea of the law in Paul's letters might be a good example. In Rom. 7.4 believers are said to have died to the law, but in Gal. 6.2 they are urged to fulfil it. These two uses of the law are obviously different and seemingly contradictory to each other. Considered in its context, however, the law to be rejected in Rom. 7.4 clearly refers to the law that claims to be able to save people out of the wrath of God though in reality it can only condemn, and so believers, already redeemed by Christ, have nothing to do with it. On the other hand, the law in Gal. 6.2 in its context refers to the law of Christ and the will of God, so it ought to be obeyed in a redeemed life. These two ideas are definitely different from each other but they both belong to Paul. Hence, such a binary-composite mode of thought is

47. 'Binary relation' is a mathematic notion often used by anthropologists and sociologists to measure and describe, e.g., kinship. See D. Sills (ed.), 'Mathematics', in *International Encyclopedia of the Social Sciences*, X (New York: MacMillan & Free, 1968), p. 71.

As linguist Roman Jakobson found 'binary oppositions' in phonemic, word and sentence structure, so did Levi-Strauss see binary oppositions underlying the mental structure in totemism and myth. See C.R. Badcock, 'Culture as Language', in *Levi-Strauss: Structuralism and Sociological Theory* (New York: Holmes & Meier, 1976), pp. 33-67, esp. 50-51. I use the term 'binary-composite' to characterize the inclusive and synthesizing tendency of Chinese minds.

48. J.B. Henderson, *Scripture, Canon, and Commentary: A Comparison of Confucian and Western Exegesis* (Princeton: Princeton University Press, 1991), p. 171; D.W. Chappell, 'Hermeneutical Phases in Chinese Buddhism', in Donald S. Lopez, Jr (ed.), *Buddhist Hermeneutics* (Honolulu: University of Hawaii Press, 1988), pp. 175-206, esp. 180.

useful for the appreciation of complicated issues such as the law in Paul.[49] Also remarkable is Chia's view that Jesus is the divinization of personality (*jen-ge shen-ge-hwa*). It is similar to an Adoptionist view, but it is coupled with another statement that says Jesus is the personification of divinity (*shen-ge jen-ge-hwa*). It is also similar to the idea of exaltation in the Christ hymn (Phil. 2.9-11), but Chia sees this as referring to Jesus' divinization, not glorification; though he does underline Jesus' perfect practice of virtues as Paul had emphasized the exemplary humility and obedience of the kenotic Christ (Phil. 2.6-8). In fact, Chia's view of 'divinization through virtues' is very close to a Confucian theory that says a man can become *shen-jen* (holy man) when he cultivates his morality and achieves virtues. It is also close to a popular Buddhist's belief that says all people can become Buddha if only they try it. Divinization is certainly not the same as becoming *shen-jen* or Buddha, but, in a similar way, Jesus' divinization resulted from his perfect practice of the virtues.

2. *On the Three Stages of Sanctification (pp. 352-59)*. Chia begins this chapter by saying that believers have been born again, justified and saved, so they should seek the maturing of their Christian life and improve their relationship to Christ. Then he uses the temple in Jerusalem as a central metaphor to discuss three types of Christians. (1) Christians with sanctified status share the death and life of Christ and are like people who have the experience of walking through the court yard. (2) Christians with sanctified life live a selfless life for Christ's sake and are like people who have the experience of offering sacrifice in the court of the priests. (3) Christians with accomplished sanctification live a victorious life for Christ and are like people who have the experience of entering the Holy of Holies to be in union with God.

Chia assembles a great number of passages out of the Bible to present this uplifting but 'mosaic' chapter. He not only uses metaphors and ideas, but also cites exact words from the Chinese Bible. It is appealing to Christians but concealing to outsiders. What is remarkable, however, is his synthesizing tendency to include and draw together seemingly disparate ideas, different from the analytic tendency of historical critics. His

49. E.P. Sanders, *Paul, the Law, and the Jewish People* (Philadelphia: Fortress Press, 1983), *passim*. In this book, Sanders successfully encompassed and accounted for all disparate ideas of the law in Paul's letters and demonstrated a 'both–and' attitude in working out a system of Paul's view on the law.

use of the entire canon as the explanatory framework for biblical themes is also in contrast to the limited use of one individual book by historical critics, but similar to the efforts of recent canonical criticism.[50]

Second Period: 1945–1975

This period began with the rule of Communist Party[51] and ended with the renewed contact with the West when president Nixon of the USA visited Beijing in 1972. Shutting its door to the Capitalist countries in the West, China had become independent of, but also alienated from, most countries in the West. After long years of Communist experiment, the promises of collective prosperity and social justice did not seem to be realized, so people began to feel disillusioned and frustrated. Meanwhile, the constitution recognized only atheism as a legal religion, and the Communist regime tightened its control over all other religions, Christianity in particular[52] because it was closely connected with foreign countries through missionary societies and church affiliations.

The most remarkable event for Chinese Christians in this period was the Three-Self Movement[53] led by Wu Yau-tsung, who urged Christians to cut their ties with foreign churches, end the missionary era, and

50. B.S. Childs, *Biblical Theology in Crisis* (Philadelphia: Westminster Press, 1970); J.A. Sanders, *Torah and Canon* (Philadelphia: Fortress Press, 1972); J.A. Sanders, *Canon and Community: A Guide to Canonical Criticism* (Philadelphia: Fortress Press, 1984): especially ch. 3, 'Canonical Hermeneutics', pp. 46-60.

51. For the religious policy of Communist China in this period, see D.E. MacInnis, *Religious Policy and Practice in Communist China* (New York: Macmillan, 1972); D.E. MacInnis, *Religion in China Today: Policy and Practice* (Maryknoll, NY: Orbis Books, 1989). Two volumes of conference papers (*Vol. I: The Theological Implications of the New China* [the Ecumenical Seminar held in Bastad, Sweden, 1974] and *Vol. II: The Christian Faith and the Chinese Experience* [the Ecumenical Colloquium held in Louvain, Belgium, 1974] are published together in *Christianity and the New China* (South Pasadena, CA: Ecclesia, 1976).

52. For a short history of Chinese Church under the Communist rule, see G.T. Brown, *Christianity in the People's Republic of China* (Atlanta: John Knox, 1983), pp. 75-100; For a book-long study, see P.L. Wickeri, *Seeking the Common Ground: Protestant Christianity, the Three-Self Movement, and China's United Front* (Maryknoll, NY: Orbis Books, 1988).

53. For the original documents of this movement, see a convenient collection: F.P. Jones, *Documents of the Three-Self Movement: Source Materials for the Study of the Protestant Church in Communist China* (New York: National Council of the Churches of Christ in the USA, 1963).

mature to be an independent Chinese Christianity. He promoted the three principles of self-governing, self-supporting, and self-propagating, which in 1951 were accepted by 151 Protestant leaders in Beijing.[54] In 1950, he also drew up a document called 'The Christian Manifesto' and asked Chinese Christians to pledge their allegiance to the Communist government and follow its lead to purge the so-called imperialist influence in the church and in the nation. While some Christian leaders cooperated with the government in signing the Manifesto, others refused to do so and were persecuted in the Accusation Meetings. Wang Ming-tao was the most celebrated case. We will discuss him after Hsieh Fu-ya.

Hsieh Fu-ya (= N.Z. Zia, 1892–1991)
Hsieh Fu-ya was professor of Chinese Literature in Lin-nan, Chung-san and Chin-lin universities. One of his great contributions to the Chinese church was his translation of Kant and Schleiermacher, among others, in the series of *Historical Christian Classics*.[55] Many of his own writings were intended to wed Christian faith with Chinese culture as Wu Lei-ch'uan did, because he also believed that the gospel of Christ can transform[56] Chinese culture and at the same time complement it in strengthening the moral fabric of Chinese society. In distinction to Wu Lei-ch'uan, however, he benefited from a familiarity with Christian thought in the West.[57] We will look at two excerpts from his book,

54. Y.T. Wu, 'The Present-Day Tragedy of Christianity', *Tian Feng* (April 1948); Y.T. Wu, 'The Reformation of Christianity: On the Awakening of Christians', *Shanghai Daily Ta Kung Pao*, July 16–18 (1948), in Jones, *Documents*, pp. 1-5, 12-14.

55. F.Y. Hsieh (trans.), *Kant's Moral Philosophy* (Hong Kong: Fu-ch'iao Press, 1960); F.Y. Hsieh, *Schleiermacher: Religion and Feeling* (Hong Kong: Chinese Christian Literature Council, 1967).

56. Richard Niebuhr had discussed five types of relationship between Christ and culture in the history of Christianity: Christ against culture, the Christ of culture, Christ above culture, Christ and culture in paradox, and Christ the transformer of culture. See: H.R. Niebuhr, *Christ and Culture* (New York: Harper & Brothers, 1951). Hsieh held a 'dualist but not dualistic' view, in Niebuhr's terms, on Christ and culture. He tried to hold together and distinguish at the same time between loyalty to Christ and responsibiltiy for culture (see Niebuhr, *Christ and Culture*, p. 149). He also regarded Christ as the transfomer of Chinese culture.

57. L.C. Wu, 'The New Ideas in Christianity and the Basic Thoughts of Chinese People', in W.H. Lam (ed.), *Chin-dai hwa-jen shen-hsueh wun-sien (A Source Book of Modern Chinese Theology)* (Hong Kong: China Graduate School of

Chi-du-chiao yu chung-kuo szu-siang (Christianity and Chinese Thought, 1971).[58]

1. *On the Word that Dwelled among us (pp. 30-34)*. Hsieh believed that John the evangelist had a mystical spirituality, so he could recognize Jesus as the Word of God that became flesh and dwelled among us. Based on what the boy Jesus said to his parents, 'Did you not know that I must be concerned about my Father's affairs?' (Lk. 2.49), Hsieh inferred that Jesus must have had an intensive preparation for his ministry since his childhood. When disappointed by the corrupted leaders, he must have felt *dang jen pu jang* (no hesitation to practice *jen*) and began his attempt to rejuvenate the traditional culture of his people, namely, the prophetic messages of Hebrew Scriptures. Hsieh also pointed out that Jesus' refusal to turn stones into bread, in the temptation story, demonstrates clearly his determination to *sha shen ch'en jen*; willing to starve to death rather than to live ashamed. Finally, in describing Jesus' teaching on the kingdom of heaven, Hsieh used a popular saying of Chinese Buddhism, 'Put down the butcher's knife, and at once you become Buddha', to emphasize the immediacy and easiness of receiving that message. He urged Chinese people to repent and enter the kingdom of heaven.

It is evident that Hsieh freely cited Confucian ideas to describe Jesus' thoughts and actions, just as Wu Lei-ch'uan did. What interests me, however, is his discovery of what is presumed between the lines of the gospel narrative. He pointed out the significance of Jesus' sense of calling as already shown in his childhood and his strong indignation against the corruption of his people and their leaders as we can see attested by his cleansing of the temple (Mk 11.15-17). Judged by historical criteria, Hsieh's exegesis is not uncritical and is indeed revealing concerning the motivation of Jesus' mission. How, then, did he find that? One of the vantage points he had, I believe, was the agonizing experience that he went through as a Chinese scholar watching his traditional culture systematically destroyed by Mau Zedong's Cultural Revolution (1966–76)[59] in the name of which the Red Guards relentlessly eradicated the

Theology, 1986), pp. 445-61. He discussed five basic ideas of modern Christianity: Humanism, Meliorism, Experimentalism, Socialism and Practicalism.

58. Pub. by Chinese Christian Literature Council in Hong Kong.

59. Y. Zhu, 'The Causes of the "Cultural Revolution"' *Beijing Review* 24 (September 14, 1981), pp. 15-18.

so-called 'old ideas, culture, customs and habits'.[60] His own heart-breaking experience enabled him to empathize with Jesus in respect to the solemn sense of calling and strong indignation.[61] The fact that he used a Buddhist idea to explain a Christian message to a good effect also indicates how helpful a cultural expression can be in conveying the meaning of the Bible.

2. *On the Traits of Chinese Christianity (pp. 307-11)*. Hsieh argues that Christ is the head of the church and the church the body of Christ. In history, the Christian church has absorbed different kinds of nutrition, namely, Roman Catholic, Greek Orthodox and Protestant churches; therefore, legitimately, Hsieh argues, there will also be a Chinese church. This Chinese church should have three traits: (1) critical inclusiveness, (2) dynamic golden mean, and (3) mystical practice. It should include all Christian traditions and engage itself in critical dialogue with other religions. It should also strike a balance to find the golden mean between the conservative and liberal theologies. In addition, since Chinese people are inclined to experience faith through practice, as opposed to Westerners who like to prove faith through knowledge, Chinese Christians should involve themselves in social service, and the key to an effective social service is the mystical union with God. It is not until all Christians are unified, as Jesus and the Father are (Jn 10.38; 14.10, 11; 17.11), and all Christians are transformed to be new people, that the gospel of Christ can be spread in China.

Like Chia Yu-ming, Hsieh shows a binary-composite mode of thought in his discussion of the ideal traits of Chinese church. The tendency of Chinese people to *experience* faith, as he points out, can be helpful in their reading of the Bible, too, because the Bible contains ancient believers' experiences in faith events. Both Chinese and ancient believers take interest in life experiences.

---

60. See 'Decision of the Central Committee of the Chinese Communist Party concerning the Great Proletarian Cultural Revolution', *Peking Review* 33 (August 12, 1966), p. 6. For the impact of this revolution on Christian churches in China, see Wickeri, *Seeking the Common Ground*, pp. 179-85.

61. F.Y. Hsieh, *Chi-du-chiao yu chung-kuo szu-siang* (*Christianity and Chinese Thought*) (Hong Kong: Chinese Christian Literature Council, 1971), p. 297.

Wang Ming-dao (1900–1991)

Wang Ming-dao was a highly respected pastor to a large independent church in Beijing and a well-known itinerant evangelist in the nation. He refused to sign The Christian Manifesto of 1950 because he disagreed with the liberal theological views of the leaders of the Three-Self Movement[62] and he did not think that Christians in principle should be involved in the political arena. As a result, he was arrested three times and jailed for twenty-two years. Persecution for the faith made up a good part of his life and it is reflected in his reading of the Bible. We will look at two samples of his Bible reading.

1. *On Christ's Brides (Collection,*[63] *IV, pp. 2-25).* This is a thematic exposition on 'Christ's brides' under three questions. Who are Christ's brides? What are the promises for them? And how can we become Christ's brides? Believing that the best commentary on the Bible is the Bible itself, Wang used the principle of *scriptura scripturae interpres* in searching for answers. Like many conservative Christians in the West, he also believed in the literal meaning of the biblical text and always paid close attention to the details. For instance, he noticed that, besides Christ and his brides, there are guests in the wedding feast (Mt. 22.2-14; Rev. 19.9). Who can they be? The fact that these guests are second to the brides in terms of glory and joy in the wedding feast leads him to see a parallel in Paul's exhortation for Christians to run a good race in life so as to win the prize from heaven (1 Cor. 9.24; Phil. 3.13, 14). In this metaphor, presumably some Christians would fall behind and become second in glory and joy to the winners. They are, by analogy, the kind of people represented by the guests who are less glorious and joyful though also attending the feast. The lesson is therefore clear: strive for the best witness in your lives so as to become Christ's brides and enjoy the utmost glory in the final judgment. Somewhat out of place but typical of him, he ended this exposition with an earnest exhortation for Christians to endure sufferings for their faith. He said that persecution always accompanies those who determine to obey God, because the world they live in is evil (Jn 15.18-20). He urged his readers to reject the way of the world and faithfully endure all tribulations,

62. M.T. Wang, *Jen n'en chien-she tien-kuo ma?* (*Can Man Construct the Kingdom of Heaven?*) (Hong Kong: Shuen-dao Press, 2nd edn, 1962), pp. 1-16.

63. C.C. Wang (ed.), *Wang Ming-dao wun-kuh* (*Wang Ming-dao Collection*) (Touliu: Conservative Baptist Press, 1976–1978).

because Christ will be pleased to take them to be his brides.

Because he believed that beyond individual books there is coherence in the entire Bible, Wang took seriously all details of biblical texts and always tried to weave them together for his readers. He approached the Bible with a binary-composite mode of thought, as did Chia Yu-ming and Hsieh Fu-ya. His exegesis also betrays a typical motivation shared by many Confucian commentators on the Classics, that is, the intention to edify and to nurture moral aspirations.[64] Finally, his long years of imprisonment by the Communists gave him a similar life experience to that of Paul who wrote many letters in jail, and naturally his reading of Paul is often sympathetic and penetrating. To many readers, his stark persistence in faith undoubtedly increases the impact of his exhortation.

2. *Who is Jesus? (Collection, VII, pp. 136-37; 148-62)*. In this article, Wang listed nine categories of biblical evidence trying to prove that Jesus is indeed the Son of God. They are the prophecies in the Old Testament, the announcements of the angels, the testimonies of the saints, the witness by John the Baptist, the declaration of God, the actions of Jesus, the recognition of evil spirits, the fulfilment of Jesus' prediction, and especially the resurrection of Jesus. Since all evidences are drawn from the Bible, only Christians, like himself, who have accepted the authority of the Bible will be convinced. In terms of exegesis, he used typological[65] principles, for instance, to see Jesus as the woman's offspring who will engage in combat with the snake, as is written, 'The offspring of the woman will strike your head' (Gen. 3.15). It is also interesting to note that, while Wu Lei-ch'uan and Hsieh Fu-ya were attracted to Jesus' personality and morality, Wang found his divine sonship most important. In fact, he intended to fight the liberal scholars of his time who denied the divinity of Jesus.[66] In cases such as these, an exegete's theological prejudgment often predetermines what he or she will find in the Bible.

64. J.B. Henderson, *Scripture, Canon, and Commentary: A Comparison of Confucian and Western Exegesis* (Princeton: Princeton University Press, 1991), pp. 121-29. The 'moralizing' tendency of Confucian commentators can be found even in their interpretation of love songs. See Sze-Kar Wan's paper herein, 'From Philo Judaeus to Confucius and Back, or Allegorical Interpretation East and West'.

65. W.H. Lam, *Wang-Ming-dao yu chung-kuo chiao-hueh* (*Wang Ming-dao and the Chinese Church*) (Hong Kong: China Graduate School of Theology, 1982), p. 181.

66. Lam, *Wang-Ming-tao*, pp. 155-59.

Third Period: 1975–1990

This period began when China reopened its door to the West in the 1970s. Prior to that in the cold war era, China had cut off its relations and stopped activities of exchange with the West. It had also closed theological seminaries and almost all the churches. Taiwan and Hong Kong, on the other hand, were allied to the West in developing democracy and economy, and gradually became active members of the global community. Many of their people became informed world citizens, and a great number of Christian scholars pursued their theological education in the West. As a result, critical studies of the Bible and liberal theological views were quickly transported into these two areas. Meanwhile, encouraged by the ecumenical movement, stimulated by the liberation theology of Latin America, and supported by their Asian colleagues,[67] Chinese scholars there began to engage themselves in interreligious dialogues, undertake the contextualization of Christianity, and create their own theologies to meet their special needs.[68] We will discuss C.S. Song and Chow Lien-hwa as representative scholars of this period.

Song Choan-seng (= C.S. Song, 1929–)

Formerly president of Tainan Theological Seminary in Taiwan, C.S. Song now teaches at Pacific School of Religion in Berkeley and at South East Asia Graduate School of Theology. Educated at Edinburgh and Union Seminary in New York, he has served as Associate Director of the Faith and Order Commission of the World Council of Churches and Director of Study for the World Alliance of Reformed Churches. These experiences in ecumenical institutions gave him a frame of reference crossing many cultural boundaries. Nevertheless, his concern and compassion remain focused on the suffering and dreams of his own people and neighbors in Asia. We will look at two excerpts from his book, *Jesus, the Crucified People* (1990).[69]

---

67. D.J. Elwood, *What Asian Christians are Thinking: A Theological Source Book* (Quezon City: New Day, 1976).

68. C.S. Song, *Theology from the Womb of Asia* (Maryknoll, NY: Orbis Books, 1986); S.C. Wang, *Taiwan siang-tu shen-shueh lun-wun-chih (Taiwan Homeland Theological Essays)* (Tainan: Tainan Theological Seminary, 1988). See also articles published in *Ching Feng*, a quarterly journal devoted to the dialogue between Chinese culture and Christianity, pub. by Tao-Fong-Shan Ecumenical Centre in Hong Kong.

69. Pub. by Crossroad in New York.

1. *Who do you Say that I am? (pp. 145-64).* Song first noted that
Gospel writers did not claim to write a history of Jesus nor did they hide
their ambivalence about him. Their honesty, he observed, betrays their
love for Jesus as a human friend and human master, though he was
already in the process of being divinized. Following a statement about
his method which allows Gospel stories to converse with today's stories,
he began an exegetical study on Jesus' question in Caesarea Philippi,
'Who do you say I am?' (Mk 8.27-30 and par.). Then, he discussed the
issues of Jesus' identity arguing that Jesus could not have regarded himself as a Davidic Messiah, because the Davidic kingdom was only a
short-lived political regime which would not make a good model for his
mission. Song surmised that Jesus knew that such a Jewish nationalistic
Messiahship would become a stumbling block for his mission beyond
Jewish borders, so his Messiahship must have rather been based on the
historical and faith event of the Exodus with which even the suffering
people in the Third World today can identify. Finally, he questioned the
validity of Christian insistence on exclusiveness if Jesus himself had
superseded his Jewish traditions.

It needs to be seriously considered whether or not the uniqueness of
Jesus Christ has been lost in Song's insistence on inclusiveness, which
presents an easy path towards religious syncreticism. However, in this
exegesis, Song shows a remarkable sensitivity to historical-critical issues
such as the evangelists' ambivalence about Jesus and the short existence
of the ancient Davidic kingdom. It is also evident that his personal
experience of the plight and desires of Asian peoples has led him to
discern a Messiahship, in Jesus' consciousness, which is patterned after
the Exodus event rather than the Davidic kingship the narrow nationalistic significance of which had been transformed by Jesus himself
according to the Gospel writers.[70] In other words, he has found, in the
Exodus event, a theological reason for Jesus' refusal to serve as a
Davidic Messiah.

2. *Jesus is the Crucified People (pp. 209-32).* The question in this
chapter is whether or not Jesus himself thought that he was a paschal
lamb, so Song did an exegesis on the gospel account of the last supper.
Comparing it to the Passover narrative in Exodus 12–13, he pointed out
that there are two special elements in the last supper, the bread for

70. M. de Jonge, *Christology in Context: The Earliest Christian Response to
Jesus* (Philadelphia: Westminster Press, 1988), p. 211.

Jesus' body and the wine for his blood. Another significant difference, he claimed, was that God passed over the paschal lamb but stayed with Jesus while he was on the cross, and therefore the cross surpassed the Passover. Then Song argued from silence to say that, since Jesus did not mention Exodus at all in the last supper as prophets often did, he must have regarded the cross event as superseding the Exodus event in terms of God's salvation. Finally, Song discussed various meanings of Jesus' Eucharistic words 'for many' in Greek and contended that it should be understood as 'in behalf of and representing all peoples'. Thus, on the cross Jesus is the crucified people.

Appealing as it may be, Song's comparison between the last supper and the Passover is open to question. His argument from silence is not certain and his view of God being with Jesus on the cross is debatable (what, then, is the meaning of Jesus' cry 'My God, my God, why hast thou forsaken me?' Mk 15.34). However, his exposition of Jesus' words 'for many' makes a strong case and his thesis that Jesus is the crucified people is a significant insight which as we can see is testified in Paul, 'Christ redeemed us from the curse of the law, having *become* a curse for us—for it is written, "Cursed be every one who hangs on a tree"' (Gal. 3.13). It greatly enriches our understanding of and appreciation for Jesus' special relationship, even identity, with the sinful people who are cursed, similar to what Wu Lei-ch'uan had found about the Holy Spirit. Since the 'hermeneutical circle' in this case begins with Song's experience with and concern about the daily struggles of Asian peoples, it offers another example of the simple fact that an experience analogous to that of the Bible is a great asset in doing biblical exegesis.

Chow Lien-hwa (1920–)
Chow Lien-hwa is a distinguished Baptist pastor, professor of Systematic Theology, and Chinese Bible translator in Taiwan. He is also the general editor of *Chinese Bible Commentary*.[71] We will look at two examples of his reading of the Bible.

1. *On the Trinity (Theological Outline,*[72] *pp. 86-105)*. Chow discussed this difficult doctrine in three sections: (1) biblical evidence, (2) the problems, and (3) the truth of the Trinity. He argued that the idea of the

71. Pub. by Chinese Christian Literature Council in Hong Kong.
72. L.H. Chow, *Shen-sheuh kang-yao (Theological Outline)* (Taipei: Dao-shen, 1979).

Trinity is attested in the New Testament. Jesus the Son reveals God the Father (Jn 14.6) and the Holy Spirit makes people know God as Father (Rom. 8.14-16; Gal. 4.6). In order to explain the problem of the three-in-one, he used the analogy of *f'en-shen* (to split body), a theatrical idea for an actor to play different roles in the same performance. A question follows: how can God the Father remain the same when he *f'en-shen* to play the role of the Son? To answer it, Chow referred to the idea of numbers in *I Ching* (*The Book of Changes*) which explains that when the number I increases to number II, there is a change in terms of quantity but the quality of the number I remains inside of number II.

While discussing biblical evidence, Chow twice emphasized that to see God the Father through Jesus the Son is not only a teaching of the New Testament but also a common experience of believers. When discussing the relationship between the Father and the Son, he twice asserted that their intimacy could be understood in practice as well as in theory. Evidently he intended to appeal to Chinese minds which place experience and practice above argument and theory when it comes to the test of truth, as can be seen in the fact that Confucius taught mostly the truth of life that is practicable. As for the idea of *f'en-shen* and the change of numbers in *I Ching*, they are obviously Chinese notions that he employed to explain the mystery of the Trinity.

2. *Can Everybody Become Christ?(Communication and Transformation,*[73] *pp. 39-51).* This extract is one of Chow's answers to Tsai Jen-hou, a Neo-Confucian philosopher, who raised six controversial questions that seem to separate Confucianism and Christianity on the level of basic doctrine and which need to be discussed before a meaningful communication between the two belief systems and any transformation of either can take place. The question under discussion here is whether or not every ordinary person can in theory become Christ. Confucianism teaches that everybody can become *Iao* or *S'un* (the two perfect sage-kings in ancient times) as long as he or she practices *jen*. Buddhism also teaches that everybody can become Buddha, and Taoism teaches the idea of *ch'en-jen* (the authentic person), though following different processes. Chow's answer is positive, because, he argued, Jesus himself had said, 'What I have done, those who believe me will also do',

73. J.H. Tsai, L.H. Chow and Y.C. Liang, *Hueh-tong yu chuan-hwa, chi-du-chiao yu sin-ju-chia deh dueh-hwa* (*Communication and Transformation: A Dialogue between Christianity and Neo-Confucianism*) (Taipei: Cosmic Light, 1987).

and Paul wrote that believers are already united with Christ through baptism, so Christ will live within them.

Chow's reading of the Bible in this extract is quite questionable.[74] The context of his quotation from Jesus (Jn 14.12) shows that Jesus meant to say to Philip that his believers should continue his 'works', in the sense of his mission to reveal and glorify God,[75] not the mere miracles,[76] and that they would do even better with the help of the Holy Spirit when he went away to the Father (cf. 15.27). The two quotations from Paul (Rom. 6.4; Gal. 2.20) refer to a new life 'in Christ' that his believers will live. As such, his scriptural quotations are related to what Christians should do 'as' Christ has done. Christians can and should become like Christ, but they can not become Christ himself except in a figurative way. Chow's answer to the Neo-Confucian question of 'becoming Christ', therefore, shows that a question from another culture, incompatible with that of the Bible, can sometimes misdirect our search for the original meaning of the biblical text.

Implications for 'Cultural Exegesis'

Hans Küng is very perceptive when he writes that Chinese Christians face an enormous challenge from their compatriots, because they have dual religious citizenship, dual cultural citizenship and dual citizenship in faith.[77] In reality, such a dual citizenship between Chinese and Christian cultures has become both a curse and a blessing to them. Often, it makes them the marginalized people in either of the two communities, but it also makes them privileged because they are constantly informed and nurtured by both. Life in a border town is always adventurous and challenging, but it can also be rewarding and refreshing. Indeed, we biblical scholars will find it a pleasant surprise and incredible benefit, too, if

74. See Tsai Jen-hou's response, in Tsai, Chow and Liang, *Hueh-tong yu chuan-hwa*, pp. 137-43.

75. R. Bultmann, *The Gospel of John: A Commentary* (trans. G.R. Beasley-Murray, R.W.N. Hoare and J.K. Riches; Philadelphia: Westminster, 1971), pp. 610-11.

76. R.E. Brown, *The Gospel according to John XIII–XXI* (Garden City, NY: Doubleday, 1970), p. 633; R. Schnackenburg, *The Gospel according to St John*, III (trans. D. Smith and G.A. Kon; New York: Crossroad, 1987), p. 71.

77. H. Kung and J. Ching, *Christianity and Chinese Religions* (New York: Doubleday, 1989), pp. 273-84.

we sometimes walk over the cultural fence to visit our neighbors' back-
yard and appreciate their rose garden.[78] A cultural exegesis of the Bible
will surely be rewarded by colorful blossoms of new visions.

What do we learn from this survey of Chinese readings of the Bible?
First of all, it shows that a reading informed by Chinese culture and
Chinese experiences very often finds exactly the same meanings of the
Bible as the historical critics do. Sometimes, however, it is highly
questionable, and yet, again, sometimes it reveals meanings of biblical
texts never found before. Thus, a diagram indicating the relationship and
compatibility among the cultures of the Bible, the West and Chinese,
begins to emerge.

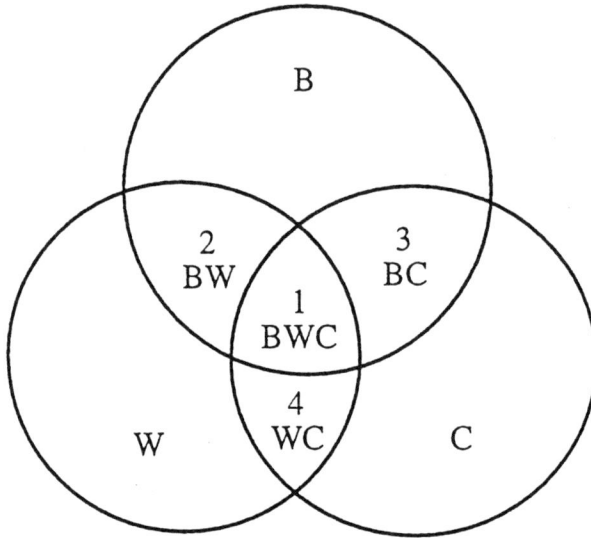

The three circles B, W and C represent Biblical, Western and Chinese
cultural worlds. They overlap with one another in area 1 (BWC) which

78. Two recent books by Western scholars deliberately written from a Third–
World point of view remarkably demonstrate the kind of fresh insights that can be
found: R.M. Brown, *Unexpected News: Reading the Bible with Third World Eyes*
(Philadelphia: Westminster, 1984); D.J. Adams, *Cross-Cultural Theology: Western
Reflections in Asia* (Atlanta: John Knox, 1987).

represents the universal human 'nature',[79] so it is possible for both Western and Chinese peoples to exegete and understand the Bible though it was written in ancient times. But they also differ from one another in important aspects, not only in their world views but also their ways of 'cognitive functioning'.[80] The cultural differences between the biblical and Chinese world views are evident because they have been developed in different environments and circumstances. Western culture, after the time of the Renaissance and the rise of science, has also qualitatively removed itself from its cultural roots in the Bible, so much so that it is now as distant from the Bible's culture as is Chinese culture. Historical-critical reading of the Bible developed in the West is therefore also a kind of cultural reading, just as Chinese, or any other reading, is.

As this diagram illustrates, we find four areas of compatibility among the three cultural worlds. Area 1 (BWC) is what both Western and Chinese readings can detect and comprehend in the Bible. More comparative study of Western and Chinese readings of the Bible can therefore confirm and expand more of such understanding. Area 2 (BW) is what only Western reading can detect and comprehend in the Bible because it retains some cultural traditions of the Bible. Area 3 (BC) is what only Chinese reading can detect and comprehend in the Bible. As our survey indicates, because they have been shaped by similar life experiences and concerns of the Bible, Chinese minds are sensitive to and compatible with certain biblical traditions that have become incomprehensible to Westerners. Finally, area 4 (WC) is where Western and Chinese readings agree on their explanation of the Bible but they do not really recover any original meaning of it, because they share modernity which is lacking in the Bible. This reminds us to respect the limitations of modern culture and cautions us not to be overly confident in our ability to recover all meanings of the Bible.

---

79. 'Nature' here is used in the sense of hereditary and necessary features universally shared by members of the human species as opposed to the arbitrary and contingent cultural codes developed in different societies; see C. Levi-Strauss, *The Elementary Structures of Kinship* (trans. J. Harle Bell and J. Richard von Sturmer; ed. R. Needham; Boston: Beacon, 1969), pp. 3-11.

80. R.A. Shweder and E.J. Bourne, 'Does the Concept of the Person Vary Cross-Culturally?', in R.A. Shweder, *Thinking Through Cultures: Expeditions in Cultural Psychology* (Cambridge, MA: Harvard University Press, 1991), pp. 113-55 [155]; cf. also R.A. Shweder and R.A. LeVine (eds.), *Culture Theory: Essays on Mind, Self, and Emotion* (Cambridge: Cambridge University Press, 1984).

Secondly, this survey has revealed three features of Chinese reading of the Bible. (1) *Experience*. As a minority group in their society, Chinese Christians are constantly forced to explain and justify their faith and deeds, and are sometimes persecuted. This minority experience is similar to that of the Jewish people in the Exile and the early Christians in the Roman empire, so Chinese scholars are sensitive to the adverse social contexts presumed between the lines of biblical texts (Wu, Hsieh, Wang, Song, Chow). (2) *Values*. They are also attentive to the questions of relationship and function, be it the issue of historical Jesus or Holy Spirit, maybe because of their corporate society and pragmatic nature[81] (Wu, Chia, Song, Chow). (3) *Mode of Thought*. They also show an binary-composite mode of thought which seeks to bring all disparate parts to a totality, even if they are contradictory. They appreciate paradoxes (Chia, Hsieh, Wang).

Thirdly, the three periods of time which we have surveyed are conspicuously marked by ever changing situations and new problems for Chinese Christians. Although some of their basic cultural perspectives remain the same, the horizon of their concerns always changes with the time. Therefore, we ought to remember that any serious effort in cultural exegesis has to take this variable factor into account. In fact, we may never reach a final version of cultural exegesis.

The question for cultural exegesis is not any more whether or not we can do it, but rather how we do it. If in recent studies of the Bible we have learned and benefited from the questions and perspectives of sociology and social science which are mostly developed from social groups in modern times and foreign to the culture of the Bible,[82] certainly we can also discover new exegetical directions and insights from a critical study of various cultures and their ways of reading the Bible. This survey has shown that a comparative study of different cultural readings can be very fruitful. A full scale of comprehensive comparison is therefore called for between Chinese and Western readings, and between many others. Of course, cooperative work among scholars of kindred spirit who are experienced in various cultural backgrounds is also required if we want to gather adequate as well as accurate data.

---

81. K.S. Latourette, *The Chinese: Their History and Culture* (New York: MacMillan, 1964), p. 680.

82. A brilliant sociological study of the Bible which gives rise to the inquiry of cultural exegesis is D.L. Smith, *The Religion of the Landless: The Social Context of the Babylonian Exile* (Bloomington: Meyer–Stone Books, 1989).

Only through such cooperation and critical dialogue can we begin the integrative theoretical endeavor to formulate a new approach or method of cultural exegesis.

ALLEGORICAL INTERPRETATION EAST AND WEST: A METHODOLOGICAL ENQUIRY INTO COMPARATIVE HERMENEUTICS*

Sze-Kar Wan

The Stoic commentator of Homer, Pseudo-Heraclitus, defines allegory (ἀλληγορία) as 'The manner of saying one thing but meaning something else'.[1] This etymological definition is intended not as an objective description of Homer's intentionality but rather as a description of the hermeneutical principle behind the commentator's own allegorical *interpretation*. In an attempt to defend Homer against his detractors, the Stoics developed a hermeneutical strategy according to which the author really intends to say 'something else' other than what he literally says.[2] The appearance of illogicality, impossibility and immorality[3] are but intended signs by the author inviting the reader to allegorize. Similarly, President O'Malley has remarked that 'the absurd is the sign of allegory'. It is only by allegorical interpretation that the 'intended' message

---

* In the course of revising this paper for publication, I have received valuable help and criticism from Professor Irene Eber of Hebrew University.

1. ''Ο γὰρ ἄλλα μὲν ἀγορεύων τρόπος, ἕτερα δὲ ὧν λέγει σημαίνων, ἐπωνύμως ἀλληγορία καλεῖται' (Ps.-Heraclitus, *Quaestiones Homericae* 5.2); cf. Heraclitus, *Allégories d'Homère*, (ed. F. Buffière; Paris: Société d'édition "Les belles lettres", 1962), pp. ix-x; C. Thompson, 'Stoic Allegory of Homer: A Critical Analysis of Heraclitus' Homeric Allegories' (PhD dissertation, Yale University, 1973).

2. Criticisms of Homer probably began with Plato in his debates with the Sophists. See J. Tate, 'Plato and Allegorical Interpretation', *Classical Quarterly* 23 (1929), pp. 142-54. For a discussion on the origins of allegorical interpretation, see J. Tate, 'The Beginnings of Greek Allegory', *Classical Review* 41 (1927), pp. 214-15; 'Plato and Allegorical Interpretation', *Classical Quarterly* 23 (1929), pp. 41-44; 24 (1930), pp. 1-10; 'On the History of Allegorism', *Classical Quarterly* 28 (1934), pp. 105-14.

3. See a summary of criticisms in Aristotle, *Poetica* 25.

of Homer can be uncovered. The method was a reverse of the author's supposed procedure of saying one thing and meaning something else.

In this respect, allegorical interpretation is not so different from the historical-critical method.[4] Both are concerned with recovering the authorial intention and both manipulate the text to arrive at the desired result. What is different, of course, is that while the historical critic sees the hermeneutical gap as that which is created by the historical and epistemological distance between the text and the interpreter,[5] the allegorical interpreter sees the gap as primarily a doctrinal one. The historical critic must bridge the hermeneutical gap by means of historical tools and a canon of criticism, while the allegorical interpreter must construct a system, a set of principles, cultural assumptions, and so on, to reproduce the author's intended meaning. If this is the case, we, the onlookers (though by no means indifferent), have no way of understanding the allegorical interpreter's claim unless we know the underlying doctrinal system. The task of evaluating an allegorical interpretation is therefore the task of understanding the internal, often unstated, logic of the allegory and of delineating the pattern of the *tertium comparationis*, the middle term between the text and the desired results.[6] It should be clear that this is the very reason why I have chosen allegorical interpretation as the means of comparing two drastically different cultures, that of the Hellenistic and Roman periods of Late Antiquity on the one hand and,

4.   The vehement objection raised by nineteenth-century biblical scholars against allegorical interpretation notwithstanding: such objection has to be seen as part of the revolt against a 'dogmatic' or 'doctrinal' interpretation of the Bible. See, e.g., the dismissal of the allegorical method by W. Wrede, *Über die Aufgabe und Methode der sogenannten neutestamentlichen Theologie* (Göttingen: Vandenhoeck & Ruprecht, 1897); (ET 'The Task and Methods of "New Testament Theology"', in R. Morgan (ed.), *The Nature of New Testament Theology* [Naperville, IL: Allenson, 1973], pp. 68-116).

5.   See the classical formulation of this *Problematik* by F. Schleiermacher, *Hermeneutics: The Handwritten Manuscripts* (trans. J. Duke and J. Forstman; Missoula, MT: Scholars Press, 1977).

6.   To present the problem as a discovery of the allegorical interpreter's assumptions, philosophical presuppositions and prejudices is not to imply that a historical critic is free from such problems. The very work of Heidegger indicates the indispensability of prejudice (*Vorverständnis*) in interpretation. R. Bultmann, furthermore, has answered decisively the impossibility (and by implication the undesirability) of presuppositionless exegesis. Cf. 'Is Exegesis without Presupposition Possible?', in *Faith and Existence* (New York: Meridian Books, 1960), pp. 289-96.

on the other, that of Pre-Han and Han China. Allegorical interpretation points to and highlights the prejudices, presuppositions and cultural assumptions of the interpreter and his or her readers.[7] A comparison between different practices of allegorical interpretation, east and west, is one avenue into the heart of cultural exegesis.

This paper has four parts. Parts I and II consist of discussions of Philo's allegorical interpretation of the Septuagint,[8] a mode of interpretation that has had a profound impact on western hermeneutics, and the

7.   The order of presentation here that goes from a theoretical discussion of allegorical interpretation to the apologetic practice of that method is, of course, ahistorical. Allegorical interpretation probably arose as a defense of Homer (most likely by the Stoics) against his critics. See p. 124 n. 2 above.

8.   The assumption here is that Philo should be read first and foremost as a commentator of the Bible. Scholars have variously attempted to see Philo as a philosopher (cf. e.g. J. Drummond, *Philo Judaes, or the Jewish Alexandrian Philosophy in its Development and Completion* [2 vols.; Amsterdam: Press, 1969; first pub. London, 1888]; H.A. Wolfson, *Philo: Foundations of Religious Philosophy in Judaism, Christianity, and Islam* [2 vols.; Cambridge, MA: Harvard University Press, 1947]; and most recently D. Winston, *Logos and Mystical Theology in Philo of Alexandria* [Cincinnati : Hebrew Union College Press, 1985]; as a *mystic* (cf. e.g. the classic work of J. Pascher, Ἡ βασιλικὴ ὁδος: *Der Königsweg zu Wiedergeburt und Vergottung bei Philon von Alexandreia* [Paderborn: F. Schoningh, 1931]; E.R. Goodenough, *By Light, Light! The Mystic Gospel of Hellenistic Judaism* [New Haven, CT: Yale University Press, 1935]; and as a Jewish Mystic, in E. Bréhier, *Les idées philosophiques et religieuses de Philon d'Alexandrie* [Paris: Librairie philosophique J. Vrin, 3rd edn, 1950]; H. Lewy, *Philosophia Judaica: Philo* [Oxford: East and West Library, 1946], esp. 7-25). The recent works of V. Nikiprowetzky, *Le commenataire de L'Ecriture chez Philon d'Alexandrie* (Leiden: Brill, 1977), and I. Christiansen, *Die Technik der allegorischen Auslegungswissenschaft bei Philon von Alexandrien* (Tübingen: Mohr, 1969), however, have revived the enduring view of Philo as an exegete of Scripture. This is, of course, the predominant view among the early church fathers, whose love for Philonic exegesis, more than anything, was the very reason for the collection, edition and preservation of the Philonic corpus after the destruction of the Alexandrian library. This is also the view of C. Siegried, *Philo von Alexandria als Ausleger des Alten Testaments an sich selbst und nach seinem geschichtlichen Einfluss betrachtet* (Jena: Hermann Dufft, 1875). For an up-to-date survey of the *status quaestionis*, see J. Morris, 'The Jewish Philosopher Philo', in G. Vermes, F. Millar and M. Goodman (eds.), *Emil Schürer: The History of the Jewish People in the Age of Jesus Christ*, 3.2 (Edinburgh: T. & T. Clark, 1987), pp. 809-89; and T. Tobin, *Creation of Man: Philo and the History of Interpretation* (Washington: Catholic Biblical Association, 1983), pp. 1-4.

Confucian commentarial traditions of the *Shih Ching* (*Odes*) during the Pre-Han and Han periods. In Part III of the essay, I will compare these two types of allegorical interpretation and attempt to discern what cultural factors might have been, at least partly, responsible for the formation of quite different shapes of cultural exegesis. I will conclude in Part IV with some general observations and conclusions about interpretation and cultural exegesis.

1. *The Allegorical Interpretation of Ps.-Heraclitus, Philo and Paul*

A Stoic commentator calling himself Heraclitus deals with the opening scene of the *Iliad*, in which Apollo is described as smiting the Achaeans in anger:

> How indeed does one explain why Apollo, who had been eager to shoot his arrow, then sat down apart from the ships and let fly a shaft; terrible was the twang of the silver bow [*Il.* 1.48-49]. For if he [*sc.* Apollo] were shooting in anger, the archer would have had to stand near those whom he wounded. But as he [*sc.* Homer] wants to speak allegorically (ἀλληγορῶν) of the sun, he quite fittingly supposes that its cargo of plague-ridden rays comes from afar (*Quaest. Hom.* 13.4-5).[9]

The seeming inconsistency (Apollo's shooting from afar instead of near) indicates to the Stoic commentator that Homer's *original intent* was to speak about the sun and the deathly plagues. Once this initial identification is made, the rest of the story (*Il.* 1.50-58) is allegorized by the same Stoic principle (*Quaest. Hom.* 14–16). The description of the 'white-armed Hera' (*Il.* 1.55), in like manner, according to our commentator, is not superfluous but is in fact intended as a reference to the purifying *white light of air* (*Quaest. Hom.* 15.6),[10] and the sacrifice of Odysseus in *Il.* 1.472-76 is read as a sacrifice to the sun-god, for the Achaeans reveled until 'the setting of the sun' (*Quaest. Hom.* 16.1-2). Lying behind allegorical interpretation is the concern to equate the textual narrative (i.e. the Achaeans' misfortunes) to an order or reality outside the immediate scope of the text (i.e. Stoic cosmology). The initial point of contact is the identification of Apollo as 'sun'.

9.   Translation found in Tobin, *Creation*, pp. 98-99.

10.   In good Stoic fashion, the interpretations are not restricted to physical explanations; moral and psychological explanations of the Homeric texts are also found in *Quaest. Hom.* 17-20. See Heraclitus, *Allégories d'Homère*, pp. xxi-xxix, for a list of various allegorical interpretations represented in the commentary by Buffière.

Philo was no innovator of the allegorical method of exegesis. This is clear even from a cursory glance of the authors cited by Ps.-Heraclitus: many of the physical and ethical allegorical interpretations of the Homeric texts found in Ps.-Heraclitus are also reflected in Philo's commentaries of the Bible.[11] But more influential to Philo were the generations of Greek-speaking Jewish scholars before him. From them, Philo inherited both their allegorical method and their allegorical results.[12] Philo, in other words, did not work in a vacuum but worked within a long exegetical tradition.[13]

But Philo was no eclecticist aimlessly adopting the exegeses of his forbears either. All the things that he learned and collected were channeled into an overriding motif for his writings (most of which were commentaries): *the allegory of the soul*. The works of P. Boyancé, J. Daniélou, and, most recently, the cogent arguments of Thomas Tobin have demonstrated, persuasively I think, that what distinguishes Philo from his predecessors is his consistent effort of reading external events—the creation story, the fall, and the patriarchs in Genesis—as internal struggles of our soul on its tortuous journey to perfection.[14] See, for example, Philo's treatment of Gen. 2.8-9, which reads,

> God planted a garden in Eden facing the sunrising and placed there the man whom he had fashioned (ὅν ἔπλασεν). And out of the ground God made every tree that is pleasant in sight and good for food and the tree of life and the tree of knowing good and evil.

In *De opificio mundi*, Philo first dismisses the notion that Paradise refers to a physical garden, for no one has yet witnessed such things as the trees of life and knowing good and evil. This idea is so absurd and empirically false, according to Philo, that it must be an invitation to read

---

11. See p. 126 n. 8 above and Tobin, *Creation*, pp. 99-100.

12. The traditional character of Philo's exegesis is especially championed by B.L. Mack; see e.g. 'Exegetical Tradition in Alexandrian Judaism: A Program for the Analysis of the Philonic Corpus', *Studia Philonica* 3 (1974–75), pp. 71-112.

13. W. Boussett, *Judisch-Christlicher Schulbetrieb in Alexandria und Roin* (Göttingen: Vandenhoeck & Ruprecht, 1915), has gone so far as to suggest that Philo belonged to an 'Alexandrian exegetical school'. A somewhat modified view is presented by Nikiprowetzky, *Commenataire*, p. 179.

14. P. Boyancé, 'Etudes philoniennes', *Revue des études Grecques* 76 (1963), p. 68; J. Daniélou, *Philon d'Alexandrie* (Paris: Artème Fayard, 1958), pp. 135, 137; Tobin, *Creation*, pp. 45-54.

the biblical passage allegorically. This Philo does by identifying Paradise as 'mind' and the trees as 'virtues' planted as 'standards in the soul':

> While the man was still leading a solitary life and the woman was not yet made, it is said that Paradise was planted by God like nothing familiar to us (Gen. 2.8-9). For the wood is soulless in these [earthly gardens], which are full of all sorts of trees: some ever-blooming to give unremitting visual delight while others blooming with young shoots every spring; some bearing fruit for human beings—not only for necessary nourishment but also for luxurious enjoyment of life—while others bear a different fruit that is necessarily given to beasts. As for the divine Paradise, on the other hand, all plants are ensouled and rational that bear as fruit virtues and, beside it, steady insight and discernment—in which beauty and ugliness are known—and disease-free life, incorruption, and everything like it.
>
> This description, it seems to me, is to be interpreted symbolically rather than literally, for never before on earth have trees of life or knowledge appeared, nor is it likely that they will in the future. But probably by Paradise it symbolizes *the governing power of the soul*, which is full of so many opinions as of plants. By the tree of life [it symbolizes] the greatest of the virtues, *reverance toward God*, through which the soul becomes immortal. And by the tree of knowing good and evil [it symbolizes] *prudence which is middle*, by which matters that are by nature opposite can be distinguished.
>
> After he set up these boundaries in the *soul*, He watched as a judge to which [of the two] it would incline. When He saw it inclining towards wickedness, and despising piety and holiness—from which immortal life is retained—He naturally cast it out and drove it from Paradise, thus dashing any hope for the soul that had committed the incurable and irremediable [sins] of a subsequent return [to Paradise], even though the cause of the error was highly blameworthy, which it is not proper to pass over in silence (*Op. mund.* 153-55).[15]

These identifications prepare Philo for the interpretation of the planting of the Paradise as the placement of virtues in the human mind, which in turn allows him to read the story of the fall allegorically (or psychologically if you will). By this schema, Adam is 'mind', Eve is 'sense-perception', and the serpent is 'pleasure' that tempts sense-perception into giving up the pursuit of virtue (*Op. mund.* 156-70). This elaborate allegory of the soul begins by identifying Paradise as mind and closes by subsuming all external events of the fall under the internal struggles of the soul.

15. My translation.

Another example of this procedure can be found in Philo's interpretation of Gen. 12.6: '[Leaving Haran] Abram passed through the land to the place at Shechem, to the oak of Moreh'. In *Migr. Abr.* 216-20, Philo first identifies Abraham as (what else?) our mind that is capable of being freed, and in fact must be freed, from the confines of our body. Thus prompted, Philo is able to represent Abraham's travel to Canaan as the inner striving of the soul for learning.

> The mind, when it has gone forth from the places about Haran, is said to have travelled through the country as far as the place of Shechem, to the lofty oak-tree [Gen. 12.6]. Let us consider what is meant by 'travel through'.

> Love of learning is by nature curious and inquisitive, not hesitating to bend its steps in all directions, prying into everything, reluctant to leave anything that exists unexplored, whether material or immaterial. It has an extraordinary appetite for all that there is to be seen and heard, and, not content with what it finds in its own country, it is bent on seeking what is in foreign parts and separated by great distances. We are reminded that merchants and traders for the sake of trifling profits cross the seas, and compass the wide world, letting stand in their way no summer heat nor winter cold, no tempestuous nor contrary winds, neither youth nor age, no sickness of body, neither the daily intercourse with friends nor the pleasure too great for words which we take in wife and children and in all else that is our own, nor the enjoyment of our fatherland and of all the gracious amenities of civic life, nor the safe use of money and property and abundance of other good things, nor in a word anything else either great or small. If so, it is monstrous, such speakers urge, when we stand to gain a thing most fair, worth all men's striving for, the special prerogative of the human race, namely wisdom, to refrain from crossing every sea, from exploring earth's every recess, in the joy of finding out whether there is in any place aught that is fair to see or hear, and from following the quest of it with utmost zest and keenness, until we can come to the enjoyment of the things that we are seeking and longing for.

> Travel through man also, if you will, O my soul, bringing to examination each component part of him. For instance, to take the first examples that occur, find out what the body is and what it must do or undergo to cooperate with the understanding; what sense-perception is and in what way it is of service to its ruler, mind; what pleasure is, and what desire is; what pain and fear are, and what the healing art is that can counteract them, by means of which a man shall either, if he falls into their hand, without difficulty make his escape, or avoid capture altogether; what it is to play the fool, what to be licentious, what to be unjust, what the multitude of other sicknesses to which it is the nature of pestilential wickedness to give

birth, and what the preventative of these; and on the other hand, what righteousness is, or good sense, or self-mastery, courage, discretion, in a word virtue generally and moral welfare, and in what way each of them is wont to be won.

Travel again through the greatest and most perfect man, the universe, and scan narrowly its parts, how far asunder they are in the positions which they occupy, how wholly made one by the powers which govern them, and what constitutes for them all this invisible bond of harmony and unity. If, however, in your investigation, you do not easily attain the objects of your quest, keep on without giving in, for these 'need both hands to catch them', and only by manifold and painful toil can they be discovered (LCL translation).

This interpretation follows a well-planned rhetorical form. First, the text is mentioned (Gen. 12.6). Second, a *lemma* is singled out for interpretation ('Let us consider what is meant by "travel through"'). Third, the phrase 'passing through' is related to 'love of learning' (τὸ ἱλομαθές). 'Love of learning' is an appropriate analogy, because it is 'by nature curious and inquisitive, not hesitating to...pry into everything'. Once this identification is established, Philo is able to discuss the *soul's* 'learning' and its pursuit of wisdom. A supplement is added to show the importance of the search of wisdom: if merchants, seekers of earthly goods, risk danger 'traveling through' different lands to reach their destination, the pursuer of wisdom surely ought to be that much more diligent 'exploring earth's every recess, until we can come to the enjoyment of the things that we are seeking and longing for' (217-18). Fourth, Philo exhorts the soul to 'travel through' a human body, so as to examine its every part (219). Fifth, Philo exhorts the soul further to search through the mystery of the cosmos, for the cosmos is the 'greatest and most perfect man'. The same five-step procedure is repeated in §§221-22, this time focusing on a different *lemma*, 'Shechem'. Examples of this sort can be multiplied throughout the Philonic corpus.

Lest we think such allegories are found only in non-Christian writings, no less august a writer than Paul practices the same art. In the course of addressing the question of the Lord's Supper and in particular the question whether it is legitimate for a believer to participate in pagan worship, Paul offers in 1 Cor. 10.1-5 a piece of allegorical exegesis on the Israelites' experience in the wilderness (Exodus 32). The exegesis centers on the comparison between the Corinthians and the Israelites, the latter being 'types' (τύποι) of the former:

> I want you to know, brothers and sisters, that our fathers were all under
> the cloud, and all passed through the sea, and all were baptized into
> Moses in the cloud and in the seas, and all ate the same supernatural food
> and all drank the same supernatural drink. For they drank from the super-
> natural *Rock* which followed them, and the *Rock was Christ*.
> Nevertheless with most of them God was not pleased; for they were
> overthrown in the wilderness. Now these things are warnings for us, not
> to desire evil as they did. Do not be idolaters as some of them were; as it
> is written, 'The people sat down to eat and drink and rose up to dance'
> [Exod. 32.6]. We must not indulge in immorality as some of them did,
> and twenty-three thousand fell in a single day. We must not put the Lord
> to the test, as some of them did and were destroyed by serpents; nor
> grumble, as some the them did and were destroyed by the Destroyer.
> Now these things happened to them as a warning, but they were written
> down for our instruction, upon whom the end of the ages has come.
> Therefore let any one who thinks that he stands take heed lest he fall. No
> temptation has overtaken you that is not common to man. God is faithful,
> and he will not let you be tempted beyond your strength, but with the
> temptation will also provide the way of escape, that you may be able to
> endure it (1 Cor. 10.1-13, RSV).

To understand what Paul is doing here, one must begin not with the
original Exodus text but with what Paul intends to do with the text. We
have to work backward in order to understand what provides the
middle term (*tertium comparationis*) between his results and the texts.

What Paul wants to achieve at the end is the citation of Exod. 32.6 in
v. 7b, where 'eating', 'drinking' and 'idol worship' ($\pi\alpha\acute{\iota}\zeta\epsilon\iota\nu$) are
explicitly linked up. Paul's proof, first of all, is a terminological one. The
Israelites 'ate and drank' just as the believers have eaten and drunk the
food and wine of the Lord's Supper. But the participation of the
Israelites in the meal provided by God did not protect them from his
wrath when 2300 of them fell as a result of idolatry (v. 8). But to
accomplish that, Paul must overcome a major problem: the original text
of Exod. 32.6 is not about a sacramental meal; the eating and drinking
of the Israelites are at best tangentially connected to the sacrifice. Paul
realizes this and he tries to head it off by adding references that are
meant to prove that the Israelites' eating and drinking are in fact
sacramental as the Lord's Supper. This Paul does in vv. 1-3.

1 Cor. 10.1-3 has some peculiar language. 'Cloud' and 'sea' are obvious references to Exod. 14.20, 22 (cf. 13.21), but Paul thinks of them as
'baptism': not just any baptism but 'baptism into Moses' (v. 2), a phrase
that is unparalleled in Jewish literature. Paul then identifies the food

consumed by the Israelites as 'the same spiritual food' (τὸ αὐτὸ[16] πνευματικὸν βρῶμα, vv. 3-4). Paul here is clearly reading Christian terms back into the Exodus account. The peculiar phrase 'baptism into Moses' can make sense only when compared to the Christian 'baptism into Christ'. Only then are 'cloud' and 'water' understood in terms of the Christian baptism.

But since the proof here is a terminological one, Paul wants to be more precise. He introduces the drinking and eating of the Israelites, an act he calls πνευματικόν. It is unclear whether Paul means by it 'spiritual', 'supernatural' or even 'allegorical' (since the word was used as a technical term for allegorical interpretation in some quarters). But the overall comparison is clear enough: the Israelites ate and drank, as a result of being baptized into Moses; the Corinthians, too, ate and drank, having been baptized into Christ. But if, in spite of the participation in the meal, the Israelites fell because of immorality, how much more so would the Corinthians? Implicit here is a comparison between two historical events, which Paul sees as parallel. It is within this parallelism that Paul wishes to provide the punch-line for his case: 'Do not be idolaters as some of them were; as it is written, "The people sat down to eat and drink and rose up to dance". We must not indulge in immorality as some of them did, and twenty-three thousand fell in a single day' (10.7-8).

What enables Paul to make the comparison, the fixed point around which the Israelites and the Corinthians revolve, is the identification of Christ with the 'spiritual rock that followed' the Israelites. The 'rock' is well-known in Jewish wisdom speculation. In Philo, *Leg. All.* 2.96, the 'rock' is the Wisdom of God (cf. also 3.162) and in *Det. Pot. Ins.* 118, the 'rock' is the Word of God. It was supposed that the same rock followed the Israelite wandering in the desert. Paul in 1 Corinthians historicizes the Wisdom of God and localizes it in Christ. It is this identification of the rock with Christ that enables Paul to use 'spiritual' (πνευματικόν) in this passage, a term now applied to the 'rock' and 'drink' of v. 4. Whether Paul here has in view of Christ's actual, pre-existent presence as Wisdom in the wilderness need not deter us. For our purpose it is enough to note that this piece of typological allegory[17]

---

16. αὐτό is omitted in 𝔓[46] and A. But it is difficult to see why it would be added if it were not original, since its presence has added obscurity rather than clarity to the text.

17. I will not discuss the supposed distinction between typology (historical comparison) and allegory (ahistorical comparison), a distinction favored by those

begins with the procedure of identifying the rock as Christ and, then and only then, the inevitable restructuring and reinterpreting of the Exodus account in this new light as a consequence. Christ is the *tertium comparationis*.[18]

All three authors, Ps.-Heraclitus, Philo and Paul, therefore, allegorized, albeit in varying degrees of complexity and arriving at different results. Ps.-Heraclitus was concerned with reconciling the Homeric text to Stoic cosmology, Philo was concerned with drawing out the allegory of the soul from the biblical account, and Paul was concerned with seeing Christ as the fulfilment of Israelites' wilderness experience. Their methods, however, were not arbitrary but followed well-established procedures of allegorical interpretation: all three began with a symbolic identification used as a key to unlock the rest of the text. The identification was most likely traditional and required a minimal amount of justification. None of the interpreters approached the text in isolation; all three appropriated it as part of their own exegetical traditions.

The Odes and the Confucian Commentatorial Tradition

The *Odes*, part of an earlier Chinese canon,[19] are a collection of songs, court poems, love sonnets and epithalamia dating to the first half of the first millennium BCE. The *Odes* were widely studied and commented upon, much as the Homeric poems and the Pentateuch, though in genre and form they are closer to the Song of Songs. Confucius and his

---

who would like to safeguard Paul's attention to historical veracity. Suffice it to say that I see typological interpretation as a subspecies of allegorical interpretation. According to the former, a certain view of history (usually eschatological) instead of a metaphysical formulation (e.g. Philo's allegory of the soul) is used to determine the middle term of comparison. See further p. 145 n. 38 below.

18. Other examples can be adduced: cf. Gal. 3.1–4.11, in which Paul's midrashic argument pivots around the first identification that Christ is the 'seed' (3.16: σπέρμα, singular) that was promised to Abraham in Gen. 12.7; 13.15; 17.7; 24.7, etc.).

19. That is the *Five Classics*, the standard canon from the Han Dynasty (third century BCE to third century CE) onward. They were replaced by the *Four Books* in the Southern Sung, at the initiative of Chu Hsi (1130–1200). The *Four Books*, which consist of less lengthy, more metaphysical writings and excerpts, were compiled for the purpose of bringing out the 'true meaning' of the *Five Classics*. The process of canonization, in China as in the Christian West, was inextricably bound up with the question of hermeneutics.

followers all discussed and commented on the *Odes*;[20] it is their interpretation, in fact, that placed the stamp of orthodoxy on the *Odes* and it
is their interpretation that would decisively mold the character of pre-
modern Chinese hermeneutics.[21]

One of the earliest hermeneutical positions on the *Odes* is summed up
in the pithy phrase, 'The *Odes* articulate aim' (*shih yen chih*), which
gradually became a commonplace by the first century CE. The phrase
has a complex history and, as all such aphorism, has acquired a great
deal of traditional baggage. Steven van Zoeren has recently proposed to
read two dialogues in the *Analects* as reflecting the growing prominence
towards the late Chou of the 'moral adept' whose importance lies in his
standing behind the *Odes* and defining their 'aim'. The first is found in
Anal. 5.26, in which Confucius the 'moral adept' oversees the disciples'
attempts to articulate their aims:

> Yen Yüan and Chi-lu [disciples of Confucius] were in attendance. The
> Master said, 'I suggest you each tell me what your aim (*chih*) is'.
>
> Tzu-lu said, 'I should like to share my carriage and horses, clothes and
> furs with my friends, and to have no regrets even if they become worn'.
>
> Yen Yüan said, 'I should like never to boast my own goodness and never
> to impose onerous tasks upon others'.
>
> Tzu-lu says, 'I should like to hear what your aim (*chih*) is'.
>
> The Master said, 'To bring peace to the old, to have trust in my friends,
> and to cherish the young'.

The second citation in *Anal.* 11.26 is much longer but nevertheless
shows essentially the same concern with defining and articulating the
'aim':

20. Confucius and his disciples were of course not commenting on the *Odes* as
canon, since the *Five Classics* were not fixed until some three or four centuries later.
One can argue, in fact, that it was largely due to the moralizing interpretation of
Confucian interpreters that the *Odes* could have survived and become canonized. In
this respect, their acceptance into the Chinese canon parallels the similar process of
acceptance of the Song of Songs in rabbinic circles.

21. Such is the intriguing thesis of S. van Zoeren, *Poetry and Personality:
Reading, Exegesis, and Hermeneutics in Traditional China* (Stanford: Stanford
University Press, 1991). The topic of this paper owes much of its inspiration and, as
it will become clear, a good deal of its reference to literature in the *Odes*, to P. Yu,
'Allegory, Allegoresis, and the *Classic of Poetry*', *Harvard Journal of Asiatic
Studies* 43 (1983), pp. 377-412.

When Tzu-lu, Tseng Hsi, Jan Yu and Kung-hsi Hua [all disciples of Confucius] were seated in attendance, the Master said, 'Do you feel constrained simply because I am a little older than you are. Now you are in the habit of saying, "My abilities are not appreciated". But if someone did appreciate your abilities, do tell me how you would go about things.'

Tzu-lu promptly answered, 'If I were to administer a state of a thousand chariots, situated between powerful neighbors, troubled by armed invasions and by repeated famines, I could, within three years, give the people courage and a sense of direction.'

The Master smiled at him. 'Ch'iu, what about you?'

'If I were to administer an area measuring sixty or seventy *li* square, or even fifty or sixty *li* square, I could, within three years, bring the size of the population up to an adequate level. As to the rites and music, I would leave that to abler gentlemen'.

'Ch'ih, what about you?'

'I do not say that I already have the ability, but I am ready to learn. On ceremonial occasions in the ancestral temple or in diplomatic gatherings, I should like to assist as a minor official in charge of protocol, properly dressed in my ceremonial cap and robes.'

'Tien, what about you?'

'What harm is there in that? After all each man is stating what he has set his heart upon.'

After a few dying notes came the final chord, and then he stood up from his lute. 'I differ from the other three in my choice.'

'In late spring, after the spring clothes have been newly made, I should like, together with five or six adults and six or seven boys, to go bathing in the River Yi and enjoy the breeze on the Rain Altar, and then to go home chanting poetry.'

The Master sighed and said, 'I am all in favor of Tien'.[22]

Without forcing too fine (not to mention speculative) a reading of these two dialogues, suffice it to say, for my purpose, that the phrase, 'the *Odes* articulate aim', implies a need for proper interpretation of the *Odes* even at this early time of its formulation and compilation. In other words, the *Odes* could not be accorded their proper authority unless the orthodox interpretations espoused by Confucius and his immediate

22. Van Zoeren, *Poetry and Personality*, p. 11 and *passim*.

followers was first adopted.[23] This emerging orthodoxy is found summarized in two *logia*, which in turn record two variations of the same theme: one has to do with proper, orthodox thought and the other has to do with the application of the *Odes* to the arena of governance. *Anal.* 2.2 defines how the *Odes* are supposed to have a proper effect on one's thought:

> The Master said, 'There are three hundred *odes*. One saying covers them all, "Thought without deviation"'.[24]

Anal. 13.5 deals with the proper application of the *Odes* to Government:

> The Master said, 'What good is knowing three hundred *odes* by heart but failing when given the government at home and being incompetent while sojourning as ambassador abroad?'

There was therefore a growing orthodoxy, both epistemologically and morally or politically,[25] imposed on the *Odes before* they were canonized. This is perhaps the only way by which the *Odes*, which contain some highly romantic materials, materials not otherwise assimilated easily into the strait-laced morality of the Confucianism of the Pre-Ch'in or any other period, could be integrated into the Confucian canon.

This process of moralization and politicization can be illustrated by one of the most famous, certainly the most discussed, odes, *kuan chü*, which also opens the collection. The title of this poem is drawn from the first line, a way of entitling a work not unlike that of the Psalms in the *Tanakh*. The ode was probably originally an epithalamium set against an agricultural background. It describes a young man's longing for his love while she goes about her business of harvesting water plants. I here quote the ode in full:

---

23. In this regard, the treatment of the *Odes* is quite similar to the treatment which the Song of Songs received at the hands of the rabbinic and patristic interpreters. Both the Song of Songs and the *Odes* contain such highly romantic and erotic compositions that they can be used by 'puritanical' traditions within rabbinic Judaism, Christianity and Han Confucianism only if they are accompanied by proper introduction and interpretation.

24. My translation. James Legge has 'Having no depraved thoughts'; and Lau, 'Swerving not from the right path'.

25. The Chinese, especially during this period, do not sharply distinguish the moral and the political; both are covered under the same term *ch'eng*.

Kuan kuan[26] cry the ospreys
On the islet of the river.
Lithe and lovely that beautiful, young lady,
A good match for the lord.

Here and there the water plants;
Left and right she passes among them.
Lithe and lovely that beautiful, young lady,
Waking and sleeping he wishes for her,
wishing but not getting.
Waking and sleeping he thinks of her,
longing, longing,
tossing and turning.

Here and there the water plants;
Left and right she harvests them.
Lithe and lovely that beautiful, young lady,
Zithers and lutes befriend her.
Here and there the water plants;
Left and right she culls them.
Lithe and lovely that beautiful, young lady,
Bells and drums delight her.[27]

The earliest comment on this ode by Confucius appears to be not so
much an exegetical discussion as a commendation of its musical quali-
ties.[28] In *Anal.* 3.20, Confucius is given to say, 'As regards the *kuan chü*
there is joy without licentiousness, sadness without sorrows'. This saying
is at first peculiar for its emphasis not on moral teaching (as one would
expect) but on the assumed power of the ode to evoke emotions and to
solicit a deep resonance in the human psyche. But the peculiarity disap-
pears when the ode is understood in the light of musical performance.
Such a practice is explicitly mentioned in *Anal.* 8.15: 'The Master said,
"When Chih the Master Musician begins to play and when the *Kuan
chü* comes to an end, how the sound fills the ear!"'[29]

In spite of the relatively scant discussions of exegesis in the *Analects*,
there are two passages tying the reading of the *Odes* to an exegetical

26. '*Kuan kuan*' is possibly the mating call of ospreys.
27. My translation.
28. As pointed out recently by van Zoeren, *Poetry and Personality*, pp. 27-31.
29. The difference between seeing the *Odes* as moral teaching and seeing them as
performance is most plausibly explained by the different oral traditions collected in
the *Analects*, a problem not unlike the Synoptic problem associated with Gospel
studies.

technique called *hsing*—literally 'to rise or raise', 'to stimulate', or 'to take its start from (something)'—a technique that would have a profound influence in Chinese hermeneutical theories. In a short and cryptic saying, even by the standard of Chinese classics, Confucius says, 'Start (*hsing*) with the *Odes*; stand on rites; complete with Music' (*Anal.* 8.8). This is obviously a formulaic saying intended to summarize the hermeneutical stance *vis-à-vis* the *Odes*. In the other passage, Confucius exhorts the young people to study the *Odes* (in a manner reminiscent of Plutarch's appeal to young aristocrats to study Homer): 'Why not study the *Odes*? With the *Odes* one can be stimulated (*hsing*),[30] investigate, learn sociability, control one's emotions, serve the father at home and serve the lord abroad...' (*Anal.* 17.9).[31] Neither passage defines precisely what *hsing* is, though both disclose a pattern of emotional, educative or political development in one's upbringing[32] that begins with the study of the *Odes*.[33]

There would be no point entering into a discussion of the long and complex history of *hsing* in traditional and modern Chinese literary theories;[34] for the purpose at hand, it is enough to examine the use of

30. Or 'The *Odes* can stimulate'. Classical Chinese does not distinguish between the active and the passive.

31. This translation is tentative. Cf. Lau's paraphrastic (and less precise) translation: 'Why is it none of you, my young friends, study the *Odes*? An apt quotation from the *Odes* may serve to stimulate (*hsing*) the imagination, to show one's breeding, to smooth over difficulties in a group and to give expression to complaints. Inside the family there is the serving of one's father; outside, there is the serving of one's lord' (*The Analects* [New York: Penguin Books, 1979], p. 145). Lau acknowledges the difficulty by pointing to possible text corruption (p. 145 n. 4).

32. The 'educational', 'behavioral' and 'political' are not three distinct spheres but continuous stages of development in the Han conception of cultivation.

33. Such is the case as regards not only the *Odes* but also such a historical writing as *Spring and Autumn Annuals*. Cf. J. J. Y. Liu, *Chinese Theories of Literature* (Chicago: University of Chicago Press, 1975); and D. Holzman, 'Confucius and Ancient Chinese Literary Criticism', in A. Rickett (ed.), *Chinese Approaches to Literature from Confucius to Liang Ch'i ch'ao* (Princeton: Princeton University Press, 1978), pp. 21-41.

34. See the classic survey by Hu Nien-yi, '*Shih Ching chung de fu pi hsing*', *Wenhsueh Yich'an Ch'engk'an* 1 (1957), pp. 1-21. Cf. also Yu, 'Allegory, Allegoresis,' pp. 392-95; Van Zoeren, *Poetry and Personality*, pp. 89, 268 n. 24, who sees *hsing* as applied only to a textual lemma, whereas *pi* ('analogy') is applied to the whole ode. Contemporary scholarship on *hsing* is summarized in C.H. Wang, *The Bell and the Drum: Shih Ching as Formulaic Poetry in an Oral Tradition*

hsing in the immediate generations after Confucius. The term is connected to the movement from poetry to personal emotion to government in one the earliest glosses on *kuan chü*. Following a citation of the first line of *kuan chü*, the glossator comments,

> This is called *hsing*; '*kuan kuan*' is a harmonious sound. The 'osprey' is a kingly bird. It is a bird of prey, and keeps apart [from its mate]. An 'islet' is a place in the water where one can stand. The Consort was delighted by her lord's virtue; there was nothing in which they were inharmonious. Moreover, *she did not debauch him with her beauty*. She resolutely kept herself hidden away [in the women's quarters], just as the osprey keeps apart [from its mate]. This being the case, it was possible to transform the empire. [For] when husbands and wives keep a proper distance, then fathers and sons will be close. When fathers and sons are close, then lord and minister will be punctilious. When lord and minister are punctilious, then the court will be rectified. When the court is rectified, then the kingly transformations will be accomplished.[35]

The glossator begins by classifying the ode as *hsing*, thus determining the manner in which he intends to interpret the romantic lines of the ode. He then applies the technique to the first line of the ode, '*Kuan kuan* cry the ospreys', and reads '*kuan kuan*' onomatopoetically as 'harmonious sound' and 'osprey' as 'a *kingly* bird'. The kingly osprey lives apart from its mate, thus immediately setting his ensuing comments within the context of a courtly—but *chaste*—relationship. The second line, 'On the islet of the river', strengthens his argument, for an islet stands isolated in the middle of the river. In other words, once the opening, naturalistic scenes are identified as referring to the pure and virtuous relationship between the kingly bird and its mate, the glossator feels justified to take off from this starting point and discuss in earnest the proper expression of relationship between husband and wife, the proper expression of relationship between father and son, and the proper expression of behavior between king and subject. The glossator goes further: he identifies the ospreys as King Wen and his Consort, the legendary King and Queen of the Chou Dynasty, during which rituals were correct, all relationships were proper, and the country was peaceful. The entire exegetical development hinges on the opening identification of the osprey as a 'kingly bird' that maintains proper decorum with its mate. That done, it is only a matter of working out the precise

(Berkeley: University of California Press, 1974), pp. 6-22.

35. Adapted from Van Zoeren, *Poetry and Personality*, p. 87.

elements to turn a love song into a moral exhortation for chastity (between husband and wife!), ritual correctness and benevolent governance.

A preface to the *Odes* took shape some time later and continued the same exegetical tradition of moral and historical interpretation:

1.   As for the *kuan chü*, the virtue of the Consort.
2.   It is the first of the *Airs* (or It is the beginning of the suasion), and it is that whereby the world is transformed and husband and wife put right. So it was performed at the village meetings and at the gatherings of the feudal lords.
3.   'Air' (*feng*) means 'suasion' (*feng*); it means 'teaching'. Suasion is exerted in order to move [one's prince?], and teaching aims at transforming [the people].
4.   The *Ode* is where the aim goes. While in the heart, it is the aim; manifested in words, it is an Ode.
5.   Emotion moves within and takes shape in words. Words are not enough, and so one sighs it. Sighing it is not enough, and so one draws it out in song. Drawing it out in song is not enough, and so all unawares one's hands dance it and one's feet tap it out.
6.   Emotion is manifested in the voice. When voice is patterned, we call it tone.
7.   The tones of a well-governed age are peaceful and happy; its government is harmonious. The tones of a chaotic age are resentful and angry; its government is perverse. The tones of a lost state are sorrowful and longing; its people are suffering.
8.   So for putting right the relations of gain and loss, moving Heaven and Earth, and affecting the manes and spirits, nothing comes close to the *Odes*.
9.   The early kings therefore used them to regulate the relations between husbands and wives, to perfect filiality and respect, to enrich human relations, to beautify the tutelary transformation [of people], and to change mores and customs.

The exegetical details are different, but the tack is the same. The technique *hsing* gives rise to the same development from the emotional to the personal and ultimately to the political.

Allegorical Interpretation West and East

To what extent, then, can we call *hsing* an allegorical technique? Insofar as one thinks of allegorical interpretation as relating the text to a well-organized, *transcendent* system in the manner of Philo's allegory of the soul or the Stoicism of Ps.-Heraclitus, *hsing* is obviously not allegorical. A transcendent world-view would not even be a 'rejected possibility'[36] for the interpreters of the *Odes*. But insofar as one could conceive of the use of an allegorical method in a non-dualistic world view and insofar as we concentrate on the method as technique, the *hsing* of the *Odes*-interpreters is clearly allegorical. By means of *hsing*, the text is broken open with a single identification and on the basis of the identification other elements of the text are made to relate to an order or realm outside the text. In the interpretation of *kuan chü*, the opening scene of the osprey and the islet is first identified as a virtuous queen who for the sake of not appearing licentious is determined to live apart from her husband. Once this identification is made, the rest of the narrative is allegorized, element by element, to the virtuous conducts of the King Wen and his consort and to the proper relationships between father and son, between superior and subjects, and so on. As Pauline Yu concludes,

> The predominant mode of defining and explicating the *hsing* suggests that most traditional commentators on the *Odes* saw some relationship of similarity or analogy linking it with the main topic of the poem. The image then provides a means of placing the situation at hand within a larger, more general context—of linking it with other members of the category to which it belongs, be it proper (or improper) male–female behavior, as in the *Guan ju* [=*kuan chü*] and numerous other marriage and courtship songs, or filial relationships...[37]

In spite of the structural similarity between the techniques of the Confucian commentators and the authors of Late Antiquity, however, two major differences between *hsing* and western allegory stand out. First, before the Confucian interpreters launch an elaborate identification

---

36. I owe this felicitous phrase to Professor Benjamin Schwartz.

37. Yu, 'Allegory, Allegoresis', p. 398. Yu's observation is sound, but her narrow definition of allegorical interpretation (or 'allegoresis' as she calls it) does not allow her to appreciate the allegorical impetus behind this form of interpretation. This understanding of *hsing* is closer to the pseudo-Kung An-kuo's definition as 'Drawing out a comparison on the basis of categorical analogy'; cited in Yu, 'Allegory, Allegoresis', p. 392 n.34.

of the text, they first make an internal comparison between the natural imageries (i.e. the osprey in the islet) and the narrative proper (i.e. the lord's longing for the young lady). They are made to correspond to each other because of the implied separation in both cases (the islet as a symbol of isolation; the lord's longing implies separation). It is only after this internal comparison has been made do the interpreters move to identify osprey as king and the king as King Wen of the Chou Dynasty. Such a comparison is in fact part and parcel of the kind of correlative thinking that is characteristic of the Han Dynasty, according to which every thing and every event is connected to each other; nothing, not even poetic imagery, takes place in isolation. There is therefore an *internal* ethos of correspondence first before that correspondence is extended to include *external* events, even if the events might belong to the distant past. Secondly, the end result of the Confucian technique of *hsing* clearly does not deal with the journey of a soul through the cosmos but with concrete, historical events and personages. Its main concern is with contextualizing the poem, populating it with well-known sages from previous, admired generations, and finally localizing the poetic images in history.[38] This is perhaps to be expected: it may be the only way in which a non-dualistic cosmology could engender allegorical interpretation. If interpretation is the process of vesting the text with

38. By focusing my discussion on the allegorical techniques of Philo and Ps.-Heraclitus on the one hand and on the other the *hsing* of the *Odes* interpreters, I am not claiming these are the only, or even the best, representatives of their respective exegetical traditions. Philo's allegory of the soul was but one among many in the first century. The *pesher* method of the Qumran community and their close ally, the fulfilment exegesis of the Gospel of Matthew and the *Epistle of Barnabas* would provide significant variations to the Philonic method. Though the distinction between typology and allegory is, in my view, largely an artificial one (see e.g. R.P.C. Hanson, *Allegory and Event: A Study of the Sources and Significance of Origen's Interpretation of Scripture* [Richmond: John Knox, 1959] and p. 135 n. 18 above), they nevertheless represent two different approaches within the general phenomenon of allegorical interpretation. On the Chinese side, already in as early a writing as the *Preface to the Odes*, *hsing* is mentioned alongside two other types of handling the *Odes*: they are *fu* ('description, recitation') and *pi* ('comparison, analogy'). Boundaries among these three types of interpretation shift and different interpreters take them to mean different things, but it remains true that *hsing* is but one technique among others. The comparison between *hsing* and allegory is still important, however, not only because they are obviously similar in structure but also because they both call upon cultural resources for their generation.

authority, for the Chinese interpreters it is *history*, not revelation, that is the locus of authority.

On a more general level, the comparison between the interpretation of the LXX by Jewish interpreters like Paul and Philo and the interpretation of the *Odes* by Confucian scholars has its obvious limitations. Not the least is that the *Odes*, primarily a collection of love poems, are closer in genre to the Song of Songs than to Genesis. But the choice of Genesis for this comparative study is deliberate; it was chosen to highlight not only the similar allegorical techniques used in these vastly different and clearly independent traditions but also the different characters of these two types of canonical texts. It is well-known that the present Chinese canon, drawn up mainly by the courtly Confucian guild, lacks the kind of creation myth that is readily found in Mesopotamian and Greek literature. This lack, of course, reflects a Confucian prejudice against the mythological, since fragments of creation myths are found in other, competing traditions, the Taoist, for example. Thus purged, the Confucian canon exerts an enormous influence on generations of scholars and thinkers, at least in their public life.[39] It cultivates an underlying metaphysical conception of the world drastically different from that of the west.[40] Without having to deal with creation myths, the Confucian world view is then able to posit a continuum between heaven and earth and between the past and the present. Unlike the West, it does not conceive of an absolute disjuncture between the divine and the human. This is especially true in the so-called 'correlative cosmology' formulated during the Han Dynasty.

Given this world-view, then, there is little wonder that the glossator of the *Odes* and the writer of the *Preface* are legitimized—philosophically and metaphysically equipped—to tie an epithalamic ode to actual historical figures who are moral exemplars of the virtue of propriety. In so doing, they arrive at exactly the opposite sentiment from that which evoke the primary imageries of the ode. Instead of a song celebrating the young man's intense desire for his love, we now have an orthodox version, bowdlerized, extolling the values of maintaining a distance

---

39. Their private leanings towards and yearnings for mystical Taoism, however, are a different story.

40. This approximation, which suffices for a comparison between the Jewish and Christian West and *Confucian* China, remains just that, an *approximation*. It therefore can and perhaps must be refined and supplemented by the numerous views and mythologies, notably those of the Taoists, excluded by the Confucian canon.

between husband and wife. Such propriety calls for other forms of propriety, thus resulting in the successful administration of the kingdom. There is a continuum that begins with the proper control of emotion and ends with the correct governance of the kingdom.

The type of allegorical interpretation practiced by Early Jewish and Christian authors, on the other hand, is thoroughly otherworldly. The underlying metaphysical structure is a Middle-Platonic one,[41] in which the intelligible (νοητός) world is sharply distinguished from the sense-perceptible (αἴσθητος) one, or an eschatological-messianic one, which is nourished by a special, linear view of history rushing toward a catastrophic climax. According to these schemata, the soul, for whom the proper place is the intelligible realm, can strive for virtue and acquire perfection only when it is freed from the encumbering body (so Philo and his fellow-Platonists); or the believer must wait for the final revelation of Christ, at the *parousia*, when time (history, kingship, etc.) and space (body, Jerusalem, heaven and earth, etc.) will come to an end and receive new meaning. Their basic points of identification are extra-historical and extra-sensory entities.

A caveat: the point of my comparison is not to reduce these two conceptions of allegorical interpretation to their corresponding cultural and philosophical backgrounds, but to compare instead these two modes of interpretation in their proper cultural *mileux*. In spite of the differences in exegetical intent, these two types of allegorical interpretation share a similar technique. In the case of Ps.-Heraclitus in *Quaestiones Homericae*, for example, it is the seeming lack of consistency in Apollo's shooting from afar that prompts the commentator to suggest a physical interpretation. Philo's identification of the Paradise as 'mind' also hinges on a perceived roughness of the text, namely, how can an ordinary garden sustain soulful trees. On the basis of such difficulties,[42] an

---

41. See J. Dillon, *The Middle Platonists 80 BC to AD 220* (Ithaca, NY: Cornell University Press, 1977), pp. 168-71.

42. The rise of literary criticism and, later, commentary writing was most likely closely connected to supposed difficulties associated with Homer. The first defenders of Homer, among whom is Aristotle (*Poetica* 25 and his now lost Ζητήματα Ὁμηρικά), would raise and resolve well-known critical problems of Homer. The relationship between the Zetematic literature (ζητήματα καὶ λύσεις) and commentaries (ὑπομνήματα) remains unexplored, but a strong case can be made that the two trace their origins back to the similar concern of trying to smooth out difficulties one encounters in the texts (of Homer and later of Plato).

interpretation that accords with the world-view of the readers and interpreters alike is proposed. But the formulation of the problem as textual
irregularity suggests that the interpreters conceive of their hermeneutical
task as essentially an epistemological task. That is to say, the text is in
need of interpretation because its literal meaning (whatever 'literal'
means) creates an epistemological crisis when measured against the prevailing notion of logicality. The resolution of this crisis, therefore, must
also accord with the same prevailing standards of reason and
understanding.

The impetus standing behind the exegetical traditions of the *Odes*, on
the other hand, points to a *relational* definition of the hermeneutical
task.[43] By 'relational' I mean two things. First, it refers to the interpreters' concern to make the past, the golden age as it were, into a real-
izable and practical model for the present. Secondly, it refers to the
interpreters' concern to situate themselves in the exegetical tradition of
the past, to bind themselves to a tradition that begins with the event that
gave rise to the text, accentuated with the inscripturation of the text, and
continually sustained by exegesis. In other words, one exegetes not just
to acquire wisdom of the past through the text but also to belong to a
historically alive and traditionally rich stream of relationships. As a result,
commentaries on the *Odes* as a rule include the text itself, the *Glosses*
and the *Preface*, as well as exegetical notes by generations of readers
and interpreters—provided, always, that they pass the test of orthodoxy—each adding and legitimating the previous layers of commentary.[44] History is not the temporal gulf that must be bridged but an
unbroken stream of tradition in which each commentator must find a
proper place.

The hermeneutical task, according to the Confucian interpreters, is
therefore not an epistemological one, but a moral one. The problem is
not so much how one can understand the thought of the original author,

43. If what follows is correct, then 'hermeneutics', which connotes understanding and rational characterization, is obviously a misnomer. I will continue to use the
term and its derivatives to refer to the elaboration or exposition of text, without
restricting it to the merely epistemological.

44. The form of this type of commentary resembles midrashic commentaries. See
S.D. Fraade, *From Tradition to Commentary: Torah and its Interpretation in the
Midrash Sifre to Deuteronomy* (Albany, NY: SUNY Press, 1991), pp. esp. 1-23;
and D. Boyarin, *Intertextuality and the Reading of Midrash* (Bloomington, IN:
Indiana University Press, 1990).

and the solution does not lie with closing the 'breach of inter-subjectivity'.[45] The Confucian formulation of the hermeneutical task (if the term is meaningful in this context) is: how does one become moral and where in this tradition does one find oneself. Exegesis is designed to induce, to provoke, to stimulate[46] the reader to moral action and to orthodoxy. It is only in this connection can one explain the movement from emotion to personal relations to government.[47]

Is Cultural Exegesis Possible?

Is, then, 'cultural exegesis' possible? On one level the answer is obvious. If the examples of Ps.-Heraclitus, Philo, Paul and the commentators of *Odes* are any indication, exegesis cannot help being 'cultural'. According to Martin Heidegger and Rudolf Bultmann,[48] understanding is impossible without 'preunderstanding' (*Vorverständnis* or *Vorsicht*). The interpreter brings with him or her all the prejudices, all the moral and cultural standards, all the criteria of truth that inevitably condition the mode of his or her questioning. Hans-Georg Gadamer has defined the hermeneutical problem explicitly as a historical one. Ever since Friedrich Schleiermacher, history has been viewed as the gulf that must be bridged. Gadamer, however, proposes that interpretation does not and, indeed, cannot take place in isolation, apart from history. History is the precondition for understanding and understanding has to be seen in the larger context of 'effective history' (*Wirkungsgeschichte*). All these authors write in the context of the western culture, but what is true for the west is even more true for China. For the Confucian interpreters, history itself *is* the locus of authority. 'Cultural exegesis' is therefore redundant. In Confucian exegesis, as in all other types of exegesis, interpretation cannot help being part of a tradition.

45. In the words of David Linge, in H.G. Gadamer, *Philosophical Hermeneutics* (trans. and ed. D. Linge; Berkeley: University of California Press, 1976), p. xii.

46. These three functions—'to induce', 'to provoke', and 'to stimulate'—are of course the variant translations of the technique *hsing*.

47. One should also remember that when the *Five Classics* were adopted as the basis of provincial and imperial examinations, the curriculum included not just the texts of the *Five Classics* but also accompanying commentaries which espoused orthodox views.

48. See M. Heidegger, *Being and Time* (trans. J. Macquarrie and E. Robinson; London: SCM Press, 1962); and R. Bultmann, 'Is Presuppositionless Exegesis Possible?' (p. 125 n. 6 above).

On another level, however, that is to say on a 'cross-cultural' level, the question can benefit from the study of comparative hermeneutics. Is '*cross*-cultural' exegesis possible? If so, how does one pursue it? If my analysis of the Chinese exegetical tradition is on the mark, then it would not simply be a straight-forward reading of, say, the Bible in a Chinese environment. That is because the Chinese mode of exegesis is both *historical* (i.e. an event in history) and *traditional* (i.e. as a process arising out of and returning to the continuum that is the Chinese tradition). Modern Chinese biblical exegetes are very suspicious of the formulation of *Heilsgeschichte* in the Christian West,[49] not so much because it is traditional and historical but because it is the wrong history and the wrong tradition. Because Chinese interpreters are so aware of the traditional and historical conditionality of any interpretation, they are much more concerned with grounding it in the *right* (read *Chinese*) tradition. They turn instead to the creation story, supposedly being cosmic and universal, while bypassing the rest of the Old and New Testaments.[50] An integral part of the Chinese 'horizons' (to use Gadamer's term) is the 'unity of the Way' (*tao t'ung*) that forges an intimate relationship between the present and the past. Exegesis of any text falls short if it fails to foster and maintain that unity. Protestant exegesis since the Reformation has been a continual effort of liberating the exegete from the restraints of tradition and its hold on human imagination. Chinese exegesis, on the other hand, begins with the premise that one exegetes *in order* to be a part of the tradition and *in order* to find a place for oneself. It is only then that the exegete can have the proper condition for self-cultivation and for moral realization.

I would like to propose four hypotheses regarding the question of 'cultural exegesis'. These hypotheses can be construed as the Chinese reading of the biblical text, but I think they dovetail very nicely with Gadamer's proposal that interpretation can go on only in history or in tradition.

First, exegesis is always related to self-understanding. Exegesis is a community's process of self-reflection. The primary focus of exegesis is not apologetic: its purpose is not to defend a given tradition against criticisms from the outside or to persuade outsiders of the supposed validity

49. See the critiques by, e.g., C.S. Song, *The Compassionate God* (Maryknoll, NY: Orbis Books, 1982).

50. Cf. e.g., C.S. Song, *Third-Eye Theology: Theology in Formation in Asian Settings* (Maryknoll, NY: Orbis Books, 1979).

of the tradition. It, rather, to quote George Lindbeck, aims at producing 'communally authoritative teachings regarding beliefs and practices that are considered essential to the identity or welfare of the group in question...[and] indicate what constitutes faithful adherence to a community'.[51]

Secondly, this definition of exegesis is not relativistic but requires following caveats regarding the notion of objectivity.

Thirdly, this definition of exegesis is 'objective' not in the sense of relying on abstract ideas floating somewhere above us. It is 'objective' in the sense that it is tied to a community in all its socio-economic and political reality. The notion of objectivity I am working with here is closely related to Michael Polanyi's 'fiduciary community', in which there is general commitment and shared vision and faith. The problem confronting us today is that there is a new, emerging community and we do not know what it is like. The distinction between 'us' and 'them' is no longer as clearly defined as before and one of the goals of the Casassa Conference, as I perceive it, is to ask ourselves what this new community is. Exegesis, in association with dialogue based on that exegesis, engenders and fosters that self-understanding.

Fourthly, this definition is objective in the sense that exegesis must be historical. This means, exegesis is not merely a manipulation of text in a symbolic fashion but is rather a historical reading that takes into account the events attending the formation of the text, the inscripturation of the text, the editing of the text, the history of interpretation generated by the text, the history of the community or communities associated with the text. Historicality implies a twofold emphasis: community and tradition. 'Cultural Exegesis', or, as I propose, '*Cross*-Cultural Exegesis', is not just a question related to the text; it is also a call to communal reflection.

---

51. *The Nature of Doctrine* (Philadelphia: Westminster Press, 1984), p. 74.

THE CORNELIUS STORY IN THE JAPANESE CULTURAL CONTEXT

Hisao Kayama

The purpose of this paper is to analyse the Cornelius story in the Book of Acts in terms of the problem of purity and impurity. This biblical text has relevance for understanding other cultural contexts. The problem of purity and impurity, we shall see, is also at the core of Japanese Shinto and Buddhist tradition. In fact, we could say that this problem provides a point of contact for two vastly different cultural worlds and historical contexts. This paper is a modest attempt of a cross-cultural exegesis of the Cornelius story from a Japanese perspective.

I. *The Cornelius Story in the Lukan Context*

One of the most serious and perplexing problems in early Christianity was the issue of Gentile mission. Judaism, the matrix of Christianity, had had a long history of encountering with non-Jews. In Deuteronomy 24.17-22, for example, aliens are found living under care of Israelites—'You shall not pervert the justice due to the sojourner or to the fatherless, or take a widow's garment in pledge; but shall remember that you were a slave in Egypt and the Lord your God redeemed you from there; therefore I command you to do this' (vv. 17-18); 'When you gather the grapes of your vineyard, you shall not glean it afterward; it shall be for the sojourner, the fatherless and the widow. You shall remember that you were a slave in the land of Egypt; therefore I command you to do this' (vv. 21-22). In Deut. 14.21, the problem of clean and unclean foods is taken up and aliens are given freedom to eat anything—'You shall not eat anything that dies of itself; you may give it to the alien who is within your towns, that he may eat it, or you may sell it to a foreigner; for you are a people holy to the Lord your God'. Furthermore, Trito-Isaiah reflects a post-exilic theological stance, prophesying of the salvation of Gentiles in the end time:

Let not the foreigner who has joined himself to the Lord say, 'The Lord
will surely separate me from his people'; and let not the eunuch say,
'Behold, I am a dry tree'. For thus says the Lord: 'To the eunuchs who
keep my sabbaths, who choose the things that please me and hold fast my
covenant, I will give in house and within my walls a monument and a
name better than sons and daughters; I will give them an everlasting name
which shall not be cut off' (56.3-5).

Likewise, R. Jehoschua in the Tannaic period (ca. 90 CE) states that
pious Gentiles will also have a share in the future world (*t. Sanh.* 13.2).
As a matter of fact, the missionary successes of Judaism in late antiquity
were quite impressive throughout the Roman Empire as reported by
Philo and Josephus.[1] Non-Jews had easy access to Judaism through the
synagogue service and many became interested in Judaism. Judaism was
presented to the world as a universal religion.

Nevertheless, the non-Jews (*gôyim*, or 'Gentiles') are basically rejected
and hated by God; hence the law-abiding Jews must remain cautious not
to get defiled by associating themselves with the unclean Gentiles. The
law-abiding Jews must beware particularly of the Gentiles' idolatry,
bloodshedding and unchastity.[2] Therefore, non-Jews who are away from
these forbidden factors are at the threshold of divine salvation as God-
fearers, even though they are not fully accepted yet into the Jewish
community, because they are uncircumcised.

Cornelius, a Roman centurion, was such a God-fearer; he was not
merely 'a devout man who feared God with all his household', but
'gave alms liberally to the (Jewish) people, and prayed constantly to
God' (Acts 10.2). Therefore, he was already at the threshold of salvation
according to the Jewish criterion, but not a proselyte yet. Most probably,
Luke adopted the Cornelius tradition and editorially remodelled it so that
it might suitably play an integral role in the context of salvation history.
It is, however, hard to tell with precision which parts go back to the
original tradition and which parts to Luke's hand. Fortunately, it is not
my primary task in this essay to distinguish between tradition and
redaction. It seems to me, at least, that the major part of Peter's vision

---

1. D. Georgi, *The Opponents of Paul in Second Corinthians* (Philadelphia:
Fortress Press, 1986), pp. 83-151. See also Philo, *De Vit. Mos.* (2.17-18) and
Josephus, *Apion* (2.279-95).
2. Str–B IV.1, pp. 353-411; K. Lake, 'Proselytes and God-Fearers', in
F.J. Foakes-Jackson and K. Lake (eds.), *The Beginnings of Christianity*, V (Grand
Rapids: Baker Book House, 1979), pp. 74-96.

(10.28-48) and the entire portion of the report and explanation of the event within the Jerusalem community (11.1-18) are Luke's redaction.

The Cornelius story, the longest single story in Acts, consists of five scenes: (1) Cornelius in Caesarea and the vision he sees, in which he hears the heavenly voice to send for Peter (10.1-8); (2) Peter in Joppa and the vision he sees, in which he is shown all sorts of animals descending from above and is told to slaughter and eat them (10.9-16); (3) Cornelius's servants visit Peter in Joppa (10.17-23); (4) Peter goes to Caesarea, accompanied by the servants and his Jewish Christian companions; the Holy Spirit is poured out upon the Gentile household, to whom Peter is preaching (10.24-48); (5) Peter's report and the discussion of that matter in the Jerusalem community (11.1-18).

The whole issue at stake in the story is the problem of the Gentile mission which is most acutely and symbolically presented to the reader in the second scene: 'Peter went up to the housetop to pray (v. 9). The motif of prayer corresponds to Cornelius's prayer just prior to the vision he saw in the preceding scene; the prayer motif suggests their Jewish piety. And then, 'Peter became hungry and desired something to eat' (v. 10a). Therefore, people prepare something to eat. At the same time, the hunger motif prepares for the vision of clean and unclean foods. 'Falling into a trance', which reminds us of Paul's similar experience (cf. Acts 22.17-18; 2 Cor. 12.1ff.), 'Peter saw the heaven opened, something descending, like a great sheet, let down by four corners upon the earth. In it were all kinds of animals and reptiles and birds of the air. And there came a voice to him, "Rise, Peter, kill and eat"' (vv. 10b-13).

The Jewish food regulations are written in detail in Lev. 11.14 and Deut. 14.3-21, according which only those animals which are cloven-footed and chew the cud are clean and edible; everything in the waters that has fins and scales, whether in the seas or in the rivers, is clean and edible; among the birds, twenty-one kinds (the eagle, the vulture, the ostrich, the hawk, the owl among others) are declared unclean and to be abominated. And all the swarming things that swarm upon the earth are unclean. In Peter's vision, all kinds of animals and reptiles and birds, both clean and unclean according to the Jewish cultic law, descended from the heaven. The sight itself would have been puzzling to Peter, because to the Jew 'nothing unclean descends from the heaven' (*b. Sanh.* 59b). And what is more puzzling or rather shocking is undoubtedly God's command to Peter, 'kill and eat!' Peter was a law-abiding Jew as proven by his regular prayer and temple worship (3.2), hence he naturally refused to obey, saying, 'No, Lord; for I have never eaten anything that is common or unclean' (v. 14). Peter's answer somehow corresponds to Ezekiel's reply to God who predicts the Israelites' self-defilement by eating their unclean bread: 'Ah Lord God! behold, I have never defiled myself; from my youth up till now I have never eaten what died of itself or was torn by beasts, nor has foul flesh come into my mouth' (4.14). God does not accept Peter's refusal, however: 'What God has declared clean, you must not call common' is the reply (v. 15a). 'What God has declared clean' is synonymous with 'what God has cleansed' (RSV). When did God make such a declaration? We are not told. However, these words at least remind us of the story of God's creation (Gen. 1.28-29); when God created the fish of the sea and the birds of the air and every living thing that moves upon the earth, 'he saw everything that he had made, and behold, it was very good' (Gen. 1.31). Therefore, the vision Peter saw is apparently grounded upon the viewpoint of creation theology, through which the distinction between the clean and the unclean animals is already relativized.[3]

The vision might be regarded as an allegory;[4] the 'clean' and the 'unclean' being gathered together in the same sheet points toward the future fellowship of the 'clean' and 'unclean' people in the same community. The meaning of this vision is later clearly stated before Cornelius and his household through the mouth of Peter; he says that 'You yourselves know how unlawful it is for a Jew to associate with or to visit anyone of another nation; but God has shown me that I should not call any man common or unclean. So when I was sent for, I came without objection' (vv. 28-29). God has made the 'unclean' people clean by inviting them into the eschatological redemptive community. God proves it true by outpouring the Holy Spirit upon Cornelius and his household, while Peter is still preaching the Gospel. Therefore, from the viewpoint of our story-teller, it is in fact the story of Peter's conversion[5] more than that of Cornelius's. Peter had indeed experienced the outpouring of the Holy Spirit at the Pentecost, which proves that he was genuinely a Christian. From the Jewish point of view, Peter went beyond the boundary of Judaism that was being guarded with the idea and practice of purity and impurity. Accordingly, talking about Peter's

---

3. K. Löning, 'Die Korneliustradition', *BZ* 18 (1974), p. 13. A. Weiser, *Die Apostelgeschiche Kap. 1–12* (Siebenstern, 1981), p. 264.

4. J. Roloff, *Die Apostelgeschichte* (NTD, 5; 1981), p. 170.

5. Cf. Roloff, *Die Apostelgeschichte*, p. 165.

conversion here is not an overstatement. In that sense, Peter was the key figure rather than Cornelius; yet, to be more exact, it is God who is at the center of the story. As a singular event of this sort, the conversion of the Ethiopian eunuch had already taken place through Philip's witness in Samaria (8.26ff.), which was the first event of Gentiles' conversion recorded in Acts. This could perhaps be viewed as an unexpected event that happened to a single God-fearer. Furthermore, in this case, there was no problem related to the Jewish law or to table fellowship with the Gentiles. In the Cornelius story, on the other hand, the problem of purity and table fellowship with the Gentiles were the issues at stake. In other words, Luke used this story of Peter and Cornelius in order to elaborate a fundamental Christian principle;[6] this becomes particularly clear in the final two scenes of the drama. Even the seemingly unintentional prosaic concluding sentence ('Thus they asked him to remain for some days', 10.48b) indicates something quite unusual for a law-abiding Jew.[7] In fact, Peter became the object of criticism for his behavior among the Gentiles, when he returned to the community in Jerusalem.

The last scene is most likely Luke's own composition and hence reveals more directly his own theological perspective. Upon hearing the report of the Gentiles' salvation the circumcision party criticized by saying, 'Why did you go to uncircumcized men and eat with them?' (11.3). Then Peter gives a summary report of the vision and outpouring of the Holy Spirit upon them, and concludes with the following justification: 'If then God gave the same gift to them as he gave to us when we believed in the Lord Jesus Christ, who was I that I could withstand God?' (11.17). With this they were silenced and glorified God who had granted salvation even to the Gentiles.

The Cornelius story is to be told again at the Jerusalem council in chapter 15. Paul and Barnabas of the church of Antioch were under the same attack from the Jerusalem circumcision party and they went up to Jerusalem in order to make an appeal to the Apostles. Peter explained to the assembly that 'God made no distinction between us and them, but cleansed their hearts by faith' (v. 9). Furthermore, with James's reconciling proposal the entire Jerusalem church agreed in principle to recognizing the Gentile Christian mission. Nevertheless, the content of the agreement, namely the apostolic decree, does present to us a very

6. H. Conzelmann, *Acts of the Apostles* (Philadelphia: Fortress Press, 1987), p. 80.
7. Str–B, pp. 263-78.

serious problem. The church legitimated the Gentile Christian mission but under the condition of 'abstaining from what has been sacrificed to idols and from blood and from what is strangled and from unchastity' (11.29). These stipulations basically repeat the cultic regulations required of the alien residents in Israel, to which we already referred.[8] How do we reconcile the apostolic decree with the divine declaration that there is no longer any distinction between the clean and the unclean?

Historically speaking, Paul, who attended the Jerusalem council, never mentioned the apostolic decree in his letters. His report of the council, that '...those who were of repute added nothing to me' (Gal. 2.6), would seem to contradict the compromise solution seen in the apostolic decree. Most probably, the stipulations of the decree were relevant for the conflict in Antioch which occurred shortly after the Jerusalem council. According to Paul's own report (Gal. 2.11ff.), Peter later withdrew table fellowship with the Gentiles, fearing James and the circumcision party; and along with him Barnabas and the rest of the Jewish Christians of Antioch withdrew. Paul harshly condemned their attitudes and began independent missionary activities.

In his letter to the church in Rome Paul wrote the following regarding the clean and unclean foods: 'One believes he may eat anything, while the weak may eat only vegetables. Let not him who eats despise him who abstains, and let not him who abstains pass judgment on him who eats; for God has welcomed him' (Rom. 14.2-3). Here we can see that Paul firmly stands on the principle of Christian freedom and love. Paul, a former Pharisaic rabbi, received this principle from Jesus, as he explains: 'I know and am persuaded in the Lord Jesus that nothing is unclean in itself; but it is unclean for anyone who thinks it unclean' (Rom. 14.14). It would have taken some time before Paul's clear-cut understanding of the food problem was widely accepted in congregations composed of both Jews and Gentiles. More than three decades later, when Luke writes, 'the issue of table-fellowship in mixed congregations was no longer a live issue'.[9] Why, then, has Luke paid serious attention to the apostolic decree as something binding to the Gentile Christians? 'For Luke, it no longer has the ritual or ethical significance; the significance is for Luke rather salvation-historical, since the decree provided continuity between Israel and the church, which was free from the Law', as

8.   Str–B, pp. 353ff.; K. Lake, *Beginnings*, V, pp. 74ff.
9.   Conzelmann, *Acts*, p. 80.

Hans Conzelmann points out.[10] If the decree was still in practice in
Luke's congregation, it would perhaps be primarily a matter of wisdom
for the dominant Gentile Christians to enable the Jewish Christians to be
part of a mixed congregation.

As mentioned above, Paul's understanding of foods free from the
cultic law of purity and impurity was rooted in the teaching of Jesus.
Luke's interpretation of the Cornelius story is similarly rooted in the
teaching of Jesus. The depiction of Cornelius as a pious God-fearer
resembles the faith of the Roman centurion whose servant was healed
by Jesus (Lk. 7.1-11/Mt. 8.5-13). Like Cornelius, he loved the Jewish
people and even built a synagogue for the Jewish community. Both the
Cornelius story and this Q pericope have the same *motivation*, namely,
to legitimize the reception of godfearers into the church by referring to
the words and action of Jesus.[11] Jesus' teaching regarding defilement
(Mk 7.1-23; cf. Mt. 15.1-20) is even more directly related to the
problem. Jesus' statement that 'there is nothing outside a man which by
going into him can defile him; but the things which come out of a man
are what defile him' (Mk 7.15) may have been editorially reworked by
Mark.[12] Nevertheless there is no reason for refusing to see Jesus' basic
intention and thought in these words, when we remember his frequent
association with sinners and those suffering from unclean diseases. 'This
reflects a very substantial lack of concern over the details of ritual
defilement'.[13] Mark has concluded this pericope by stating that 'Thus he
(Jesus) declared all foods clean' (v. 19b)[14] and by presenting a list of
things that come from within and defile a person (vv. 21-23).

Our discussion of Luke's Cornelius story, as well as other related
texts, has focused on the problem of purity. This was indeed the key
issue at stake between Judaism and Christianity at the earliest stages of

10. Conzelmann, *Acts*, p. 110.

11. Roloff, *Die Apostelgeschichte*, p. 166.

12. C.E. Carlston, 'The Things That Defile (Mk. 7:15) and the Law in Matthew
and Mark', *NTS* 15 (1968), pp. 75-96; *idem*, *Parables of the Triple Tradition*
(Philadelphia: Fortress Press, 1975), pp. 162-67.

13. Carlston, *Triple Tradition*, p. 167.

14. This passage is Mark's editorial comment. Lake and Cadbury refer to this
passage as a possible allusion to the vision of Peter (Acts 10.15). It is unlikely,
however. The contrary is more plausible. The Markan passage of Jesus' words
declaring that all foods are clean may have occurred to Luke's mind, when he wrote
the divine declaration in Peter's vision. Cf. Lake and Cadbury, *Beginnings*, IV,
p. 115.

Christian mission. This issue, however, is not confined to Jewish tradition. We must now consider the universal significance of the problem in relation to other religions and cultural contexts.

II. *Purity as a Universal Problem*

The idea of purity and impurity is present in every religion and culture. This universal phenomenon has been illuminated most clearly in the work of Mary Douglas. As a cultural anthropologist, she has clarified the meaning and social significance of purity in human culture. Her scholarly contribution consists of not only uncovering the existence and implications of purity and pollution, but also in providing the methodology and framework for identifying the characteristic of a given sociocultural group in terms of group and grid. Before elaborating this group–grid framework in the *Natural Symbols: Explorations in Cosmology* (1970),[15] she had published the pioneering work *Purity and Danger* (1965),[16] in which she argued that the idea of purity was the basic concept ordering a sociocultural system. For Douglas the concept 'purity' is a technical term that refers to the lines and boundaries that maintain the order of a society, whereas the contrary concept 'pollution' stands for the violation of such lines and boundaries of a sociocultural system. In the preceding section we briefly mentioned Jesus' attitude toward the issue of purity and impurity. The Pharisees criticized Jesus and his disciples for their violation of the purity rules defined by Jewish tradition. Jesus reinterpreted the meaning of defilement in terms of the will of God and thereby relativized the traditional Jewish understanding of purity.

Douglas's approach has been applied to biblical scholarship, particularly in the United States by such scholars as Jacob Neusner,[17] Bruce J. Malina,[18] Jerome H. Neyrey,[19] John H. Elliott,[20] and Leland J. White.[21]

---

15. M. Douglas, *Natural Symbols: Explorations in Cosmology* (London: Barrie & Jenkins, 2nd edn, 1973), pp. 77-92.

16. M. Douglas, *Purity and Danger: An Analysis of Concepts of Pollution and Taboo* (London: Routledge & Kegan Paul, 1966).

17. J. Neusner, *The Idea of Purity in Ancient Judaism* (Leiden: Brill, 1973); *idem*, 'History and Purity in First-Century Judaism', *HR* 18 (1987), pp. 1-17; *idem*, 'Map without Territory: Mishna's System of Sacrifices and Sanctuary', *HR* 19 (1979), pp. 103-27.

18. B.J. Malina, 'Normative Dissonance and Christian Origins', *Semeia* 35

A most illuminating application of Douglas's group and grid framework theory can be seen in Malina's *Christian Origins and Cultural Anthropology* (1986). In this work he elaborated Douglas's theory using various combinations of group and grid in his analysis. Group refers to the degree of social pressure on a given social unit to conform to the norms of a society. In this framework strong group refers to high pressure toward social conformity, whereas weak group indicates a greater degree of individual freedom. Grid refers to the degree to which socially held values and individual experience match; high grid means a higher degree of integration, whereas low grid means a low degree of such integration. A pyramid type of social structure such as, for example, the society of the Sadducees or the Herodians in New Testament times, can best be explained in terms of strong group–high grid quadrant.[22] On the one hand, this strong group–high grid quadrant at the top level features strong concern for purity or boundary, making lines in order to maintain the social structure. On the other, this strong group–high grid quadrant has within it a number of horizontal lines of disinctive *castes*. Malina regards the strong group–low grid quadrant as the most significant framework for New Testament studies, since, in his view, almost all the New Testament writings, except for the Gospel of John, derive from persons socially and emotionally anchored in this quadrant.[23] Although there tends to be a low degree of integration in the sociocultural system, this quadrant resembles strong group–high grid as far as ritual is concerned. This is because it also generates societies of fixed rituals like baptism for Christians and circumcision for Jews. Malina maintains that the various Palestinian factions like the Pharisees, the Zealots and the Jesus movement group can best be understood in

(1986), pp. 35-59; *idem*, 'The Received View and what it Cannot Do: III John and Hospitality', *Semeia* 35 (1986), pp. 171-94; *idem*, *Christian Origins and Cultural Anthropology: Practical Models for Biblical Interpretation* (Richmond, VA: John Knox Press, 1986).

19. J.H. Neyrey, 'The Idea of Purity in Mark's Gospel', *Semeia* 35 (1986), pp. 91-128; *idem*, 'Body Language and I Corinthians: The Use of Anthropological Models for Understanding Paul and his Opponents', *Semeia* 35 (1986), pp. 129-70.

20. J.H. Elliott, 'Social Scientific Criticism of the New Testament and its Social World: More on Method and Models', *Semeia* 35 (1986), pp. 1-33.

21. L.J. White, 'Grid and Group in Matthew's Community: The Righteousness/ Honor Code in the Sermon on the Mount', *Semeia* 35 (1986), pp. 61-90.

22. Malina, *Christian Origins and Cultural Anthropology*, pp. 29-30.

23. Malina, *Christian Origins and Cultural Anthropology*, pp. 37-44.

terms of this cultural script of high group–low grid. In this theoretical framework, Jesus and Paul can best be understood as weak group–low grid individuals. According to Malina, 'What such individuals envision is not a change in the shape of society but a change in the values of society'.[24]

According to Douglas's model, one can say that Jesus shifted his basic attitude from strong group–low grid to weak group–low grid,[25] when he left John the Baptist and began preaching the gospel. This has even been referred to as the 'conversion of Jesus'.[26] If we reconsider the conversion of Peter in the Cornelius story in terms of Douglas's model, Peter's conversion can also be best explained as a basic shift from strong group–low grid to weak group–low grid orientation, even if the historical Peter may not have behaved in quite the same way.

In this paper I do not intend to focus on Douglas's model nor do I seek to review its application to biblical materials in detail. The purpose here is simply to point out that the concern for purity and boundary maintenance is a phenomenon that can be found in every culture. In this sense, the generalization and abstraction of purity rules of a given society can function as an important tool for analysis. Nevertheless, this framework and approach has its limitation when it comes to textual analysis. In our present context, it is sufficient simply to point out that Douglas's model sensitizes us to the problem of purity in diverse cultural situations ranging from first-century Judaism to contemporary Japan.

III. *The Idea of Purity in the Japanese Cultural Context*

The Japanese culture has been formed predominantly upon the basis of Shinto, which literally means the 'way of the gods'. Although the history of proto-Shinto as nature religion is as old as Japanese history, there is evidence that by the *Yayoi* period (3rd century CE) Shinto consisted of shamanistic rituals related to rice cultivation. In the succeeding

24. Malina, *Christian Origins and Cultural Anthropology*, p. 56.

25. Malina, *Christian Origins and Cultural Anthropology*, pp. 56-57. According to Neyrey, Jesus' change is only a matter of difference of grid, not group, because 'Jesus bases his own reform on those same Scriptures, but viewed from a different perspective' ('Idea of Purity', p. 119).

26. P.W. Hollenbach, 'The Conversion of Jesus: From Jesus the Baptizer to Jesus the Healer', *ANRW*, II.25.1, pp. 196-219. Cf. Malina, *Christian Origins and Cultural Anthropology*, p. 203.

Kofun period (ca. 300–710), many clan states were brought under the control of the Imperial House, whose tutelary god Amaterasu (the sun goddess) extended considerable influence for the unification of Japan as a nation.

Unlike Buddhism or Christianity, Shinto has never undergone significant theological and doctorinal development. One consistent feature of Shinto is its ritual emphasis. As a ritual religion, Shinto penetrated in and influenced Japanese culture in various ways, often more socio-psychologically than ideologically. In the words of a historian of religions,[27]

> In order to cope with the mysterious and often threatening powers of the universe, Japanese folk religion (Shinto) developed an all embracing system of ritual comprising of festivals, annual observances, rites of passages, ceremonies of exorcism and taboos. Most are supposed to secure immediate, concrete benefits in this world, protection from danger, fertility, growth, healing, warding off evil.

The nature of Shinto as a this-worldly religion is closely related to its traditional concept of impurity (*kegare*). Shinto especially considers death unclean. Not only the deceased but also those who touch them are considered defiled. Therefore, funeral services are mostly conducted at Buddhist temples, funeral houses or in the home of the deceased by Buddhist priests, but seldom conducted at Shinto shrines. It is customary that ones who attend funeral services are given salt for purifying themselves outside the entrance of their homes or place of worship. At the entrance of Shinto shrines is a font that visitors may wash their hands with purification water. Inside the shrine, Shinto priests perform a purification ceremony before the worshippers by waving a purification wand.

The most pervasive and painful outcome of the idea of purity and impurity in the Japanese society is the creation of some three million 'outcasts' called '*Burakumin*'; they used to be called '*Eta*' which literally means 'much pollution'. Although the historical origin of the *Burakumin* has not been firmly established, most scholars would agree that the history goes back to the *Heian* period and that it is closely connected to the idea of purity and impurity of Shinto and Buddhism; the latter had already been brought into Japan in the middle of the sixth century from China through Korea. Yoshino and Murakoshi explain:

27. T. Imoos, 'Shinto', *Indian Missionary Review* (January edn, 1986), pp. 42-43.

In the early part of the Heian period (794–1185) the coexistence of Shinto and Buddhism became well established. Concomittantly, the Shinto idea of pollution and avoidance of defilement (which was associated with death) was linked to the Buddhist teaching against the killing of animals. Those who were engaged in the unpleasant but essential tasks of handling the deceased and disposing of dead animals from the temple grounds were considered polluted and they were prohibited from participating in religious rites. Moreover, since defilement was thought to be contagious, contact with the so-called polluted people was shunned. Those whose livelihood involved dealing with death, butchering and processing raw skins were ostracized and forced outside the mainstream of society.[28]

The first visible ghettos were thus founded around the ninth century in Kyoto on marginal lands set apart for the purpose of grazing cattles and burying the dead. It is reported that today some 6000 segregated 'buraku' (ghettos) exist throughout Japan. Buddhism, originally a religion of aristocrats in Japan, successfully spread among the Japanese people at large in the medieval period, including the Burakumin (some 90 per cent of whom today belong to the *Jodo-Shinshu* sect founded by Shinran). It was lately discovered that *Burakumin*'s graveyards had also been segregated and that discriminatory posthumous Buddhist names (*kaimyo*) had been given to them by priests such as 'Leather-Man', 'Leather-Woman', 'Animal-Man', 'Animal-Woman' and the like.

Today, the great majority of the Burakumin no longer make a living by killing animals or what their ancestors were forced to do.

Yet, the stigma that Burakumin are somehow polluted through hereditary traits remains deeply embedded in the latent thoughts of the older generation. Thus, prior to marriage and employment, it is still a prevalent practice to investigate a person's family background and check for so-called 'bad-blood'.[29]

In recent years, a number of organizations to foster liberation, equality and integration have been founded and become an incentive for the Government to establish an Integration Policy. One of the earliest such liberation movements was '*Suiheisha*' (Levelers Association) founded in 1922. Their deeply inspiring declaration for human liberation and equality is considered one of Japan's first statements on human rights. Its principal author Mankichi Saiko used the ideas of Christianity, as well

28. T.R. Yoshino and S. Murakoshi, *The Invisible Visible Minority: Japan's 'Burakumin'* (Osaka: Buraku Kaiho Kenkyusho, 1977), p. 26.
29. Yoshino and Murakoshi, *The Invisible Visible Minority*, p. 121.

as Marxism and Buddhism, as the cross of thorns emblem of their movement symbolically suggests. In fact, Saiko and his fiends visited Toyohiko Kagawa, one of the most influential Christian leaders in Japan, for consultation. Later, however, the friendship between the Kagawa and Suiheisha movements broke down, because Kagawa rejected their most potent method of confronting discrimination through censure or through denouncement. In fact, he referred to their actions as the 'gospel of hatred'. That separation was quite unfortunate not only for Kagawa and the Suiheisha movement, but also for the Christian church in Japan. Kagawa has recently been criticized by a group of Christians who have actively participated in the Buraku liberation movement, because Kagawa used a number of words and descriptions discriminatory to the Burakumin in the voluminous book, *A Study of the Psychology of the Poor* (1914), which he authored at the age of twenty-five while living in a slum in Kobe.[30] Kagawa is still recognized as a 'saint' by many people; indeed, he was a most active leader in the history of Protestant mission in Japan. Even though there may be various reasons why he used discriminatory language, he must nevertheless be criticized. Through our criticism of Kagawa we have begun to understand that he represents, in some way, Peter before his encounter with Cornelius and his subsequent transformation.

In 1991 *A Theology of the Crown of Thorns: Buraku Liberation and Christianity* by Teruo Kuribayashi was published. This book, which is regarded as one of the first books of indigenous Japanese theology, has forced serious rethinking of the issues of Buraku discrimination upon us and the Japanese Christian church. According to Eiichi Kudo, in early Protestant mission work in Japan there were a few sporadic efforts to reach the Burakumin. The Burakumin showed considerable interests in the Christian gospel of equality and human liberation and some became Christians. But later, one unfortunate incident caused a separation of Burakumin Christians from other non-Burakumin members. In those early days, members of a congregation used the same chalice for the Holy Communion. Non-Buraku members refused to do so because of their inherited traditional idea of the Burakumin as the polluted. This situation closely resembles the problem associated with the church in Antioch. As we already discussed, the problem of table fellowship

---

30. Kirisuto Shimbon Sha (ed.), *A Collection of Sources: Kagawa's Writings and Buraku Discrimination: Hinminshinri no Kenkyu* (A Study of the Psychology of the Poor) (Tokyo: Kirisuto Shimbun Sha, 1991).

between Jews and Gentiles was closely connected to the idea of purity and impurity defined by the Jewish tradition. Similarly, the issue of the Holy Communion in the Japanese Christian church was rooted in the idea of purity and impurity of the Shinto and Buddhist traditions. Much like the Gentile in the Jewish society, the Burakumin have had to bear the stigma of religious, cultural taboos and have been regarded as outcasts in Japanese society. The idea of purity and impurity thus still continues to be influential within the church in Japan. Kuribayashi's important contribution is his attempt to build a bridge between the Burakumin and Christianity; he does this by viewing Jesus Christ and his movement from the position of both marginal people in Jewish society and the Burakumin of the Japanese society. In his words,

> The context of Jesus' missionary movement was mainly among the poor people of first-century Palestine. What made his work unique was his fellowship with 'sinners' (*hamartoloi*) and his declaration that they are the ones who will inherit the 'Kingdom of God'. Our analysis shows that, unlike modernistic definitions, sinners described in the Scripture refer to people in several occupations discriminated against in terms of a religious code of purity and impurity, comparable with the historically discriminated against people in Japan and Korea (and elsewhere). Jesus was free from such a religious code of purity and impurity and set them free from the oppression of that code [my translation].[31]

Kuribayashi's consistent viewpoint is that of the Burakumin, from which the Gospel of Jesus Christ can best be understood. Therefore, in that viewpoint we can have a hermeneutical advantage for interpreting the biblical truth of human liberation. He also intends to go even beyond the Latin American theology of liberation in that his theological enterprise has the task to serve for human liberation from discriminatory culture.

IV. *Concluding Remarks*

I have briefly discussed the Cornelius story in terms of the problem of purity and impurity, which is the key issue at stake in the narrative and historical context. I argued that the meaning of the text is not confined

31. T. Kuribayashi, *Keikan no Shingaku: Hisabetsu-Buraku Kaiho to Kirisutokyo* (Tokyo: Shinkyo Shuppan Sha, 1991), p. 319. This is the enlarged Japanese publication of a doctoral dissertation he wrote under D. Sölle and K. Koyama at Union Theological Seminary in New York City, 1986: *Towards a Theology of the Crown of Thorns*.

to the Jewish tradition, but has universal significance, even in the contemporary situation of Japan. This universal problem was clarified by the framework elaborated by Mary Douglas. Furthermore, I discussed the problem of purity and impurity rooted in Japanese society, particularly with reference to the Burakumin. Through this study, I noted significant cross-cultural continuity from the first-century Jewish situation to contemporary Japan.

To the Japanese reader of a given biblical text, however, the meaning becomes clearer and more familiar by considering the text from the particularity of each situation. Each culture faces similar and corresponding issues. The Japanese reader will better understand the problem of purity and impurity in the Cornelius story by viewing it from the position of the Burakumin. Indeed, the Burakumin himself or herself will be able to more existentially grasp the meaning of our text. If this is true, their voice must be attentively heard. Just as Peter was transformed through the vision and encounter with Cornelius, we may be similarly transformed by reconsidering this vision and by our encounter with the Burakumin.

In conclusion, I would like to make two final remarks. First, the problem of purity and impurity is one of many issues at stake in the Scripture. However, it is not simply one of many issues; the problem of purity and impurity is a key issue for understanding the religious, cultural and historical situations in which the biblical texts were written. Unless we correctly understand this problem, we will lack a clear understanding not only of the Cornelius story, but of other biblical texts. Secondly, I repeatedly referred to the problem of purity and impurity as a universal phenomenon rooted in every sociocultural situation. The Burakumin is specifically a Japanese phenomenon. There are undoubtedly other 'Burakumin' in other societies, however. And if so my presentation will hopefully have some relevance for the task of biblical interpretation and provide a hermeneutical advantage in these other social contexts.

A *DHVANI* INTERPRETATION OF THE BIBLE:
ACCORDING TO INDIAN TRADITION

Matthew Vellanickal

Until recently biblical scholarship susbcribed to an objectivist, one-dimensional hermeneutic, which assumed that the text of the Bible has only one true meaning, independent of any cultural or religious conditioning of the reader. The fundamentalist, for whom the Bible is the inspired Word of God spoken directly to and recorded immediately by the biblical author, will find this 'true' meaning not in the obvious literal sense of a biblical text, but as it is read within the tradition of his or her community. The critical scholar, on the other hand, is keenly aware of the fact that the Bible is the product of a long and complex process involving different oral and written traditions and literary editions, and will look for the 'true' meaning of a biblical text in its original meaning, intended by its original author. One will try to recover this meaning from the layers of traditions that have accumulated around it by means of a diligent application of the historical critical method.[1] The historical-critical method has become almost everywhere the standard method for interpreting a biblical text.[2]

In India, there have been attempts to search into the meaning of the biblical text different from the fundamentalist and the historical-critical approaches. This is especially true regarding the Gospel of John.[3] There

---

1. V.S. Polyttres, 'Analysing a Biblical Text: Some Important Linguistic Distinctions', *SJT* 32 (1979), pp. 113-37.

2. For information on the origin and history of historical critical method, cf. E. Krentz, *The Historical-Critical Method* (Philadelphia: Fortress Press, 1975), pp. 6-32.

3. C. Duraisingh and C. Hargreaves (eds.), *India's Search for Reality and the Relevance of the Gospel of John* (Delphi: ISPCK, 1975); G.S. Prabhu (ed.), *Wir werden bei ihm wohnen: Das Johannes-Evangelium in indischer Deutung* (Herder, 1984).

were attempts to make the biblical text meaningful and relevant to the complex and multi-cultural and religious context of India. However, the approaches and the methods of interpretation are various.[4] These works range from exegetical and theological studies[5] to meditative and artistic presentations along the lines of Buddhist and Hindu meditational techniques.[6] There are also some individual attempts for a sort of Indian interpretation of the Bible from the point of view of a traditional Hindu world view.[7] Some authors have attempted to give a social interpretation of the biblical text to make it more relevant to the socio-political situation in India.[8] There have also been studies from the point of view of interreligious dialogue.[9] Finally, distinct from all these approaches, there have been attempts to apply a traditional Indian method of interpreting the Scriptures, namely, *dhvani method* to the biblical text.[10] This is the method that I am trying to present in this paper, and this will involve applying it to one of the passages in St John's Gospel.

The Historical Background

It is actually the limitations of the historical-critical method which has given rise to other approaches and methods in the field of biblical studies. In practice the historical-critical method analyses the biblical text by subjecting it to a series of techniques, the so-called criticisms (text and

4.   M.R. Spindler, 'Recent Indian Studies of the Gospel of John: Puzzling Contextualizations', *Exchange* 9 (1980), pp. 1-55, for an overall view of the Indian approaches.

5.   M. Vellanickal, *Studies in the Gospel of John* (Bangalore, 1982).

6.   J. Sahi, 'An Artist Looks at the Fourth Gospel', in Duraisingh and Hargreaves (eds.), *India's Search for Reality*, pp. 78-92.

7.   M.A. Amaldoss, 'An Indian Reads St. John's Gospel', in Duraisingh and Hargreaves (eds.), *India's Search for Reality*, pp. 7-21; Sr Vandana, 'From Death to Life', in Duraisingh and Hargreaves (eds.), *India's Search for Reality*, pp. 25-38.

8.   C. Duraisingh, 'The Gospel of John and the World of India Today', in Duraisingh and Hargreaves (eds.), *India's Search for Reality*, pp. 41-53; S. Rayan, SJ, 'Jesus und die Armen in vierten Evangelium', in Prabhu (ed.), *Wir werden bei ihm wohnen*, pp. 81-98.

9.   M. Vellanickal, 'Dei Kirche im Dialog mit den religiösen und Kulturellen Traditionen in Umfeld des Johannes evangeliums', in Prabhu (ed.), *Wir werden bei ihm wohnen*, pp. 48-70.

10.   The whole issue of *Bible Bhashyam: An Indian Biblical Quarterly*, published from St Thomas Apostolic Seminary, Vadavathoor, Kottayam, India, was dedicated to this new method of interpretation (cf. *Bible Bhashyam* 5.4 [1979], pp. 261-318).

literary, form and redaction), through which a rigorous textual, philological, grammatical and stylistic analyses attempt to recover the original form of the text and determine its original meaning.[11] It claims to be the scientific method for the study of the Bible and thus to be valid always and everywhere, transcending all bounderies of place and culture.

This kind of objectivity and a certain absoluteness characteristic of the historical-critical method, though useful to a great extent, has given rise to some hesitation as to its effectiveness in interpreting the biblical text, which is not scientific but religious.[12] Its inadequacy is manifested in different ways. The historical-critical method has proved, in many contexts, ineffective, irrelevant and ideologically loaded.[13]

It is ineffective because of its inability to arrive at conclusive results. After more than two centuries of painstaking studies, the historical-critical method has left us with a heap of hypothetical possibilities.[14] In most of the cases the conclusions arrived at by historical-critical method are questioned and criticized. For example, the widely accepted dating of the New Testament books is being questioned.[15] Or, take the apparently conclusive demonstration of Joachim Jeremias that 'Abba' as an address for God is a usage distinctive of Jesus.[16] This is challenged by Braun, who questions the uniqueness of the 'Abba' formula.[17] The two-source theory of Synoptic origins, once almost a dogma of critical orthodoxy, is now being questioned by some who claim that Luke used Matthew and that Mark summarized Matthew and Luke.[18] The historical-critical method seems incapable of ever reaching any universally accepted conclusions, because the assured results of today are challenged tomorrow.

The historical-critical method is also to a certain extent irrelevant because of its objectivism and consequently its inability to respond to concrete personal and communitarian needs. 'Scientific' biblical studies

11. H. Zimmermann, 'Neutestamentliche Methodenlehre', *KBW* (1968).

12. W. Wink, *The Bible in Human Transformation* (Philadephia, 1975); G. Maier, *The End of Historical-Critical Method* (St Louis, 1977).

13. G.S. Prabhu, 'Towards an Indian Interpretation of the Bible', *Bible Bhashyam* 6 (1980), pp. 151-63.

14. P. Stuhlmacher, *Historical Criticism and Theological Interpretation of Scripture* (London, 1979).

15. J.A.T. Robinson, *Redating the New Testament* (London, 1976).

16. J. Jeremias, *'Abba' in the Prayer of Jesus* (London, 1967), pp. 11-65.

17. H. Braun, *Spät-jüdisch-häretischer und frühchristliche Radikalismus*, II (Tübingen, 1957), pp. 155-56.

18. W. Farmer, *The Synoptic Problem* (London, 1964).

have become purely academic without touching problems that really matter to people. Most of the studies are also not intelligible to the ordinary person.

Alternative Methods

It is against this background that a wide variety of alternative methods have been developed to make the biblical interpretation more effective and relevant. Thus the existentialist hermeneutics,[19] structural exegesis,[20] rhetorical criticism,[21] and other similar methods have been developed. However, the situation today remains a bit confused, yet open to new experimentation and methods in the field of biblical interpretation.

Indian Methods of Biblical Interpretation

It is in the context of this process of developing new methods of biblical interpretation that India also has its contribution to make. The Indian exegesis is greatly concerned about relevance and it is reluctant to accept the academic barrenness which afflicts the 'scientific' exegesis of today. Relevance has always been key to the nature of the traditional Indian religious background, both Christian and Hindu. Among the Hindus a study of the Sacred Books was never a merely academic exercise but always a squarely practical quest for liberation. Among the Christians the explanation of the biblical text was pastorally oriented and inspirational.

The Dhvani Interpretation

The *dhvani* interpretation of the Scriptures belongs to this category of approach and methodology. The *dhvani* theory was first proposed by

19. R. Bultmann, 'New Testament and Mythology', in H. W. Bartsch (ed.), *Kerygma and Myth* (New York, 1961), pp. 1-44; J. Robinson and J. Cobb, *The New Hermeneutic* (New York, 1964).

20. R. Polzin, *Biblical Structuralism* (Philadelphia, 1976).

21. A. Wilder, *Early Christian Rhetoric* (London, 1964); R. Funk, *Language, Hermeneutic and the Word of God* (New York, 1966).

Anandavardhana of Kashmir in his *Dhvanyalokal* (ninth cent. CE) and it is a theory developed in the world of Sanskrit poetics.[22]

Dhvani: The Suggested Meaning

Dhvani is the suggested meaning and it is not to be equated with the primary or expressed meaning (in Sanskrit *abhidha*) of a word. The primary or expressed meaning is the dictionary meaning, something fixed in the sense that whenever the particular word is heard its fixed meaning is conveyed because of its significative power.

The suggested meaning is also not the secondary meaning of a word (in Sanskrit *laksana*), already known to the linguists. This occurs when the primary meaning of a word is not suitable in a particular context, and so a meaning other than the usual meaning has to be assumed. And that meaning is somehow related to the primary meaning by popular usage. For example if I say 'the hamlet on the Ganges', the primary meaning is 'on the Ganges river'. As it does not suit well, we take it to mean 'on the bank of the river Ganges'. This is the secondary meaning. Here we can see that the secondary meaning is still in the realm of the primary meaning in the sense that this meaning is fixed by convention or usage. The main task of the secondary meaning is to remove the incompatibility created by the primary meaning.

Dhvani, on the other hand, provides an additional meaning or suggests something new which is not strictly the function of the primary (*abhidha*) or secondary meaning (*laksana*). The example of 'the hamlet on the Ganges' suggests an atmosphere of peace, prayer and holiness associated with the sacred river. This is the role of *dhvani*.

The Relation of the Suggested Meaning to the Expressed Meaning

How is the suggested meaning related to the primary or secondary meaning and yet different from it? According to Anandavardhana the suggested meaning is something like the charm of a young lady.[23] This charm which is unmistakable cannot be identified with any individual limb or with the ornaments she wears, but it stands out over and above the individual limbs or the particular ornaments of the lady. So too the suggested meaning shines above the word and its meaning, its

22. A. Amaladass, SJ, 'Dhvani Theory in Sanskrit Poetics', *Bible Bhashyam* 6 (1979), pp. 261-75.

23. Krishnamoorthy (ed. and trans.), *Anandavardhana's Dhvanyaloka* (Dharwar: Karnatak University Press, 1974), pp. 6, 18-19.

arrangements in terms of style, diction, structure and the like.

However, the suggested meaning can only be grasped after the expressed meaning. Though the suggested meaning is different from the expressed meaning, it can only operate through the expressed meaning and so they are closely related. This is explained by a well-known maxim of 'the lamp and the pot'.[24] The lamp illumines itself and at the same time reveals the pot nearby. After revealing the pot, the lamp does not cease to be, but continues to be there, though our attention is shifted to the pot. The lamp serves the purpose of revealing the pot and once the pot is discovered the lamp seems to recede into the background, giving way to the newly discovered object. The lamp, so to say, subordinates itself so that the new object may come into the limelight. The expressed meaning subordinates itself like the lamp, revealing the suggested meaning. Thus the suggested meaning is dependent upon the expressed meaning but distinct from it.

The expressed meaning arises from the words, but the suggested meaning can emerge from a word, part of a word, a sentence, the whole passage, its style or other features. In other words, the suggestive factor can be anything in a given context of the expressed meaning. The expressed meaning can be understood by anyone who is well-versed in the rules of grammar, but the suggested meaning can result from dynamics beyond what the rules of grammar sanction, from the contexts or external elements.

Suggested Meaning and the Reader
There is also a difference in the effects the different meanings produce on the readers. The expressed meaning brings a cognitive perception, whereas the suggested meaning creates an atmosphere of surprise and a thrill of discovery. The expressed meaning is the same for all those who know that language, because it is something fixed in a context. But the suggested meaning can vary from person to person depending on each one's background. For example, the phrase 'the sun has set' may come across differently to different people according to circumstances. To a lover it may mean 'it is time for a rendezvous'; to a soldier it may mean 'it is time to attack the enemy'; to a religious person it may mean 'it is time to begin the evening worship', and so on.[25]

---

24. Cf. Krishnamoorthy (ed.), *Dhvanyaloka*, pp. 200, 10-12.
25. Mammatas, *Kavyaprakasa V.vrtti* (Poona: B.O.R.I., 1965), p. 240.

Poetic and Religious Language

Dhvani or the suggested meaning, which is also called the evocative meaning, is characteristic more of a poetic language or a religious language. For *dhvani* to function, the text (be it a poem or a Scripture) must possess a special evocative quality which is its predominant purpose, and the reader should be attuned to this quality. Both the relaying quality of the text and the receiving antenna of the reader together make the *dhvani* broadcast possible. The attuned antenna of the reader alone would not suceeed in catching the *dhvani* message if the text did not transmit. And the transmitting text will remain sterile if the reader is deaf and not attuned to it. The concept of *sahrdaya*, namely, the empathetic reader, is an important one in the history of the *dhvani* theory.[26]

Communication and Communion

'Communication' has primarily to do with information and information is communicated through fixed and clear-cut categories. A category is a definite and commonly accepted way of looking at things. Because of this, things can be spoken of and referred to. The aim of communication is to make the hearer or reader acquainted with one or another way of looking at things. Therefore, communication is characteristic of the expressed meaning, primary or secondary.

But 'communion' has to do with 'subjects'. That is with 'subjects' inasmuch as they are 'lit up' by awareness or consciousness. So communion is 'subjective' though not subjectivistic. Communion is union of subjects. What is characteristic of *dhvani*, therefore, is communion.[27]

Dhvani and the Scripture

Because of this 'communion' aspect of *dhvani* theory, it is specially applicable to sacred Scriptures. 'Scripture' is not just what is written but that reality which puts us in contact with the world of the 'subject'. Scriptures deal with the significant and meaningful. Significance is transmitted only through *dhvani*, because it is ineffable. Since Scriptures speak of the ineffable, they are revelation. And revelation is never descriptive or informative. The language of revelation is always transformative. What *dhvani* does is to transport the reader to that dimension of reality where communion takes place.

26. Krishnamoorthy (ed.), *Dhvanyaloka*, p. 304.

27. F.X. D'Sa, SJ, 'Dhvani as a Method of Interpretation', *Bible Bhashyam* 5 (1979), pp. 280-84.

Dhvani in New Testament Exegesis Today

The interpretation of a *biblical* text through *dhvani* resembles recent attempts at understanding the parables of Jesus as metaphor.[28] Rhetorical criticism concentrates on the parable itself taken as a metaphor, with little interest in its origin (who uttered the parable) or its effect (how the parable was understood by those to whom it was spoken). It will focus on the text-meaning of the parable, rather than on its author or original reader meaning. The rhetorical critic will try to enter into the parable itself, and resonate to the curious combination of realism and strangeness ('the disclosure of the extraordinary in the ordinary') through which the parable is able to evoke in us the 'limit-experience' of the Kingdom.[29]

As an extended metaphor evoking such a limit experience a parable obviously cannot be conceptualized. One can never reduce it to a neat set of propositions or lessons. Like any metaphor a parable is open to the future, and will continue to disclose an indefinite sequence of new meanings as it is spoken into a succession of new situations.[30]

Clearly, then, in interpreting the parables of Jesus as metaphor, rhetorical criticism is relying on *dhvani*—that is, on that use of language through which either (or both) the primary or secondary meaning takes the reader to a depth of meaning which is experienced rather than expressed.

But unlike *dhvani*, which, since it functions through primary as well as secondary meanings, can occur anywhere in a text, interpretation through metaphor would, strictly speaking, be confined to the explicitly figurative portions of the New Testament. There is, however, a growing awareness that the metaphorical process can occur beyond the boundaries of metaphor proper, and that the whole New Testament can in fact be treated metaphorically, since it is the story of Jesus who is 'par excellence the metaphor of God'.[31] The familiar mundane story of Jesus is a way through which one arrives at the experience of God. This insight, unfortunately, has not been followed up and we have hardly any example of a metaphorical interpretation of non-parabolic New

28. Funk, *Language, Hermeneutic and the Word of God*, pp. 133-62.
29. P. Ricoeur, 'Biblical Hermeneutics', *Semeia* (1975), pp. 170-78.
30. S. Witting, 'A Theory of Multiple Meanings', *Semeia* (1977), pp. 75-103.
31. S. Te Selle, *Speaking in Parables* (Philadelphia, 1975), p. 37.

Testament texts. A fruitful field for exploration lies open here. We in India have made an attempt in this direction.[32]

A Dhvani Interpretation of John 1.1-18

The prologue of St John's Gospel is poetic in style, and it is loaded with symbolisms and riven with the tensions that suggest the straining of language called upon to express a limit experience. It thus lends itself admirably to an interpretation through *dhvani*.

The Formation of the Prologue

Normally historical criticism will start with the questions of the formation of the prologue, relation of the prologue to the Gospel and so forth. We do not want to enter into these problems, nor will it contribute anything to the *dhvani* interpretation of the prologue. We only note here that most of the exegetes agree that the prologue of the Fourth Gospel was originally a hymn and was later adapted to be the introduction to the Fourth Gospel. But when they try to identify what verses belonged to the original hymn and how it was joined to the Gospel, there is no agreement among the scholars.[33] Whatever the process of formation is that the prologue has undergone, we take the text as such and try to interpret it through the *dhvani* method.

The Structure of the Prologue

In order to see the presentation of the themes and the movement of the argument, it is important to look into the structure of the prologue.

There are several studies made on the structure of the prologue based on the literary indications.[34] They can be classified into two main categories: one, those who propose a concentric structure (Boismard, Feuillet), and the other, those who propose a circular or spiral structure (Lacan, Ridderbos, Panimolle), though in details they may differ again one from the other.

32. G.S. Prabhu, 'A Dvhani Reading of the Stilling of the Storm', *Bible Bhashyam* 5 (1979), pp. 295-308; M. Vellanickal, 'Drink from the Source of the Living Water', *Bible Bhashyam* 5 (1979), pp. 309-18.

33. R.E. Brown, *The Gospel according to John*, I (New York, 1966), pp. 18-23.

34. M. Vellanickal, *The Divine Sonship of Christians in the Johannine Writing* (Rome, 1977), pp. 124-36; in this I give a panorama of the different studies on the structure of the prologue.

I follow the opinion that the prologue has a concentric structure and we give below the text of the prologue indicating the concentric structural procedure.

1.1-2	A	In the beginning *was* the Word...*was* with *God*...*was* *God*...*was*...with *God*.
1.3-4	B	All things *were made through* him...what *was*...*made*...in him was life...light of men.
	C	The light shines...darkness *did not receive it*
1.6-8	D	There *was*...*John*...*he came* for *witness*...*to bear witness to* the light...To *bear witness to*...
1.9-10	E	The light...was coming into the world...and the world did not know him
1.11	F	He came to his own and his own *received him* not
1.12-13	F'	Whoever *received him*...who believe in his
1.14	E'	The Word *was made* flesh and dwelt among us...We saw *his* glory...as of...the...Son.
1.15	D'	*John bore witness to* him and cried *he* who *comes*...*was*...
1.16	C'	From *his* fulness *we have* all *received* grace for grace
1.17	B'	For the law...*through*...grace and truth *was made through* Jesus Christ.
1.18	A'	No one...*God*...the only begotten Son who *is* in the bosom of the Father...

The words put in italics mark the literal parallelism between the first and the second halves. In the development of the theme also we can find the same parallelism; the different aspects of the general theme are developed in a parallel structure. The different aspects may be described as follows: 1. Jesus Christ in his relation to God, which enables him to be the salvific revealer (vv. 1-2, 18 = AA'); 2. His relation to the world (vv. 3-4, 17 = BB'); 3. Response and participation—negative and positive (vv. 5, 16 = CC'); 4. John the Baptist bearing witness to Christ (vv. 6-8, 15 = DD'); 5. Response—negative and positive (vv. 9-10, 14 = EE'); 6. Response—negative and positive and result of the positive response (vv. 11-13 = FF').

The Scheme of the Structure

For a clearer perception of the movement of the argument I present below a scheme of the structure in terms of the themes:

1-2	A	Word the revealer
3-4	B	Word's role in creation and salvation as life and light
5	C	Salvific revelation in terms of light, response negative
6-8	D	The testimony of John the Baptist

9-10	E	Salvific revelation in terms of light being present in the world, response negative
11	F	Salvific revelation in Christ, response negative
12-13	F′	Salvific revelation in Christ, response and participation positive
14	E′	Salvific revelation in terms of the incarnate Word, response and participation positive
15	D′	The testimony of John the Baptist
16	C′	Salvific revelation in terms of grace, response and participation positive
17	B′	Jesus Christ's role in salvation as grace and truth
18	A′	The only begotten Son the revealer.

The main theme in the prologue is the divine–human encounter in Christ with its negative and positive results.

In presenting the theme and its different aspects, the second half of the prologue (vv. 12-18) uses a vocabulary that is distinct from that of the first half (vv. 1-11), the two halves remaining, however, parallel to one another. This, of course, presupposes that the whole prologue deals with the incarnate Word, Jesus Christ.[35] The second half makes use of a vocabulary which reflects the concrete Christian experience, with the terms such as 'Jesus Christ', the 'only begotten', 'his glory', 'his fulness', 'grace and truth', 'the Father' and so on. These are certainly more concrete expressions of Christian experience than those found in the first half, such as the 'Word', 'God', 'All things', 'life', 'light', 'world' and so on, but nevertheless parallel to them. It is no wonder that the vocabulary of the second half is so distinctively Christian because it is precisely in the second half that the positive response to and participation in the Christ-event is expressed.

The Expressed Meaning
The expressed meaning of the passage of the prologue is that God revealed himself in Christ and received a two-fold response, negative and positive, and those who gave a positive response came to share in what Christ is. In one word, it is the description of the Christ-event as experienced by John. In presenting this Christ-event or God's self-manifestation in Christ, the evangelist distinguishes three different stages:

35. S. De Ausejo, 'Es un himno a Cristo el prologo de San Juan?', *EstBíb* 15 (1956), pp. 223-77; 381-427.

1. In the creation and cosmic religious traditions (vv. 5, 9-10);
2. In the life of Jesus (vv. 11-13);
3. In the life of the Church (vv. 14-16).

1. In the creation and non-Christian religious and cultural traditions (vv. 5, 9-10). In these verses John continues to meditate on the 'light' coming to humankind from the 'Logos'. The present tense 'shines' and the aorist 'did not receive it' seems to show that the evangelist is concerned both with the ever-present Logos as light or self-revelation of God in this world on the one hand, and the historical rejection of the incarnate Word on the other. This complex thought is expressed also in v. 9 where the light that enlightens every person was coming into the world. The 'was' in v. 9 probably looked back at the beginning of creation, but at once one thinks of the present reality of the incarnate Word and adds 'coming into the world'.

2. In the life of Jesus (vv. 11-13). The section 11-13 forms the transition passage in the prologue from the first part to the second part. Verse 11 with the aorist 'came' and the expression 'to his own' gives the impression that here John speaks exclusively of the historical coming of Jesus and his rejection by the Jews. But following the usual progressive style, it might be also a repetition and intensification of the thought that preceded. Verse 11 might therefore be speaking of the spiritual coming of the Logos to the world of human darkness, which closed its door, as it were, to the Logos who was so intimately akin to it. Now this coming of the Logos and its rejection on the part of the world was especially realized in the confrontation between Jesus and the Jews.

Verses 12-13 explicitly speak of the specific Christian encounter with the mystery of Christ, but on a more personal level. The words 'accepting Christ', 'believing in his name', 'were given the power', 'to become children of God', all are indications of this specific Christian response.

3. In the life of the Church (vv. 14, 16). In these verses the mystery of the divine–human encounter in Christ takes on the ecclesiological dimension. The 'we have seen' of v. 14 and the 'we have received' of v. 16 seem to be a reference to the apostolic witnesses, who are testifying to their ecclesial experience of the Christ-event, of course, based on their experience of the historical Jesus.

The Negative and Positive Response

As John presents the divine–human encounter in the three different stages, the response is two-fold: negative and positive. Writing out of his own ecclesial experience of Christ, naturally he is inclined to say that the response on his part and on the part of his church is positive. Note the phrases, 'to all who received him', 'who believe in his name' (v. 12), 'we have seen his glory' (v. 14) and 'we have all received from his fulness' (v. 16). Furthermore, when he thinks of the response given to the mystery of Christ as present in the creation at large and the non-Christian religious and cultural traditions, he is inclined to say that as a whole humanity failed to give an adequate response. Note the phrases, 'the darkness has not overcome it' (v. 5), 'the world knew him not' (v. 10) and 'his own received him not' (v. 11).

The Dhvani Meaning

The *dhvani* meaning in the prologue is open to numerous possibilities depending on the reader. Therefore it is not possible to pinpoint or formulate exactly the *dhvani* meaning of the prologue. However, I can suggest some of the lines of the *dhvani* meaning of the prologue.

The Experience of the Ineffable Mystery of God's Self-Revelation

The evangelist, through his poetic presentation of the Christ-event with the different stylistic and structural movements in developing its different aspects, creates an atmosphere in which the reader is invited to stand before the ineffable mystery of God's self-revelation to humankind. Every self-disclosure of God from the beginning of the world reflects and partakes of the One Word who is the complete self-utterance of God and will share in the Word's incarnation as well. The self-revelation of God existed from the beginning of the world in one form or other in nature and in the religious and cultural traditions of humankind.

This evokes an experience in the reader, an experience of awe, reverence and respect for the great mystery of God's all pervading self-manifestation. At the same time the reader is also invited to recognize and respond to the various experiences of God's self-manifestation.

The parallel presentation in two parts (vv. 1-11 and 2-18) with the generic and specifically Christian terminology respectively will evoke in its readers an experience of solidarity between their Christian experience and their religious experience outside Christianity.

The negative response that characterizes the first part of the prologue, where the presence of the mystery of Christ in the creation and the cosmic religions is stated, indicates that there is a real distinction between the cosmic religions and Christianity in the mode of the presence and operation of the mystery of Christ. Taken in its entirety, Christianity implies the full revelation of the mystery and the highest form of its visible mediation and of its presence in the world. While in non-Christian religions the mystery of Christ is imperfectly revealed and his grace imperfectly mediated, Christianity implies the full disclosure of the mystery and perfect mediation of grace. The parallelism between the specifically Christian experience of the mystery of Christ in the second part of the prologue (vv. 12-18) and the generic presentation of it in the first part (vv. 1-11) shows the 'latent Christianity' in the cosmic religions.[36] That would mark the unity between the cosmic religions and Christianity. At the same time, the negative response recorded in the first part in contrast to the positive response in the second part seems to mark the distinction between Christianity and the cosmic religions— namely, the imperfect character of the revelation and visible mediation of the mystery of Christ in the latter.

The Experience of Christianity as the Privileged Means of Salvation
The parallel and progressive presentation of the mystery of Christ in the prologue will evoke in the reader an experience of Christianity as the privileged means of salvation.

Christianity contains the mystery of Christ in the complete visibility of the eschatological community of salvation established by him, and is ideally destined by God for all, but is in reality not granted to all. In that sense, Christianity becomes the normative and privileged means of salvation. It is one thing to receive the Word which God speaks to human beings through the mediation of the seers who have heard it in the innermost of their being and transmitted it to others. It is another to hear the decisive Word which God speaks to human beings in his incarnate Son who is the fulness of his revelation.[37] It is one thing to come into contact with the mystery of Christ through the symbols and ritual practices that have through the centuries sustained and given visible form to humanity's response in faith. It is another to meet the same mystery

---

36. G. Thils, *Propos et problemes de la theologie des religions non-chretiennes* (Tournai, 1966), p. 194.
   37. Heb. 1.1-2; Jn 10.35-36.

represented in the sacramentality of the symbolic actions instituted by Christ himself and entrusted by him to the Church.

Reaching Out to the Fulness through Dialogue

The solidarity and unity between the Christian and cosmic revelations of the mystery of God will evoke in the reader a thirst for reaching out to the fulness of that God-experience through dialogue.

Though the mystery of Christ is directly and infallibly encountered in the sacramental sign of the Church, its actual efficacy remains dependent on each person's response in faith to God's gracious advance in Christ. And it is on this experiential level that John is presenting the mystery of Christ or the divine–human encounter in his prologue. Therefore, the negative and positive responses should not be taken exclusively as corresponding to the revelation of this mystery in the cosmic religions and Christianity respectively. As the non-Christian religions reflect a ray of the same truth or the mystery of Christ, the Light that enlightens all (cf. Vatican II, *Nostra Aetate*, no. 2), the two-fold response, negative and positive, is valid for both. Hence the actual attainment to the fulness of experience of the mystery of Christ remains something to be sought out and realized gradually. In this attempt the hindrances affect both Christianity and the cosmic religions. Hence our approach should be one of common attempt and searching to reach out to the fulness through mutual dialogue.

THE ROLE OF READING IN MULTICULTURAL EXEGESIS

Stephen Breck Reid

Growing up in a black working class family, my parents taught me to tell the truth and pursue the good life. Living now in a black middle class academic world, I find that the understanding of 'truth' and 'good life' seem in flux.

How do we find truth and the good life? Paul gives us a polarity or dialectic for a multi-cultural society. On the one hand in Christ there is no Jew or Gentile, male or female (Gal. 3.28). On the other hand, we have this treasure in earthen vessels (2 Cor. 4.7). We still have categories such as Gentile and Jew, male and female. A multi-cultural exegesis seeks a reading of Scripture and life that understands the truth of both of Paul's positions.

A cultural reading of texts has import for the society. Two impulses drive our examination. 1. the transformation of self-understanding in North America. The melting-pot myth lies dying on the North American horizon. Multi-cultural contexts present the modern reader in new ways every day. The encounter with these contexts engenders new construals of the form and content of truth.

2. The changing multi-cultural landscape requires an attentiveness to the metamorphosis of women's roles in North American cultures. Any serious look at interpretation and reading of Scripture must address the issue of truth. However, the issue of 'truth' must confront the issues of race, class and gender. This involves making use of the research on such matters in places where it may have a bearing on exegetical method.

The psalter opens with a promise of the good life, 'happy is...' In order to understand the good life in this age we must have a sense of the multi-cultural context we live in and the reading of Scripture that we share.

Psalm 1 does not refer directly to truth as its subject matter. Rather it describes the nature of the good life. However, the reader must posit the truth claims as valid in order to appreciate the description of the good life in the Psalm. Therefore we must address the issue of truth briefly. In that discussion we will contrast an idealist view of truth to an interactive/relational view of truth.

An Intrinsic Reading of Psalm 1

The psalm begins *'ašᵉrê* 'happy is...' Here we have the Hebrew counterpart of the good life. The term functions as a source for the strong exhortation.[1] The poet uses *'ašᵉrê* (happy is) instead of the more liturgical *bārûk* (blessed is).[2] 'In form, vocabulary and topic Psalm 1 is a creation of literary conventions found in Proverbs.'[3]

The structure of the passage alerts us to the theme of the psalm. It begins with a proverb. Then the psalm breaks into three interwoven parts marked by three *kî* (for, because) clauses (see vv. 2, 4b and 6). The first *kî* clause marks an adversative clause. The behavior in v. 2 contrasts that described in v. 1. The way of the wicked differs from the path of the righteous. The second *kî* clause also marks an adversative clause. The writer contrasts the righteous ones of v. 3 to the wicked one in v. 4. The third *kî* clause functions differently. Here in v. 6 the *kî* clause functions as a kind of result clause. Verse 6 provides the theological and ethical punch line. It is theological in the sense that the verse describes what God knows, and ethical in the sense that we must stand in proper stance to the knowledge of God.

The *kî* clauses are themselves connected by two phrases, *lo' kēn* 'It is not thus...' and *'al kēn* 'Thus...' The phrase *lo' kēn* 'It is not thus...' sets up the adversative *kî* clause. The phrase *'al kēn* 'Thus...' prepares us for the final *kî* clause which recounts the fate of the wicked.

Structurally, the writer has used these syntactical devices to make a simple point. We find life-giving communities and death-dealing communities. Only those who affiliate with the right community will find the good life.

1. E. Gerstenberger, *Psalms*, I (FOTL, 14; Grand Rapids: Eerdmans, 1988), p. 42.
2. C. Stuhlmueller, *Psalms*, I (Old Testament Message, 21; Wilmington, DE: Michael Glazier, 1983), p. 59.
3. J.L. Mays, 'The Place of the Torah-Psalms in the Psalter', *JBL* 106 (1987), p. 8.

The vocabulary of the psalm makes the same point. Happiness belongs to those who do not walk (*hālak*) in the counsel of the evil. Three points come to mind in this regard.

First, the Hebrew term walk involves more than the movement from one place to another. How one walks in Hebrew Scriptures shows an orientation to the world, a matter of behavior (See Isa. 33.15; Ps. 15.2; Prov. 6.12; 15.2; 30.29). How well this captures a piece of black experience. Ask almost any teenager: a walk is more than a walk, it is a statement. Do you shuffle or do you stride with power? Do you avoid eye contact or stare down all would-be adversaries?

Secondly, a walk involves a corporate side. How you walk tells the company you keep. I remember as a teenager wanting to walk like the quarterback of the football team. Now I question my teenage son where he learned this or that walk. We can clearly see that a walk remains a statement but also a reflection of one's community and commitments.

Thirdly, the company we keep reflects 'the words of our mouths and the meditations of our hearts' (Ps. 19.14). The person who strays with the men and women of evil counsel will never find the good life.

The psalmist continues to use language of orientation and ethics. This community will not prosper: 'the sinners shall not stand' (*'āmād*). The term *'āmād* means 'to stand' but also 'to take a stand' (See 2 Kgs 23.3; 2 Sam. 15.2). The third verb (*yāšāb*) 'to sit' does not often refer to an ethical position. For the Psalmist continues, 'and on the seat the scorners will not sit (*yāšāb*). The three verbs walk (*hālak*), stand (*'āmād*), and sit (*yāšāb*) often metaphorically refer to righteous behavior.[4]

The psalmist links the three negative verbs with three anti-communities through metaphors of orientation: counsel of the wicked, path of the sinners, and seat of the scornful. These are the scorners. Traditionally the books of Psalms and Proverbs describe the scorners (*lêṣîm*) as the opponents of the wise and righteous. Typically, in wisdom literature, the three nouns wicked (*rᵉšaʿîm*), sinners (*hattaʿîm*) and scorners (*lêṣîm*) denote those who behave out of tune with the righteous.[5] Path (*derek*) occurs 66 times in the Psalms. The term seems to come into vogue during the exilic period. The presence of the term primarily in Jeremiah and Ezekiel corroborates such a historical context.

---

4. L.G. Perdue, *Wisdom and Cult: A Critical Analysis of the Views of Cult in the Wisdom Literature of Israel and the Ancient Near East* (SBLDS, 30; Missoula, MT: Scholars Press, 1977), p. 270.

5. Perdue, *Wisdom and Cult*, p. 270.

In those occurrences in Jeremiah and Ezekiel we often find the term referring to ethical orientation.[6]

As noted above, then, we move to an adversative clause introduced with (*kî 'im*). 'Therefore, if a person delights in the *tôrāh* (law, teaching, instruction) of the LORD, and on God's *tôrāh* he/she meditates day and night, that one shall be like the tree planted on the banks of a stream which gives fruit and makes leaves' (Ps. 1.2-3).

The key verbs provide important reminders of themes for multi-cultural exegesis. The first verb, 'delight' (*ḥapaṣ*), connotes the 'joy' of religious experience. Here we see the way in which the encounter of the *tôrāh* and the believer gives forth a brilliant burst of positive religious experience. We might call it the Holy Ghost. The passage does not end with the religious experience. We also meditate on the *tôrāh*. We think. It is not enough for people of color to 'feel' in the *tôrāh*, we must reason in the *tôrāh* as well.

Here we see the combination of critical thinking and the religious experience that characterizes black church tradition from Sojourner Truth, to W.E.B. DuBois, Martin Luther King Jr and Malcolm X to this very day. The term 'meditate' (*hāgāh*) here describes thought, or critical reflection as a holistic enterprise. It can be a verbal thought in humans or the meditation of animals such as lions over prey (Isa. 31.4) or a hurt pigeon (38.14).[7]

Before we get caught in the euphoria of the potential good life, the psalmist returns us to the lot of the evil. 'As a result, the evil, therefore, will be like the chaff, which is driven by the wind. So, the wicked will not rise over the just (*mishpat*) nor the sinners over the congregation of the righteous *ba'dat ṣadîqîm*' (Ps. 1.5). The term congregation ('*ādāh*) occurs only three times in the psalter (Pss. 1.5; 74.2; 111.1). Ps. 111.1 provides the closest parallel to the use of the term in Psalm 1. Psalm 111 like Psalm 1 brings together praise and wisdom themes (Ps. 111.1, 10). The congregation of the upright are those who fear the LORD hence the persons with wisdom. There is an implicit recognition that some are foolish. The conflict of Psalm 1 finds an echo in Psalm 111. Likewise, Psalm 74, a prayer for deliverance likewise assumes some conflict. The congregation of course is on God's side, the psalmist clearly draws the enemies in this psalm (Ps. 74.4-11).

6. Stuhlmueller, *Psalms*, I, pp. 59-60.
7. Kraus, *Psalms 1–59* (Minneapolis: Augsburg, 1988), p. 117; Stuhlmueller, *Psalms*, I, p. 60.

The text reminds us of the competition between the just and the evil. The Psalms from the first to the last bring to us issues of advocacy. The beat for which we search comes from the divine metronome. The beat of Psalms captures this in the heartbeat of God. The heartbeat of God is praise and justice.

The good life has roots in the Torah. The good life finds expression in the congregation of the righteous. The conflict inherent in the use of the term congregation tells us something of the worldview of the Psalter. The conflict between the righteous and the wicked is played out in many ways. One of these is shame and social access.

This is a wisdom psalm. As such, questions about the nature of truth seem altogether reasonable. However, the Torah, not wisdom, constitutes the source of understanding the ways of the righteous.[8] The issue moves beyond the rugged individual seeking truth and the good life.[9] An intrinsic reading of this psalm indicates relational or associative knowledge and meditation on Torah as an instrument of truth leading to the good life. However, relational truth found in the context of the congregation, an issue discussed later, comes in the midst of conflict. Before we move any further in terms of the demonstration of a method we should ask what the definition of truth as relational truth does as we think about method.

I. Truth

A. Questions of the Form and Content of Truth
Women's ways of knowing and contemporary ways of reading. The work on women's epistemology provides helpful hermeneutical insights. The concept of relational truth resonates with feminist epistemology. Mary Field Belenky and a team of psychologists examined the ways women know and from that view of reality construe truth, knowledge and authority.[10] As they developed their model they also instructed us on how women might read texts. The ways of knowing presented by Belenky and her team in *Women's Ways of Knowing* parallel three

---

8. G.T. Sheppard, *Wisdom as a Hermeneutical Construct: A Study in the Sapientializing of the Old Testament* (BZAW, 151; Berlin: Walter de Gruyter, 1980), p. 138.

9. Kraus, *Psalms 1–59*, pp. 9 and 121.

10. M.F. Belenky *et al.*, *Women's Ways of Knowing: The Development of Self, Voice, and Mind* (New York: Basic Books, 1986), p. 3.

literary theories: formalist (rhetorical analysis), historical-genetic (everything else), and reader-response. First, there is *the Silent Knower*. However, those caught in silence seldom get to college and provide for us merely a reminder of how tenuous our voice remains. No literary theory parallels the silent knower.

The Received Knower. This is the first step beyond silence. Received knowers trust in words, as someone in my home congregation put it, 'simple Bible truths'. 'While received knowers can be very open to take in what others have to offer, they have little confidence in their own ability to speak. Believing that truth comes from others, they still their own voices to hear the voices of others.'[11]

Part of what the received knower contributes to the knowing and reading process is the affirmation of listening as a way of knowing, a way of relationship and power, a sociology of knowledge. For example:

1. Listening to friends: 'Young received knowers have a literal faith that they and their friends share exactly the same thoughts and experiences'.[12] Often their friends function as their voice.

2. Listening to authorities: '...those who think that they should *receive all* knowledge are more apt to think of authorities, not friends, as sources of truth'.[13] Friends become the voice of the received knower; authorities and experts become their power and truth. 'Received knowers are intolerant of ambiguity... They are literal.'[14] The received knower does not read a text until someone has told them what the text means ahead of time. Even though such an epistemology accents listening as a vehicle for reading and knowing on the one hand, on the other hand it so thoroughly sabotages the reading process that it has no easy counterpart in literary theory. Nonetheless, received knowers find a comfortable niche in either formalist or historical-genetic readings of others, that is to say, readings rendered by experts.

The Subjective Knower. For the subjective knower all truth is internal. All reading in this position becomes a proof testing for experience. In this case experience becomes the only hermeneutic. Now, theologically this presents us with the problem that community falls away and ultimately the only truth we have is the individual truth. Reader-response resonates with the subjective knower.

11. Belenky *et al.*, *Women's Ways of Knowing*, p. 37.
12. Belenky *et al.*, *Women's Ways of Knowing*, p. 38.
13. Belenky *et al.*, *Women's Ways of Knowing*, p. 38.
14. Belenky *et al.*, *Women's Ways of Knowing*, p. 42.

The Procedural Knower. Here we find the 'voice of reason' speaking in measured tones: 'knowing requires careful observation and analysis'.[15] The procedural knower no longer trusts the inner voice and experience. The procedural knower knows through 'method'. For some this gives a great sense of control. If one can just find the correct method of reading, everything else will take care of itself. Here methodological fundamentalism replaces a dynamic hermeneutic. Theologically we fall into works righteousness. We can save ourselves, that is to say, through our reading science and method.

At the same time the procedural knower values perspective, and talk. This is a far cry from either the silent or the subjective knower. Objectivity comes back. Objects, that is to say, the external world, comes to life in this way of knowing. Under the rubric of the procedural knower two categories emerge, the separate and the constructed knowers. These styles dominate the debate of hermeneutics and culture today.

The Separate Knower. The separate knowers use doubt creatively. 'Separate knowers are tough minded.'[16] Even ideas that 'feel right' meet with a hermeneutic of suspicion. In fact one could characterize separate knowers as those who organize their reading and knowledge through a hermeneutic of suspicion.

Separate knowers separate positions from persons; hence debate and argument do not threaten relationships for separate knowers. We can afford to listen to reason. '...many students become adept in playing the academic game of separate knowing.'[17] Separate knowers learn skills that allow them to protect themselves from the authorities in their lives. The reading becomes a public reading. The reading and voice become specialized. Here we find echoes of the procedural knower. The voice is a public and specialized voice but there is a loss of the inner voice, a loss of the self.

'Separate knowers' procedures for making meaning are strictly impersonal.'[18] The fear of self-interest looms so large that objectivity involves the ability to speak dispassionately. The separate knowers find the formalist and historical-genetic model of reading most rewarding. Like the received knowers they gravitate toward those models of

15. Belenky *et al.*, *Women's Ways of Knowing*, p. 94.
16. Belenky *et al.*, *Women's Ways of Knowing*, p. 104.
17. Belenky *et al.*, *Women's Ways of Knowing*, p. 107.
18. Belenky *et al.*, *Women's Ways of Knowing*, p. 109.

reading. Unlike the received knowers, separate knowers are active in the process of reading texts.

The separate knower model dominates the American scene. However, its hegemony faces strong critique. In 1987 Allan Bloom gave a clarion call to the impending death of American culture through the excesses of higher education. He claimed that the relativity of truth has become a moral dictum in higher education.

'The true believer is the real danger.'[19] This motto or dictum conflicts with the moral goal of education. 'Democratic education...wants and needs to produce men and women who have the tastes, knowledge and character supportive of a democratic regime.'[20] The suspicion of 'truth' extending beyond one's own demographics eats away at all democratic institutions. Each person or group has a truth but sociologically and philosophically it becomes difficult to think of truth that is more than cultural bias.

Bloom connects truth with ideas. We should begin with a receptivity to the 'Truth' and return to certain 'founding ideas'. As a Plato scholar, he expounds Plato's understanding of truth as ideas. Bloom understands truth and ideas as existing as external entities free from the interests of a given community. The recovery of founding ideas holds the potential to stem the present malaise. History provides the best vehicle for the recovery of our unity in the ideas of democracy.

Bloom reconstructs the present crisis by a particular construal of our intellectual history, in which the idea of openness replaced the ideas of founding, and history became an instrument of deconstruction. The pursuit of openness has lead to anomie.

A similar challenge comes from the 'left' as well as the 'right'. Itumelang Mosala launches a severe critique of black theology for this 'ghetto' approach to truth. 'Indeed, black theology is simply contextual theology, that is, white theology in black clothes.'[21]

E.D. Hirsch proposed that American higher education suffered from an epidemic of 'cultural illiteracy'. If the form of truth is the collection of founding ideas, then the content is cultural literacy. Bloom understands

19. A. Bloom, *The Closing of the American Mind: How Higher Education Has Failed Democracy and Impoverished the Souls of Today's Students* (New York: Simon & Schuster, 1987), p. 25.

20. Bloom, *The Closing of the American Mind*, p. 26.

21. I.J. Mosala, *Biblical Hermeneutics and Black Theology in South Africa* (Grand Rapids: Eerdmans, 1989), p. 22.

the form of truth and ideas as external. Hirsch describes an erosion of the teaching of the content that conveyed the truth and ideas of Western civilization. Bloom argues on behalf of a separated knower. Connected knowers and constructive knowers find such a position locked in the futility of the Enlightenment. Bloom and Hirsch set off a debate about the future of higher education. Henry Louis Gates Jr, among others, argues that we must not allow the views of Bloom and Hirsch to squelch new voices in the academy. The debate reflects on the nature of a multi-cultural approach. They correctly point to a need for intellectual identity formation in higher education. But I would argue that the way forward is not in losing the Euro-American voice but rather letting new voices into the chorus of higher education.

The Connected Knower. 'Connected knowers begin with an interest in the facts of other people's lives, but they gradually shift the focus to the people's ways of thinking.'[22] As the feminist writer Susan Griffin once said, 'I can think like a man or I can think like a woman'. 'Connected knowers learn through empathy.'[23] The text can be the recipient of this empathy. 'Connected knowers try to understand a text by imagining themselves into the author's head.'[24]

Three characteristics seem to be part of the connected knower's epistemology: 1. sharing small truths, 2. refusing to judge ('Connected knowing requires forbearance'[25]), and 3. collaborating in groups committed to connected knowing. The operative hermeneutic is an egalitarian one. 'Authority in connected knowing rests not on power or status or certification but on commonality of experience.'[26] Further it is also a communal hermeneutic. Connected knowers read in groups. 'Members of connected groups engage in collaborative explorations.'[27]

The Constructed Knower. Constructed knowers integrate the other ways of knowing. In order to do this they must move beyond the given structures.[28] They have both an external and internal world; both voices receive a listening heart and a critical eye. As such they exhibit a high

22. Belenky *et al.*, *Women's Ways of Knowing*, p. 115.
23. Belenky *et al.*, *Women's Ways of Knowing*, p. 115.
24. Belenky *et al.*, *Women's Ways of Knowing*, p. 121.
25. Belenky *et al.*, *Women's Ways of Knowing*, p. 117.
26. Belenky *et al.*, *Women's Ways of Knowing*, p. 118.
27. Belenky *et al.*, *Women's Ways of Knowing*, p. 119.
28. Belenky *et al.*, *Women's Ways of Knowing*, p. 140.

tolerance for ambiguity and internal contradiction.[29]

The constructed knower takes responsibility for knowledge. 'All knowledge is constructed, and the knower is an intimate part of the known.'[30]

'Constructivists establish a communion with what they are trying to understand.'[31] They interact with the objects of inquiry, as such they are passionate knowers. Passion indicates the way that interaction feeds this style of knowing. Another mode of interaction is conversation which plays an important role for the constructivist.[32]

This interaction involves the new and different. 'Constructivist women need and value attentive strangers as well as understanding friends and colleagues.'[33] The passion and interaction construct a life as well as knowledge. Caring becomes an organizing principle. The mooring for this is commitment and action.

The form of truth that we see here is a relational truth. That truth has implications for how we read the text. 1. When we read as constructivists, we encounter texts having an internal and external life; for this reason we do an intrinsic and extrinsic reading simultaneously. By so doing we hear our voice and The Voice. 2. Further, all reading and knowledge happens in the context of community and relationships (Gilligan). The community provides the place for the question-posing and moral conflict that generates fresh reading of texts and life.

Three styles of reading predominate current biblical studies. Formalist: the form and content are so inextricably bound with meaning that the words—read literary form—drives the reading process. Hence the name formalist. 'The first requirement, they argue, is to "understand the text, as text"'.[34] In literary criticism these were the New Critics, a moribund position already in 1957.[35] Literary critics of the Bible that focus on the final form of the text and bracket the historical questions represent this sensibility.

29. Belenky *et al.*, *Women's Ways of Knowing*, p. 137.

30. Belenky *et al.*, *Women's Ways of Knowing*, p. 137.

31. Belenky *et al.*, *Women's Ways of Knowing*, p. 143.

32. Belenky *et al.*, *Women's Ways of Knowing*, p. 144.

33. Belenky *et al.*, *Women's Ways of Knowing*, p. 146.

34. L.M. Poland, *Literary Criticism and Biblical Hermeneutics* (AAR Academy Series, 48; Chico, CA: Scholars Press, 1985), p. 2.

35. F. Lentricchia, *After the New Criticism* (Chicago: University of Chicago Press, 1980), p. 4.

Historical-genetic: The assumption here says that the reconstruction of the language event through historical, grammatical, psychological and sociological analysis enables the modern reader to reexperience the mental processes of the text's author. Schleiermacher put this forth powerfully in the nineteenth century and has continued to dominate the biblical scene until recently.[36]

Reader-Response: Dissatisfied with the isolation of the reader from the process of meaning-making, Stanley Fish among others began reader-response criticism. This group is called the New Readers.

Constructed Knowers move on to cultural criticism. The conversation involves the text and the community. We have to think about the content of truth. I am proposing that we read as connected and constructed knowers.

Bloom raises a separate knower view of truth. As such a formalist or historico-genetic model of exegesis predominates. (However, even separate knowers, such as Wellhausen, were not unaffected. See the article by John Barton.) Henry Louis Gates Jr, who argues for a multi-cultural reading of texts, argues for a constructed or connected knower view of truth. Reader-response criticism fits such a model. Cultural exegesis and cultural criticism proceed from a connected/constructed knower. As such, they require a self-consciousness about what the reader brings and what the text brings as independent but related entities. Therefore, the literary positions of formalism and reader-response will be natural interpretative rubrics. Furthermore, the historical-genetic approach also reminds the reader of the otherness of the text. With all this in mind the person doing cultural exegesis will use all three literary theories. This will involve three steps. The first will be an intrinsic reading following the concerns of the formalist literary critics. Second, the reader will use traditional historical-genetic reconstruction as an extrinsic reading. Finally, there must be a reader-response extrinsic reading. The method of multi-cultural exegesis finds resonance in the interpretative clues of the Hebrew Bible itself. Psalm 1 introduces the reader of the Psalter to the rubrics for reading what follows.[37] As we understand the rubrics for reading the Psalter we learn something about multi-cultural exegesis.

36. R.E. Palmer, *Hermeneutics* (Northwestern University Studies in Phenomenology and Existential Philosophy; Evanston, IL: Northwestern University Press, 1969), p. 86.

37. J.C. McCann, *A Theological Introduction to the Book of Psalms* (Nashville: Abingdon, 1993), pp. 32-40.

B. *An Alternative Form: Relational Truth*

We have already explored and found wanting Bloom's disembodied and disinterested form of 'truth'. Rather the Psalter introduced by Psalm 1 proposes an understanding of relational truth. We find at least two resources to inform our conversation on method and relational truth: symbolic interaction and feminist psychology. As such, I choose to emphasize the connected knower and the constructed knower as the models to inform a style of reading. For the time being we will focus on the latter.

C. *An Alternative Content of Truth: Multi-Cultural*

If the form of truth we address is relational, then the content of that truth must be faithful to the diversity of the community, in our case North America. We do not forget the 'founding ideas'. Just as the constructivist uses previous styles of knowledge, so the multicultural reader includes the 'founding ideas'. African-American scholars have addressed the cultural issues involved in exegesis. Euro-American scholars have been much more quiet on the subject. Both groups have tried to provide exegetical material for particular audiences hoping for some cross fertilizing. Both of these positions come from the present context of higher education that tacitly proposes that one's exegesis and subsequent theology are so culturally conditioned that one cannot write theology or do exegesis that broadly speaks to North American culture. There is the unspoken reservation that if it were possible to do multi-cultural exegesis it would involve too much work or other retooling. This work provides an experiment in multi-cultural exegesis. One of the precursors of reader-response criticism, I.A. Richards, points out that one of the errors for reading stems from a reader's lack of reading other works. Therefore the reader cannot understand the conversation a given text. Analogously, a significant amount of error in reading in contemporary biblical studies stems from our lack of reading in non-Euro-American literature.

D. *The Particulars of Method*

The resources for this task are much closer to hand than we might think. First, *Sachkritik* of Bultmann and dialectical theology provides an interesting beginning point. Secondly, the philosophical and theological underpinnings of Brevard Childs's canon criticism and James Sanders's canonical criticism enable us to see the appropriateness of reading the text in the context of other texts. For Childs in particular, the relevant texts that we read includes church interpretation of the biblical text.

First, we move in a balanced way through the triangle but not necessarily in a linear fashion. The exegetical method I propose is quite simple. It involves the intrinsic reading of the text which gives us the basic subject matter. The reader will soon discover that I am very eclectic about the method of intrinsic reading. The text itself gives you the clues for the intrinsic reading. Intrinsic reading, used here in a narrow definition, refers to the formalist reading of the text. One extrinsic reading involves reconstructing the implied reader and speaker/author. Here we use the historical-genetic model. However, we do this with a particular eye to matters of symbolic interaction, or manipulation and power relationships. For indeed our method proceeds with a social theory.

A second extrinsic reading takes over after determining the subject matter of the text: we then seek conversation partners on that subject matter. Childs in his commentary on Exodus provides a helpful model, for his history of interpretation provides us a history of reader response. This extrinsic reading gives us an opportunity to analyse the ideologies of reader responses in Judaism and Christianity.

A third extrinsic reading involves how this subject matter finds expression in a multi-cultural world. However, given the vast universe of art, music and literature one needs to have some constraints. We will focus on the multi-cultural context of North America. Even within that context we will have limits. In order to fully understand why these limits are necessary, let us look at some racial and ethnic myths that often plague our desire for multi-cultural exegesis. It is a myth to think that all white people are the same. Euro-American heritage is not a lump out of the melting pot. All yellow people are the same. It is likewise fallacious to maintain that Asian culture is a monolith of Eastern religions. All brown people are not the same. The heritage of Latin Americans is sufficiently variegated to warrant attention. I have heard these myths not from garden variety bigots, rather on the contrary, from well-meaning academics frustrated by the complexity of a multi-cultural world but nonetheless committed to it. Here I have focused on African-American literature but one might add to the mix Mexican-American literature.

Method in Practice
Extrinsic Reading: History of Reader Response

The history of the reader response for the purposes of this discussion has three stages. The first stage examines the location of the psalm in the

Psalter. Related to this might be the location of the text in the canon of the Hebrew Bible. The second stage investigates the response to the text or theme in the New Testament and Judaism in the Greco-Roman era. The third stage jumps to the reconstrual of the text in the light of contemporary literature/culture.

A. *Extrinsic Reading: The Place of Psalm 1 in the Shape of the Psalter*

Psalm 1 provides an introduction to the entire Psalter. It bears no superscription, which is unusual. Further, we have evidence that at one time Psalm 2 began the Psalter (see Acts 13.33).[38] In fact it sets a tone for the Psalter, a tone of torah piety.[39] If one takes Psalms 1–2 together then the reader begins with the Torah and the king as the emblems of proper relationship. The tone will bring to the attention of the reader or hearer the importance of community as well as the reality of conflict with some sort of enemy. The psalm sets out a two way understanding of the world.[40] Therefore we begin to understand multi-cultural exegesis with the primer of reading, the beginning of the Psalter.

B. *Extrinsic Reading: Judaism and New Testament*

The New Testament plays on this psalm in two different emphases. a. Paul quotes a selection of this Psalm in the book of Romans (7.22). Traditional Christian interpretation claims that the individual cannot accomplish the tasks set out in the Psalms, therefore Christ must have done all this for us.[41] b. As noted above, the two way (Ps. 1.6) theme has similarities with the Sermon on the Mount (Mt. 7.13-14) and Hellenistic Judaism.[42]

If we had more time we could explore profitably how this theme finds expression in terms of love and knowledge in Judaism and Christianity.

C. *Extrinsic Reading: Contemporary Literature*

The themes of congregation and community burst forth from the pages even before the novel *Beloved* begins. The novel portrays a type of relational truth. Morrison quotes Rom. 9.25, 'I will call them my people

---

38. J.T. Willis, 'Psalm 1—An Entity', *ZAW* 91 (1979), pp. 381-401.

39. G.H. Wilson, *The Editing of the Hebrew Psalter* (SBLDS, 76; Chico, CA: Scholars Press, 1985), pp. 206-207.

40. P.C. Craigie, *Psalms 1–50*, (WBC, 19; Dallas: Word Books, 1983), p. 61; Kraus, *Psalms 1–59*, p. 121.

41. Kraus, *Psalms 1–59*, p. 121.

42. Craigie, *Psalms 1–50*, p. 61.

which were not my people, and her beloved which was not beloved'.[43]
The characters in the novel *Beloved* are Baby Suggs the grandmother,
Sethe the mother, Denver her daughter, Howard and Buglar the run-
away sons, Halle Suggs (Sethe's husband?), Paul Garner and Beloved.
The characters move between 'Sweet Home' which was not a Sweet
Home but the location of slavery in the South.

The role of the congregation of righteousness, as central, points to the
nature of human existence. Sethe did not create the slave experience
that provided the context for her behavior. Therefore it seems reasonable that rugged individualism presents an inadequate defense against
structural evil and oppression. She did not get herself into slavery and
she could not get herself out.

We see the role of the congregation in three scenes. The congregation is
present at the loss of her children. They are there when she tries to kill
them rather than allow them to return to slavery. The congregation is
there when Beloved consumes Sethe's life. The congregation is there
when the daughter Denver asks for help in sending away Beloved, the
demon.

Conclusion

The test of an approach to the text is exegesis. Luther and Bultmann
both argued that their style of *Sachkritik* found its earliest expression in
the text. Likewise I will argue for relational understanding of truth in
Scripture. A look at Psalms, in particular Psalm 1, makes clear a pre-
occupation with truth in relational context.

We balance authorial, affective as well as formalist school. These
methods are surrounded by symbolic interaction and conflict theory.
The goal is not to find the wrong but to interact and talk.

43. See also Hos. 2.23.

BEFORE THE TEXT AND AFTER: THE SCANDINAVIAN SCHOOL AND THE FORMATION OF SCRIPTURE

Roger Syren

At a congress convened to contemplate the impact of various cultural surroundings on the understanding of biblical texts and stories, it must be both right and timely also to ask questions about cultural dependencies in biblical studies generally and biblical scholarship specifically. Surely, ideas, theories, 'schools' and so on in this field must be somehow related to a cultural setting, but is it possible to trace these relationships immediately to the surrounding environment? I am not sure. First, biblical scholarship was born and bred on European soil, and this means that European culture was common ground for the scholars themselves. Secondly, biblical scholars traditionally had a very broad education and were often equally at home in at least one other field apart from the Bible. This comes to light in a preference for importing ideas and philosophies of the day into the Bible, reading 'in' rather than 'out'. Thereby they seem to have abstracted more or less from their own background.

In the case of the 'Scandinavian school', I shall ask in this paper whether the attribute stands for anything discernible in Scandinavian culture or not. I do this on the explicit request of the congress organizer, and I start from a broad look on Scandinavia from a cultural aspect.

1. Scandinavia—A Cultural Entity

Geographically as well as historically, the countries of the Scandinavian peninsula, together with Denmark and Finland south and east of it, are traditionally seen as one entity, situated as they are on the northern fringes of Europe. Their unity is based and upheld on a common history and culture as well as a common language; that is, Swedish, Norwegian and Danish form one family of Northern Germanic, and one language or dialect is easily understood by speakers of the other two, at least after some practice or a few lines of reading. Iceland is situated in the Atlantic Ocean at a far distance from Scandinavia, but it belongs to the same cultural sphere since its population is Scandinavian. Finland, although its majority population, the Finns proper, are of non-Scandinavian descent, and although the Finnish language belongs to a totally different type altogether, the Finnish–Ugric group, has a long common history with Sweden of which it was a province until 1809. In that year it came under Russian sovereignty and remained so until 1917 when it gained independence. Denmark and Norway likewise share a common history and belonged together until 1814 when Norway was united with Sweden under a common sovereign, the King of Sweden. In 1905 that union was dissolved and Norway became an independent monarchy. Further, Finland has a minority of almost 300,000 Swedish speakers, guaranteed equal rights by the Finnish constitution, which also acknowledges Swedish as an official language alongside Finnish. The Laps or the Saamis, living in an area which covers the northernmost parts of Norway, Sweden and Finland, form the one and only ethnic minority within the boundaries of the Scandinavian area (apart from modern immigrants). They actually represent the original inhabitants of large sections of the area, gradually pushed northwards by subsequent waves of colonization from the south and by the development of dominating central forces. Toponyms in the southern parts still preserve reminiscences of their age-old presence there.

Ever since Christian missionaries first arrived to the central regions of Scandinavia in the ninth and tenth centuries, it has had close contacts culturally and politically, as well as religiously, with Germany and the European continent. Germany as the central area of influence was brought even more to the fore after the Lutheran reformation and the emergence of national Lutheran churches in the sixteenth century. All countries of Scandinavia adopted the Lutheran faith within the time span of less than a century. It is no wonder, then, that Scandinavian biblical scholarship should be dominated by a strong German influence, which articulates itself in the sort of questions asked and the methods chosen. Of course this is due also to the eminent position taken by German scholarship universally in this area, from whatever direction one happens to look towards Germany, but for Scandinavia the German impact is doubly in force. Indeed, an Eastern influence was able to make any lasting inroads in eastern Finland only. The Finnish national epos,

Kalevala, in itself a nineteenth-century compilation of age-old poems, chants and charms, reveals a Christian influence at least in the figure of Marjatta, a Finnish diminutive of 'Maria' or 'Mary'. In Poem 50 she is 'a man-shy youngest child' and becomes a virgin mother by picking the 'puolukka', 'whortleberry':

> I am neither an unmarried man's nor a married man's. I went to the rise for a berry, to pick a red whortleberry; I took the berry with pleasure, next put it on my tongue. It went into my throat, then slipped into my belly. From that I swelled up, from that I got full, from that I got pregnant.[1]

This very broad and brief survey of what characterizes Scandinavian culture would suggest that the 'cultural conditioning' of 'the Scandinavian School' is either to be sought in the particular Scandinavian environment and history, or it could in some way reflect the powerful German impact on that environment and history. A third possibility is that both factors are at work.

What Makes the 'Scandinavian' School Scandinavian?

Considering the strong German influence, to speak of a distinctly Scandinavian school in biblical studies in the first place is in itself a cultural demarcation. In the common usage of the term, the term has a rather limited coverage, denoting a propensity for emphasizing *oral transmission* as crucial when it comes to understanding the formation of the Bible. For an adequate appreciation of the content of the biblical literature, on the other hand, as it has come down to us, the idea of *divine kingship* as part and parcel of a common religious ideology in the ancient Near East is central to this school of thought. In a recent publication, *A Dictionary of Biblical Interpretation*,[2] George W. Anderson of Cambridge in Britain, a real *connoisseur*, writes on 'Scandinavian Old Testament Scholarship'. In his application, the term 'Scandinavian scholarship' refers to distinct group of scholars whose most renowned representatives are Pedersen in Copenhagen, Mowinckel in Oslo and Engnell in Uppsala. He begins with Johannes Pedersen to whom the two latter readily admitted their debt. Pedersen, in his turn inspired and

---

1. E. Lonnroth and P. Magoun (trans.), *The Kalevala or Poems of the Kaleva District* (Cambridge, MA: Harvard University Press, 1963).

2. G.W. Anderson, *A Dictionary of Biblical Interpretation* (London and Philadelphia: SCM Press and Trinity Press International, 1990), pp. 609-13.

influenced by another Dane, the anthropologist V. Gronbech, wrote an imposing work, *Israel: Its Life and Culture* in four volumes (1st edn 1920) in which he attached a very great importance to the psychological and mental side of the Israelite conception of humanity and human ways of thinking, allegedly very different from the modern. The work, as indicated, was greatly to influence subsequent Scandinavian studies.

Anderson's application of the term is in line with the common understanding of it, including mine, and in order to give a profile to it I shall give a presentation of Ivan Engnell, the founder and main representative of the 'Uppsala' (broadly synonymous with 'Scandinavian' in this context) school, and Sigmund Mowinckel. I do this from two angles: first their view of the formation of the Old Testament literature in general; secondly, their distinct way of handling Isaiah, the text, his person and his message. Thirdly, I turn my attention to H.S. Nyberg and his study on Hosea as another (besides Pedersen) major source of influence on Engnell in particular. Finally, I return to the question of the cultural setting of the Scandinavian school.

3. Engnell's and Mowinckel's Understanding of the Formation of the Old Testament

Ivan Engnell (d. 1964) did not actually publish much, and although his theories about the growth of the Old Testament are laid out quite extensively in his book *Gamla Testamentet: En traditionshistorisk inledning* (Uppsala, 1945), his presentation is in broad terms only and several questions remain open. The book was published by a Church of Sweden publisher and is rather popular in nature. Moreover, he intended it as the first part of a larger work; his plans for a second part, in spite of his promises in the foreword, were never realized.

Engnell's work may be influenced and inspired by Pedersen, but it also quite explicitly represents a reaction against the German schools, and Wellhausen in particular, whose conclusions were in Engnell's opinion based on a number of anachronistic conceptions and should be abandoned altogether. Other approaches, such as Gunkel's form criticism, receive a much more favourable comment, although form criticism, too, should be applied only with caution. The religio-historical method, in contrast, was approved of and acclaimed since it allows for due consideration of the various aspects of Israelite and Near Eastern religious thinking, and especially the cultic pattern common to them all.

Engnell explicitly distanced himself from Wellhausen's conception of the development of Old Testament religion.

According to Engnell, the key to understanding the emergence of the Old Testament literature and the basic principle in its formation was oral transmission. Oral transmission was a main characteristic of the Near Eastern cultures, and accordingly it should be applied to the Old Testament as well. Narratives and tales were handed down within narrow circles and schools, and thus passed on to ensuing generations. Only against this background is it possible to understand at all how and why the Old Testament literature survived the severest of crises, the exile. There had never been any redactors, only groups of traditionalists, differently termed depending on the *genre* of material under their supervision: scribes for wisdom literature, priests and singers for the Psalms and the Law, disciples of prophets for the prophetic literature (referring to Isa. 8.16). The eventual commission into writing of these bunches of traditions was no revolutionary process, merely a sign that people had ceased to revere the spoken word in the context of a general crisis in Israel's respect for its old traditions in general, in exilic and post-exilic times. The agent in this process might have been none other than the last one in the chain of oral traditionalists. He was certainly no 'theologian' in his own right: what he did was merely to deliver as faithfully as he possibly could the received material.

Engnell chided the German literary critics for not having appreciated the true nature of the Hebrew mind—and he reverted to Pedersen for support at this point. Also they did not duly consider the peculiarities of the Old Testament narrative style in its various dimensions. But the literary critics chosen as targets for his attack were not any famous German names, but two fellow Scandinavians, Aage Bentzen and E. Hammershaimb, both of Denmark, who had shortly before written on the subject. On the other hand, he sought support from H.S. Nyberg, the famous orientalist whose opinion on the Pentateuch as a 'compilation of traditions from different periods' he recommended. Nyberg had assigned a date not later than the period of the Monarchy to the constituent elements of the Pentateuch. But Engnell deemed that there had never been any Pentateuch as we perceive of it, but instead a sharp distinction should be made between Deuteronomy and the pre-ceeding four books, the 'Tetrateuch'. In his view, Deuteronomy intro-duced the Deuteronomistic work as its first section. The Tetrateuch, in turn, was made up of diversified materials, which he designated

'narrative' and 'law'. The kernel and the nucleus from which it all had
started was Exodus 1–15, the cultic legend of the *pesaḥ* (an idea borrowed, again, from Pedersen[3]), around which the bulk of the other
material had been build up. The one responsible for the last stage of the
transmission and also for its commission to writing he called 'P'. 'P'
was, again, only a reproducer, not a producer of original ideas.

Although it is possible, and indeed customary, nowadays to refute
most of Engnell's arguments and conclusions, one should take seriously
his objections to the routines of literary criticism. And though his considerations seem to have had little effect on main stream scholarship, he
exerted influence for a time at least through a number of successful
pupils, among them Helmer Ringgren in Uppsala and the late Gösta
Ahlström in Chicago, who both, however, later distanced themselves
from Engnell. And although time may have made many of Engnell's
considerations obsolete—many were in fact neither original nor conclusive—it is nevertheless interesting to note in his arguing elements which
still deserve attention, and perhaps more so today than a decade ago. At
the present time, voices are raised against the simplifications of the
literary-critical analytical approach, with its sometimes vaguely and
weakly founded separations and isolations of supposedly detached
elements. These new voices who emphasize the synthesis of the text in
all its dimensions, formal, stylistic, artistic and the rest, may surprisingly
enough find some common ground with Engnell, although he of course
looked upon the text as a compound and shared with the literary critics
their interest in the prehistory of the extant text, rather than its final
appearance. Several of his arguments against the source-critical school
are similar to those brought forward by representatives of the synthetic
approach, and his references to 'oral transmission' would only have to
be exchanged for the 'artistic skill of the author' or the like in order to
serve the new and different purpose. All in all, one perceives behind
Engnell's arguing a conscientious, not to say an obstinate, effort to find
arguments of his own to underline his case.

Sigmund Mowinckel, by far the most well-known Scandinavian biblical scholar, is renowned for his *Psalmenstudien* in 6 volumes, and his
hypothesis, built on Babylonian evidence, about an annual New Year
Festival. In a little book called *How the Old Testament came into Being*
(*Hvordan det Gamle Testamentet er blitt til*, Oslo, 1934), which

---

3.   J. Pederson, 'Passahfest und Passahlegende', *ZAW* 52 (1934), pp. 161-75.

contained a number of lectures in popular form, he had come out firmly in support of the classical source hypothesis, allocating to J, E and P their own role in the formation of the Pentateuch and the designation JE given to the redactor who fused together the works of J and E respectively. As earlier in his *Psalmenstudien (I–IV)*, he paid much attention to questions of form, and distinguished between such *Gattungen* as prophetical legend, prophetical biography, entertainment literature (which was his designation for Job, Ruth and Esther), and so on. In a memorial volume on the centenary of Mowinckel's birth,[4] Magne Saebo, Mowinckel's fellow Norwegian, characterizes Mowinckel's position concerning the literary-critical school as one of shifting attitudes, and he describes it as 'a continuity with creative renewal'. By this is evidently meant Mowinckel's combination of methods, literary, form-historical and traditio-historical. In *The Disciples of Isaiah* (1926 on Micah, Zephaniah, Nahum and Habakkuk), Mowinckel spoke of 'circles of disciples' and 'schools' rather than 'redactors', and Saebo finds that Mowinckel increasingly employed the terminology of the traditio-historical school. But he never gave up literary criticism as a tool for retrieving the history of texts and traditions. Moreover, in his study *Prophecy and Tradition* (1946), he levelled severe criticism at Engnell for a very static conception of 'tradition'. In Mowinckel's view, 'tradition' should be thought of as a dynamic process and a real history. His search was for a 'historical understanding of the Testament', hence his methodical flexibility. On the relationship between Mowinckel and the Uppsala school in general, Helmer Ringgren points out in the same memorial volume that the discussion between Mowinckel and the Uppsala school mostly concerned details, while their general outlook was similar.[5] However, at one point they took definitely different positions, namely concerning the character of Israelite kingship and Messianism. Mowinckel understood it in eschatological terms and in connection with his idea of the Enthronement Festival (*Han som kommer*, 1951, ET *He That Cometh*, 1956); Engnell, on the other hand, thought in terms of an elaboration of the ideological concept of divine kingship (*Studies in Divine Kingship in the Ancient Near East*, 1943).

If Engnell's traditio-historical approach came in *reaction* against the

---

4. M. Saebo, 'Sigmund Mowinckel in his Relation to the Literary Critical School', in H.M. Barstad and M. Ottosson (eds.), *The Life and Work of Sigmund Mowinckel*, *SJOT* 2 (1988), p. 35.

5. H. Ringgren, 'Mowinckel and the Uppsala School', *SJOT* 2 (1988), p. 41.

German literary school, one could say that Mowinckel *supplemented* it: he recognized its potentials but also its shortcomings. The same is largely true also of Mowinckel's *Psalmenstudien* in which he elaborated on the forms of the Psalms, and added a number of *Gattungen* to those worked out by Gunkel.

4. *Engnell and Mowinckel on Isaiah*

Mowinckel published a popular study on Isaiah in 1949, part of a series on 'Great Men of Religion'. He described in it the setting of the calling of Isaiah as occurring during the great Festival of the New Year in 742 or 741. This Festival, also celebrated as the Day of Yahweh, had its roots in Canaanite fertility rites heralding the advent of the rainy season and Nature's revival. On this occasion, Yahweh was greeted as mighty Creator, Ruler and King, in a cultic representation of his ascent to the throne. The great festive procession had reached the Temple on the seventh day of the Feast, the sacrifice was completed and the sacrificial meal under way as Isaiah, prostrating himself in prayer, received a vision, and was told about his mission. His message got its pregnancy from the impending threats against Israel's future. Some years earlier, in 745, Tukulti-apil-esjarra III had gained access to the throne in Assyria and the political situation had turned precarious. Mowinckel also pointed to the internal tensions in Judah, with huge rifts between landowners and merchants in the capital and the peasants and half-nomads in the rural areas and on the borders. The old tribal organization and inherited moral values were in decline. The splendour and wealth spent on the cult was not matched by any corresponding esteem of moral standards and righteousness in the social sphere, although that was the essence of what the covenant between Yahweh and Israel required. In Mowinckel's view, Isaiah's message was clearly one of doom, but he was also willing to ascribe to the original prophet the promise about the returning 'rest'. The 'rest' was originally to be equated with Judah in its entirety, but later the prophet did change his mind to let it include only a tiny minority. Mowinckel made a clear distinction between the cultic prophets, *nebi'im*, organized in special classes or groups, and other prophets who like Amos did not belong in such professional groups. Isaiah's, Hoseah's Jeremiah's and others' association with the cult, however, was by that time only formal. At certain festivals they performed their task of representing the godhead in a way contrary to expectation, by proclaiming what was not prescribed in the liturgy, nor desired by the audience: they preached doom and gloom in stead of salvation and a bright future.

For his part, Engnell again voiced harsh criticism against the literary cliche concerning what a prophet of doom must or must not proclaim, what is original and what is conversely considered secondary. Along with Pedersen and Mowinckel he found an institution of prophets in Israel attached to the Temple, in the pattern of common Near Eastern and Canaanite practices. Such circles of prophets associated with the cult developed a formulaic style which allowed for a constant interchange between periods of need and periods of bloom, and accordingly, over an extended period of time, they would proclaim judgment as well as salvation. Any literary-critical dissolution of such complexities would result in the destruction of the transmitted pattern. The hallmarks of the specifically prophetic style were change of speaking subject (the prophet identifying himself completely with Yahweh and speaking in I-me form), clairvoyance with circumlocutions and evasive language in general, symbolic actions, and also the use of the perfect, in this context categorized as 'prophetic perfects', the *incipit* 'Thus says the Lord (*āmar yaweh*):' and the formulas, frequently at the end of the oracle, and so on.

In Engnell's perception, ch. 6 constituted a program in which the very burden of Isaiah's message was given in concentration. The designation 'the rest' refers to none other than the prophet's disciples who are to form the kernel of the new Israel. The theme of the surviving 'rest' was certainly one integral to Isaiah's message from the outset, and there is no way of tracing any evolutionary stages in that message from this respect at least.

Thus, Mowinckel and Engnell agreed that Isaiah's message contained doom as well as salvation, although Engnell underlined that particular point more strongly. On other points they disagreed, and Engnell in fact criticised Mowinckel for not grasping the true nature of Old Testament prophecy, and its psychological side in particular, and also for being much too influenced by literary (i.e. source) criticism. On the other hand, Mowinckel did not accept Engnell's theory on the introduction from Canaanite religion into Israel of the idea of divine kingship, and its influence on Israelite religion. Mowinckel's criticism was certainly justified along with R. de Vaux[6] and Gerhard von Rad,[7] one should note

6. R. de Vaux, *Ancient Israel: Its Life and Institutions* (London: Darton, Longman & Todd, 1962), p. 112.

7. G. von Rad, *Theologie des Alten Testaments*, I (Edinburgh: Oliver & Boyd, 1965), p. 318.

the differences in this respect between the various Oriental cultures. Along with Abraham Heschel,[8] one would expect in the prophets some reflections of that idea. In de Vaux's words, 'they accuse the kings of many crimes, but never of claiming divinity'. Engnell considered the composition of the 'book' of Isaiah to be wrongly understood by the literary critics; in reality it was to be seen as built around a set of traditions, defined as three parts or collections which stemmed from different circles of transmitters. His view that the so called *Ebed Yahweh* songs or poems form integral parts of their surroundings and should be interpreted in the light of their context is, on balance, reverberated by a modern Scandinavian scholar, Tryggve Mettinger of Sweden, who carries the idea further to deny altogether the existence of any separable Songs.[9]

5. *H.S. Nyberg's Studien zum Hoseabuche*

Henrik Samuel Nyberg was the son of a Minister in the Church of Sweden and a prodigy showing an early talent for Latin and languages in general. Although his main field was to become Persian studies, he also wrote a Hebrew Grammar and a study on Hosea, published in 1935. In this study expressed a very high appreciation of the reliability of the Hebrew (Masoretic) text, and this at a time when interferences with the shape of that text had become habitual—in Nyberg's view really without any valid motivation, and often resting merely on the scholar's personal opinion articulated in a self-sufficient *Ich lese*, 'I read!' The basis for the habitual textual emendations is the tacit assumption that the Old Testament emerged as a literary work, that its creators were *Schriftsteller* and its sources written—furthermore, the Masoretic text was taken by the literary school to render the biblical text not only in its most recent form, but also in a state seriously corrupt. Textual transmission amounted to a process of its continuous degeneration. The ancient versions, on the other hand, had preserved the text in an earlier and less corrupt state. Nyberg revolted strongly against such assumptions, and listed a number of antitheses to them, stressing the principally oral nature of Oriental transmission of traditions. He referred to Islamic and Persian literature for support; the Qur'an is traditionally learnt by

8.   *The Prophets*, p. 476.
9.   T. Mettinger, *A Farewell to the Servant Songs: A Critical Examination of an Exegetical Axiom* (Scriptora Minora; Lund: Almqvist & Wicksell, 1982–83).

heart and recited to an audience. As far the ancient versions were concerned, they have had their own history of transmission and undergone a long process of recensions. Any textual emendation on the basis of a version is of necessity only tentative and should not be considered otherwise. By and large, the consonantal Masoretic text, although not without corruptions, was to be preferred, whereas both Peshitta and still more the Septuagint contain a lot of secondary readings and corruptions.

Nyberg's requests for a more careful consideration of the Masoretic text to Hosea did have some effect and were taken seriously in the ensuing scholarly treatment of Hosea, for example in commentaries (Rudolph, Wolff, Jeremias and others). But for the most part, he was not credited by them for his insights and his name was hardly even mentioned. His views did not otherwise meet much response or approval. According to Martti Nissinen, a Finn who recently published a doctoral thesis on Hosea,[10] this was because Nyberg was more or less an outsider and did not belong to any school of the day. Neither did he himself seek support from them, although a form-critical analysis might have strengthened his case considerably. Thus, the reaction against him came to be mainly negative—and Nyberg's peculiar philological method which enabled him to find totally new meanings even in common and familiar Hebrew words like *melek*, was particularly frowned upon. Nissinen, however, credits him for at least asking essential questions, and thereby opening a discussion with lasting relevancy for understanding the growth of the prophetical books.

6. *The Cultural 'Conditioning' of the Scandinavian School*

I began by pointing to the major German influence on Scandinavian culture and scholarship. Also in the cases of Engnell and Nyberg, one may easily detect that influence. To a very great extent their perception of key issues and their choice of arguments was conditioned by the German literary-critical school (albeit in the names of Bentzen and Hammershaimb), whose assumptions and conclusions, in many cases, they were at pains to refute. Accordingly, the question arises what caused this reaction, and what was at the root of their approach.

To me it would seem that the answer is *not* to be sought primarily in

---

10. M. Nissinen, *Prophetie, Redaktion und Fortschreibung im Hoseabuch* (Neukirchen–Vluyn: Neukirchener Verlag, 1991). Nissinen stresses the processes of redaction and continuing reinterpretation: 'Fort*shreibung*'!

the particularly Scandinavian environment and history. Oral transmission forms, it is true, an essential part of the Scandinavian cultural heritage, as it does in others. The Dane Axel Olrik (d. 1917) formulated a number of laws pertaining to epic folklore. But the old Norse literature and Icelandic sagas attest as much to the importance of the written word in Scandinavian culture, and it would hardly have been tenable for Engnell to argue his case from them. Rather, I would argue for two other background-factors as essential. First, there will have been an urge to find an identity for Scandinavian scholarship and in distinction from Germany, and secondly a kind of (neo-) romantic reversion to a fascination for every aspect of contemporary (early) Oriental life and phenomena.

Missionaries and visitors to the Orient still in the nineteenth century recognized biblical landscapes and scenes. Among them was the Finn Georg August Wallin whose itinerary took him in 1845 to Mecca, appearing as a Muslim in disguise. Nyberg's education and standing made him well equipped to give this sort of fascination an academically acceptable form. He was looked upon as the great master and teacher in the field of Orientalia. He was also made a member of the Swedish Academy, the body which selects annually most of the Nobel prize winners. His influence on Engnell is visible not least in the latter's use of Arabic terms for certain phenomena and traditional forms such as *hadith*, a term that covers a legitimation narrative of a peculiar custom like the sacrifice of the Passover lamb in Exod. 12.26-28, *diuan* (taken from Nyberg's Hosea-study) denoting a collection of traditions stemming from the prophet or built around him, and *raui'* for the traditionalists themselves. He also adopted Nyberg's method of coping with textual difficulties in the Hebrew not by emendations but by reverting to other Semitic languages and finding relevant data from them, such as roots or word-meanings which could illuminate some Hebrew lexical item. This method was later to be implemented almost to the extreme by other scholars, mainly non-Scandinavian.

Any major trend in contemporary Scandinavian biblical scholarship is difficult to discover. At least there is little, if any, serious effort made to carry on Engnell's work. His pupils are likely to remain his last followers. A retrospective collection of essays on the Uppsala school by Scandinavian university scholars was published in 1984.[11] They

---

11. K. Jeppesen and B. Otzen (eds.), *The Productions of Time: Tradition*

conclude the book by posing the question whether the contributions by the earlier generation will be found helpful at all in finding new pathways, rather than impede such efforts. The question receives the very Scandinavian, middle-of-the-road answer, that the break with the past has not, after all, been complete.

History in Old Testament Scholarship (Sheffield: Almond Press, 1984).

RECONSTITUTING THE AZANIAN *MIŠPĀḤÔT* (CLANS):
LAND, CLASS AND BIBLE IN SOUTH AFRICA TODAY

Itumeleng J. Mosala

The Bible is inseparable from the modern history of South Africa. It was there at the founding of modern South Africa when white colonizers dispossessed the Africans of their land and created out of them a wage class with nothing but their labour power to sell. When apartheid, as a specific ideology of racial oppression and exploitation was established, it was there. The Bible is there in the present constitution of the South African government. The Bible is there in every aspect of South African life in curious and often violently contradictory ways.

Not only was the Bible present at the moment of the enslavement of black South Africans, but it became the mechanism through which and the reason why a settler colonial group of white people took 'the land of black people.

Lest any political confusion is created, let me explain my use of the word 'clans' in the title of this paper. While the term may be perfectly clear to those who are familiar with its use in the Hebrew Bible, its application to the South African situation without explanation can be dangerous. It is my intention to avoid as much as is possible any connection with the idea of tribes which for us in South Africa has caused us much pain through the policy of Bantustans or Homelands which the government imposed on us.

Clans in this paper translates the Hebrew term *mišpāḥôt*. The social phenomenon represented by the latter term has been chosen in order to posit, using the Bible, a project for the reconstruction of a liberated nation, economy and culture of Azania, committed to a permanent struggle against racism, sexism and imperialism. I translate *mišpāḥôt* with Norman Gottwald sociologically to mean a 'protective association of families'. The functions of the biblical *mišpāḥôt*s as identified by Gottwald resonate with the functions of a number of African traditional institutions, notably the two known as Letsema and Mophato. These functions have played a major role in influencing socialist thinking among many South African political activists. Gottwald summarizes his reflections on the Israelite clans or *mišpāḥôt* in the following way:

> From passages we have examined, the *mishpaha* stands out as a protective association of families which operated to preserve the minimal conditions for the integrity of each of its member families by extending mutual help as needed to supply male heirs, to keep or recover Land, to rescue members from debt slavery, and to avenge murder. These functions were all restorative in that they were emergency means to restore the normal autonomous basis of a member family, and they were all actions that devolved upon the *mišpāḥôt* only when the *beth-av* was unable to act on its own behalf. The very existence of such a protective association gave vital reassurance to Israelite families, while the overt action of the protective association was always an exceptional measure of the last resort.[1]

The protective association of Israelite clans (the *mišpāḥôt*) presupposed the freedom and autonomy of Israelite households (*bêt 'ābôt*). It is clearly the case, however, that this presupposition expresses a right on the part of the households to be free and to be autonomous; but as the *gō'ēl* or liberator function of the *mišpāḥôt* firmly indicates, the reality was often oppression, indebtedness, dispossession and death.

For a socialist, committed to a materialist reading of the Bible, it is difficult not to detect strong roots of socialism in the traditions of the Bible. There are deep cultural connections between the values of the struggles of the people of God in the Bible and those of our own. Of course, in the canonical form of the Bible, these values of socialist organization and action occupy a subordinated position. But is there a cultural hermeneutics of liberation that can free the Bible from the ideologies of the dominant classes of its time and of our own time? Or is it doomed to play the colonial role which it has played and continues to play in the hands of ruling classes?

The ongoing and resilient commitment to the traditional cultural values of solidarity and mutual help, freedom and liberation among many oppressed peoples of the world has caused some of us in Bible scholarship to return to similar concerns in the Bible. It is the case, of course, that we have too often claimed uncritically that the Bible is

---

1. N.K. Gottwald, *The Tribes of Yahweh: A Sociology of the Religion of Liberated Israel, 1250–1050 BCE* (Maryknoll, NY: Orbis Books, 1979), p. 267.

dominated by these values. I have argued elsewhere, and I do again here, that on the contrary the values of freedom and liberation, solidarity and mutual help have only a precarious existence in the Bible. They are themselves not free. Consequently and like the Bible, they must be freed in order for them to be able to free.

In South Africa today, therefore, three issues are bound up together in a significant way. They are the issues of land, class and Bible. It is almost impossible to touch on the one without touching on the other. The land question has always been at the heart of the South African struggle for liberation. No liberation movement worthy of its name could totally ignore this issue which actually defines, in significant ways, the real nature of the oppression of blacks by whites. Hence all the black liberation movements include something in their programmes about land. There are of course significant differences among the organizations of the oppressed as to the extent to which the land question dominates their respective ideologies.

In the Bible and in the statements and programmes of South African political organizations, the land question is undergirded by an underlying social class perspective. It is this social class perspective which readers of the Bible, if they are committed to a reconstruction programme along the lines of liberation, need to isolate and interrogate. Already the absence of a class analysis, both in the way in which we read the Bible and in the proposals for reconstructing the Azanian society, are getting us into trouble.

The Land Question and the Bible

The most important question facing Christians working with and in popular movements in South Africa today is, how does the most crucial issue for Africans, namely, the land issue, inform our reading of the Bible? What kind of hermeneutics can we develop that can liberate us and the Bible for a future such as the one the people of the Bible seem always to have envisioned, if only in suppressed forms? I mean a hermeneutics that can make Micah's vision of liberated *mišpāḥôt*s or clans come true. This is the vision:

> They will hammer their swords into ploughs, and their spears into
> pruning knives. Nations will never again go to war, never prepare for
> battle again. Everyone will live in peace, among his own vineyards and
> fig-trees, and no one will make him afraid. The Lord Almighty will has
> promised this (Mic. 4.3-4).

The task of Yahweh's people is to liberate the possibilities of their own liberation. Crucial among these is the struggle against patriarchy in all its forms. Micah's vision is, therefore, only truly liberating when it itself shall have been liberated from its patriarchal prison. Once freed from its own enslaving tendencies, it can be asserted that it is more than what Professor Brueggemann is willing to permit it. He writes,

> Micah 4.1-5 is a radical assertion of a poetic promise, designed to lead Israel to an alternative reality. Admittedly, this is not a political strategy or a concrete action. It is only a practice of imagination which presents an unthinkable, underived future. Those who heard this oracle (as well as those who spoke it) were called to realities they could not see or identify. Nor could they discern how such an anticipation could become a reality.[2]

According to Professor Brueggemann, in this text:

> The poet is in touch with deep agrarian dreams. He presents what must be Israel's most elemental social hope. That hope is not simply for a disarmed world. It is much more personal. What one wishes for is to be secure enough to produce and enjoy produce unmolested, either by lawlessness or the usurpation of the state... Obviously, there can be no such personal well-being as long as there is war and threat of war. But what denies that personal hope is not simply hostility and the threat of hostility. Rather, the main threat to 'vine and fig trees' is the economics that sustain and require war. What usurps vines and fig trees is not just invading armies, but the tax structure and the profit system which are both cause and effect of military dangers.[3]

That Brueggemann is on target with these assertions there is no doubt. The point needs to be made, however, that in the Hebrew Bible as in our times the words of Micah do not reflect simply the deep dreams of poets. The many stories of the Israelite clans, like their Azanian counterparts, are rooted both in the historical reality and the social struggles of their past, present and future.

The land question is not only an issue for Africans. Nor is it a purely South African concern. I submit that the oppression and exploitation of all communities and groups is in some way related to the power of landownership which oppressors and exploiters all over the world wield. That is the one matter.

The other matter, which we need to keep firmly in mind, is that the

2. W. Bruegemann, 'Vine and Fig Tree: A Case Study in Imagination and Criticism', *CBQ* 43 (1981), p. 190.

3. Bruegemann, 'Vine and Fig Tree', pp. 190-91.

liberation of the land is for us Christians not simply a secular issue. The liberation of the land is a thoroughly spiritual business. For the Africans in Azania, the monopolization of land by white people constitutes a double injury. It is at once a condition of spiritual impoverishment and a denial of the dignity of Africans.

Already different perspectives have been emerging influenced by the different and often conflictual positions of the different players. It is instructive to see the influence that the historical popular movements and perspectives are playing in this matter, as well as to see how their social class commitments determine the use to which the Bible is put. The whole situation underlines the argument that there can be no neutral reading of the Bible. This is true even within the broad framework of liberation.

In a recent newspaper article a white South African, evidently informed by rightist popular thinking of the kind that is supported in the Bible by the conquest traditions, writes,

> Sir—Will somebody point out on a map of our country where this land is which the whites are supposed to have usurped from the blacks. Will such a person also try to explain why the whites were so stupid as to have driven these blacks from the arid western part of the country, instead of e.g. from the eastern Cape with its fertile soil and high rainfall.
>
> Black people traditionally do not, and cannot own land in their father-lands. The land they live on belongs to the monarchs or the government.[4]

Another report in the newspapers representing a white business perspective on the land question, which can also be linked to a particular perspective in the Bible, probably texts such as the one where Abraham buys land from the Canaanites to bury his dead or for his cattle and sheep, reads like this:

> The Land Bank should provide direct financial support to prospective black farmers to enable them to buy land directly from owners, Development Bank of Southern Africa senior divisional manager Johan van Rooyen said.[5]

Evidently sympathetic with this approach, the African National Congress (ANC) unsuccessfully tried to buy land in an area adjacent to a white suburb. The land was needed in order to house returning ANC exiles. The effort failed because the more powerful white rightists, who

---

4.   S. Pretorius, in *The Sowetan*, Monday, July 8, 1991.
5.   *Business Day*, July, 1991.

obviously did not want blacks on that land, combined their financial resources to defeat the ANC in an auction for the land.

In another development reported in the media recently, Archbishop Desmond Tutu is said to have led a delegation from a section of the Xhosa tribe known as the Fingos to Mr F.W. De Klerk, the white President of South Africa, to appeal for the return of their land in the Tsitsikama area of the Cape. Here also there are biblical connections which derive from where one stands in the popular movements. I am thinking especially of the Nehemiah project in the Old Testament. It is a return to the land under the sponsorship of the Persian oppressors of the Jews. A strain of the popular movement will be led by their political-ideological perspective to take this view of where we are in the struggle in South Africa.

Two other positions are identifiable. One corresponds to a community and a man who suffered a reversal of what appeared at first as a position of advantage. The City Press, a black newspaper in South Africa, reported as follows:

> The mystery of an assault charge laid against Afrikaner Weerstandsbeweging [a right wing white organisation] leader Eugene Terre Blanche by a 70-year old farm labourer deepened this week when the Transvaal Attorney General referred the docket back to the Ventersdorp police. Instead, the old man will now be charged with possession of dagga [marijuana].[6]

This experience will lead many activists in the popular movements to take seriously Jesus' decision not to utter a word to Pilate in self-defense during his trial. It is dangerous for black people to show any confidence in the institutions of white people. It is difficult for black people not to call into question the strategy of Paul when he appeals to his citizenship of Rome and of Judah as a source of power and strength in face of a repressive state.

Finally, there is a story of a community in a black township called Alexandra where, in desperation, African people have moved to take residence in a cemetery for lack of land to build their homes. The report goes:

> In Alexandra, where close to 2,000 people daily go about their business skirting graves and tombstones, the answer given with monotonous regularity is 'poverty'. 'Give us a place', the cemetery squatters said, 'and we

6. *City Press*, June, 1991.

will move immediately. We are not happy living here, but where can we go'. They have been living on the doorstep of a cemetery for three years. Residents say they have been forced to live with the dead by Alexandra Town Council, which, they said, embarked on a shack-destroying campaign.[7]

Leaving aside how white people read the Bible, these are the different conditions in which the Bible is read. The specificity of the reading is highly influenced by popular political frameworks to which Christians belong. The question is, in these different situations, which texts of the Bible will speak more fundamentally to the deep aspirations of the people, especially on the burning question of the restoration of the Land? Is it going to be the Jubilee texts in Leviticus? Will it be the Nehemiah strategy of national reconstruction? Or can the Exodus speak to us despite having been spoken to our oppressors and having provided them with the ideological arsenal to clear us off? Or will we resort to the abstract and elitist message of the prophets? How will we know what to choose? Is it possible that at different times we shall choose different texts? What are the hermeneutical implications of this?

One thing is clear: the Bible is yet to be the terrain of fierce struggles. Indeed, much blood may yet be shed as a result of, over or through the Bible.

I submit that the problem of a liberative biblical hermeneutics is not solved by choosing 'the right' text for my situation or struggle. In reading the Bible from the people's perspectives, namely, the perspective of liberation, we must confront the fundamental question of the nature of the biblical Text. Biblical study has to revisit this question in the light of the many formerly suppressed struggles, if it is not to reinforce again the use of the Bible as an instrument of oppression and exploitation.

For myself I find help in the suggestion by Terry Eagleton that as cultural workers, we should read all texts, written or historical, in 1. A Projective way, intending the effects of the political and human project to which we are committed. 2. A Polemical way, critically exposing the rhetorical structures of the texts and their underlying political and ideological mission. And in this regard it is not true that the experiences of ordinary people cannot offer the critical tools needed to undertake this task. The academy has no monopoly on the production of critical tools.

7.   *The Saturday Star*, July 20, 1991.

3. An Appropriative way, reading those texts that represent the perspectives of the dominant and oppressive classes against themselves.

Allow me at this point to engage some ideas which come out of the economic policy, and especially the section on agricultural transformation, of the political organization of which I am a member, and former President, The Azanian People's Organization. This is the organization founded by Steve Biko who will be more familiar to you than me. I quote from one part:

> A process of integrating the rural and modern industrial economic sectors will be set in motion and the national economic integration will be geared towards strengthening the predominance of the socialist mode of production, distribution, and exchange. In the rural and agricultural sector priority will be given to a process of transforming large-scale, and capital intensive farms that are historically and currently owned by white landlords into publicly owned enterprises. These farms will be expropriated without compensation by the socialist state and AZAPO government.

The biblical *mišpāḥôt*s, in their role as *gō'ēl* or liberator are expected by Israelite tradition and social commitment to liberate or recover the land, restore the freedom and autonomy of the people, to rescue members from slavery and to avenge murder. This is in line with the agricultural economic policy of the Azanian *mišpāḥôt*s or clans as envisioned by the Black Consciousness Movement.

Furthermore, the Azanian clans, inspired by the values and strategies of the biblical *mišpāḥôt*s, understand structural transformation and emancipation of agriculture in a liberated and reconstituted Azania to involve a two-fold process:

> Firstly, to engage in a process of transformation of the racist capitalist mode of production, concomitant superstructures and tribal ownership of the land. Secondly, to alleviate and ultimately eradicate completely all forms of dependence upon the world market demand generated by the predominance of world capitalist dominance on the Azanian economy.

There is a great deal of material we can draw from in the Bible to inform our struggle for human emancipation. We in Azania are greatly encouraged by the critical work of scholars who take seriously the struggle in the Bible and refrain from narrow idealization of traditions whose class perspectives can never really emancipate and liberate our people.

Without liberating the land our people will never be genuinely liberated. To reconstitute one Azania and one nation we need mishpahothic structures nurtured in the best socialist traditions to restore the normal autonomous basis of member families, extend mutual help among member families, to preserve minimal conditions for the integrity of member families, to recover the land, to rescue members from debt slavery, and to avenge murder.

This struggle, indeed this vision, is a matter of culture. It is culture not simply as an ethnic issue, or racial issue, or geographic issue, but, in the words of Amilcar Cabral, culture as a factor of struggle:

> The time is past when, in an attempt to perpetuate the domination of peoples, culture was regarded as an attribute of privileged peoples or nations and when, out of ignorance or bad faith, culture was confused with technical skill, if not with the colour of one's skin or the shape of one's eyes. The liberation movement, as representative and defender of the culture of the people, must be conscious of the fact that, whatever the material conditions of the society it represents, the society is the bearer and the creator of culture.[8]

The cultural practice of the oppressed people of the world today must make the Bible speak the words of those who are silent in its pages. It must expose and enter into struggle with the class character of biblical cultures. For this reason, culture and ideology must enter into critical dialogue in producing a cultural exegesis and hermeneutics that liberates the text and us. As Willis and Corrigan put it,

> 'Ideology' is not only the 'content' of the 'discourses' but the particular 'preferred' relation of their silences to each other as well. It is working culture, or its cultural praxis, which makes this silence speak—but not in words, or not in words with the verbal 'discourse' of its meaning at their centre. The various discourse positions which to a greater or lesser extent base themselves on language thus write out working class meaning, destroy the real agency of its subjects, and banish sense and knowledge from all but bourgeois 'discourses'—we have the largest social tautology masquerading as science: and its cost is the eradication of the working class from history.

Only a materialist cultural hermeneutics of liberation can prevent the permanent eradication of the biblical working class. And if that one survives, this one must survive.

---

8. *Unity and Struggle: Speeches and Writings* (Heinemann: London, 1982).

DREAMING: AN ABORIGINAL INTERPRETATION OF THE BIBLE

Anne Pattel-Gray*

Australian Aboriginal people have much to offer in the area of cultural exegesis, as we have lived in harmony with the Creator and the creation for—literally—tens of thousands of years. Since the Dreaming, passing on stories of how we came to be, who we are and what things mean through corroborees and ceremonies—song, dance and music. We have lived in relationships of justice and peace with each other and with the land.

It is only recently that we have encountered a different interpretation of the transcendent. For the last two centuries our experiences of white, Western Christianity have had a lasting impact on us. In all of this time, true Aboriginal exegesis has been bound. It is time it was freed. This conference is one step towards that goal.

I hope to introduce you to Aboriginal interpretation by shedding some light on how we have been manipulated by Western colonial eisegesis and by providing a glimpse of Aboriginal exegesis.

204 Years of European Eisegesis—A Historical Summary

For the past 204 years, Aboriginal exegesis has been blocked by European eisegesis. That is, our access to the biblical text has been very limited and has been controlled by white, Western Christianity. Our encounter with Scripture has been interpreted through the European filters of both secular colonization and theological imperialism. This has been marked by false assumptions, methodological mistakes and missing interpretative tools.

* Anne Pattel-Gray is the Executive Secretary of the Aboriginal and Islander Commission of the National Council of Churches in Australia and the author of *Through Aboriginal Eyes: The Cry from the Wilderness* (Geneva: World Council of Churches, 1991) and *The Great White Flood: Racism in Australia* (forthcoming).

False Assumptions

Colonizing European society made a number of false assumptions when it arrived 'to save us'. One of these was the mistaken idea that God was not here. Social, cultural and religious arrogance blinded them from seeing God from our perspective. We have known God all along, from the beginning of time. In the words of Aboriginal theologian, the Revd Djiniyini Gondarra,

> The Aboriginal Christians are convinced and believe that the God of the bible was with us and our people in the dreamtime. He was very active in our history. He has come to us in many different ways and many different forms to reveal His presence. He spoke to us through his creation, the beauty of the nature that clothes itself in God's glory that convinced us and made us believe that he is also the God of the Aboriginal race in Australia.[1]

Fortunately, the error is understood today. The Revd Dr Emilio Castro, General Secretary of the World Council of Churches, put it succinctly in his sermon at the Opening Worship of the WCC Seventh Assembly: 'God was with them [the Aboriginal people] before we came'.[2]

Another false assumption was patriarchy. Scripture scholars Hayes and Holladay write, 'The social structures presupposed by the writers of biblical materials were patriarchal and authoritarian'.[3]

Similarly, when the British introduced their form of Christianity in Australia, they too 'presupposed patriarchal and authoritarian social structures' in the Aboriginal culture which they encountered. But they were wrong! Our culture *was not* patriarchal then, and *is not* patriarchal now! In fact, Aboriginal society was *matriarchal*, and over time became egalitarian.[4] A number of traditional Aboriginal leaders have stated that it was the women who were the creators of the ceremonies, the keepers of the sacred objects.[5] Indeed, women had the wisdom. Thus, cultural

1. D. Gondarra, *Father, you Gave us the Dreaming* (Darwin, NT: Bethel Presbytery, Northern Synod, Uniting Church in Australia, 1988), p. 3.

2. E. Castro, Opening Worship Service, World Council of Churches, 7th Assembly, Canberra, Australia, 7 February 1991.

3. J.H. Hayes and C.R. Holladay, *Biblical Exegesis: A Beginner's Handbook* (London: SCM Press, 1983), p. 15.

4. M. Yunupingu, author's interview, North East Arnhem Land, Australia, May and August–September 1991.

5. G. Yunupingu, author's interview, Sydney, Australia, 31 January 1992.

patriarchy became theological patriarchy and patriarchal Christianity became patriarchal missions.

Methodological Mistakes

The colonizers also made many methodological mistakes. For example, they put down—or at least completely misunderstood—the centrality and importance of the Aboriginal *oral* culture. They brought a written document—the Bible—and expected Aboriginal people to understand it.

A second methodological mistake was that in most places the coloniz-. ers chose not to learn the language of the people, and worse, they imposed English. Indeed, indigenous languages were prohibited.[6] In 1944, the National Missionary Council of Australia wrote,

> ...no full effort was made by the missionaries to learn the Aboriginal language. There were so many tribes, and the number of languages was also so great that the missionaries often thought that the best [thing] was to teach the natives about the Lord Jesus Christ [and] was to teach them English first and then give them the Gospel story in that language. Even today, because the population of the tribes is so small, some people consider that it is not necessary to learn the languages.[7]

Similarly, a third methodological mistake was that in most places colonizers never learned the culture of the people, and worse, they imposed their own. They never bothered to look for the tribal laws, customs, values, ethics, morals, and other social codes of the people. Had they done this, perhaps they would have struck a common chord and there could have been profound, sincere dialogue and mutual growth—and significantly less bloodshed.

A fourth methodological mistake was that in most places.colonizers used coercion and force to communicate the message of Christianity. Mr Rronang Garrawurra, of the Northern Territory, remembers that when he was a small boy missionaries used *food* as a *weapon* in the 'battle for souls'. In his own words,

> ...the missionaries used to force us—if you come to school you would have food.
> 'We'll give you food. If you come to Sunday School, we'll give you food. If not, we will not give you [any].'

6. R. Garrawurra, author's interview, Sydney, Australia, 9 February 1992.

7. National Missionary Council of Australia, 'A Day of Remembrance of the Aborigines', *Minister's Bulletin* 5 (January 1994), p. 5.

That's why I said they forced us to come. [At] the same time they proclaim the Good News and [at] the same time force us to accept it.[8]

In what some may consider virtual *proof* of the grace of God—in spite of this amazing methodological mistake—Mr Garrawurra is now the Revd Garrawurra—an ordained minister of the Uniting Church in Australia and indeed Assistant Principal of Nungalinya Theological College!

Last—and most certainly—a fifth methodological mistake was that colonizing Christianity brought and practised a fatally flawed hermeneutic model. Theologian Clodovis Boff describes the 'hermeneutic circle' where elements are held in tension and together contribute to meaning and understanding.[9] He also discusses a model of hermeneutic meditation called the 'Correspondence of Terms' which seeks to establish proportionality between, for example, Jesus and his political context and today's Christian community and the current political context.[10] It seems that the colonizing European society which came to Australia followed this model, by seeking to establish proportionality between the faithful of Jesus' day and the mission to the Gentiles, on the one hand, and the Christian community of the colonial era and the missions to the Aboriginal people, on the other. It seems to have believed that being faithful to God meant a direct correspondence between what early Christians did then and what they did later.

Clodovis Boff points out that this model is seriously flawed and unacceptable because of its focus on political results rather than hermeneutical integrity. Thus, he offers the alternative 'Correspondence of Relationships' model, where Scripture relates to its context and at the same time we (and our theology of the political) relate to our context—all existing in a hermeneutic circle. As Boff puts it,

> We need not, then, look for formulas to 'copy', or techniques to 'apply', from scripture. What scripture will offer us are rather something like orientations, models, types, directives, principles, inspirations—elements permitting us to acquire, on our own initiative, a 'hermeneutic competency', and thus the capacity to judge—on our own initiative, in our own right—'according to the mind of Christ', or 'according to the spirit', the new, unpredictable situations with which we are continually

8.   Garrawurra, interview (see n. 6).
9.   C. Boff, *Theology and Praxis: Epistemological Foundations* (trans. R.R. Barr; Maryknoll, NY: Orbis Books, 1987), pp. 135-39.
10. Boff, *Theology and Praxis*, pp. 142-50.

confronted. The Christian writings offer us not a *what*, but a *how*—a manner, a style, a spirit.[11]

Thus, to complete our example, the colonizing European Christianity which came to Australia sought, found and implemented the *what* of the Scriptures, but failed miserably at grasping and living the *how*. They undertook the mission imperative, speaking of a God of love and justice, and then proceeded to take Aboriginal land, kill Aboriginal people, destroy Aboriginal spirituality and culture, take Aboriginal babies from their mothers, place Aboriginal children in mission compounds against their will, impose harsh physical punishment and forced labour on Aboriginal 'unbelievers'; and the list goes on and on. Their actions had no love, and certainly had no justice. The European Christianity which colonized Australia held—and implemented—a hermeneutic method which was flawed, quite 'fatally'.

Missing Tools

Aboriginal people have never been given all the tools that were available to grasp the roots of the deep knowledge that is the basis of the biblical text. From the very beginning, white European contact with our people has led to our being kept away from the liberating truths of the gospel. The colonizing culture thought itself superior to ours. As a result, both the theology they practised and the theological method they used were flawed. The Bible became bound up in mystery, threat and oppression—a written document which our oral culture was not accustomed to and a book the profound interpretation of which we were not privy to.

The Revd Gondarra writes of the dialogue between Western culture and both the Christian and the Aboriginal context.

> The Reformation gave Western culture the freedom to explore that dialogue in many directions. The Western Church has not, in turn, given that same freedom to Aboriginal people to explore dialogue through their own culture. We now want, and must explore, that dialogue.[12]

In other words, Aboriginal people have not been given an opportunity to encounter the Christian Gospel *on our own*. Indeed, missionaries saw Christianity as an extension of their own culture and used it as a tool to

11. Boff, *Theology and Praxis*, p. 149.

12. D. Gondarra, *Series of Reflections of Aboriginal Theology (Let My People Go)* (Darwin, NT: Bethel Presbytery, Northern Synod, Uniting Church in Australia, 1986), p. 14.

Westernize our people. In the words of the Revd Graham Paulson, an
Aboriginal Baptist theologian,

> The anthropological textbooks tell us that in Western Australia the mis-
> sionaries were sent in after all other attempts had failed to *subjugate* the
> Aboriginal; so the missionaries were sent in as a Western tool to
> Westernise rather than Christianise.[13]

The interpretation that has already been given by European invaders
is one of oppression and indoctrination, which meant that it called for us
to abandon our religion, our ceremonies and our cultural life. The colonizers never told us anything about God favouring the poor and
oppressed (e.g. Amos 2.7; 4.1; 5.7-13; Lk. 4.18-19; 16.19-31). They
never told us of the New Testament passages where God invites all
people to the table (e.g. Lk. 13.29) and rejects any form of
discrimination (e.g. Lk. 13.29; Acts 8.27ff.).

We have not been able to do that because Christianity imprisoned the
Aboriginal people and kept us from more knowledge which, in fact, we
could have read—then and now. Even today, scriptural teaching in the
church is marked by superficiality and shallowness. We are taught biblical stories, as if we were sitting in a Sunday School of 100–200 years
ago. Indeed, narrow-minded fundamentalist theology is very strong
among Aboriginal communities all across Australia. Modern biblical criticism is not introduced—and certainly not encouraged.

Even for us today, to sit and challenge our own people to come up
with our own indigenous interpretation of the Gospel is very difficult
because some of our people keep mimicking the rhetoric that has been
instilled in us for these past 200 years. We continually repeat the missionary theology and words that have imprisoned us for so long. As
Aboriginal people, we need to stop, to think, 'How does the gospel
relate to me and where am I at this moment?'

60,000 Years of Aboriginal Exegesis—An Untold Story

Exegesis—Both Old and New

Exegesis is both old and new to Aboriginal people. We have been
'doing' exegesis for literally tens of thousands of years, for as long as we
have been on the Australian continent. Our entire worldview is centred
around harmonious relationships between Creator and creation, between

---

13. G. Paulson, author's interview, Sydney, Australia, 17 January 1992.

people and land, and between ourselves and our brothers and sisters. Those relationships are discovered and made timeless through the passing on of our Dreaming stories and our complex family connections. We have been 'living' exegesis for a long, long time.

Only recently, however, have we begun to 'write' exegesis. As a few of our people come into contact with post-colonial and liberation theologies from the East and South, we begin to see that our own indigenous theology—which we have been 'living'—is in fact speaking the same language. As we begin to transcend the mission and church structures which have bound us, we begin to understand how to communicate our own spiritual and theological insights and methods to the West—including to the people whose forbearers oppressed us then, and who themselves continue to oppress us today.

Aboriginal people are now reinterpreting the gospel and making it relevant to our culture, spiritual, ceremonial and religious way of life so that we may embrace the whole of the gospel, and not just parts of the gospel—which is what was given and taught to us. We are starting to interpret the Bible our own way—reading it in a way that relates to us—and we are becoming empowered, we are becoming strong.

We Aboriginal people have much to share of ourselves—including our own profound spiritual and cultural insights—as we encounter the text of the Christian gospel and communicate through Dreaming stories, songs and dances and ceremonies.

Interactive Exegesis

Aboriginal people are not critical of other cultural interpretations. We do not criticize others because we know we are not the 'be all and end all' of biblical interpretation. But what we do object to is the oppressive interpretations of the gospel and the ways in which these are applied in Australia to our people.

This is why our conference this past week has been very important in terms of what we can learn from each other. If we stick our head in the sand, and fail to relate to any other culture or people, then we cannot say we are practicing of participating in any form of exegesis—we are in fact, applying eisegesis. We know that it is very important to keep open the ways of communication.

In communicating with each other, we are giving respect to other people's interpretation, their culture and their belief—in the hope of developing some understanding. In many cases, we share common

cultural characteristics. For example Native American Indians—as well
as many other oppressed indigenous nations—are oral people, the same
as we are. They too have a great connection to the Creator and to the
creation. Both of us have a deep and abiding interest in the cultural
practice in religion, a strong understanding and sense of being in harmony in our lives and practice. And we both share elements of our
application of cultural exegesis.

Even though there are cultural differences, still we understand the
depth of each other's spiritual connections—to Creator, to land, to each
other.

Non-Aboriginal people do not have this connection to the Creator or
to the creation, as their practise is related to an institution and not to
creation. Their worship is done within buildings—indeed they create
buildings in order to worship. They have set forms of liturgy. They limit
God, whereas Aboriginal people worship within creation itself and see
God's connection through the trees, the rivers, the mountains, the
valleys and all food that is bountiful. We spend more time communicating with the Creator, for the Creator is the significant source and
provider of our life. We share with other indigenous people our love,
desires, connection, ceremonies, practice for the Creator. Through this
we all find liberation for our people.

Non-Aboriginal people have institutionalized God, theorized God and
misinterpreted God to the point that wealth, greed, status and power
have become the main focuses of their God—whereas Aboriginal communities focus mainly on the communal and ceremonial life, stewardship
and equality for all humankind.

All oppressed indigenous people have this focus because of common
elements we suffer: oppression, cultural genocide, dispossession and
indoctrination. We are all working towards the empowerment and
liberation of our people.

Respect for Others

Something else we have to share with other cultures and other people of
the world is our acceptance and respect for other people's cultures and
what they have to offer. We know that in our culture we have a vast
richness that has been totally ignored—if not simply dismissed. Similarly,
we know that other cultures also have this vast richness, so we seek to
acknowledge and learn about other people's riches and their cultures.

We do not come in and become dominant; we do not totally suppress other people's religion, culture, interpretation and just enforce our own. As the Revd Paulson has correctly pointed out, Aboriginal people

> learned this process of contextualisation within a multi-cultural context, whereas in most countries it's just bi-cultural. Australia, after Israel, is one of the most multicultural countries in the world and that's hard to imagine. And yet it's the Aboriginal people who are learning to come to grips with all of these other pressures from all of these other points of view. So our context is more multi-cultural than many countries in the world in learning to come to grips with a whole range of input factors. We are learning to take the Gospel and say, 'Hey, this is me, this is where I'm at, and this is how the scripture relates to me'.[14]

In many ways, the perspective that white churches have about the Aboriginal form of living by the gospel is neo-colonial. Basically their attitude is that, since they have somehow 'conquered this land' and are in the majority, they have some kind of God-given monopoly over the Word of God, its interpretation, its application and its propagation. Authentic, indigenous exegesis is considered to be a quaint cultural oddity, of less-than-equal standing with the 'long' tradition of European, Enlightenment scholarship. In some scenarios, Aboriginal exegesis is held as theologically unfeasible; in others, it is put down as demonic or at least syncretistic. But from the Aboriginal point of view, as the Revd Paulson reminds us,

> culture and law and religion are so inextricably bound that we don't compartmentalise like the [West does] so, in other words, our culture and our law and our religion are much more closely tied and there is much less syncretism in our law then there is in theirs [white churches].[15]

Practical Problems

Some churches have begun to accept and seek out Aboriginal spiritual and theological insights. Yet, even these churches have failed to make any kind of significant progress in terms of incorporating elements of the insights into their own corporate and individual lives. For example, for the past few years the Uniting Church in Australia has begun a process of indigenization, where Blacks and Whites work together towards self-determination, justice, understanding and reconciliation. But, the process is stalling. The church has developed a Uniting Aboriginal and Islander Christian Congress but this has structural, political and certainly

14. Paulson, interview (see n. 13).
15. Paulson, interview (see n. 13).

financial limitations. A project of covenanting between Aboriginal and non-Aboriginal members is at a virtual standstill. The hierarchy is still mostly white. Theological education for Aboriginal people is still *below* even the undergraduate level. The models of worship and liturgy are only minimally changed (and in some cases represent the worst of paternalism and tokenism). Even the Uniting Church's own leaders, both Aboriginal and non-Aboriginal, recognize that 'We have a long way to go'.

Moving Forward

We need a liberation from the limited theological methods which were taught to us in the past. We need to free ourselves from the oppression that was placed on us through heretical and destructive interpretations of Christianity. We need to probe the depths of the biblical witness, to learn the skills of modern scholarship and to be able to relate those learnings with our own spiritual and cultural ways. Already we have an inclusive and empowering theological method and now, we are moving toward expressing ourselves for our own benefit as well as the benefit of others.

Applying Aboriginal Exegesis

Dreaming. As I have mentioned, Aboriginal people have been 'doing' exegesis for a long time. Our 'lived exegesis' is intimately connected with our Dreaming. In the words of the Revd Djiniyini Gondarra,

> To me as a tribal Aboriginal, dreaming is more than just an ordinary dream which one would dream at night or day. To us, dreaming is reality, because it takes in all of Aboriginal spirituality. When the religious tribal elders say 'This mountain is my dreaming' or 'that land is my dreaming', he is really saying that this mountain or that land holds very sacred knowledge, wisdom and moral teaching, passed on to us by the spirit of the creator, who has created for us the holy sacred sites and sacred mountains which exist today.
>
> Therefore the Aboriginal dreaming is based on three fundamental areas in Aboriginal lifesystems. They are religious, social and political. One cannot be divided from the other, because if it is destroyed or interrupted, it takes away the uniqueness of what was designed and entrusted to us by our creator spirit.[16]

16. Gondarra, *Father, you Gave us the Dreaming*, p. 2.

Similarities to the Bible

An interesting observation is the tribal law and its parallel to biblical law, such as the law of Moses' day. It is surprising—not only to myself but also to many white people—how the culture they set out to annihilate, in fact, has laws that are closer to the Bible than their own white laws. Some of us wonder whether the gospel—or the Lord's teachings— weren't with us from day one, because of the parallels between our ancestors and the forefathers of the Bible. They were so parallel, so close in what they were doing. The Revd Gondarra writes,

> Aboriginal people practise their religious life in such ways to love, respect and honour their creator in whom they believe, just as the Hebrews prac- tised their religious life of love, respect and honour their God Yahweh. Discipline, self respect, pride and dignity are part of the religious behaviour of Aboriginal people, so is the language, kinship, moiety and subsection. All that is expressed in the religious manner, is practiced in the social life cycle of the Aboriginal people.
>
> There is a unique relationship established among the tribal communi- ties. Sharing things together is a symbol of love, respect and acceptance. That is why our culture is very rich. It brings us together in harmony. Aboriginal cultural patterns cannot be destroyed or transplanted by assimi- lation: that would bring genocide in the whole cycle of Aboriginal lifestyle and ceremonial systems. When Aboriginal leaders take up the leadership in religious, social and political areas, they are bound by the Aboriginal code of law which is called *rangga/madayin* of his people. To take away from his true Aboriginality is to destroy who he is, his pride and dignity. In him there is a religious behaviour that cannot be taken away by the pre- sent foreign political, religious and social system, because he has been ordained into leadership by the great creator spirit. In him there is knowl- edge, wisdom and understanding bestowed upon him by the creator spirit. There is a special name given by Aboriginal people to this office which is called *Djerrikay and Dalkarra*.[17]

Indeed, Aboriginal culture has many symbols which reflect biblical parables and elements. The results of Aboriginal exegesis are 'recorded' in many different ways, including Dreaming stories and totems. There is one Dreaming which is very similar to the Christian 'Lord's Supper'. The Revd Rronang Garrawurra recalls the time when

> our ancestors used to have a special ceremony every so often to bring all the different tribes together. This was in the middle of the year when there was a dry season... Part of the ceremony is to restore the relationship

17. Gondarra, *Father, you Gave us the Dreaming*, pp. 2-3.

between different tribes, because our ancestors used to fight each other and there they used to have tension between tribes... and the only way we used to bring them together is to have the special ceremony. They used to ask all the women to make a cyprus palm nut bread [which is poisonous if not prepared in a special way]. We would get the wild grapes and crush them together, but in the different stages. They have this meal inside the sacred ceremony—which would include only the old people, the elders— to restore the relationship, to have that special meal, and they have that Holy Communion when there are lots and lots [of people]. Outside, ladies can have that, or the whole community can have it. And the story relates closely to Jesus and the disciples.[18]

This special ceremony was close to eucharist—each time Aboriginal people performed this ceremony, it was renewing the relationship. Similarly, each time we take part in eucharist, it renews our relationship with God.

Another way Aboriginal exegesis is recorded is through 'totems'. In the words of the Revd Gondarra,

In Aboriginal culture, when persons approach a sacred site, a sacred object, or a totem, it is as if they are approaching the tablets of stone Moses brought down from the mountain. In special places in Australia a kind of Law from long ago is thought to be retained. We would suggest that sacred objects which outsiders have called 'totems' may be better compared to the tablets of stone enshrined in the ark of the covenant.[19]

Thus, Dreamings and totems show many similarities to the biblical texts.

Distinctiveness

Aboriginal culture is also characterized by uniqueness. The Revd Graham Paulson has stated that what is distinctive about Aboriginal exegesis is its ability to make

the application of the biblical principles that are in the word of God, directly to the cultural basis of the Aboriginal people.

The distinctive is not in the biblical principle itself but in the application of what the biblical principle does or how... that impacts on what is the Aboriginal cultural value. And I think that most exegesis that we have on our bookshelf has to do with application within a western cultural context and unfortunately, for Aboriginal students, we have to learn about that. I think not enough emphasis is given to the application within the terms of

18. Garrawurra, interview (see n. 6).
19. Gondarra, *Father, you Gave us the Dreaming*, p. 4.

biblical principles to the distinctive Aboriginal context and I think that is probably one of the major failings of Christianity within Australia in the last 200 years. They have said so much about the application of Christian principles to Aborigines but it has always been in the framework of its application to a western cultural context, not to an Aboriginal cultural context.[20]

This distinctiveness is best conveyed in a Dreaming story told by Aboriginal theologian, the Revd George Rosendale:

> [A] myth [which is] helpful in illustrating the Passion of our Lord is about the brolga, the jabiru, and the emu. A long time ago, brolga and jabiru were sisters; they lived on the mud flats and near lagoons. The emu, their cousin, lived over the hills, in the high country. One day, the emu decided to visit her cousins. when she came to the top of the ridge, she saw dust on the plains below. Realising her cousins were fighting, she ran down as fast as she could, and got between them to stop them. Just then, one of the sisters swung her yam stick and accidentally hit the emu across the back. The emu's blood got on the neck of brolga and the legs of jabiru. To this day, indeed, the brolga has a red neck and the jabiru red legs; and the emu has a hump on the back. Jesus, our peacemaker, carries the scars on hands, feet, and side. Many biblical passages could be related to and illustrated by this story, as, for instance, John 20:26-29, Romans 5:8-11, and I John 1:7.[21]

This—as well as many other Dreaming stories—shows both the similarities to the Bible and the distinct features of Aboriginal exegesis.

Conclusion

Aboriginal exegesis and interpretation of the biblical texts is rich and full of vitality. It is a unique form of scholarship, often conducted in close contact with God's creation. It is an expression of our daily lives, our family systems, our connectedness to everything around us. The strength of our culture, the endurance of our traditions, the resilience of our people—all come together in our Dreaming. We have known the Creator from the beginning of time and we look forward to sharing elements of our continuing Dreaming with our brothers and sisters all across the creation.

20. Paulson, interview (see n. 13).

21. G. Rosendale, 'Aboriginal Myths and Customs: Matrix for Gospel Preaching', *LTJ* 22.3 (1988), p. 5.

INDIGENOUS BIBLICAL HERMENEUTICS:
GOD'S REVELATION IN NATIVE RELIGIONS AND THE BIBLE
(AFTER 500 YEARS OF DOMINATION)

Pablo Richard*

1. *The Indigenous Trauma Facing the Bible*

The first experience of the indigenous peoples with the Bible was traumatic. In the conquest and colonization of America, the Bible was normally utilized as an instrument of domination and death. A popular Guatemalan saying states, 'When the Spaniards arrived, they told us to close our eyes and to pray. When we opened our eyes, we had their Bible and they had our land'.

This is a harsh saying, but it expresses well the trauma that indigenous peoples undergo when confronting the Bible. This trauma is deepening today with the experience of manipulation in fundamentalists sects that still turn many biblical churches against the religion and faith of the natives.

Furthermore, the best-intended biblical interpretations often ignore or undervalue the indigenous religious traditions and the Bible itself becomes a cause of ignorance or lack of interest in the revelation of native traditions. One time an indigenous Panamanian told me, 'You people with your Bible have wounded our soul'. It is sad to hear this, but it is true.

Once we have listened to the profound insights of the indigenous culture and tradition, we who are biblical scholars or non-indigenous teachers also live with a problem concerning the Bible. We are so astonished with the indigenous religious tradition, with the experience of God in oral tradition and with the native religious force that has survived 500 years despite Christianity, that to us it seems *inadequate* to speak of our

*   Translated by David Arias.

Bible; so distant in time and space, and so culturally alienated in its Western colonial interpretation.

All of the preceding facts oblige us to create a liberating hermeneutic in the context of the last 500 years of evangelization, colonization and spiritual conquest.

2. *God's Revelation in Indigenous Religious Tradition*

a. *Insufficiency of Theological Instruments and Traditional Magisterials of Discernment*

At the beginning, the dominant opinion of the missionaries was to consider the native religion as pagan, idolatrous and inclusively demonic. Even today, the attitude towards the native religions is one of ignorance, suspicion or disrespect. However, these opinions are, at least 'officially', over with. The Second Vatican Council exhorted the faithful who work amongst the non-Christian populations to 'familiarize yourselves with their national and religious traditions; discover, with joy and respect, the seeds of the Word which are contained within them' (*ad Gentes* 11). Similarly it asked for 'a sincere and patient dialogue in order to discover the riches that God has generously distributed to the people' (*ad Gentes 11*).

> With her work [the Church] gathers all the good that is sown in the hearts and minds of humanity and in all the rites and cultures of these populations, not only to keep it from vanishing, but also so it may be purified, ennobled, and made perfect for the glory of God (*Lum. Gen.* 17).

The Council recognizes a preparation of evangelical revelation:

> God, creating and protecting the universe by his Word [cf. Jn 1.3], offers to mankind in creation a perennial testimony of himself [cf. Rom. 1.19-20]…and after he continually cared for the human race, to give eternal life to all who sought salvation with perseverance in good deeds… In this way, God was preparing an Evangelical path through the centuries (*Dei Verbum* 3; cf. also *Lum. Gen.* 16).

The Church's teaching also speaks of revelation in a universal and optimistic tone:

> The Holy Ecclesiastical Council professes that man can certainly know God with natural reason, mediated through creation [cf. Rom. 1.20]; and teaches that, thanks to oral revelation, all persons, in the present human condition, are easily able to know, with absolute certainty and

without error the divine realities, that in fact are not inaccessible to reason (*Dei Verbum* 6; cf. also *GS* 58 about the relation between Evangelism and culture).

Paul VI in this same line, referring to religious non-Christians, mentioned teaching that we would be able to apply to our millennial (see below) indigenous religions:

> The Church respects and esteems these non-Christian religions, as they are the living expression of the soul for vast groups of people. These religions carry with them the echo of thousands of years of the quest for God; an incomplete search, but frequently made with sincerity and honest hearts. They possess an impressive heritage of profoundly religious texts. They have taught generations of people how to pray. All are filled with innumerable 'seeds of the Word' and they constitute an authentic 'evangelical preparation' (*Ev. Nuntiandi*, 53).

I have also heard various missionaries, in their attempts to give value to the native religions, say that the native religions represent in Latin America what the Old Testament meant for the New Testament.

All of the preceding signifies an enormous progression from the colonial position and the previous fundamentalism of the Church. The Church's teachings are useful and necessary references, but our actual experience and reflection carries us farther away from them, without denying their value.

Today, after 500 years of diverse attempts at evangelization, we have discovered that the experience of God of the native peoples, is a millennial experience (the testimonies go back at least ten thousand years, although in the last three thousand years a more expressive and elaborate theology has developed), whose development and profundity fills us today with admiration and respect. The indigenous religions, in addition to flourishing for millennia in the life of the indigenous peoples, have survived 500 years of political, cultural and theological aggression. Even more, the native religions have been the means that have allowed the native peoples to resist and survive, many times in spite of Christian evangelization. The indigenous religious tradition has also demonstrated an immense vitality for incorporating the best parts of the Christian tradition, incorporating and interpreting them in its own religious and cultural structures. The indigenous faith has been the creator and bearer of the best folk religious traditions and has arrived at its own theological synthesis. As a result, the designation of the indigenous religious tradition as 'evangelical preparation' or as the bearer of 'the seeds of the

Word' is correct, but insufficient. I believe that in the native religions we not only find the 'seeds' of the Word, but also revelation that has been unfolded in them like a robust tree, with roots, a trunk and broad branches. It is also insufficient to speak of 'evangelical preparation', since the indigenous theologians and sages had greater capacity than the missionaries to appreciate and identify the gospel when it arrived confused and misconstrued from the conquest and colonization of America. Not only were they capable of correctly taking possession of the gospel, but they had been capable of sheltering and saving the gospel from the manipulations that the conquest and 'evangelization' had caused. By this, we are neither canonizing nor sanctifying the indigenous religions, but rather only questioning the criteria with which we discern and judge.

b. *Some Theoretical Elements for an Indigenous Biblical Hermeneutic*
It is necessary to construct a new hermeneutical instrument to interpret indigenous religious traditions. A primary element for that construction is the traditional and orthodox distinction between the Bible and the Word of God. The Bible is an instrument for the revelation of the Word of God. This Word of God is a reality much broader than the Bible: it is in the Bible, but also before and after it. God is a living God, who has been communicating with us since the creation of the world and continues to communicate today. The Bible transmits to us in a bountiful way, with inspiration and authority, the Word of God, but the Bible does not exhaust the whole Word of God. The Bible certainly reveals the Word of God to us, but it also reveals where and how God has shown himself in all of humanity and where and how he reveals himself today in our history. This force of the biblical text was named by the Church Fathers, 'Spiritual Sense'.[1] Consider two texts from the Church Fathers that can help us in this search. The first, from St Augustine, says,

> The Bible, the second book of God, was written to help us decipher the world, to give back to us the view of faith and contemplation, and to transform all reality into a great revelation of God.[2]

The second text is from Caisano:

---

1. This is the central theme of my article, 'Lectura Popular de la Biblia en América Latina: Hermenéutica de la Liberación', in *Revista de Interpretación bíblica latinoamericana* 1 (1988), pp. 30-48.
2. Cited by Carlos Mesters in *Flor sin Defensa* (*CLAR*, 16; Bogotá, 1984), p. 28.

> Taught by this that we ourselves feel, we no longer perceive the text as
> something we only hear, but rather as something that we experience and
> touch with our hands; not as a strange and unheard-of history, but rather
> as something that we give birth to from the deepest depths of our heart, as
> if they were sentiments that form part of our own self.
>
>   We insist: it is not the reading that makes us enter into the meaning of
> the words, but rather from our own experience acquired previously in the
> life of each day.[3]

Let us now apply the above to the indigenous religious traditions. In
light of St Augustine's text, we would be able to say that the cosmos,
the native culture and religion, is the *first* 'book' of God.[4] There the
Indians discover the revelation of God and engage God in dialogue. The
Bible is the *second* book of God, given to help us to decipher the first
indigenous 'book' containing the revelation of God. The reading of the
Bible returns to us the expression of faith and contemplation (which we
lost due to the conquest and the dominant occidental ideology) in order
to grasp the native cosmic, cultural and religious reality as a grand divine
revelation. This spiritual reading of the Bible neither undervalues nor
destroys God's revelation in the indigenous religious world, but on the
contrary considers it (indigenous religion) to be the first Word of God
which is thus considered to be a great epiphany of God. This method of
reading is antagonistic to the fundamentalist and colonizing reading of
the Bible, which ignores or destroys God's revelation in the book of life,
and finally also in the Bible itself.

The citation from Caisano carries us still farther and responds better to
the religious experience of the native peoples. The indigenous religious
world is so rich and profound, that when the Indians read the Bible, they
not only read and hear it, but they construct it, they give birth to it,
beginning with their own religious experience. It is not the reading of the
Bible alone that brings them to penetrate the sense of the words, but
rather the previous Indian religious experience coupled with the reading
of the biblical text. In the indigenous interpretation of the Bible there is a
production of consciousness that comes with the previous religious
experience, which the natives have developed throughout thousands and
thousands of years.

3. *Collationes* X, p. 11.
4. I use the word 'book' in an analogous, comparative and symbolic sense. The
indigenous religious traditions are sometimes expressed in texts, but also in rites,
symbols, myths and in oral tradition.

The classical hermeneutic speaks to us about the Bible as canon. This can be understood in both a passive and an active sense. In the passive sense, the Bible is canon because it contains the books accepted by the Church as inspired books. When the apostolic period ended the canon consisting of inspired books was closed. But also the Bible is canon in an *active sense*. Canon means measurement. A meter, a liter, a kilo are all measurements or established canons used to measure or weigh things. In a similar manner the Bible is a canon, which is to say, a 'measurement' which 'measures' the Word of God. The Bible is the established criterion to discern God's Word in history, in humanity and in the cosmos. We are unable to discern the revelation of God using arbitrary methods or formulas. We ought to discern in a 'canonical' manner, which means, in accordance with the Bible as established canon. Therefore, to speak of the Bible as canon, is not to reduce all of God's revelation to the biblical text (as fundamentalists do), but to utilize the revelation contained within the Bible as criteria for the discernment and interpretation of the Word of God in all of human history, from creation until the end of the world. If we apply this to the indigenous religious world, we can affirm that the reading of the Bible will not substitute or annul the native religious tradition, but rather that it will be an instrument for discerning the presence and revelation of God in the indigenous tradition. Thus the Bible recovers the *spiritual authority* which is its own and ceases being an authoritarian instrument of religious and cultural repression, as it was used in the conquest and spiritual destruction of America.

The principal hermeneutic that we have expounded (the spiritual sense of the Bible, the Bible as the second book of God, the Bible as active canon for discernment) is a liberating hermeneutic for the indigenous religious tradition, with the condition that it be combined with another equally important hermeneutic principle: that the beginning of textual appropriation and of biblical interpretation as a part of evangelization is transformed simultaneously within the evangelical subject. This is the principle that recognizes in the indigenous the possibility and capability of being *subject* to the reading and interpretation of the Bible. The Bible allows us to discover God's revelation in the indigenous tradition, with the condition that the Bible is read and interpreted by the indigenous peoples in the native cultural and religious structures that are their own.

The Bible is canon (or the criterion for discernment of the Word of God) in the native religious traditions, as long as the Bible is appropriated by the indigenous community. The conditions or mediation of this

appropriation are various. In the first place, this Indian appropriation of
the Bible grows out of an ecclesiastical community, which supposes the
construction and existence of the local native church. In the second
place, the native appropriation of the Bible entails an adequate appropriation of theoretical methods (historical, linguistic and cultural tools). This
is necessary for the indigenous people themselves to familiarize themselves with the text (literal sense) and the history behind the text (in a
historical sense), resulting in a recovery of the Bible from all its perverse
interpretations. In the third place, the native appropriation of the Bible
necessitates that the reading and interpretation of the Bible be accomplished in accordance with the *historical process of native liberation*
(the political, cultural and religious process).

These three conditions or mediations (the native ecclesiology, the theoretical preparation and the historical condition) will enable the Indian to
be an active subject and creator in the interpretation of the Bible. This
native interpretation of the Bible transforms the native from an evange-
listic object (the one who is preached to) to the subjective evangelist, and
creates an indigenous method of reading and interpreting the Bible.

3. *Indian Theology: Theoretical Framework for a Native Biblical Hermeneutic*

The presence and revelation of God in indigenous culture and religion is
the root of an Indian theology that is as ancient as the indigenous
peoples themselves.[5] We begin by saying very clearly that the *subject* of
this Indian theology is the indigenous community itself:

> The subjects of Indian theology are the indigenous communities rooted in
> the same ground out of which arise and grow their rites and myths.

---

5.   Recent literature regarding indigenous theology includes, *Teología India:
Primer Encuentro taller latinoarmericano* (Mexico Cenami: Ecuador Abya Yala,
1991), p. 329; 'El Dios de nuestros Padres', *Christus* 7 (1991); E. López, 'La
Teología en el Istmo de Tehuantepec', Mimeo (1991); E. López, '500 años de
resistencia y de lucha de los pueblos de América contra la opresión', Mimeo (1991);
M. Marzal *et al.* (eds.), *Rostros Indios de Dios: Los amerindios cristianos* (Mexico
Cenami: Ecuador Abya Yala, 1991), p. 322; C.L. Siller, 'Religíon Indígena en
Mesoamérica', *Esquila Misional* (1991); E. Tamez, 'Quetzalcóatl y el Dios cristiano:
alianza y lucha de Dioses', *Pasos* 35 (1991); D. Irarrazaval, 'Teología Aymara:
Implicancias para otras teologías', Mimeo (1991).

This community lives the experience of God, Father–Mother in its development, the reflection joined together with their wisemen and women—legitimate interpreters of their beliefs—and expresses and celebrates this through their daily existence and through their rites. The ordainment of this theological experience corresponds to the members of the same community and to those among the community tuned into their projects.[6]

The creation of an Indian biblical hermeneutic that permits us to read and interpret the Bible from the Indian culture and religion ought to have this Indian theology as a theoretical framework for reference. Indian theology ought to give us the theory, the method, the objective and forms of expression for this Indian hermeneutic. This Indian hermeneutic is but a chapter of Indian theology. Today we see the general features of a native theology, especially the specific elements necessary in order to construct an Indian hermeneutic. Here I will briefly try to reflect on the texts of native theologies and expand from there, as a non-Indian exegete, on some hermeneutical reflections. I am well aware of what the above text says about the *indigenous community* as the *subject* of the native theology. That same text, nevertheless, permits me to enter the end of the process, in the ordination of the indigenous theological experience, in the measurement that enables me to feel a part of the indigenous community and in profound sympathy and solidarity with all their projects.

a. *Definition of Indian Theology*

Native theologians distinguish between an Indian-Indian theology and an Indian-Christian theology. The first is prominent among indigenous groups in order to recover their own theological thinking, whose existence reaches some ten thousand years back to their origins.[7] The second theology is prominent amongst native theologians active inside the Church and in dialogue with Christianity. There is an essential identity and continuity between the two, but in the scope of this essay I am interested in the Indian-Christian theology that has been developing since the conquest and continues into our time.

E. López, an Indian theologian, defines native theology as the 'Giving reason to/for our millennial hope'. More precisely, 'It is reflective

6. *Teología India*, p. 315.

7. For information concerning native thology before the conquest see the two articles by E. López cited in n. 5 above.

discourse that accompanies, explicates and guides the paths of our native peoples through all of history'.[8] Later, he enumerates this theology's characteristics: it is a concrete theology, an inseparable companion from the life project of the indigenous. It is an integral theology that globally reflects on village life, where God is radically implicated. It is a theology with a markedly religious language that is overlaid with symbol, myths and rites, that express in a radical and total form the sense that animates life. Finally, it is a theology that has as its subject the village itself, which elaborates belief and thought in a collective form.

The name *Indian* is not the name of aboriginal peoples. Instead they are called *Nahuas*, *Zapotecas*, *Mayas*, *Bribis* and so on. Indians have existed since 1492, as it was the conquistadors who made them into Indians by subjugating and oppressing them. Indian theology consciously assumes the adjective 'Indian', not as a name, but rather as an indication of the oppressed condition:

> The condition of the Indians, even though offensive, brings us closer to the rest of the poor in America and in all the world. None of us choose to be Indians just as none of the other exploited choose to be exploited. It was the wickedness of men that made us into Indians, the Blacks into slaves, and the poor into the exploited. Because of that, we Indians have to fight for our liberation as well as that of all of the poor of the earth. In this sense, Indian theology forms part of Latin American theology, which is the theology of liberation. And it is more, for the actual Latin-American theology is a continuation of the resistance theology which was begun 500 years ago by our ancestors.[9]

We now see the different attitudes and responses facing the conquest and colonization as being as much a part of the indigenous peoples as they are a part of the Church, and especially as that response which made possible the uprising of an Indian-Christian theology.[10]

The following responses to the conquest were made by the indigenous peoples:

1. *Frontal assault*: with all available military strength against the invading armies.

2. *Passive resistance*: waiting in silence in order not to be killed (which did not mean backing down but hiding oneself).

---

8. E. López, 'Teología India Hoy', *Christus* 7 (1991), p. 22.

9. López, 'Teología India Hoy', p. 24.

10. For information concerning the following evidence see the article already cited by López, '500 años de resistencia'.

3. *Alliance*: with the dominating forces to resolve inter-ethnic conflicts between dominant indigenous peoples and the dominated.

4. *Collective suicide.*

5. *Indigenous cultural and religious reformulation in the colonial systemic context*: dialogue to attain a vital synthesis, where the native cultural and religious tradition might be able to continue being itself without betraying its identity, and while assuming the religious and cultural values of the dominant Christianity. Not only was it concealed in part by an occidental and Christian overlay, but in addition was withheld from the conqueror: his ideological, cultural and religious weapons were appropriated by the conquered in order to demonstrate that they themselves were Indians, with their own traditions, who lived and expressed the gospel message more coherently than the European Christian conquistadors themselves. With this methodology, the indigenous appropriated the Bible for themselves, reading it and interpreting it in accordance with their own experience of God and their religious traditions.

The European Church sought to verify its involvement with the following proposals:

1. *Total identification of the church with the colonial conquest and domination* (this was the dominant attitude).

2. *Church collaboration with the colonial system*: in order to obligate the colonial system to dedicate itself to the service of evangelization (evangelization was thus conceived as the very reason for the conquest—because of this the Church tried to ensure that the conquest might be accomplished according to gospel ethics). This attitude resulted in legitimation of the conquest and perpetuation of the notion of Indians as pagans and idolaters.

3. *Church marginalization by the colonial structure* (the Church acted from the margins of the system, accepting the system's brutalities as inevitable). This attitude brought about the construction of acts of charity for the indigenous people as well as the formation of indigenous submission.

4. *Prophetic denunciation of the colonial system as contrary to evangelization* (a challenge which had been quite significant, but had no great success since it was rather quickly silenced).

5. *Cultural contextualization of the gospel to the native world or indigenous appropriation of the gospel* (by way of the formation of native intellectuals, who made possible the re-encounter with the

peoples' past and the reformulation of the gospel in accord with indigenous traditions).

The indigenous proposal for dialogue (number 5 above) and the ecclesiastical proposal of acculturation and appropriation (number 5 also) were complementary to and made possible the rise of an indigenous Christian theology. The fundamental aspect in this proposition, both indigenous and ecclesiastical, was the transformation of the Indian into evangelist. The native now evangelizes the native. Little by little, the indigenous peoples ceased being the object of evangelization in order to transform themselves into the subjects of evangelization. The best and most ancient example of this is found in the well-known account of Nican Mopohua, an indigenous narrative about the apparitions of 'Our Lady of Guadalupe'. But there are many other expressions of it: indigenous accounts of the conquest, creation myths, symbols and rites of existence, as well as others disseminated throughout the Christian tradition in Latin America, and the creation of a popular religiosity of indigenous roots, and the entire indigenous theological development to date.

I would like to end this section by citing an actual indigenous theological text which originated in the South Andean region of the indigenous world. It is a profound and poetic synthesis of all I have intended to communicate. The account runs,

> Between us it was sown
> —It's going to be 500 years—
> ambition together with doctrine
> destruction together with baptism
> and we knew to resist without impatience.
> Supporting the wars, the lies,
> the blizzards, the dispossession, the rains and droughts,
> the thousand plagues of insects and enemies.
> We have sowed life in our soil,
> selecting and caring for the grains of the gospel
> among the harsh lands of plundering and of disdain we suffer.
> We made our ideas germinate
> to know to survive in the midst of such hunger,
> to defend ourselves from much scandal and attacks,
> to organize ourselves amidst such confusion,
> to make ourselves happy despite such sadness
> and to dream transcending desperation.
> We did not dream of accumulating abundance:
> our sole abundance will be life in the Kingdom of God.

We dreamt of sufficiency to distribute,
because we are brothers thanks to the love of God.[11]

4. *Point of Departure and Initial Steps toward an Indigenous Biblical Hermeneutic*

Vatican II relates that, 'Scripture must be read and interpreted with the same Spirit with which it was written' (*Dei Verbum* 12). The difficulty is that throughout the centuries the Christian Bible has been read and interpreted fundamentally with *another* spirit, with a devoid spirit. It has been read with a spirit of Hellenistic philosophical abstraction, with the imperialistic spirit of Constantine, with the European spirit of conquest and colonization, with the Western patriarchal and erudite spirit, with the individualistic spirit of modern liberalism. It is necessary to rescue the Bible from this captivity in order to enable another reading and interpretation with the Spirit with which it was written. To do so, we need a *non-occidental* point of reference (non-Hellenistic, non-imperialistic, non-colonial, non-patriarchal, non-liberal and non-modernistic). We need to recover the Bible by way of the reverse position of historical occidental domination. My view is that the indigenous peoples, with their culture and religion, are able to give us a non-Western point of reference, or that reverse of history from which we can read and interpret the Bible with newly refreshed eyes, and re-encounter the Spirit with which it was written.

The indigenous theologian Eleazar López tells us,

> The most profound yearnings of our people are also those of Christ. The differences are merely superficial in form, not in content. Even more, much of the content is better preserved among our peoples, because of the purity of heart possessed by the poor, than in the contaminated vessels of the Church.[12]

The indigenous peoples, with their millennial history, with their cultural and religious tradition, and recently, with their own native method of evangelization and their native theology, are much better prepared to read and interpret the Bible than the Western European Christian who has a millennial history of violence and conquest, impregnated with the erudite, liberal and modern spirit. I have

11. Taken from, 'Proclama final del Congreso Teológico-Eucaristico y Mariano en el sur andino', *Pastoral Andina* 63 (1987).
12. 'Teología India Hoy', p. 25.

arrived at this conclusion after having worked for 6 years in biblical workshops with the Kunas Indians from Kuna-Yala (Panama), rigorously applying the hermeneutical principles mentioned in this essay. The indigenous people have appropriated the Bible, acculturating it to their own cultural and religious traditions. With the Bible in hand, mind and heart, they have also made a critical discernment concerning the revelation of God in their own religious tradition. As was mentioned above, the indigenous peoples have read and interpreted the Bible (the second 'book' of God) in order to discern in the native religious tradition (the first 'book' of God) the great epiphany of God's revelation.

There exists a theological principal in native theology, which is fundamental for the creation of this indigenous hermeneutic. It is expressed by theologian Kuna Aiban Wagua:

> Paba is very big, Paba is immense; Nana is very big, Nana is immense.[13]
> He is not trapped by one people, one people cannot know all of his paths, nor can they comprehend him in totality. Because of this, Paba created many peoples upon the earth. Paba did not create only one people, as Nana did not create only one people upon this earth. For this same reason, when a people says, 'that which I know of Paba is better and more exact', such is evidence that this people does not know Paba; such a people remains far from understanding his message; such a people believes that Paba is something small, also that Nana is something small. As Kunas we say that Paba and Nana are in the heavens.[14]

Eleazar López holds a similar view. After noting the diversity of the pre-Hispanic people and the theologies of the indigenous, he says,

> no people was considered absolute owner of God, but rather they only participated in the vision of a transcendent reality which was equally shared with other peoples. Due to this, they were able to enter into faithful dialogue with other peoples and adjoin their beliefs and religious symbols with those of their neighbors with admirable facility.[15]

This indigenous principal permits direct contact between today's indigenous peoples and the people and historical cultures that remain behind the biblical texts. Thus a dialogue between the indigenous and the Bible is established which serves as groundwork for inter-ethnic and inter-

---

13. The Kuna Indians always refer to God as 'Paba' and 'Nana', which might be translated analogously as God (Father and Mother).

14. A. Wagua, 'Las Teologías Indias ante la globalidad de la Teología Cristiana', *Christus* 7 (1991), p. 34.

15. López, 'Teología India Hoy', p. 25.

religious dialogue, as a point of departure in order to read and interpret together all of the biblical texts.

The profound structure of the history of salvation enables us to discover as much in the indigenous religious traditions as there is in the Bible. It is surprising to study the coincidences, the convergences, the common points of contact and the common spirit which animates both traditions.

I am not in agreement with the view that the indigenous tradition is like the Old Testament, or is a base for the comprehension of the New Testament. In the first place, the Old Testament is not 'Old' in the archaic sense that it ought to be transcended by the 'New'. The Old Testament can never be transcended and ought never to be abandoned in the understanding of the New Testament. It is better to speak of the 'Hebrew Bible' or the traditions of the Israelites. In the same vein, neither can the indigenous religious tradition be considered 'Old', as something which ought to be surpassed by the Christian New Testament. On the contrary, the cultural and religious indigenous traditions ought to be the matrix for the reading and comprehension of the Old and New Testaments. Dialogue between the Bible and indigenous religion is dialogue from Genesis to Revelation. We cannot relegate the native tradition solely to the Old Testament, even if it may fit there more to our liking, where it may raise less contradictions and where it may be easier to encounter a common point of departure. The dialogue between biblical and Indian religion ought to arrive at the heart of the New Testament itself.

In the New Testament the point of departure for an Indian-Christian reading is always the historical Jesus—Jesus the Jew, Jesus 'before Christianity'.[16] The mystery of the incarnation greatly impacts native theology: 'The Word became Indian and dwelled among us and we have seen its glory'.[17] The indigenous comprehension of the acts and sayings of Jesus, and above all his plan of the Kingdom of God, comes directly and almost naturally to native tradition.

Among all indigenous peoples exists some analogous tradition to Jesus as prophet and teacher. Take, for example, Quetzalcoatl in all of meso-America or Ibeorgun among the Kunas. The comprehension of the cross of Jesus has come to be seen as that of the Indians who were crucified

16. See A. Noland, *¿Quien es este hombre? Jesus, antes del Cristianismo* (Santander: Sal Terrae, 1981).
17. This is how a Kuna Indian paraphrased Jn 1.14.

throughout history. The history of Christian mission, as historically founded in the resurrection of the messiah and in the experience of the Holy Spirit, is appropriated as part of the profound religious and spiritual experience of all indigenous peoples. The indigenous religious experience is a spiritual experience, a 'life according to the Spirit'. Finally, the book of Revelation enthuses through its vision of history and through its use of symbols and myths, that which permits a reconstruction of the consciousness of the undergoing crises of the oppressed, their oppression and persecution.[18]

Natives are very interested in becoming familiar with the New Testament in order to understand the birth of Christianity, as well as to be able to critically assess it in its later development. They are interested to know what the Jesus movement *before* Christianity was like; what the apostolic mission and the force of the Spirit *before* the institutional organization of the Church were like; and finally, how the Church left to us by the apostles was organized *before* the constitution of occidental and colonial Christendom. Such a remembrance of Christian origins has great impact on native tradition, aiding in the recovery of its own identity. But also, the recovery of Christian origins has a great impact on the reconstruction, in critical form, of an authentic Indian-Christian identity.

Dialogue between indigenous cultural and religious traditions and the Bible is bringing about a profound respect for their distances and differences. There is an absence of concordism and fundamentalism. There exists a dialogue where the native people appropriate the Bible, where the Bible is understood as part of indigenous tradition and as interior to its categories, and where the Bible is read in order to better understand and discern the native traditions themselves. This reading of the Bible is a constant and common practice today in many places within Latin America. Here we have given some features of this practice simply to provide a feeling of it. We will have to wait many years more to see this practice produce all of its potential fruits. For the moment we listen, each time more closely, to the testimony of the indigenous peoples saying, 'We better understand the Bible as part of our native traditions; We better understand our own native traditions as part of the native reading and interpretation of the Bible'. While we continue listening to this

18. The Náhuatl text named 'Nican Mopohua' has great apocalyptic measure, which essentially accomplishes in native history the same function as the Book of Revelation: namely, the reconstruction of the consciousness of an oppressed people through symbols and myths, in a time of chaos and crisis.

testimony, we know that we are moving along the right path and that in the practice we are constructing an indigenous hermeneutic. Such a dialogue holds much mutual respect, mutual appropriation and acculturation; where no one destroys any one else and all are enriched in the quest for the Word of God. The biblical appropriation process on the part of natives is transcending the indigenous trauma with the Bible that I commented on at the beginning of this essay. The indigenous peoples are not talking about returning the Bible to the Pope, but exactly the opposite: appropriating the Bible in order to work within the liberating evangelization to Christians still colonized, and in the evangelization to the Church still held captive by colonial idolatries and perversions. The encounter of native theology with the Bible and the rise of a liberating indigenous hermeneutic is certainly a sign of hope, finally, after 500 years.

THE TEXT AS OTHER:
TOWARDS A HISPANIC AMERICAN HERMENEUTIC

Fernando F. Segovia

The world of biblical criticism today, in the mid 1990s, is very different from the world of biblical criticism in which I was trained as a student in the early to mid 1970s and within which I began to function as a critic and educator in the late 1970s. In the course of these twenty years, the field has undergone a fundamental shift, a shift of such magnitude and consequences that it cannot be reasonably compared to any other development in the discipline in the course of the century. This shift has been like no other, and it is by no means over yet; in fact, as the present conference on cultural exegesis clearly indicates, its impact has only just begun. Indeed, among its manifold and far-reaching consequences, the shift has allowed for a thorough and ongoing reformulation of the proper role of experience and culture in the task of biblical criticism and interpretation. It is this particular issue that I should like to address in this study.

The shift left many practitioners of the field—above all, older scholars fully established in the discipline and the profession—quite *démodé* and under unexpected attack. It left them not only in bewilderment and consternation but also with a marked degree of bitterness, with that sense of realized and sarcastic eschatology that often accompanies the evaluation of newfangled ideas by an aging generation, accustomed to power and authority but now seriously called into question (the after-me-comes-the-deluge syndrome).[1] Of those who were not willing to be left behind and who opted for change—a much easier decision for younger scholars with less vested interest in the professional or disciplinary status quo—

---

1. E. Freund, *The Return of the Reader: Reader-Response Criticism* (New Accents; New York: Methuen, 1987), pp. 1-20; C. Roland and M. Corner, *Liberating Exegesis: The Challenge of Liberation Theology in Biblical Studies* (Louisville: John Knox, 1989), pp. 35-69.

the shift has demanded a thorough retooling. Such retraining involved a new way of seeing altogether, grounded in wide and massive reading in fields which had not formed part of their original training in the discipline and which were in themselves undergoing major changes at the same time. For many such people, including myself, the shift has proved to be a truly liberating force.

The shift to which I am referring concerns the long dominance and swift demise of the historical critical model of interpretation, in unquestioned control for the first three quarters of the century but in broad retreat during its last and present quarter.[2] Though the sequence as well as the aims and tools of its various methodological movements (source criticism; form criticism; tradition criticism; redaction criticism; composition criticism) are well-known, its basic strategy for reading and underlying theoretical orientation are not, since the model itself did not require theoretical sophistication of its practitioners, only practical expertise. In other words, the model had little critical self-consciousness, either of itself as a model or of its relationship as model to other models of interpretation.[3] I should like to begin, therefore, with an overview of the

2. The first notes of concern or warning begin to appear in the course of the 1970s. Thus, for example, Petersen speaks of 'a process of potentially revolutionary change' with the future of the method as a 'lively question' (pp. 9-10): N. Petersen, *Literary Criticism for New Testament Critics* (Guides to Biblical Scholarship; Philadelphia: Fortress Press, 1978). Similarly, Stuhlmacher speaks of the method as 'involved in a war on many fronts,' with its 'relevance... in part subject to serious doubt in theological and ecclesiastical circles' (pp. 19-21): P. Stuhlmacher, *Historical Criticism and Theological Interpretation of Scripture: Toward a Hermeneutic of Consent* (trans. R.A. Harrisville; Philadelphia: Fortress Press, 1977).

3. Such theoretical myopia had inevitable consequences. For example, its concentration on acquiring the basic methodological tools for interpretation allowed it to think of itself, quite unreflectively and uncritically, as 'the' method, as the one view of criticism shared by all, without any realization of its own theoretical and ideological foundations. Likewise, its failure to enter into critical exchange with other interpretative models, varied as they were during the course of the century, not only reinforced this provincial view of itself as 'the' model but also prevented it from responding satisfactorily to the theoretical challenges that eventually emerged, adding thereby to the consternation and frustration of its practitioners. Its focused attention on the wherewithal of exegesis rendered any concern for its theoretical rationale unnecessary, and, as such, devoid of theoretical sophistication. It was left basically defenseless.

basic principles underlying the model and its strategy for reading a text.[4] A critical exposition of this model as model will make it easier to address the very important issue of experience and culture in the reading of the Bible.

1. *Historical Criticism: The Search for Universality and Objectivity*

First, the historical critical model approached the biblical text as historical evidence from and for the time of composition. As such, the text was to be read and analyzed within its own historical context and regarded as a direct means for reconstructing the historical situation that it presupposed, reflected and addressed. Within this overall historical conception of the text, its character as a religious document was specially emphasized, with a corresponding focus on its theological content and message. For the model, the meaning of the text was seen as residing either in the world represented by the text or in the intention of the author of the text, or both.[5] Consequently, an analysis of the text as text never really formed part of its methodological repertoire until the very end, and then the entire model began to collapse.

Secondly, since the model did not regard the biblical text as a literary, rhetorical and ideological production in its own right, there was little conception of the text as an artistic, strategic and ideological whole. In fact, as it presently stood, the text was often regarded as quite problematic and even unintelligible, full of 'aporias'—textual unevennesses, difficulties or contradictions—of a stylistic, logical or theological sort. The presence of such aporias led to a view of the text as the end result of a long process of accretion and redaction and to an analysis of such a text in terms of an excavative reading involving the separation and reconstruction of its constitutive literary layers, often in conflict with one another. In fact, it was the juxtaposition of such layers that created the aporias, which served in turn as guideposts for the process of

4. R. Collins, *Introduction to the New Testament* (Garden City, NY: Doubleday, 1983), pp. 41-69; P. Stuhlmacher, *Historical Criticism*, pp. 22-60.

5. In terms of M.H. Abrams' useful typology of critical theories, historical criticism would qualify as a combination of mimetic and expressive theory: M.H. Abrams, *The Mirror and the Lamp: Romantic Theory and the Critical Tradition* (London: Oxford University Press, 1953), pp. 3-29; M.A. Powell, *What is Narrative Criticism?* (Guides to Biblical Scholarship; Minneapolis: Fortress Press, 1990), pp. 1-10.

composition and analysis.[6] The reading involved was, therefore, a reading from the ground up rather than from beginning to end.[7]

Thirdly, the model had a strong positivistic foundation and orientation. The meaning of the text was univocal and objective, and it could be retrieved if the proper methodology, scientific in nature, was rigorously applied. Further, since the text presupposed, reflected, and addressed a historical situation, the path of history itself, likewise univocal and objective in nature, could be scientifically reconstructed as well. To be sure, disagreements in such retrievals and reconstructions were constant and profound, leading to criticism of works other than one's own as somehow defective in conception or application; intrinsic to historical criticism was the methodological exposé or demolition of previous scholarship, usually carried out at the beginning of any work in a section generally known as the history of scholarship. Scholarship was thus seen as ultimately progressive and evolutionary in principle, though subject to serious deviations and aberrations, rather than in terms of different strategies of reading.

Fourthly, given its scientific basis and approach, the model called for a very specific kind of reader—the reader as a universal and informed critic. The biblical critic assumed a position of neutrality and impartiality with regard to the text through a careful application of the proper methodological tools of the discipline; as a result, the critic brought nothing to the text in the process of interpretation. Thus, in order to recover the objective meaning of the text, the critic assumed an air of objectivity, divesting himself (gender emphasized) of all presuppositions, whether theological or sociocultural. It was the function of such a disinterested critic to approximate the meaning of the text, unpack it, and make it available to everyday, untrained readers. In the process, to be sure, the position of the critic emerged as a highly authoritative and

6. For a recent and sharp exposition of this procedure, in the area of Gospel studies, see: R.T. Fortna, *The Fourth Gospel and Its Predecessor: From Narrative Source to Present Gospel* (Minneapolis: Fortress Press, 1988), pp. 1-11. Interestingly enough, this technical term of historical criticism becomes very important as well for deconstruction, with 'aporia' as that point where the self-contradictory meanings of the text can no longer be resolved. While in historical criticism the 'aporia' leads to earlier versions of the text, with varying degrees of reconstruction, in deconstruction the 'aporia' leads to a view of the meaning of the text as undecidable.

7. For the evolutionary theory of literature underlying the model, see Petersen, *Literary Criticism*, pp. 11-20.

powerful one, within a hierarchical system consisting of text, critic and reader.

Fifthly, the model possessed a strong underlying theological stance to the effect that Christian doctrine and life were subject to the guidance and judgment of the Word of God. Since the texts possessed a univocal and objective meaning, and since this meaning could be retrieved by means of a properly informed and conducted scientific inquiry, the meaning uncovered was a meaning for all times and all cultures. Consequently, a proper hermeneutical appropriation and application of the text was ultimately based on such a meaning and such an interpretation of the text. In other words, it was the original meaning of the text, properly secured and established, that dictated and governed the overall boundaries or parameters for Christian doctrine, life and stance vis-à-vis the world.

Finally, the model presupposed and entailed a very specific and universal pedagogical model: all readers, regardless of theological persuasion or sociocultural moorings, could become such informed and universal critics, if the right methodological tools were properly disseminated and acquired. It was a pedagogical model of learned impartation and passive reception, highly hierarchical and authoritative in character, with strong emphasis on academic pedigree (who studied under whom) and schools of thought (proper versus improper approximations to the text). Not surprisingly, this educational model closely paralleled the interpretive model, with students and readers ultimately dependent on teachers and critics for an account of the text and its meaning.

From the point of view of experience and culture, the model may be seen as a mixed model. While it took into account the social context of the work under analysis, it deliberately bypassed the social context of the critic reading and interpreting such a work. Thus, while the culture and experience underlying the texts themselves were regarded as essential for sound scholarship and proper interpretation, as something to be avidly pursued, the culture and experience informing the readers of these texts were looked upon as intrusive and unscholarly, as something to be avoided at all cost, so as not to vitiate or contaminate the whole process of interpretation. The rightful task of the critic, it was often repeated, was exegesis, not eisegesis—a reading of the text, not a reading into the text; allowing the text to speak on its own terms rather inserting one's words into the text.[8] To be sure, such a task was in principle a noble and praiseworthy one, but ultimately quite naïve as well as quite dangerous.

On the one hand, given its search for the social context of the biblical text, the critical task demanded the acquisition of such varied methodological tools as a mastery of the pertinent ancient languages, familiarity with textual criticism, and a command of the scholarly tradition on the text or topic under investigation, thus making quite necessary as well the learning of several modern languages seen as essential to the development and direction of the discipline—(in order of importance) German, English and French. Given the emphasis on the theological character of these texts, the task also called for thorough acquaintence with the theological tradition, its traditional categories and terminology. Further, given the focus on recovery and reconstruction of the past, the task also involved intensive knowledge of the period and area under consideration, its historical framework, social institutions, cultural conventions, forms of religious expression, and literary production and forms. With such expertise on hand, the critic became fully equipped and ready for the rigorous exercise of the discipline.

In retrospect, however, such methodological expertise did have a number of salient weaknesses. First, although biblical criticism is clearly a form of literary criticism, involving the criticism of ancient texts, the training did not require an informed and thorough grounding in the

8.　J. Hayes and C.R. Holladay, *Biblical Exegesis: A Beginner's Handbook* (Atlanta: John Knox, 1982), pp. 5-29. Here the language of exegesis/ eisegesis, proper scientific tools, and meaning of the text still predominate. The authors do specify that the meaning of the text is virtually inexhaustible and hence only partially available to any particular kind of exegesis. At the same time, the role of the reader as reader is almost completely bypassed. In the end, eisegesis is described in terms of either asking the wrong questions of the text or answering the right questions wrongly. See also the beginning remarks to an introduction to New Testament exegesis meant for the German student: H. Conzelmann and A. Lindemann, *Interpreting the New Testament: An Introduction to the Principles and Methods of N.T. Exegesis* (trans. S.S. Schatzmann; Peabody, MA: Hendrickson, 8th edn [1985], 1988), pp. 1-5. Once again, the language of exegesis/eisegesis, scientific study and criteria, and proper understanding of the text are very much in evidence. The authors do point out that the exegete must be aware of his own presuppositions, conceived in purely theological terms; however, such awareness is seen as necessary in order to avoid reading such presuppositions in and into the text. A focus on the reader as reader, therefore, remains at a very minimal level indeed.

wider world of literary theory, whether European or American. Thus,
how this particular approach to the texts stood within the history of literary theory or how it conformed to or differed from other contemporary approaches was never considered a subject of interest or discussion.
As a result, why this approach did what it did, in the way that it did do
it, was never addressed explicitly, much less in a critically comparative
fashion. Similarly, in its study of the ancient world and culture—a world
far removed from that of its modern students and a study requiring
close attention to the problems inherent in any type of cross-cultural
analysis—no appeal was made to sociological or anthropological models
employed in cross-cultural studies. Given the absence of a properly
informed theoretical basis, the approach to the social context of the
texts, detailed and learned as it was, remained throughout at a rather
impressionistic level.[9] Finally, in its overriding concern for the theological content and message of the texts, the training fostered a rather
provincial and idealistic approach to the texts, with a focus on biblical
theology but without a corresponding appreciation for the literary and
rhetorical dimensions of the texts as texts, the social conditions underlying the production and reception of these texts, or the broader ideological stance represented and espoused by the texts. Consequently, the
early Christian movement was seen almost exclusively in terms of
theological positions, conflicts, and developments.[10]

On the other hand, given its eschewal of subjectivity, its aversion to
any regard for the social context of the interpreter, the critical task also
called for a negation of the critic's own particularity and contextuality.
In the end, however, such a negation was far more apparent than real.

First, the model revealed a serious tension between aim and praxis,
with its exegetical results belying and undermining its theoretical goals.
Despite its stated objectives, its interpretive findings did not yield any
type of univocal or objective meaning, accepted by all. Scholarly disagreements were constant and profound with regard to any text, large

    9. B.J. Malina, 'The Social Sciences and Biblical Interpretation', in
N.K. Gottwald (ed.), *The Bible and Liberation: Political and Social Hermeneutics*
(Maryknoll: Orbis Books, 1983), pp. 11-25; 'Why Interpret the Bible with the Social
Sciences?', *American Baptist Quarterly* 2 (1983), pp. 119-33.
    10. R. Scroggs, 'The Sociological Interpretation of the New Testament: The
Present State of Research', *NTS* 26 (1979-80), pp. 164-79; S.K. Stowers, 'The
Social Sciences and the Study of Early Christianity', in W.S. Green (ed.),
Approaches to Ancient Judaism (BJS, 5; Atlanta: Scholars Press, 1985), pp. 149-81.

or small, or any issue, major or minor. Whatever consensus there emerged, it was frequently either highly ephemeral in nature and/or directly attributable to the particular school of thought, religious tradition, or even nationality at work. In fact, the discussion often turned out to be an in-house discussion. For example, as the footnotes invariably showed, it was clear that, for the most part, the Germans read and interacted with one another, as did the English and the French.

Secondly, the model was incredibly naïve. Even when presuppositions—always understood in terms of theological or religious traditions—on the part of the interpreter were acknowledged, such presuppositions, it was argued, could be effectively accounted for and obviated, yielding in the end a fairly objective account of the text and its meaning. As a result, what were in effect personal and social constructions regarding texts and history were advanced as scholarly retrievals and reconstructions, scientifically secured and hence not only ideologically neutral but also methodologically unassailable, though, as already indicated above, such reconstructions and retrievals were immediately subjected to sharp criticism by a bevy of similarly-intentioned practitioners of the discipline.

Finally, the model was inherently colonialist and imperialistic. Despite its denial of particularity and its pursuit of impartiality, the model clearly emerged not only out of a European setting but also out of a male European setting. As such, it was and remained thoroughly Eurocentric, indeed thoroughly male-Eurocentric, at every level of discourse and inquiry. The model unreflectively universalized its bracketed identity, expecting on the surface all readers everywhere to become ideal critics, informed and universal, while in actuality requiring all readers to interpret like male European critics. The entire discussion, from beginning to end and top to bottom, was ultimately characterized and governed by the fundamental concerns, questions, and horizons of this particular group, uncritically disguised as the fundamental questions, concerns, and horizons of the entire Christian world. To become the ideal critic, therefore, was to enter into a specific and contextualized discussion—a European discussion.[11]

---

11. On this point, with a specific focus on African American students and critics in graduate programs and academic institutions governed by Eurocentric interests, see the interesting essay: W.H. Myers, 'The Hermeneutical Dilemma of the African American Biblical Student', in C.H. Felder (ed.), *Stony Road We Trod: African American Biblical Interpretation* (Minneapolis: Fortress Press, 1991), pp. 40-56.

In the end, the historical critical model collapsed from within and without. From within, it simply got to the point where its own methodological development was no longer able to address the emerging new questions, concerns, and challenges. On the one hand, with the change in the 1970s from redaction criticism to composition criticism, a turn to literary theory became inevitable.[12] Once a consideration of the role of the author shifted from an analysis of the changes introduced into the received tradition—the heart of redaction criticism—to an examination of the finished product in terms of its overall (theological) arrangement and development—the goal of composition criticism—the need for literary theory became obvious. On the other hand, with the pronounced interest of both redaction and composition criticism in the social context of each text and its underlying community, a turn to social theory—of whatever sort, whether sociological, anthropological, or economic— became imperative as well. The traditional tools of the discipline were simply no longer able to address such challenges satisfactorily; new tools were very much in order, and new tools began to be imported en masse into the discussion.

From without, ongoing developments in a wide number of disciplines, including systematic theology, involving a focus on theory as perspective with its own ideological and social foundations, made any claims for a disinterested objectivity in interpretation simply untenable and subject to critical exposé. In the theological world the validity and ideology of such claims came under increasing attack from a wide variety of quarters, as more and more outsiders entered the theological disciplines, both in the Euro-American world and in the Third World, and began to claim their own voice in theology and interpretation. Once again, the traditional stance of the discipline was simply unable to meet such emerging challenges adequately; new orientations were urgently needed, and new orientations were adopted en masse within the discipline.

In retrospect, one may say that on one level the historical critical model, under the guise of neutrality and impartiality, dehumanized the reader, asking for the divestiture of all those factors which constitute and

---

12. Redaction criticism begins in the 1950s, solidifies in the 1960s, and begins to yield to composition criticism in the 1970s. For a brief account of redaction criticism see R.F. Collins, *Introduction to the New Testament*, pp. 196-230; and N. Perrin, *What is Redaction Criticism?* (Guides to Biblical Scholarship; Philadephia: Fortress Press, 1969); *idem*, 'The Evangelist as Author: Reflections on Method in the Study and Interpretation of the Synoptic Gospels and Acts', *BR* 17 (1972), pp. 5-18.

characterize the reader as reader—such as gender, ethnic or racial background, socioeconomic class, sociocultural conventions, educational attainment, ideological stance. On another level, however, such divestiture was not a dehumanization at all but rather a rehumanization, insofar as objectivity and impartiality were cover terms for Europeanization, given the thoroughly Eurocentric contours and orientation of the discipline. Thus, while the experience and culture of readers and critics were seemingly sacrificed in the pursuit of truth, in effect it was the experience and culture of some critics and readers that were sacrificed to the experience and culture of other critics and readers. Again, the ideal was praiseworthy but hopelessly and dangerously naïve; its result was a situation of classic neocolonialism, where the interests of the colonized or margins were sacrificed, subtly but surely, to the interests of the center or colonizers.

2. *Text as Other: The Irruption of Contextuality*

As the title for the present study suggests, I believe that the time has come to introduce the reader, the flesh-and-blood reader, fully and explicitly into the practice of biblical criticism and interpretation; to acknowledge that no reading, informed or uninformed, takes place in a social vacuum or desert; to allow fully for contextualization, for culture and experience, not only with regard to texts but also with regard to readers, with a view of all readings as proceeding from, dependent upon, and addressing a particular social location or matrix, however defined. This irruption of contextuality I see not as a harbinger of anarchy and tribalism, as many who insist on impartiality and objectivity often claim, but rather of justice and liberation, of resistance and struggle against a subtle authoritarianism and covert tribalism of its own. In effect, I regard the admission and intromission of contextuality as an acceptance of the world for what it is, in the richness and fulness of its diversity, especially in this time of increasing and irreversible globalization in every sphere of life, including the theological and the interpretative—an acceptance of the other not as an imposed and defined other but as an independent and self-defining other.

I should like to propose, therefore, a strategy for taking the reader seriously in biblical criticism, not so much as a unique and independent individual but rather as a member of a distinct and identifiable social configuration, as a reader from within a social location.[13] This reading strategy grows out of my own social location as a Hispanic American, a readily identifiable and distinct social configuration.[14] It is a strategy that I refer to as intercultural criticism and that has as its fundamental purpose a reading of the biblical text as an 'other'—not to be overwhelmed or overridden, but acknowledged, respected, and engaged in its very otherness. It is a strategy that is ultimately grounded in a theology of otherness and mixture and a hermeneutic of otherness and engagement.

Hispanic Americans as a Social Location
As a Hispanic American, I belong to a large group of people for whom biculturalism constitutes a fundamental and inescapable way of life.[15] Such biculturalism reveals two essential dimensions. On the one hand, we live in two worlds at one and the same time, operating relatively at ease within each world and able to go in and out of each in an endless exercise of human and social translation. On the other hand, we live in neither one of these worlds, regarded askance by their respective populations and unable to call either world home. Thus, our biculturalism

13. I certainly do not mean to deny the presence of independence and uniqueness to individuals within such social groupings, but rather to focus on those aspects which characterize individuals as members of specific social groupings. In any case, such a relationship should never be conceived or formulated in terms of an either/or: individuals undergo a sustained, complex and varied process of socialization; the process itself may be questioned, resisted and altered by individuals. Likewise, I by no means present such a strategy as the sole and definitive strategy for approaching and interpreting the biblical texts; it is but one strategy. For other strategies emerging out of the Hispanic American experience, see my 'Hispanic American Theology and the Bible', in R.S. Goizueta (ed.), *We Are A People! Initiative in Hispanic American Theology* (Minneapolis: Fortress Press, 1992), pp. 21-49.

14. V. Elizondo, *Galilean Journey: The Mexican American Promise* (Maryknoll: Orbis Books, 1983), pp. 5-46; A.F. Deck, *The Second Wave: Hispanic Ministry and the Evangelization of Cultures* (New York: Paulist Press, 1989), pp. 9-25; J.L. González, *Mañana: Christian Theology from a Hispanic Perspective* (Nashville: Abingdon Press, 1990), pp. 31-53; *idem*, 'Hispanics in the United States', in F.F. Segovia (ed.), *Hispanic Americans in Theology and the Church*, special issue of *Listening: Journal of Religion and Culture* 27 (1992), pp. 7-16.

15 I operate with the following definition of Hispanic Americans: individuals of Hispanic descent, associated in one way or another with the Americas, who now live, for any number of reasons, on a permanent basis in the United States. For the rationale and attendant problems, see my 'Hispanic American Theology and the Bible'.

results in a paradoxical and alienating situation involving a continuous twofold existence as permanent strangers or aliens, as permanent others. It is a situation that I have described elsewhere as both having two places and no place on which to stand.[16] This situation of double and reinforced otherness may be further delineated as follows:[17]

a. As Hispanic Americans, our present, permanent, and everyday world is that of the United States, whether we are born or naturalized citizens, legal or illegal aliens. In this world we immediately find—much to the surprise of those of us who are immigrants, given our image of the country from the outside as a bastion of freedom, justice and opportunity[18]—that there is a script ready for us to play and follow, outside of which we dare venture only against great odds and with considerable opposition. This script involves a name, a pattern and a value judgment.

First, the name does vary, with Hispanics, Hispanic Americans and

16. F.F. Segovia, 'Two Places and No Place on which to Stand: Mixture and Otherness in Hispanic American Theology', in Segovia (ed.), *Hispanic Americans*, pp. 26-40.

17. Though Hispanic Americans constitute a distinct and identifiable social configuration, the group does encompass a variety of similarly distinct and identifiable subgroups. To be sure, any description of the Hispanic American experience and reality will bear the imprint of the describer upon it. Therefore, it is important to describe this angle of vision, given the diversity that characterizes the group—the voice and perspective that follow are those of a first-generation immigrant of Caribbean descent, a naturalized citizen and original refugee from the Cuban experience of neocolonialism and colonialism, of political convulsion and exile.

18. Such an image is not at all surprising. It is a direct product of colonialism and neocolonialism. The colonized believe—and have been taught to believe—that the world of the colonizers is a superior world, where civilization, however conceived, has reached its zenith and now reaches out to the rest of the world. As a result, whatever is autochthonous or indigenous is regarded as ultimately inferior to what lies at the seat of the empire. This image has of course its counterpart among the colonizers: to lead and guide the inferior and the primitive to civilization, with contempt and derision going hand in hand with authoritarianism and paternalism. Given this bipolar view of the world on both sides, one can begin to understand the shock of the colonized within the womb of the colonizer: the exported image of civilization is very different from every day reality, especially with regard to their own perception within that civilization. For a very interesting view of this relationship on the part of a Protestant Hispanic American, see González, *Mañana*, pp. 21-30. For a sharp description of the relationship between the dominant and the subordinate, from a feminist perspective, see J.B. Miller, *Toward a New Psychology of Women* (Boston: Beacon Press, 2nd edn, 1986), pp. 3-12.

Latinos as recurrent options. The important point in this regard, however, is the fact that none of these names are names that we employ of
ourselves. The names are given to us and thus form part of the script
itself. Secondly, the pattern behind the name is consistent and inflexible:
regardless of the geographical or social origins, we are all seen in terms
of a rather monolithic and undifferentiated mass. Again, we have but
little choice in this regard, with no amount of explanation seemingly
capable of altering the established pattern. Third, the value judgment that
underlies the pattern is not only similarly rigid and unchanging but also
quite disparaging and destructive. Its overall contours encompass such
attributes as lazy and unenterprising, carefree and sensual, undisciplined
and violent, vulgar and unintelligent. Its corresponding images in popular
culture come readily to mind: the Puerto Rican gangs of 'West Side
Story', the Mexican outlaws or *bandidos* of countless Westerns, the
drug lords and pushers of 'Miami Vice' and countless other television
programs, the Carmen Mirandas and Ricky Ricardos of this world. Thus,
the name and the pattern are by no means neutral but reveal and
convey a dominant perception of the group as primitive, inferior and
uncivilized. Once again, we find ourselves tightly locked into this external view of ourselves, with protestation or enlightenment considered
seemingly useless enterprises. In our present, permanent, and everyday
world, therefore, we begin as strangers and remain strangers
throughout—the undesirable others, the ones who do not fit.

b. As Hispanic Americans, directly or indirectly, our former, traditional, and distant world is that of Latin America, even for those whose
world was annexed by the United States, as is the case with Puerto Rico
and the formerly Mexican territories of the Southwest. Contrary to
popular perception in our present world, this former world of ours is a
world of profound differences, incredible diversity and great richness.
First, in direct contrast to the homogeneity ascribed to us via name and
pattern in our present world, we hail from many and enormously
diverse quarters—many countries and areas, each with its own distinctive history, traditions and culture—and we call ourselves mainly by our
place of origin, for example, Dominicans, Puerto Ricans, Salvadoreans.
Similarly, in direct contrast to the judgment rendered against us, we represent, in varying degrees and configurations, a new *raza*, a rich mixture
of races and cultures, encompassing European, African, American and
even Asian components. Ironically, such mixture has perhaps never
interacted before to the extent that it now does in the United States,

especially given our present numbers as equivalent to the fifth most populous nation in Latin America, so that in effect the emerging Hispanic American reality in the United States may in the end give rise to an even greater degree of biological and cultural mixture than ever before.[19]

Yet, with each passing year in our present world, we realize that this traditional world is no longer ours: our association with it has become remote, at best intermittent, and passive. In fact, from the point of view of our former world, we encounter yet another script ready for us to play and follow, outside of which we can venture, but not very far. The script has a name: the (willing or unwilling) emigrant or expatriate, such as the Mexican American *pocho* or the Puerto Rican *neorican*; an ironic pattern: getting ahead in the land of freedom, justice, and opportunity; and an even more ironic value judgment: culturally disconnected but economically superior. This script, however, is far more understandable, given our absence and distance, and much more benign, given an abiding sense of ultimate, even if conditioned, acceptance. In our former, traditional, and distant world, therefore, we gradually and inevitably become and remain aliens as well—the distant others, the ones who left.

c. We are thus always strangers or aliens, the permanent others, both where we came from and where we find ourselves. As such, we find ourselves always defined by somebody else—in our traditional world by those whom we left behind and in our present world by those with whom we live; silenced and speechless—without an autochthonous, self-conscious, and firm voice; and without a home of our own—excluded and condemned by such external definitions and such lack of voice. On the one hand, we know and understand, however regretfully and painfully, the definition of those we left behind—a permanent and living association elsewhere does remove one slowly but surely from one's traditional world. On the other hand, we suffer and fail to comprehend the definition of those with whom we live—our permanent and everyday association is disdained and rejected. Such otherness, bestowed upon us and defined for us, overwhelms and overrides us, depriving us not only of a present or self-definition, but also of a past and a future, self-appopriation and self-direction.

Such a constitutive and alienating otherness can be, as is often the case, internalized and lived out, resulting in the classic pattern of the

19. González, 'Hispanics in the United States', pp. 11-13.

colonized—passivity, submission, obedience. To be sure, this process of internalization can and does range anywhere from the truly constitutive or existential (the full acceptance of the external definition as the self-definition) to the purely strategic or tactical (the surface adoption of the external definition as a way of survival). Such otherness, however, can also be turned into a point of departure for the formulation of our own voice, a voice which not only makes explicit the spirit of independence, resistance and rebellion that so often lies beneath the surface of the friendly and hospitable colonized but also gives rise to the classic pattern of the colonizer, the pattern of manifest destiny—self-confidence, self-expression, and self-determination. For me, it is precisely this latter option that gives rise to the voice behind the theology of otherness and mixture, the hermeneutic of otherness and engagement, and the strategy of intercultural criticism.

Towards a Hispanic-American Voice

Given this social location of ours as Hispanic Americans, we must claim our otherness and turn it precisely into what it is, our very identity, using it constructively and creatively in the interest of liberation, not only on our behalf but on the behalf of others as well. I would argue, therefore, that our theological and hermeneutical voice must be grounded in and grow out of this identity of otherness.

a. To begin with, this otherness does indeed have another and much more positive dimension. While our paradoxical situation does mean having no place to stand, it also means having two places on which to stand, a second fundamental dimension which cannot be overlooked or bypassed. The very source of our alienation becomes thereby the very source of our identity. While regarded as 'others' in both worlds of our existence, the fact remains that we do live in both worlds and that we know how to proceed, at a moment's notice, from one world to the other. In other words, we know both worlds quite well from the inside and the outside, and this privileged knowledge of ours gives us a rather unique perspective: we know that both worlds, that all worlds, are constructions, solid and firm constructions to be sure, but constructions nonetheless. We know from our very experience that 'nature' is construction and its 'laws' conventions. We know what makes each world cohere and function. We can see what is good and bad in each world and choose accordingly; and we are able to offer an informed critique of each world—its vision, its values, its traditions.

This privileged knowledge allows us in the end to see our own reality as 'others' in terms of construction—understanding thereby the attributes of and rationale for our perception as 'others'; to use this reality to our own advantage—giving such 'otherness' a voice of its own; and to do so critically, not in terms of 'nature' and 'law' but rather in terms of our own power to construct ourselves as 'others'—avoiding thereby all semblance of a new romanticism or a new imperialism, a utopian or messianic interpretation of our otherness, whereby such otherness becomes idealized or exclusionist. In the end, any such glorification of our otherness would only serve to define and silence those who are 'others' to us, doing thereby unto others what others have done to us.

b. Giving a voice to this 'otherness' of ours entails a threefold critical process of self-affirmation: (1) self-appropriation, or a revisioning of our past and our history with our own eyes; (2) self-definition, or a re-telling of our present reality and experience in our own words; and (3) self-direction, or a reclaiming of our future and self-determination in terms of our own dreams and visions. Thus, the process entails, on the one hand, an active refusal to be bound by our imposed definitions, with a corresponding commitment to understand, expose, and critique such definitions. On the other hand, the process also entails an active determination to advance our own self-definitions, with a corresponding commitment not only to self-affirmation of others but also to a critical exchange with such others and their corresponding self-affirmations. As such, the process of self-affirmation envisioned is a process that confers dignity, liberation and openness not only on the group itself but on all other groups—a manifest destiny that goes against the very grain of manifest destiny, that re-defines and re-envisions the very notion of manifest destiny.

c. In this process of self-affirmation, we must fully acknowlege, embrace and integrate the fundamental characteristics of our otherness. First, we do well to remember our sociocultural past in a world where mixture is regarded as highly problematic and indeed offensive. We are a hybrid people, with a biological and/or cultural miscegenation at our very core. This indiscriminate mixture, this *mezcolanza*, brings together in many and varied ways the heritage of Europe via Mediterranean and Catholic Spain, of Africa and America, as well as of Asia (though to a much lesser extent). Though it is in large part because of such a mixture that we experience rejection in our present world, we must emphasize and embrace mixture: for us mixture is life and gives life. Secondly, we do well to remember our sociohistorical and sociopolitical past. Our mixture is by no means the result of an irenic encounter and coexistence, but rather of a harsh and cruel tradition of colonialism and neo-colonialism. Such a tradition has given rise to a history of violence and oppression, tyranny and corruption. Yet, despite such history and tradition, we have also manifested an enduring commitment to freedom, life and dignity. We must emphasize and embrace such a commitment: in the very midst of chaos and death, we struggle for life and enjoyment of life. Thirdly, we do well to remember our sociocultural present. We find ourselves not only the target of sustained discrimination, socially and culturally rejected at all levels of life, but also in a situation of widespread social devastation—politically powerless, economically deprived and educationally fragile. At the same time, we struggle to make a home under the democratic principles of the nation, hoping that our commitment to life can ultimately take root and grow. We must emphasize and embrace this struggle as well: despite often unbearable conditions, we continue to believe in and strive for our dream of freedom, justice and opportunity in a new home.

This embrace of mixture, life and struggle should ultimately provide us with an identity that recognizes the 'others' but refuses to define them, as we ourselves have been and continue to be defined; that allows such 'others' to speak and to define themselves, in contrast to our own silencing and silence; that is commited not to a placid exchange of views with these 'others' but to hard critical exchange, including the very construction of others as 'others.' Thus, the voice of our otherness becomes a voice of and for liberation: not afraid to expose, critique and provide an alternative vision and narrative; grounded in mixture as something not to be eschewed and marginalized but valued and engaged; and committed to the fundamental democratic principles of freedom and justice. From such a voice emerges a profound commitment not to overwhelm or override the other but rather to acknowlege it, value it, and engage it—a theology of mixture and otherness, a hermeneutic of otherness and engagement, and a strategy of intercultural criticism.

3. *Text as Other: Towards a Hispanic-American Hermeneutic*

The voice of otherness is thus a voice that begins with contextualization and aims for contextualization. With regard to biblical interpretation, it is in agreement with historical criticism to the effect that contextualization is imperative with regard to the biblical texts, but it goes well beyond historical criticism in arguing that contextualization is necessary as well with regard to readers and critics of the texts. In effect, it sees a genuine exchange with otherness—both with the otherness of the text as well as with the otherness of other readers of the text—as impossible without a preliminary renunciation of presumed universality and objectivity, and a corresponding admission and acceptance of contextuality. It is a voice that seeks not a dehumanization or rehumanization of the reader but a liberating and empowering humanization of the reader, of all readers, by taking fully into account the experience and culture of readers in the act of reading and interpretation. Such is the basis for a Hispanic American hermeneutic of otherness and engagement, from which emerges the proposed reading strategy of intercultural citicism.

Its theoretical foundation in literary criticism is that of reader response criticism, involving a fundamental position to the effect that no text is read, understood or interpreted without a reader and its corresponding view of meaning as the result of interaction between the reader and the text. Within this overall theoretical orientation, a broad interpretative spectrum can be readily outlined, ranging from a reader-dominant pole (with meaning coming primarily from the reader, either as an individual subject or as a member of an interpretative community) to a text-dominant pole (with meaning coming primarily from the text in terms of its own strategies and constraints).[20] Within this theoretical spectrum, I would like to locate intercultural criticism to the left of center, towards the reader-dominant pole, with a view of meaning as the result of inter-action between a socially and culturally conditioned reader and a socially and culturally conditioned text, with such a reader as an inevitable and ever-present filter in the reading and interpretation of such a text. In

20. V.B. Leitch, *American Literary Criticism from the Thirties to the Eighties* (New York: Columbia University Press, 1988), pp. 210-37; J.P. Tompkins, 'An Introduction to Reader Response Criticism', in J.P. Tompkins (ed.), *Reader-Response Criticism: From Formalism to Post-Structuralism* (Baltimore: The Johns Hopkins University Press, 1980), pp. ix-xxvi; S. Suleiman, 'Introduction: Varieties of Audience-Oriented Criticism', in *The Reader in the Text: Essays on Audience and Interpretation* (Princeton, NJ: Princeton University Press, 1980), pp. 3-45; R.S. Fowler, 'Who is the "Reader" in Reader-Response Criticism', in R. Detweiler (ed.), *Reader-Response Approaches to Biblical and Secular Texts*, *Semeia* 31 (1985), pp. 5-23; B. Lategan, 'Introduction: Coming to Grips with the Reader in Biblical Literature', in E.V. McKnight (ed.), *Reader Perspectives on the New Testament*, *Semeia* 49 (1989), pp. 3-20.

what follows I should like to explore these three basic dimensions of intercultural criticism:

a. First, the text is to be regarded, like any contemporary social group, as a socially and culturally conditioned 'other.' The question of access is crucial. Rather than positing any type of direct or immediate entrance into the text, the hermeneutic of otherness and engagement argues for the distantiation from the text as a working desideratum, emphasizing thereby the historical and cultural remoteness of the text. Such a hermeneutic begins, therefore, by recognizing that the biblical text comes from a very different historical situation and cultural matrix, a very different experience and culture; that all texts, including the biblical texts, are contextual products; and that no text—not even the biblical text—is atemporal, asocial, ahistorical, speaking uniformly across time and culture.

This operative attitude of distantiation grows out of our own bicultural reality as Hispanic Americans. First, this experience shows us that all reality is construction and, as such, profoundly historical and cultural. Second, this experience further shows us that external perceptions of ourselves as 'others' revolve around the stereotypical and fail to respect our otherness, readily overriding and overwhelming our sense of identity, with disastrous and long-lasting consequences for us both as a group and as individuals. Out of such experience emerges a key element in the theology of mixture and otherness: a commitment to understand those who function as 'others' to us—the many social groups with whom we relate and coexist, even within our own social configuration—in terms of their own words and visions, by allowing them to speak on their own, to create their own narrative, and to define their own identity. Out of this experience emerges as well a key element in the hermeneutic of otherness and engagement: a commitment to understand the biblical text—or any other text for that matter—as an 'other' to us, with its own words and visions, allowing it to speak on its own, to unravel its own narrative, and to define its own identity. In effect, if contemporary and coexisting social groups prove to be so different and so puzzling to one another, then one is justified in calling into question any type of immediate and unqualified identification with texts that come from a very different historical situation and a very different cultural framework.

For intercultural criticism, therefore, the contextuality and otherness of the text must be acknowledged, valued, and analyzed. This process of distantiation is helped immensely by a view of the text as a literary, rhetorical and ideological product in its own right: an artistic construction with underlying strategic concerns and goals in the light if its own point of view, its own vision of the world and reality, within a given historical and cultural matrix. As such, a consideration of the text as 'other' should avail itself of any variety of literary and social methodologies that would bring this multidimensional character of the text to the fore. The ultimate aim of such an enterprise would be an understanding of the text as a whole, as a world of its own, as a construct within a more comprehensive historical-cultural framework—no matter how strange or remote.

b. Secondly, the reader is also to be regarded as socially and culturally conditioned, as an 'other' to both the text and other readers. The question of critical honesty is crucial. Rather than seeking after impartiality or objectivity, presuming to universality, and claiming to read like anyone or everyone, the hermeneutic of otherness and engagement argues for a self-conscious exposition and analysis of the reader's strategy for reading, the theoretical foundations behind this strategy, and the social location underlying such a strategy. This hermeneutic further begins, therefore, by recognizing that the reader, like the text, also comes from a specific historical situation and cultural matrix, a specific experience and culture; that all readers are contextual products and that such different social locations can and do influence the process of reading and interpretation; and that no reader—not even an ideal or highly informed reader—is atemporal, asocial, or ahistorical, speaking uniformly for all times and cultures.

This attitude of self-conscious reflection also grows out of our own bicultural reality as Hispanic Americans. First, this experience shows us that all reality, as construction, has its own way of seeing and acting and that such vision and behavior have in turn their own historical and cultural roots. Second, this experience also shows us that it is possible to live and function with relative ease in more than one reality, taking on or shedding the lenses proper to each reality or world as the occasion warrants. From such an experience, once again, an important element in the theology of otherness and mixture comes to the fore: a commitment to acknowledge and allow for the voice of otherness in a world of incredible diversity. From such an experience, furthermore, an important element in the hermeneutic of otherness and engagement comes to the fore as well: a commitment to see readers, all readers and readings, as distinct and autonomous voices within such a rich diversity. In effect, if we ourselves know how to 'read' reality with more than one lens, then one is fully justified in positing an enormous variety of such lenses and readings, both in the present and in antiquity.

For intercultural criticism, therefore, the contextuality and otherness of readers must also be acknowledged, valued and analyzed. This process of conscious self-reflection is helped immensely by a view of the reader as a product, a 'text' as it were, in his or her own right: a historical and cultural construction involving a view of the past, the present and the future. Consequently, a consideration of the reader as 'other' should avail itself of any variety of social and cultural methodologies that would bring to the fore this multidimensional identity of the reader, with a systematic and sustained analysis of such factors as religious tradition and affiliation, ideological stance, political status and allegiance, socioeconomic class, gender, racial and ethnic background, sociocultural conventions, educational attainment. The ultimate aim of such analysis would be an understanding of the reader as a whole, as a world of its own, as a construct within a more comprehensive historical and cultural matrix—again no matter how strange or remote.

c. Finally, the interaction between such a text and such a reader is to be regarded not as a neutral encounter between two independent, socially and culturally conditioned entities or worlds, but rather as an unavoidable filtering of one world or entity by and through the other, of the text by and through the reader. In this regard both the question of access and the question of critical honesty are crucial. Despite the attitude of distantiation from the text, the hermeneutic of otherness and engagement argues that the historical and cultural remoteness of the text as an 'other' is in itself not a reconstruction but a construction of the past on the part of the reader. Despite the attitude of conscious self-reflection, this hermeneutic further argues that such a construction of the past is dependent as well on the reader's own social location. The hermeneutic of otherness and engagement continues, therefore, by recognizing that the very process of distantiation itself ultimately comes out of a specific historical situation and cultural matrix, a specific experience and culture; that the results of such a process are likewise contextual products, influenced by the social location of the reader in question; and that no process of distantiation—not even a properly informed and self-conscious one—is in itself atemporal, asocial or ahistorical.

This attitude regarding the interaction between the reader and the text again grows out of our bicultural reality as Hispanic Americans. First, this experience shows us that all reality, though construction, is quite resistant to change, that it is not at all easy to go against or deviate from historical and cultural roots. Secondly, this experience further shows us that the external perception of ourselves as 'others' stubbornly resists any type of critical questioning or enlightenment, often turning the whole exercise of conscientization into a frustrating Sysiphean task. Thirdly, this experience also shows us that such a fundamental sense of reality as construction is very difficult to attain within a monocultural matrix. Out of this experience emerges a key element in the theology of mixture and otherness: a commitment to critical dialogue and exchange with the other, subjecting our respective views of one another and the world to critical exposure and analysis. Out of this experience emerges as well a key element in the hermeneutic of otherness and engagement: first, a commitment to critical dialogue and exchange with the text as 'other,' subjecting our respective views of the world to critical exposure and analysis; secondly, a commitment to critical dialogue and exchange with the other interpreters of the text, both historical and contemporary, again subjecting our respective views of the text and its world to critical exposure and analysis. In effect, if contemporary and coexisting social groups prove so resistant to change with respect to one another, even in the face of sharp critique and protestations, then one is fully justified in seeing all reconstruction of the past as another form of construction, no matter how well-informed or self-conscious it may be, especially given the inability of the text to engage in a similar process of critique and protestation.

For intercultural criticism, therefore, the interchange between the reader and the text must be seen in terms of both construction and engagement. On the one hand, the process of distantiation is helped immensely by a view of all reconstruction as construction. In other words, even when attempting to understand the text as 'other' to us, historically and culturally removed, we ultimately play a major role in the construction of such otherness. Thus, even when considering the text as a literary, rhetorical and ideological product, we ultimately have a major hand in the very identification and articulation of its literary structure and development, its rhetorical concerns and aims, its ideological thrust and its relationship to its historical and cultural matrix. On the other hand, the process of self-reflection is helped immensely by a comprehensive and critical engagement with both the text as 'other' and with 'others' regarding their own constructions of the text. First, an understanding of the text as an 'other' to us demands critical engagement with it—a thorough evaluation of its world, strategy and applicability in terms of the reader's own historical and cultural context; the goal of such an engagement is none other than that of liberation itself. Secondly, in attempting to understand the text as an 'other' to us, it is necessary to understand as well how the text has been interpreted by 'others,' by readers in a variety of different historical situations and cultural frameworks. Such an understanding also demands critical engagement with these 'others'—a thorough evaluation of reading strategies, theoretical orientations, social locations, as well as interpretive results, reception, and aftereffects. Again, the goal of such engagement is none other than liberation itself.

Such, then, are the essential characteristics of the envisioned hermeneutic of otherness and engagement and the basic principles for its proposed reading strategy of intercultural criticism. In conclusion, I see this Hispanic American hemeneutic as a hermeneutic with a manifest destiny of liberation: it begins with and aims for contextualization; it opts for humanization and diversity; and it seeks not to overwhelm or override the other but rather to acknowlege it, respect it and engage it. Likewise, I see intercultural criticism not as the sole and definitive Hispanic American strategy for reading but as one strategy among many, with a similar dream and task of liberation in mind.

A NATIVE AMERICAN INTERPRETATION
OF *BASILEIA TOU THEOU*

Sr Marie Therese Archambault and Dr George E. Tinker

Introduction

We feel that this is an auspicious occasion for a conference on 'cultural exegesis'. It is, after all, 1992, the Quincentenary year of Columbus's arrival in the Americas with the resulting devastation to Indian cultures and genocide of nearly 100 million Indian peoples. We have chosen this presentation format to model the basic pre-Columbian, indigenous approach to the sacred and to all reality which in religious expression still continues today: with male and female reciprocity in a spatial configuration being a constant in native myths, creation stories and spiritual ceremonies. The feminine creative power, along with the masculine creative power, is present in the total native understanding of a spatial notion of creation. Prayers in many of our native traditions begin by invoking the oneness of the sacred mystery (God?) as it manifests itself in the reciprocal dualism of Grandfather and Grandmother, as the sacred above and the sacred below. We believe that this should be present in exegesis of the text and it is this balance that we wish to model even in our presentation.

As an aside, the title of the conference is curious enough. At least it implies that the classical Western, objective, scientific exegesis taught in the academies of Europe and America is *not* cultural exegesis, that Western, Christian scholarship is somehow culturally *neutral*. Our essay is, in part, a critique of Western, American-European 'cultural' exegesis.

1. Diverse Mythologies and World-Views

As one formed in the Jesuit-Franciscan Indian mission boarding school system,[1] and whose early life was spent totally in reservation

1. There is a growing literature on the US and Canadian governments'

atmospheres with close relatives and friends whose first language was Lakota; and on the other hand, as one who has entered with fear and trepidation into the world of scriptural exegesis, I must speak of the personal difficulty in putting these two worlds (the native and the Western academic) first, together in myself, and then into a paper such as this, *simply because these worlds are so diverse*, and it will take some scrutiny to determine where they have united even after 500 years of co-habitation.

There was a time early on when I thought that my Indian world was inferior, but as the years passed and as I gazed through an eye trained in Western learning at the rich variety of North and South American native cultures, cultures which are alive and well today through their myths, their religious practices and symbols, dances, manner of relating with all living beings, I came to know that the world of my ancestors is not inferior. But I wonder if these two worlds can ever really find a common ground.

A bird's eye view of the last 500 years, shows that the U.S. government's educational system designed to civilize the native people of this country[2] failed in its main goal, 'To kill the Indian and save the man'.[3] We native people of North and South America after 500 years continue to operate out of the profound, unconscious hold of our own indigenous cultures.

At a gathering such as this, we should be reminded that the Bible was employed by certain US government Indian agents for the purposes of civilizing native people.[4] We native people must deal with the terrible reality that the Bible, the Word of God, was used in the destruction of our cultures and identity. This historical reality stands in the background as George and I reflect upon the meaning of the *basilea tou theou*, the

residential school systems and their destructive effect upon native culture and spirit. This is dramatized in the film *Where the Spirit Lives* published by the Anglican board of Canada. It deals graphically with this historic reality for the Blood Indians of Canada.

2.   There is abundant documentation on this in the annual reports of the Commissioner of Indian Affairs which date back into the mid-1700s. In these government documents one can easily see the patterns of non-encounter, the impersonal policies set out to 'individualize', 'civilize' and 'Christianize' these people.

3.   This was the stated policy of the Hampton Institute in Virginia, established after the Civil War to 'educate' Indians.

4.   A precise example of this is the speech made by a Southern Senator in justifying the removal of South-Eastern Indian people from their land in the 1820s.

Kingdom of God for native peoples. We speak out of our relationships with reservation and urban native Christians with whom we are privileged to work on a day to day basis; and we also know many native people, baptized and at least rudimentarily taught in the Christian faith, who have abandoned the Christian churches to *seek* health and sanity in their own tribal ways. For me, what is saddest about this is the fact that most Indian people today, even those baptized, have not yet experienced the powerful and prophetic yet gentle, healing potential of the Word of God within our native spirit and soul, precisely because it is preached and bound in a Western package. Therefore, to speak *kingdom* language within a native worldview is to experience the juxtaposition of extremely diverse worldviews and ways of approaching and naming the sacred.

Not only are the worldviews diverse, but the method of approaching and studying them is also diverse. Dr Lawrence Sullivan, the current director of the Center for World Religions at Yale, has written *Icanchu's Drum*,[5] in which he describes at great length South American religions and presents *an orientation to their meaning*. But, very importantly for me, he also critiques Western methodology in studying and viewing these religions. What he says refers also to the indigenous people of North America:

> The ideology of conquest permeates every image we possess of the people of the New World, and since the Enlightenment that occurred during the Age of Exploration, has even shaped the way we think about knowledge... By conquering (simply avoiding) the obscurities of the 'savage mind' and by classifying the contents of the wild worlds where these 'savages' lived, the 'enlightened' forms of knowledge... created a new religious stance... The very history of [this] interpretation... is a methodological circumstance, a formidable fact.[6]

Sullivan urges a different scholarly methodology in the study of indigenous religions, one that takes seriously the age-old religious knowledge of indigenous peoples in the Western hemisphere, a knowledge with its own inherent logic and its peculiar non-Western manner of naming reality and the sacred. He seeks to model this proposed approach in the very writing of *Icanchu's Drum*. I agree with Dr Sullivan's work and his hypotheses as discussed at length in his study. We need only look at the formidable historical reality, that the vast majority of native people

5. L.E. Sullivan, *Icanchu's Drum: An Orientation to Meaning in South American Religions* (New York: Macmillan, 1988).
6. Sullivan, *Icanchu's Drum*, pp. 7-8.

have not wholeheartedly cooperated in the Christian endeavor even after 500 years of mission and evangelization. This fact alone speaks starkly of a profound non-encounter between the Word of God and native people.

I mention this as a preface to my remarks in this presentation about a native reading of *Kingdom of God* because it expresses a worldview which has been formed in the kingdom/conquest masculine model[7] inherent in the words kingdom of God—*basilea tou theou*. This bears heavily upon a native American understanding and reception of the *kingdom of God*, because the conceptual background for these words does not exist on the mythological level of native experience, as I will suggest. Because, with few exceptions,[8] the use of the language of *kingdom, queen* or *king* and *reign* refers to concepts and ideas which from pre-Columbian[9] times and until today, simply do not exist in most native languages, that is, as imaging the ideas of divine-right monarchs, male or female, whose power was total within certain boundaries.[10]

Now I would like to mention two myths which underlie the culture from which *basilea tou theou* comes. They demonstrate the juxtaposition between the two worlds of Mesopotamia and Native America.[11]

---

7. I have written of a more balanced approach, which includes the feminine, of native religious expressions and worldviews, pointing out that this perhaps is one reason why Christianity has in large part failed to integrate native ways. See G.E. Tinker, *Missionary Conquest: The Gospel and Native American Cultural Genocide* (Minneapolis, MN: Fortress Press, 1973).

8. A possible exception is the Aztec traditions of Quetalcoatl and Huitzilopochtli, two prominent male gods.

9. V.F. Bricker, *The Indian Christ, The Indian King* (Austin: University of Texas Press, 1981). In this book Bricker demonstrates how the Mayan people of pre-Columbian times easily adapted the Christian expressions, especially about Christ, into their own indigenous practice. Within these religious expressions, Christ had a place as a crucified king.

10. F. Lawrence, 'Language as Horizon?', in Fred Lawrence (ed.), *The Beginning and the Beyond: Papers from the Gadamer and Voegelin Conferences* (Complementary Issue of Lonergan Workshop, 4; Chico, CA: Scholars Press, 1984). 'As human beings, therefore, we concretely and actually have our world as worded, on the one hand—the *Sprachlichkeit der Welt*. And on the other hand, as human beings we performatively have our words "worlded"—the *Sachlichkeit der Sprache*. The upshot of this... is the phenomenology of perception has become increasingly displaced by a linguistic... a "hermeneutic" phenomenology' (p. 13).

11. To underline the juxtaposition a little there are two mythic figures in Western mythological history which bear heavily upon the way the Christian Scriptures have been formed and interpreted. The first mentioned is the Babylonian creation myth

The first of these myths in the long history of the words *king* and *kingdom*[12] can be traced back through its Hebrew Near Eastern roots to Babylonia in Mesopotamia. I refer to the Babylonian myth of *Enuma Elish*.[13] In this creation myth the sea-goddess Tiamat engages Marduk in a violent cosmic battle and is destroyed by him. Marduk then creates the earth and heaven from the two parts of her body. Coming out of this background along with the manifestation and growth of the Hebrew religion, we are aware that the Hebrew Scriptures no longer mention any powerful female deity figure except as the deadly enemy.[14]

Later in the Hellenistic period, the then-Hellenized but formerly Egyptian goddess, Isis,[15] and other goddesses, as the New Testament historical background attests, were also early foes for Christian missionaries.[16] The backgrounds of these two mythic figures provide possible

Enuma Elish, now commonly used by teachers of Hebrew Scriptures to describe the background from which the Genesis stories sprang. In this myth, Marduk the sky god, fights in a long bloody battle with Tiamat, goddess of the ocean, and destroys her. Her body is then torn in half to form the mythic figures of heaven and earth. The other mythic figure is Isis.

12. J.W. Perry, *Lord of the Four Quarters: The Mythology of Kingship* (New York: Paulist Press, 1966 [re-published for the Institute of World Spirituality, 1991]). For the 'Enuma Elish' discussion see pp. 75-80. Also, Perry discusses the total triumph of the male King Marduk along with the pervasive presence of this symbol in its Indo-European diffusion and multifarious manifestation in the Western world.

13. Weir comments, regarding the ancient nature of Mesopotamian myths, 'The archaic era of incarnated myth tapered off imperceptibly in Mesopotamia, for the outward forms survived two millennia of changes of dynasties and empires because of the immense prestige that accompanied these accoutrements of the rulership. It appears that the mythological forms became fully rounded in the middle of the third millennium BC, when the historical era opened, and that they were recorded in cuneiform tablets in the first quarter of the second millennium as relatively finished products'.

14. In the book of Judges the anti-Astarte passages give evidence of this.

15. There is an enormous literature on the history of Isis during a 2000-year period beginning with the 5th Dynasty and going through the Hellenistic period. See several in the Leiden-Brill Series dedicated to Isis research: J. LeClant and M. Fant, *Inventaire bibliographique des Isiacae* (Leiden-Brill Series, 1–3; Leiden: Brill, 1975).

16. This is an important moment in Western history: the destruction of the last temple of the Egyptian-Hellenistic goddess, Isis, in 534 CE by Justinian to consolidate his alliance with the Christian Western kingdom. At that point, Isis devotion had endured for over 2000 years in Egypt and had spread into the Hellenistic world. The destruction of her temple on the island of Philae off Egypt consolidated the Eastern kingdom with the kingdom in the West. 'King', 'kingdom' and later,

keys to perceiving the root and image of *kingdom*.

A worldview without the balance of feminine and masculine is a problem for native people, because native myths, as I will point out later, not only underline the importance of space and sacred place but also reveal a balanced view of the male and female in forming and perceiving that space. This is one of the reasons that the reading of *basilea tou theou* from the native perspective seems uncomfortable and imposed.

2. *'Kingdom' as Inappropriate Metaphor*

This conference is an opportunity to reaffirm the cultural otherness of the biblical text and, more importantly, to emphasize the cultural otherness of exegesis and interpretation. New Testament scholarship has always struggled with the nearly impossible task of translating a text from one language to another. Since languages are never simply codes for one another, there are always things one can say clearly in one language that may not be able to be said at all in another language. More recently, scholars have begun to understand that their task also includes the more difficult task of translating from one culture to another culture. It was the lack of this understanding that necessarily caused Christian missionaries with the best of intentions to function so genocidally with respect to native American cultures.[17]

Even when the scholar fully understands the task of translating languages and cultures, he or she must knowingly take the risk of mistranslating, not necessarily because of failure to understand the other culture or language, but because of a lack of awareness of his or her own cultural presuppositions. We all attempt to be as honest as we can about our own cultural biases as scholarly interpreters. That is not the problem. The problem is that the basis for our conscious presuppositions, the fundamental basis for our thought processes and the discursive category system that evolves out of those presuppositions, may exist at such an intuitive level that we overlook it entirely.

'divine-right kingship' have dominated Western history, theology and scriptural development until today.

17. In *Missionary Conquest*, Tinker treats the American Indian experience of genocide that was explicit and implicit in the work of even the best intentioned missionaries. The examples used in the book underscore the argument that the missionaries did much more than make naive mistakes. Their 'mistakes' resulted consistently in the perpetration of the genocide of Indian peoples as they intentionally dismantled Indian cultures and worked to destroy the very peopleness of Indian communities.

The various interpretations of the *basileia tou theou* during the past one hundred years may be a case in point. We want to argue here that the whole scholarly discussion for the last century has been predicated on an intuitive assumption of cross-cultural sameness, when otherness may have been the case. In particular, we want to argue for a primarily spatial understanding of the *basileia* as opposed to the predominantly temporal understanding argued by Western biblical scholarship over the past century. At the very least, we want to demonstrate that a native American reading of the Gospels must understand the *basileia* from a spatial perspective. We begin with the *basileia* saying in Mk 1.14-15:

> Now after John was arrested, Jesus came into Galilee, preaching the gospel of God, and saying 'The time is fulfilled, and the Kingdom of God is at hand; repent, and believe in the gospel'.

That we are dealing with a cross-cultural translation problem has become obviously apparent over the past couple of decades. We have in mind first of all, the way the language of 'kingdom', the most common English translation of the Greek word *basileia*, functions at liminal and sub-liminal levels to undergird deeply rooted notions of male domination in the predominant Amer-european culture of modern North America.

Long before women colleagues raised our consciousness of the power of sexist language to degrade the contributions of women and to ensure the social, political and intellectual domination of males in our society, we, in North America at least, should have noticed other problems with 'kingdom' language. How many of us know—really know at an experiential level—what a 'king' is? Or for that matter a 'queen'? It has been a long time since many of us in the United States or our ancestors paid homage to a ruling monarch, and some of us have ancestors who *never* knew such a thing. The very metaphor of *basileia* remains culturally radically disjunctive for any American hearer.

Obviously, the language used to mean something to someone. As a metaphor in early first-century Palestine, it must have grabbed peoples' imaginations and fired their visions of political transformation, and on the lips of Jesus it became a vision for social transformation. A metaphor, however, that speaks to one culture in one place may be unintelligible to another culture in another place. Yet we continue to insist that children learn to know the creator in terms of a reality that does not exist for them or for us. Moreover, they learn to identify the creator as quintessentially male and the act of creation as a quintessentially male activity, not requiring female participation at all, in spite of

Old Testament evidence and common sense to the contrary. The problem in a post-monarchical and post-sexist age (we may be too optimistic on both counts), is how to translate *basileia* into our place and culture, assuming that we fully understand what the metaphor means in its original gospel (Greek or Aramaic) context.

Since the emergence of eschatology as a central aspect of the interpretation of the Gospels especially in Western biblical criticism through the work of Johannes Weis and Albert Schweitzer,[18] until very recently the *basileia tou theou* has been given over completely to temporal interpretations.[19] That is, the only appropriate question to ask about the *basileia* has been, When? It is not that scholars did not consider other possibilities. In fact, the question, Where? has been consistently disallowed. Norman Perrin spoke for some seventy years of scholarly dialogue in Europe and North America when he wrote in 1967, '[the *basileia*] is not a place or community ruled by God'.[20] From Weis and Schweitzer to Perrin and beyond, the question had been, When will the *basileia tou theou* happen? When will it appear? In the course of the dialogue a wide variety of answers have been argued, each of them generating a new *terminus technicus* to label the theory. Scholars have argued between realized eschatology, actualized eschatology, immanent eschatology or future eschatology, ringing all the changes on the theme.

Curiously enough, it was Norman Perrin and his student Werner Kelber who in the mid 1970s announced a major shift in interpretation of *basileia*. Kelber first put forth arguments for a consistent spatial understanding of the *basileia* in the Gospel of Mark, linking its meaning to expanding territorial/geographical developments in that Gospel.[21] Perrin decisively articulated the metaphorical nature of *basileia* language, distinguishing between 'steno' and 'tensive' symbols and identifying *basileia* as the latter. So we now can begin to understand the

18. J. Weis, *Die Predigt Jesu von Reich Gottes* (1892); A. Schweitzer, *Das Abendmahl in Zusammenhang mit dem Leben Jesu und der Geschichte des Urchristentums* (1901); *idem, Von Reimarus zu Wrede: Eine Geschichte der Leben-Jesu-Forschung* (1906).

19. B. Chilton (ed.), *The Kingdom of God in the Teaching of Jesus* (Philadelphia: Fortress Press, 1984); W. Willis (ed.), *The Kingdom of God in 20th Century Interpretation* (Peabody, MA: Hendrickson, 1987).

20. N. Perrin, *Rediscovering the Teaching of Jesus* (New York: Harper & Row, 1967), p. 55.

21. W. Kelber, *The Kingdom in Mark: A New Place and a New Time* (Philadelphia: Fortress Press, 1974).

basileia tou theou as a 'symbol' which Perrin defines with Wheelwright as 'a relatively stable and repeatable element of perceptual experience, standing for some larger meaning or set of meanings which cannot be given, or not fully given in perceptual experience itself'.[22]

It seems obvious enough that spatial categories do not necessarily exclude the temporal, nor vice-versa. Yet the orientation assumed by the interpreter becomes crucial. Like Boring, we do not see how temporality can be excised from Mark's proclamation of the *basileia*, yet we certainly disagree with his assumption that the *basileia* sayings in Mark must be read in terms of an 'overwhelming temporal orientation.'[23] To the contrary, we want to argue for the possibility of spatial priority in language of the *basileia*, perhaps in Mark particularly.

The possibility becomes pronounced in any Native American reading of the text, because the Indian world is as decidedly spatial in its orientation as the modern Western world is temporal.[24] In fact, any Indian reader of Mark or the synoptics is bound to think first of all in terms of the question, 'Where?' with regard to *basileia*. It is in this context that we want to pursue the discussion.[25]

Consider the possibility that all of Western biblical scholarship has worked for a century with a trans-cultural blind spot. Why, after all, would the Kingdom of God not be a realm or a place where God rules

22. N. Perrin, *Jesus and the Language of the Kingdom: Symbol and Metaphor in New Testament Interpretation* (Philadelphia: Fortress Press, 1976), p. 30; P. Wheelwright, *Metaphor and Reality* (Bloomington: Indiana University Press, 1962), p. 92.

23. M.E. Boring, 'The Kingdom of God in Mark', in Chilton (ed.), *The Kingdom of God*, p. 140.

24. V. Deloria Jr, *God is Red* (Dell, 1973); *idem*, *The Metaphysics of Modern Existence* (New York: Harper & Row, 1979); G. Tinker, 'Native Americans and the Land: The End of Living and the Beginning of Survival', *Word and World* 6 (1986), pp. 66-74; *idem*, 'American Indians and the Arts of the Land', in *Voices from the Third World: 1990* (Sri Lanka: Ecumenical Association of Third World Theologians, 1991).

25. Realizing that the metaphor presents problems to modern readers, these scholars have attempted to offer new translations, emphasizing the resulting relationship between believer and God, or emphasizing as Perrin did originally, the activity of God as King. The most common translation offered is 'Reign of God', which Bultmann uses throughout his *Theology of the New Testament*. On the other hand, the translation 'Realm of God' is consistently disallowed as an unthinkable translation, because it would introduce spatiality unto the discussion.

or a community that God rules? There are, of course, reasonable arguments put forward to support the position. (For the sake of time, we must short-circuit them to offer our own analysis.) Consider the possibility that at an intuitive, subliminal level there are two very different ways of thinking, of seeing the world, of sorting out reality. Consider that those who think one way, especially if they have developed a system of discourse that has become dominant and highly differentiated in terms of categories, may have no immediate way of acknowledging those who think differently.

Our argument is that those two different ways of thinking have to do with time and space, the when and the where of the *basileia* in Mark. We would argue that space and time are not necessarily two equal coordinates in human thinking, but that usually one is primary and the other secondary for given any culture. We have already asserted that native American people tend to think out of a spatial basis. That is, space is primary and the most fundamental and powerful images, metaphors and myths have to do primarily with space and places. For the Western intellectual tradition, we would argue that the opposite is demonstrably the case, that time is primary and space is a subordinate category. From notions of progress to the casual revelation that 'time is money', from the sacred hour on Sunday morning and the seven-day cycle of work, play and spiritual obligation, to the philosophical and scientific inquiry of the West, time always reigns supreme. Think what the world might be like if Martin Heidigger had written *Being and Space* instead of *Being and Time*, or if Hegel had not had at his disposal the temporal categories that generated his philosophy of history in terms of thesis, antithesis, synthesis. Think what our world would be like if Charles Darwin had not had the temporal modalities to think through the *Origin of the Species*, or if Western theoretical physics had not developed the temporal modalities that enabled Albert Einstein to reduce the whole of the physical world to temporal categories. Indeed, in the West all of space becomes a mere function of time. It is no wonder that the Kingdom of God is also discussed consistently as a function of time.

3. *Native American Paradigms of 'Kingdom'*

Claude Levi-Strauss's structural approach to myths and their importance in cultures bears upon our understanding and references to myths in this discussion. He refers to them as a *bricolage*, that is, forms of human thought processes that are built by the human imagination and memory in the same way as a brick wall might be built, except with memories, stories and symbols which serve to express the deepest spiritual realities and values of the culture to which they belong. Each culture carries its myths as the deepest ways to express self-identity. These myths and stories form the mythological roots and psychic background to a culture's values, and frame and color the background for the meaning of space within that culture. Myths have such a powerful hold that they shape the worldview and even the history of a people.[26] With this in mind, I recall the sacred myths which underpin the Judaeo-Christian Western heritage and now contrast them with two native myths.

In the well-known creation myth of *The Tewa World* related by Ortiz[27] one sees the close and intricate relations between the myth underlying the religion of the San Juan Pueblo people and their total culture and ceremonial life. In the myth, before life on this earth began for them, the people resided below the lake. The Corn mothers, Blue Corn mother and Yellow Corn mother, decided that it was time for them to emerge from under the lake to the earth above. They sent out runners, four young men who went above to reconnoiter. Each of the young men in turn looked in one of the four directions and returned to relate that the world was not yet dry enough for the people to begin a trip up to the higher level. The myth progresses as the people gradually emerge and walk down on either side of the Rio Grande river, and every time they stop to rest another group of them remains at that place to build a pueblo and a life for themselves. Eventually all the people settle down, and this is how the Pueblo people came to be. They still live in these pueblos and the four mountains which were originally sighted by the young mythic runners, the *Towa e*, now form landmarks for the boundaries of the Tewa worldview. The people are dependent on the four mountains in the cardinal directions of the world, for all ceremonies and symbols rise from this mythical account of their origins and the place which they settled after ascending from the lake.

It was the Corn mothers who were the predominant decision-makers who declared it was time to depart from under the lake. As the people

26. V.F. Bricker, 'The Historicity of Myth and the Myth of History', in *The Indian Christ: The Indian King* (Austin: University of Texas Press, 1981); E. Leach, *Claude Levi-Strauss* (Modern Masters; New York: Viking, 1972), pp. 56-58.

27. A. Ortiz, *The Tewa World: Space, Time, Being and Becoming in a Pueblo Society* (Chicago: University of Chicago Press, 1969). The book opens with this founding myth.

emerged from the world below to this above world, their progress was not further dominated by the Corn mothers. Other leaders, such as the Hunt Chief and the Winter and Summer chiefs, arose to meet the crises and needs that arose on this primaeval journey. There was not one single dominant male whose presence resembled that of a chief God.

The entire 'coming to be' of the people was accomplished by the give and take of the people as they settled upon the space which was already there. The mountains which were discovered by the four runners remain in the sacred world of the Tewa because those mountain tops connect with the center of their village to form the sacred passageways where spirits continue to come and go in the ceremonial life of the people. The world of the people of San Juan Pueblo is profoundly set into space and it is perceived as participatory by male and female, even though the primary creative figures are Blue Corn mother and Yellow Corn mother. The *Kingdom of God* for the Tewa people would have to be here in the space where they mythically emerged, in the space that defines them. They could not be in harmony unless it were within that setting.

Another well-known myth is that of the White Buffalo Calf Woman[28] who brought the Sacred Pipe to the Lakota people of the Plains. She is one of the mythic figures who descends from the sky to give the people the way in which they should live: well and in harmony with all living beings—winged creatures, four-leggeds, the earth and two-leggeds. She emerges on earth in the form a white buffalo calf and then appears to two hunting warriors as a young woman of dazzling beauty and stately bearing. She relays a message to the chief to gather the people at a given time and she will come bring them a great gift. When that day arrives and the people are gathered, she bestows a symbol of the union of heaven and earth, the Sacred Pipe and seven sacred rituals[29] through which the people are to maintain balance and harmony with all living beings.

This myth is re-enacted each summer in the many sundance ceremonies throughout the Northern Plains of North America.[30] In this

28. There are many variants on the story of the White Buffalo Calf Woman and how she brought the pipe to the Lakota. See J. Walker, *Lakota Belief and Ritual* (Nebraska: University of Nebraska Press, 1982), p. 109.

29. J.E. Brown, *The Seven Rites of the Oglala Sioux* (Bloomington: Indiana University Press, 1959).

30. For other traditions of the sundance, see F.W. Voget, *The Shohoni-Crow Sun Dance* (Oklahoma: University of Oklahoma Press, 1984).

ceremony, always held in a sundance circle arbor, a beautiful Indian woman representing the White Buffalo Calf Woman is central to the sundance, ritually coming again, carrying the Sacred Pipe. Many native men and women[31] now participate in this sacred ritual to renew and heal their spirits. Preparation for this ritual calls for special and sacred commitment to Wakan Tanka (the Great Sacred, or sacred other) and to the people. The sundance is equivalent to any ornate liturgical celebration within a Christian Church, except that the space for its celebration must be outside, with the presence of a woman as key to it. The celebration, always done in conjunction with the position of the Pleiades star formation and with the full and waning summer moons, could also be seen as a celebration of the *Kingdom of God* because it seeks to image the world in its most balanced way, with Wakan Tanka at the center represented by a young cottonwood tree and by all created beings standing in their proper place.[32]

Perhaps there is one term which embodies a Native American analogy to *basileia tou theou*, and that is the term *mitakuye oyasin*,[33] a Lakota phrase which conveys cultural meaning in all Native American languages and communities. It means '*all my relatives*', and it is spoken at the end of every Lakota ritual prayer. It refers to all living beings and is like a statement of solidarity with all living beings. For native people, such a prayer would best express the spirit of the *Kingdom of God*. It expresses the desire to be in good relations with all those relatives, sky, earth, living beings, animals, winged creatures and all humans. In my understanding, this is what 'kingdom' means in the biblical tradition as well as what Jesus meant when he spoke of the 'kingdom'.

4. *Basileia as a Spatial Metaphor for Creation*

Creation as female and male reciprocity, as balance and harmony of all the relatives—creation as *mitakuye oyasin*: if the Indian image of creation is at all compelling, then we need to come to a new (or perhaps

---

31. In the past, men entered the sundance as an act of gratitude and to shed their blood for the people. Women were already given that privilege through childbirth, therefore it was not necessary for them to dance it. However, in modern times, many native women wishing to express commitment to the people choose to do this.

32. Personal testimonies of individual sundancers reveal that Jesus Christ is frequently visioned during the sundance.

33. C. Ross, *Mitakuye Oyasin* (Fort Yates, ND: Standing Rock College, 1989).

very old) understanding of creation in our denominational theologies and exegesis. It will be an understanding that begins to image creation as an ongoing eschatological act and not just God's initiatory act. We must begin to see creation as the eschatological basis even for the Christ event. If this is difficult, it may indeed be so because the cultures in which the gospel has come to find a home in the West are so fundamentally oriented towards temporality and so oriented away from spatiality. As a result, all the categories of analytical discourse in the Western intellectual tradition function out of a temporal base and pervade our understanding of all reality.[34] This then characterizes our theologies and especially our interpretation of key biblical themes and texts.

Let me suggest some Marcan texts which may begin to demonstrate Mark's spatiality. In Mk 10.46-52 Jesus is coming out of Jericho when a blind beggar, Bartimaeus, cries out to him for help. The important words here have to do with where Bartimaeus is sitting and where he is to go afterwards. He is sitting *para ten hodon*, that is, 'beside the roadside', or 'by the highway', or 'by the way'. After the healing, Bartimaeus is told by Jesus to 'leave' (*hupage*), that is, to return home. Instead, Bartimaeus 'follows' Jesus—a discipleship word—*en te hodo*, 'on the way'. The word *hodos* is used in both places, yet in almost all English translations there is a consistent tendency to translate the Greek word differently in each case, losing what might be an intentional play on the word by Mark. To wit, the healing of Bartimaeus comes at the end of the section beginning with the healing of a blind person in ch. eight. In between these two literary parentheses of two healings of blind people, we have just been told that the disciples who followed Jesus, even though their eyes appear to be open, are really blind. Bartimaeus, it turns out, has a greater claim to sight than do the twelve. Bartimaeus, who had been sitting 'by the way', who had not been following Jesus, has now a better claim to be following Jesus 'on the way'. Is it possible that the way here is a *terminus technicus* spelling out or pointing to the spatial bases of Mark's thinking?

The word *hodos* occurs also at the beginning of the Gospel in the quote from Malachi, and may already be a coded word in that context: 'Behold I send my messenger before thy face who shall prepare thy

---

34. R.A. Nisbet, *Social Change and History: Aspects of the Western Theory of Development* (Oxford: Oxford University Press, 1969). While Nisbet rightly sees temporality as important for understanding all Western culture, he finds this aspect to be wholly positive. I, of course, find it problematic.

way'. Is this notion of spatiality consistently there all the way through Mark? and what would this possibility mean for our interpretation of the *Kingdom of God* in Mark?[35] Lohmeyer already saw geography as an important interpretative issue in Mark, and the use of geography in the enigmatic ending of the Gospel becomes another indication of spatiality that might argue for a spatial interpretation of *basileia*.

We want to suggest that the image of *basileia* represents a symbolic value and that the parameters of the symbol might be filled in as follows: (a) The Gospels seem to view the divine hegemony as something that is in process. It is drawing near, it is emerging (Mk 1.15). Yet it is also 'among us', in our midst (Lk. 17). It is something that can be experienced by the faithful here and now, even if only proleptically. Its full emergence is still in the future. (b) The symbolic value captured by the imagery in no small part includes a view of an ideal world. And, (c) the structural definition of that ideal world is, above all else, relational and spatial.

We are convinced that the imagery of divine rule in the Old Testament is essentially creation imagery, that the ideal world symbolically represented in the image builds on the divine origin of the cosmos as an ideal past and points to an ideal future. To this extent, the ideal world is the real world of creation in an ideal relationship of harmony and balance with the creator. It is relational first of all because it implies a relationship between the created order of things and its creator, and secondly because it implies a relationship between all of the things created. As the creator, God is perforce the rightful ruler of all. Hence, the ideal world to which Jesus points in the Gospels is precisely the realization of that proper relationship between the creator and the created in the real, spatial world of creation.

Human beings may have been created as the last of all the created (Gen. 1), or perhaps a human being was created first (Gen. 2). That is inconsequential for this discussion. What is really at stake is that the harmony and balance of the created order was good. While that order

35. Any Indian person who reads these verses and who reads the story of Bartimaeus would immediately understand that the way is the Red Road, the Good Way, the Way of Life. In much of Plains Indian culture, there are two lines inscribed in a circle to form a balanced cross symbolizing not only the four directions but all of Plains Indians ethics. They are the Good Road and the Road of Difficulties, the Red Road and the Blue Road. Indian people would have little choice but to understand the Way in Mark as an ethical, spatial designation.

has been shaken by the human 'created', it is still the ideal state towards which all look forward in Christ Jesus. The process is going on now, and all of creation is a part of the process. As Paul says, all of creation groans in travail, that is, in child birth (Rom. 8.22).

Repentance

Returning now to Mk 1.15, we need not discuss at length the nature of the word for time. It is enough to acknowledge the cyclical and seasonal nature of *kairos* here over against the more linear concept of *chronos*.[36] In any case the mention of a time element should not distract us from a spatial, now creational, understanding. Nor at this point would it prove fruitful to pursue the verb *eggiken* ('has drawn near').

More important for our case is an understanding of the imperative *metanoeite* ('repent!'). And here we want to argue for the underlying Aramaic (spatial) sense of *šub* as 'return' rather than the Greek notion of 'change of mind'. Repentance is key to the establishment of divine hegemony because it involves a 'return', namely a return to God. Feeling sorry for one's sins is not a part of repentance at all, though it may be the initial act of confession. Even in the most 'Greek' of the Gospel writers, in Luke's Acts of the Apostles, repentance is not a penitential emotion but instead carries the Hebrew sense of return. In Acts 2.37, people feel penitential emotion as a result of Peter's sermon and come to him to ask what they must do. His response is to say, 'Repent and be baptized'. They already feel sorry for their sins. That is not what Peter requires of them. The Hebrew notion of repentance really is calling on God's people to recognize the divine hegemony, to return to God, to return to the ideal relationship between creator and the created, to live in the spatiality of creation fully cognizant of God's hegemony, of human createdness, and of the interrelatedness of all the 'created'. In the Native American world, we recognize that inter-relatedness is a peer relationship between the two-leggeds and all the others—four leggeds, wingeds and living, moving things. That is the real

36. If Mark is, indeed, talking about cyclical time, we ought to consider the notion that he does not have in mind some linear progression of history such as that which Western scholars have called in the past forty or fifty years 'the history of salvation' with its midpoint being the birth, the life and the death of Jesus. That has been most explicitly spelled out by Hans Conzelmann in a book about the Gospel of Luke entitled *Die Mitte der Zeit*, loosely translated into English as *The Theology of St Luke* (trans. G. Buswell; New York: Harper, 1961).

world within which we hope to actualize the ideal world of balance and harmony.

The Indian understanding of creation as sacred, of Mother Earth as the source of all life, goes far beyond the notion of such Western counter-institutions as the Sierra Club or Greenpeace. It embraces far more than concern for harp seals or a couple of ice-bound whales. It embraces all of life from trees and rocks to international relations. And this knowledge informs all of the community's activity, from hunting to dancing and even to writing grant proposals or administering government agencies. It especially concerns itself with the way we all live together. Perforce, it has to do with issues of justice and fairness in the community, and ultimately with peace. If we take seriously the spatiality of *basileia* as a metaphor for creation and the interrelationship of all the 'created' under the creator's hegemony, then it becomes very difficult to pursue acts of exploitation or oppression of one another. The reciprocity of male and female in both creator and creation necessitates a repentance, a return to relationships of balance. It mandates a model of *basileia* that obviates male-female oppression and the resulting power imbalances. Competition between human communities is replaced by cooperation or at least mutual respect. Even environmental devastation is necessarily impeded by the paradigm of *mitakuye oyasin*, because mutual respect and cooperation are then seen as extended beyond the foolish nation of two-leggeds to include all the four-legged, winged and living, moving relatives; even the trees and hills and the earth itself. Such is the *basileia tou theou*. Let those who have ears hear. *Mitakuye oyasin!*

Conclusion

If the mythological level[37] does indeed shape human beings in their deepest self-awareness and consciousness then this paper raises important questions. These address the interpretation of the biblical tradition from an entirely different background, one that cannot be ignored in the Native American reading of the biblical text.

---

37. Bricker, *The Indian Christ*, p. 4. Levi-Strauss comes under attack for his views on the historicity of myth. But the power of myth to affect the history of a people is of great interest to me because of the recent resurgence of the Lakota tradition on the Northern Plains through returning to the religious myths, one of which is that of the White Buffalo Calf Woman.

WELLHAUSEN'S *PROLEGOMENA TO THE HISTORY OF ISRAEL*: INFLUENCES AND EFFECTS

John Barton

'Cultural Exegesis' seems to have two possible senses, one positive, the other negative. Positively, it can be the name of a programme to improve understanding between people of different cultures. In interpreting texts, we can try to look over the shoulders of our fellow interpreters of other backgrounds and assumptions, and see a text as they see it. Thus the white Western male asks, What can I learn from the way a text is perceived by people who are non-white, non-Western, or non-male? Biblical texts seem especially rich in resonances which no one culture alone is able to make audible, and 'cultural exegesis' might be a good name for the collaborative effort that is able to do so. In such a task, as we learned at the Casassa conference, some of those who were last become the first, and the first become last.

But 'cultural exegesis' also has a negative sense, as a way of identifying the cultural rootedness of interpreters with whom we disagree. It belongs essentially to the world of the sociology of knowledge, and emphasizes that there are no neutral or objective interpreters. Everyone has, as people now say, 'an agenda'; everyone has an axe to grind, everyone starts from somewhere. Thus we may sometimes identify an interpreter's cultural background in order to debunk his or her interpretation. There is no surprise if those who served medieval kings interpreted the Bible as supporting kingship. What else would you expect? we ask, implying that their cultural setting has so conditioned their judgment that there is no reason to pay them any attention.

There is thus an ambivalence about the term 'cultural exegesis'. Being aware of the ambivalence, however, can help us to understand biblical interpreters—perhaps especially those from other centuries—with less naiveté, and less inclination to apportion either praise or blame. This may be especially valuable when studying the 'giants' of biblical criticism, about whom feelings can run high. One such is Julius Wellhausen (1844–1918), a founding figure for modern biblical study. His rootedness in nineteenth-century European culture is obvious. Does it 'explain' him, with no remainder? Or did it open his eyes to truth hidden from previous students of biblical culture? Certainly Wellhausen's influence is by no means uncontroversial: some regard it as positively malign. In this paper I intend to trace some of the cultural influences of his work, and to ask how far they go towards explaining it away, and how far the continuing effects of his contributions to biblical study do, and should, remain with us.

The work which made Wellhausen's name, for good or ill, was his *Prolegomena to the History of Israel*, published in 1878 when he was 34, and professor of Old Testament at Greifswald.[1] The *Prolegomena* was originally called *History of Israel I*, since it was intended to be followed quickly by *History of Israel II*. The first volume assembled the sources from which a history of ancient Israel could be written, and—most important—dated them. The second was to be the substantive history to which volume I was indeed the prolegomena. But it was not until 1894 that Wellhausen's *Israelitische und jüdische Geschichte*[2] appeared, and by then the earlier work had long been retitled *Prolegomena to the History of Israel*. Wellhausen's reconstruction of the history could in any case be predicted fairly readily from the *Prolegomena*, and it is from that work, whose implications were very quickly grasped, at least in Germany, that his influence derives.

Wellhausen's one essential insight (or mistake, as his detractors would say) is simply stated. It concerns the date of the so-called 'P' source in the Pentateuch, the material that runs from halfway through Exodus, includes virtually all of Leviticus, and ends halfway through Numbers, and which in the late nineteenth century was often referred to as the 'basic document' (*Grundschrift*) of the books of Moses. On the surface, P is the main foundation document for Israel from the time of Moses

---

1. J. Wellhausen, *Geschichte Israels: In zwei Bänden. Erster Band* (Berlin: G. Reimer, 1878); 2nd edn, *Prolegomena zur Geschichte Israels* (Berlin: G. Reimer, 1883); English translation *Prolegomena to the History of Israel* (Edinburgh: A. & C. Black, 1885); reprinted as *Prolegomena to the History of Ancient Israel* (New York: Orbis Books, 1957). On Wellhausen's time in Greifswald see R. Smend, 'Wellhausen in Greifswald', *ZTK* 78 (1981), pp. 141-76; and *Deutsche Alttestamentler in drei Jahrhunderten* (Göttingen: Vandenhoeck & Ruprecht, 1989), pp. 99-113.

2. J. Wellhausen, *Israelitische und judische Geschichte* (Berlin, 1894).

onwards, and it provides all the detailed legislation, especially about ritual, food, priesthood, festivals, circumcision, sabbath observance and purity which are still close to the heart of Judaism. Apart from the occasional eccentric such as the early nineteenth-century Wilhelm Vatke, almost everyone until Wellhausen's time assumed P to be the earliest of all Pentateuchal sources. Wellhausen's proposal, as simple as it was revolutionary, was to argue instead that it was the latest. By a detailed comparison of the early historical books, such as the books of Samuel, with their later equivalents in Chronicles, he showed (or claimed to have shown) that P must have come into being between the two bodies of material; for Chronicles showed a detailed awareness of the priestly legislation in many areas, whereas from the earlier books one would never guess that it existed at all.

P was in fact a work of the post-exilic age, of the Second Temple period as we might now call it. It was the foundation of Judaism, meaning by 'Judaism' the whole religious and cultural system we now call by that name. It was not the basis of social and religious life in *ancient* Israel, whose outlook was not yet in any recognizable sense Jewish. Ancient Israel emerges as a nation much like others in the ancient Near East; later Judaism is not a natural development from it, but an artificial religion constructed *de novo* by the priests and legislators who returned to Palestine from the Babylonian Exile. Wellhausen himself summed up his historical work on the Old Testament in the words 'Judaism and ancient Israel in their opposition'.[3] And he made no secret of the fact that his sympathies lay with ancient Israel, not with this narrow religious sect, as he saw it. Prefixed to the *Prolegomena* is a motto from Hesiod, *pleon hemisu pantos*, 'the half is greater than the whole'. In other words, the pre-exilic age, the age of J and E and D and the classical prophets, gains in stature if P and the books influenced by it are removed. Of course it would be possible to accept Wellhausen's dating without also accepting his value judgments, but in fact this has proved difficult. Those who have reacted most violently to the portrayal of post-exilic Judaism as 'artificial' have usually proceeded by redating P, returning to the pre-Wellhausen dating and claiming it for the Mosaic or early post-Mosaic age. Nevertheless, almost all modern study of the Pentateuch begins with Wellhausen's scheme, summarized in the four

3.   In a letter to J. Olshausen, 9 February 1879, cited in R. Smend, 'Julius Wellhausen and his *Prolegomena to the History of Israel*', *Semeia* 25 (1983), pp. 1-20 [9].

letters J, E, D, P arranged in that order and no other. The idea is extremely simple; the implications are so far-reaching that biblical scholarship has still not entirely come to terms with them.

From the first publication of the *Prolegomena* to our own day Wellhausen has been sharply criticised, and in a way very relevant to the theme of this conference. Of course there have been any number of detailed critiques of his analysis of the Pentateuch, and also many attempts, often highly successful, to move beyond it into the realms of form or traditio-historical criticism, redaction history or (now) 'final form' exegesis. But the really trenchant criticisms of Wellhausen have always concentrated not on the detailed analysis but on the assumptions underlying the analysis: on Wellhausen's cultural prejudices and his historical conditioning. Three such lines of attack are still current. The first is that Wellhausen was a Hegelian, who saw the history of Israelite institutions as passing through a number of phases on its way to a goal because he saw human history in general in this way. The second is that he was an evolutionist, a kind of theological Darwinian, who forced the biblical materials into the mould of gradual evolution, with J, E, D and P as successive stages in that process. And the third, and most passionately felt criticism, is that he was anti-semitic, hating Judaism and wanting nothing more than to show it up as an artificially concocted religion, designed by proto-rabbis who were the enemies of all that is natural and spontaneous in religious sentiment. The first two of these charges have most commonly been brought by conservative evangelicals, the third by Jewish scholars, but all have been influential also on those outside the particular constituency involved.

1. The allegation that Wellhausen was a Hegelian, or at least influenced by Hegelianism, was already made in the 1920s by M. Kegel: 'Hegel begat Vatke, Vatke begat Wellhausen'.[4] But it was disseminated widely by Albright in the 1950s, through his influential *From the Stone Age to Christianity*, and was accepted by important figures in Old Testament studies such as H.J. Kraus and Gerhard von Rad.[5] The association with Vatke has always been one of its strong cards, for Vatke had already come to the conclusion that P was late in the 1830s, fifty years before

---

4.   M. Kegel, *Los von Wellhausen!* (Gütersloh, 1923), p. 10.

5.   W.F. Albright, *From the Stone Age to Christianity* (Garden City, NY: Doubleday, 1957), p. 88; see L. Perlitt, *Vatke und Wellhausen* (BZAW, 94; Berlin: de Gruyter, 1965), pp. 2-3 for the references to the Hegelian accusation in Kraus and von Rad.

Wellhausen. Wellhausen expressed his indebtedness to Vatke, and Vatke was undoubtedly a Hegelian. I believe, however, that the Hegelian interpretation of Wellhausen has been decisively refuted by Lothar Perlitt in his *Vatke und Wellhausen*.[6] As he shows, Hegelianism was scarcely a viable intellectual option by the 1870s, and indeed was more or less already dead when Wellhausen was born. Vatke was a kind of throwback to earlier times, and for that very reason was more or less ignored by the scholarly community when he published his history of Israel. It was his misfortune, as Wellhausen saw it, to have linked a perfectly correct perception of the lateness of P to an impossibly outmoded philosophical framework, that of Hegel. That was why no-one had taken any notice of him. To suggest that Wellhausen's thinking in the 1870s was Hegelian is thus a hopeless anarchism.

Possibly the neatest refutation of the theory that Wellhausen was a Hegelian can be found in his own work, at the place where he is discussing the often noted patterning of history in the book of Judges. Here, he remarks, 'one is reminded of "thesis, antithesis, synthesis" when one listens to the monotonous beat with which history marches on or turns round in circles: rebellion oppression repentance rest, rebellion oppression repentance rest'.[7] No-one who would *criticise* the biblical text by drawing this comparison could seriously be a Hegelian. Rudolf Smend sums up matters by writing, 'Wellhausen stood at as great a remove from Hegelian speculation as a German historian of the nineteenth century could without falling out of context.'[8]

2. Similar things can be said about the charge that Wellhausen merely applied the theory of evolution to the Bible. Delitzsch was already remarking in 1882 that 'Wellhausen's speculations' were 'merely applications of Darwinism to the sphere of theology and criticism'.[9] The repetition of this suggestion in Anglo-American theology down to the present day is partly tied up, I believe, with a certain misreading of Wellhausen. When I learned as a student about J, E, D and P, I was taught that they represented an orderly *progress*, a growing awareness of the transcendence of God, which was assumed to be a good thing.

6.   Cf. B.S. Childs, 'Wellhausen in English', *Semeia* 25 (1983), pp. 83-88.
7.   *Geschichte Israel*, I, p. 240.
8.   R. Smend, 'Julius Wellhausen', p. 14.
9.   A comment made by Delitzsch to a Scottish visitor in Leipzig in 1882, reported in W.R. Smith, 'Wellhausen and his Position', *The Christian Church* 2 (1882), pp. 366-69; cited in Smend, 'Julius Wellhausen', p. 14.

The parts of the Priestly document drawn on to support this were not from the central legal section which was what had mostly interested Wellhausen, but from Genesis, where P is very fragmentary but contains, of course, the opening chapter of the whole Bible, the sublime creation story in Genesis 1. It was easy to argue from this that the Israelite understanding of God progressed from the primitive to the more advanced, and we were encouraged to think of P as a distinct improvement on J. From such a perspective, Wellhausen's theory does look evolutionary. But his own value judgments, of course, went in the opposite direction altogether. He saw P not as an advance on J but as a *decline* from it, in which intimate contact with the divine is replaced by a frosty legalism, and transcendence mocks the human desire for communion with God. An evolutionary view of the history of Israel would have to say something like the following:

> The history of this ancient people is in reality the history of the growth of true religion, rising through all stages to perfection; pressing on through all conflicts to the highest victory, and finally revealing itself in full glory and power, in order to spread irresistibly from this centre, never again to be lost, but to become the eternal possession and blessing of all nations.[10]

But that is a quotation from Heinrich Ewald, thirty years before Wellhausen. It was just the kind of history that Wellhausen wrote in order to refute.

If we want to understand how such erroneous interpretations of Wellhausen gained currency, we can, I think, identify two features of his work which are highly characteristic of nineteenth-century historiography, in Germany particularly, and which lend colour to charges that would otherwise seem immediately implausible. One is that Wellhausen instinctively thought in terms of stages and developments in history on what we might call a macro-scale. As P.D. Miller puts it, 'Wellhausen seems...to have wanted to schematize [the] history [of Israel]. He was in that respect a child of his times, seeing in the historical process stages in a development'. For example, he goes on, 'in his penchant for stages and phases Wellhausen saw in Amos "the founder, the purest type, of a new phase of prophecy"'.[11] It is a mistake to think that Wellhausen saw

---

10. H.G.A. Ewald, *Geschichte des Volkes Israel bis Christus* (Göttingen: Dietrich, 1843–1855); English translation, *The History of Israel* (London, 1869), p. 5.

11. P.D. Miller, 'Wellhausen and the History of Israel's Religion', *Semeia* 25 (1983), pp. 61-73 (63, 64).

progress in the history of Israel, and that is the flaw in both Hegelian and evolutionary interpretations of him. But he did see *progression*—change and development. History as a kind of positivistic accumulation of discrete facts was an idea he did not and probably could not have had. This is just as apparent in the way he presents the post-exilic age as a decline, as it would be if he saw it as an advance. In that sense he shared many of the same assumptions as Hegelians and evolutionists, though crucially turning their presentation on its head.

Secondly, Wellhausen had what Smend calls 'a total view'.[12] One reason why the *Prolegomena* is exhilarating to read, when other works of biblical scholarship from the same period are mostly somewhat yawn-inducing, is that the whole thing unfolds with such a sense of inevitability, every detail contributing to a coherent and convincing whole. Others before him had redated P—Vatke and Graf to name but two—but no-one had seen how this changed *everything* in our understanding of the Old Testament. As Wellhausen himself put it,

> Critical analysis [had] made steady progress, but the work of synthesis did not hold even pace with it… It was not seen that most important historical questions were involved as well as questions merely literary, and that to assign the true order of the different strata of the Pentateuch was equivalent to a reconstruction of the history of Israel.[13]

But of course the total view, which is Wellhausen's great strength, is also one of the features that most declares him to be a child of his time. Nineteenth-century scholarship in all fields went in for total views, for vast systems and far-reaching syntheses. We are more suspicious today of all such operations.

3. I suppose that the accusation of anti-semitism is one we are likely to take more gravely than the alleged Hegelianism or evolutionism, which for us today amount to scarcely more than the suggestion that Wellhausen is out of date. Overtly anti-semitic sentiments are hardly to be found in Wellhausen's works, but occasionally what one may call the common nineteenth-century mid-European anti-Jewish comment does indeed appear, leading one to surmise that there may have been a good deal beneath the surface in the way of largely subconscious anti-semitism. For example, 1 Chronicles 22–9 is said to be,

---

12. Smend, 'Julius Wellhausen', p. 13.

13. J. Wellhausen, 'Pentateuch and Joshua', *EB*, 9th edn, XVIII, pp. 505-14; the quotation is from p. 508.

a horrible example of the statistical phantasy of the Jews which revels in vast sums of money on paper, in artificially devised regiments of names and numbers...the monotony broken occasionally by unctuous speeches that never come to life.[14]

Hardly an amiable sentence. But more serious in a way than occasional comments like this is the allegation that Wellhausen's whole scheme is in its consequences anti-Jewish, or even that it is driven throughout by a desire to denigrate and degrade Judaism. Lou Silberman argued this case in a contribution to *Semeia* published on the occasion of the centenary of the *Prolegomena*.[15] This work, he suggests, 'like practically everything written by German Protestant theologians of the period and many subsequently and to this day, is a work of anti-Judaism'. Readers of Chaim Potok's novel *In the Beginning* may remember how the young Jewish hero is attacked by friends and family for reading Wellhausen, for they hold, as Silberman also does, that Wellhausen contributed, however indirectly, to that devaluing of Jewish life and culture whose ultimate outcome in central Europe we now know only too well.

The implication of Wellhausen's late dating of P is seen to be the accusation that the leaders of post-exilic Israel falsified the truth about the religion they wished to promote, calling it Mosaic when really they had themselves invented it. As Wellhausen puts it,

It is not the case that the Jews had any profound respect for their ancient history...The theocratic ideal was from the exile onwards the centre of all thought and effort, and it annihilated the sense for objective truth, all regard and interest for the actual facts as they had been handed down. It is well known that there have never been more audacious inventors of history than the rabbis. But Chronicles affords evidence that this evil propensity goes back to a very early time, its root the dominating influence of the Law, being the root of Judaism itself.[16]

On reading this a conscientious person may ask, What further need have we of witnesses? Should we not throw out Wellhausen and all his works? Two factors dispose me to proceed with caution even here, however.[17] First, the Judaism of his own day is not in focus for

14. Wellhausen, *Geschichte Israels*, I, p. 166.

15. L. Silberman, 'Wellhausen and Judaism', *Semeia* 25 (1983), pp. 75-82.

16. Wellhausen, *Prolegomena to the History of Israel*, p. 161.

17. A comprehensive discussion of Wellhausen's alleged anti-semitism is provided by R. Smend, 'Wellhausen und das Judentum', *ZTK* 79 (1982), pp. 249-82; reprinted in his *Epochen der Bibelkritik: Gesammelte Studien Band 3* (Munich,

Wellhausen. I do not suppose he had much idea how his contemporaries in Judaism viewed the questions with which he was concerned. He was interested in origins, in the motivations that led to the composition of the Pentateuch; and it would be entirely possible to share his estimate of what this motivation had been, and his analysis of how it worked itself out in actual literary compositions, without sharing also his value judgment on the resulting system. The empirical observations which generated his *Prolegomena* remain in place, even if one thinks his interpretation of them anti-semitic.

But secondly, and more important, I do not believe that it was really Judaism Wellhausen had in his sights at all—as Silberman to his great credit sees clearly. What Wellhausen was against in religion was empty formalism, legalism, the letter instead of the spirit, authoritarian structures instead of the freedom of the individual. The contemporary manifestations of such aberrations, as he saw them, were not in Judaism but in the Christian churches: not only in Catholicism, which like all nineteenth-century Protestants he would have accused of such abuses, but in the Lutheran church in which he had grown up but in which he had come to feel that he could no longer serve as a Professor training men for Christian ministry—with the well-known consequence that in the years after writing the *Prolegomena* he moved to Halle, and took up a post teaching Arabic studies in the Faculty of Arts. As Silberman acutely observes, what he attacked in the Judaism of the Second Temple period was, in effect, 'none other than the ecclesiastical establishment that while not attacking him made it impossible for him to retain his theological professorship in Greifswald'.[18]

If we want to explain away his conclusions, we may do it by saying that his whole cultural context—and his discomfort with it—led him to reject ecclesiastical authority; and that when he looked back into the Old Testament he saw this abomination 'reflected there' (to use his own words in another context) 'like a glorified mirage'.[19] If we want to understand him empathetically, on the other hand, we may say rather that his experience of organized religion sensitized him to the same

1990), pp. 186-215. The classic formulation of the allegation is Solomon Schechter's comment that the 'higher criticism' amounts to 'higher anti-semitism'— see p. 213.

18. Silberman, 'Wellhausen and Judaism', p. 78.

19. This is Wellhausen's well-known comment on the stories of the patriarchs; see *Prolegomena*, pp. 318-19.

phenomenon when it occurred in past ages. And as always when expli-
cating the cultural assumptions of a past writer, choosing between these
options is extremely difficult, and often reveals as much about *our*
assumptions as it does about his. For explanation by cultural assumptions lands us in a hall of mirrors, as soon as we remember that our own
stance is no more privileged than that of the writer we are studying.
Wellhausen's contemporaries seldom perceived him as anti-semitic (but
then, that may just show how anti-semitic they all were—they hardly
noticed it); but they certainly grasped the danger in his work for the
established Christian religion. 'Troubling the Church of God' was how
Delitzsch described him to a Scottish visitor.[20] 'It seems as though the
author delights in wounding the sensibilities of his Christian readers,'
wrote an early British reviewer.[21] Wellhausen's style probably annoyed
people as much as his content, for it was far from having the gravity
then expected in a work on the Bible: it was light, playful, often
irreverent. But Douglas Knight is right to say that

> at the... base of Wellhausen's opinion about [Jewish] 'distortions' of past
> history was his own anti-institutional posture, which turned him against
> the postexilic intentions—as he identified them—and drew him to the free
> spirit which he saw at play in the early period.[22]

And this anti-institutionalism, rather than the anti-semitism which was a
by-product of it, is what is central to understanding the character of his
research.

If none of these three things—Hegelianism, evolutionism and anti-
semitism—were the driving forces behind Wellhausen's work, what
was? Lothar Perlitt argues convincingly that there are two main
influences on Wellhausen, two aspects of his cultural conditioning, as we
might put it: nineteenth-century German historiography, and the
Romantic movement.

1. To take historiography first: German history-writing in the nineteenth century developed as it did not through the influence of Hegel,
but by way of reaction to him. Its achievement was to emancipate itself
from enslavement to Hegelianism, or indeed any other overt philosophy,

20. Smith, 'Wellhausen and his Position', *The Christian Church* 2 (1882),
pp. 366-69.
21. S.I. Curtiss, 'Delitzsch on the Origin and Composition of the Pentateuch',
PR 3 (1882), p. 84.
22. D.A. Knight, 'Wellhausen and the Interpretation of Israel's Literature',
Semeia 25 (1983), pp. 21-36 (73).

and to try to study ancient cultures and civilizations in all their particularity. Especially in the work of Theodor Mommsen on classical antiquity we find the insistence that good history-writing depends on the accumulation and analysis of empirical evidence, which cannot be predicted in advance on the basis of any philosophy of history. Mommsen, like all the German historians of the period, thought on a very large scale, and was interested in 'world history'. But this was conceived pragmatically, as the result of minute and particular knowledge of every relevant culture—*not* as something to be deduced from the first principles of some philosophical system. Mommsen's watchword, which Wellhausen borrowed with acknowledgment from him, is 'presuppositionless' investigation. In a work of 1901 Wellhausen wrote,

> Our vital concern is research without presuppositions: research that does not find what it is supposed to find according to considerations of purpose and relevance, but what seems correct to the conscientious researcher from a logical and historical point of view—to put it in a single word: truthfulness.[23]

Presuppositionless study is, I suppose, regarded as possible by almost no-one today, and we have already seen how very far from being free of presuppositions Wellhausen really was. Nevertheless, what he thought he was doing was research free from presuppositions, and in this he was pre-eminently the heir of German historiography in general, and of Mommsen, whose work he loved, in particular.

2. Wellhausen's antecedents in the Romantic movement are also clear, and important. Why did he have such a high regard for what he called 'naturalness', in religion as in life? Why this assumption that organized religion, ritual and law represent a decline from an earlier spontaneity in which alone the true goal of human existence is to be found? Wellhausen's early *dating* of J, with its lack of regimentation, can be defended by analysing the relevant texts; but his *valuation* of J as superior to D and P does not, obviously, derive from the biblical text itself. Not Hegel, but Romanticism, offers the best explanation of this. If we want a single source for this love of individualism and freedom from restraint, it will be Herder, who lies at the origin of so much in the traditions of German Romanticism. From him derives the idea that each age has its own particular style or character, what we might call a *Zeitgeist*;

23. J. Wellhausen, *Universitätsunterricht und Konfession* (Berlin: G. Reimer, 1901), p. 153.

and the spirits of successive ages do not necessarily manifest progress, but only change.

But also from Herder comes the belief in the primitive as often the most sublime. Human awareness of the divine does not *improve* over time; what is earlier is usually best, and the later ages of a culture represent more a decline than a progress. B.G. Niebuhr's history of Rome, which influenced Wellhausen's thinking, argued in just this way for the earliest days of the Republic as the golden age of Rome. Wellhausen's affinities with such a way of thinking should be obvious. Characteristic of Romanticism, too, was the enthusiasm for individual heroes rather than for institutions, and we have already seen enough to catch the echo of such an idea in Wellhausen. His interpretation of the prophets was a very clear case in point. If one wanted to explain Wellhausen as merely the product of his influences, German historiography and Romanticism would be the best candidates for the task; and compared with them, Hegel and Darwin are quite insignificant influences, while his anti-semitism, though not to be ignored, played a very small part in dictating the form his reconstructions took.

In a way the single most important presupposition for Wellhausen, and the one which continued (until very recently) to set the agenda for biblical study, is the presupposition he shared with the German historiographers, and to which I have already referred: the notion that research should be presuppositionless. To put it in a way that connects with the idea of cultural exegesis: Wellhausen was culturally conditioned to think that history could be written free from cultural conditioning! In his Preface to his translation of the *Prolegomena*, W. Robertson Smith argued that Wellhausen's achievement was to break free from received, inherited opinion: 'in the course of the argument it appears that the plain natural sense of the old history has constantly been distorted by the false presuppositions with which we have been accustomed to approach it.'[24] It was this plain, natural sense which Wellhausen had rediscovered. A century of philosophizing about reading and understanding texts lies between us and this great pioneer, and perhaps in nothing does he seem so dated as in his belief that he had discovered truths that would not date. Yet we should concede how much more he was than merely a child of his time. His act of synthesis, what Smend calls his 'total view' of the Old Testament, was indeed a liberation from the accumulated

24. W.R. Smith, Preface to *Prolegomena*, p. viii.

assumptions of centuries. It is hard to think of any other Old Testament scholar whose creativity, and ability to redirect the entire enterprise of Old Testament study, have ever equalled Wellhausen's. After him, nothing was ever the same again.

This may seem a strange thing to say if we think of Wellhausen primarily as the great Pentateuch critic, for in the study of the Pentateuch scarcely one stone remains on another of his elegant but maybe over-simple edifice. Some of us, it is true, do still believe in J, E, D and P in the old way, but I would guess that many more have become sceptical not only of the results but of the very methods and aims of traditional source analysis of the Pentateuch. Wellhausen did indeed set the agenda for several generations, but the modern agenda in Pentateuchal studies owes little to him.

But if we look in another direction, toward the history of Israel for which (after all) he himself regarded source criticism as mere prolegomena, then the greatness and the continuing influence of Wellhausen appear very clearly. Wellhausen, it would be fair to say, discovered the Exile. Of course people before him knew that it had happened, but so long as the Priestly Work was dated early, there was no reason to think that the Exile had changed anything in the inner constitution and temperament of the Israelites and their religion. It was an event which had happened to the body of the nation. But Wellhausen showed for the first time that it had also decisively affected the nation's soul. The experience of being exiled in a foreign land, without national institutions such as the monarchy and the Temple, had made the Israelites turn in on themselves and ask questions about their religious identity. The leading people among them had developed the blueprints for life in a restored community, where obedience to carefully devised rituals would replace the chaotic spontaneity which had encouraged the syncretistic tendencies now being punished by Yahweh. Israel could become a confessional, rather than a national community.

These were the implications of Wellhausen's dating of P, and they have become quite firmly embedded in the study of the Hebrew Bible, accepted even by many who would reject the underlying source analysis and dating. The fact that we speak of 'Israelites' before but 'Jews' after the Exile, of 'Yahwism' as the pre-exilic religion but 'Judaism' as the post-exilic, is a testimony to the pervasiveness of Wellhausen's historical reconstruction. The sense that the Exile marked a crucial change in Israel is part of our mental furniture as biblical scholars—for a detailed treatment of how and why it was crucial, one need look no further than Daniel Smith's *Religion of the Landless*.[25] All such works are the heirs of Wellhausen's *Prolegomena*. They testify to the way that his ideas have survived well beyond the historical and intellectual setting within which they were conceived. Working in a time of quite different presuppositions, they show how far Wellhausen was from being merely a child of his time. Anyone who wishes to shake off his influence will find that almost the whole basis of modern biblical study unravels in the process. For my part, I believe that his work was so rich and many-faceted that we have not yet done justice to it all; and so, far from wanting to purge our subject of his continuing influence, I should like to think that modern students of the Hebrew Bible might start to return to it for challenge and inspiration. It is the work of a large, uncluttered and creative mind; and at the same time as it demonstrates how far interpretation is influenced by cultural assumptions, it also offers hope for the human ability to transcend them and to communicate across the gulfs that divide us.

25. D.L. Smith, *The Religion of the Landless* (Bloomington, IN: Meyer-Stone Books, 1989).

WERE THE 'JUDGES' OF ISRAEL LIKE AFRICAN SPIRIT MEDIUMS?

Temba L.J. Mafico

Introduction

I grew up as a missionary protegé. Thus I was completely divorced from my African heritage. It was when I was doing graduate work at Harvard University that I began to study the Bible against the background of its ancient Near Eastern environment. To my amazement, several social and religious practices which I had been taught to disavow as African paganism and superstitions were, in actual fact, similar to those of the ancient Israelites some of which they incorporated in the worship of Yahweh. To learn more of my African culture, I then enrolled for three extracurricular courses in African traditional religions at Harvard. The knowledge I gained enhanced my understanding and interpretation of the Old Testament and ancient Near Eastern literatures. It also enabled me to appreciate why Africans prefer the Old Testament to the New Testament.

Among the many close similarities which relate African tradition to the Old Testament is the affinity between the *svikiro*, 'the African spirit medium', and the *šōpēṭ*, 'judge'. There are also close connections between the *svikiro* and the early prophets of Israel. These similarities show that the role of the *svikiro* and of the *šōpēṭ* was multifarious. Both were inspired by the divine spirit; both decided cases; some of the *svikiros* and the *šōpᵉṭîm* prophesied, others led or inspired military campaigns. In other words, the 'judges' and the African spirit mediums appeared in various statuses and performed varying functions. In the book of Judges, for instance, Deborah 'judged' and prophesied but Gideon only led military campaigns. Othniel led military campaigns but Tola only 'judged'. The African and biblical charismatic leaders, according to evidence, played different roles at different times depending on the crisis and need at hand. Though outside the purview of this article, it should be pointed out that a comprehensive understanding of the multifarious usage of the root *špṭ* elucidates the appointment and varying functions of the *šōpᵉṭîm*.

Were the African Spirit Mediums 'Judges' and Prophets?

Traditionally, the Africans[1] did not believe in a dichotomy between the sacred and the profane.[2] It is appropriate to describe Africans as being notoriously religious. Their religious beliefs determined the way they conducted their political and social life. It is therefore appropriate to describe the African traditional culture as being religio-cultural.[3] The African world was regulated by an unwritten ethical code whose observance pleased the spiritual powers of the ancestral spirits and Mwari, 'God'. Mwari and the spirits were assumed to transcend the earth and the whole universe. There is nothing which humans could do which could be hidden from the ancestral spirits and from God (cf. Ps. 136). Contact with these spirits was made through the *svikiro*, the 'spirit medium', who, by proper ritual recital, went into a trance, at which point the person became possessed by the *mudzimu*, 'ancestral spirit'. If the crisis was of tribal dimensions, a spirit medium became possessed by the *mhondoro*, the tribal spirit. The spirit mediums acted as the intermediaries between the living and the ancestors who, to the Africans, continue to live or exist among humans but in spiritual 'bodies'. They are referred to in academic circles as the living dead.[4]

The people of Zimbabwe made contact with Mwari at the sacred shrines, one in Masvingo called 'The Great Zimbabwe' and another in

1.   The term African is used here to refer specifically to the black people of Zimbabwe. However, although African religions are not identical, they have many common elements. One example is the use of lots and judgment by ordeal which were used throughout Africa and the ancient Near East. These practices were employed whenever human adjudicators had failed to resolve a dispute. Lots and judgment by ordeal were a way of detecting the decision made by the spirits and by God on the case.

2.   Cf. Mircea Eliade, *The Sacred and the Profane* (New York: Harcourt, Brace & World, 1959), p. 12.

3.   T.J. Mafico, 'African Tradition and Jewish Culture', *Patterns of Prejudice*, 16.3 (1982), p. 17. See also 'The Parallels Between the Jewish and African Religio-Cultural Lives', in *Christian-Jewish Relations in Ecumenical Perspectives* (Geneva: World Council of Churches, 1978), pp. 36-47.

4.   J.S. Mbiti, *African Religions and Philosophy* (New York: Doubleday, 1969), pp. 208-16.

Matebeleland at the Motopo Hills. However, Mwari also revealed himself at various places throughout the country, for example, at Chikore Big Tree,[5] at Mount Nyanga[6] and at Chimanimani Mountain, as well as at sacred trees, streams and hills.[7] Apart from linguistic affinities, it is the allegiance to, and the worship of, Mwari which formed the basis of unity among the many tribes living in the southern region of Zimbabwe. Collectively they became known as the Shona people. The Zimbabwe shrine also promoted the development of a harmonious relationship between historically sworn enemies, the Ndebeles and the Shonas. It is the same sacred shrine which united all the black ethnic peoples to fight against racism practiced by a white minority and oppressive government of Rhodesia, as Zimbabwe was then called.

The spirit mediums were moved to ecstasy by music, drumming and dancing. Possession by the spirit happened in the following process. A person would be seized with ceaseless yawning which was followed by the shaking of the body. Ultimately, possession by the spirit would be manifested by a person falling into a trance.[8] At this point the person became possessed by the particular spirit whose message was being sought. The spirit medium would speak in the actual voice and language of that particular spirit. The *svikiro* could not speak this language without possession. Normally, the *svikiro* would not remember what was said when they recovered from the trance.

Apart from inciting the Africans to rise up against the European colonialists, the spirit mediums played other important roles. They were able to explain why a person, family, clan or tribe was faced with an inescapable predicament. Using their power of divination, the spirit mediums were also able to summon and speak with the ancestral spirits to learn of their complaints and desires. Similarly, when Saul was in serious distress because of the Philistine military threat, he too sought

---

5.   The name 'Chikore' means a 'small cloud'. Oral tradition reports that in ancient time, a small cloud was always seen in the sky above the Big Tree, manifesting God's presence at the Big Tree, whose size was unmatched troughout the region.

6.   At Nyanga, the highest mountain in Manicaland, a cloud always covers its top, adding to its aura of sacredness.

7.   When Africans read the stories of Abraham, Isaac and Jacob, for example, they are struck by the similarities of the places where theophanies were encountered.

8.   Cf. the *muḫḫutu* of Mesopotamia who went into a trance before they disclosed oracles of the gods. They are of interest to our study because of their ecstasy and general comparision with biblical ecstatic prophets. See H.B. Huffmon, 'Prophecy in Ancient Israel', *IDBSup*, p. 698.

the services of a *svikiro*. The *svikiro* at Endor was able to recall the deceased Samuel in order that he might answer the questions posed by Saul (1 Sam. 28.3-19). In addition to calling the spirits, the mediums were also capable of invoking the presence of a distant person even living overseas. By the concept of *pars pro toto*, they were able to use a person's hair, finger nails, pieces of clothing, blood, a tooth, or some soil upon which he or she stepped, to invoke the full image of the person to whom they belonged.[9] The *svikiro* would then curse the image as directed by the person's accuser. If the person whose image is at stake was innocent of any wrong doing, the curse would not stick. As a matter of fact, if the accusation stemmed from jealousy or was motivated by other forms of malice, the curse pronounced would turn into a blessing to the innocent person. Moreover, the same curse would rebound and seriously hurt the accuser.

Retribution by a curse is reminiscent of the story of Balaam, who was summoned by the Ammonites to curse the Israelites. Following sacrifice at the seven sanctuaries of Yahweh which Balaak prepared, Balaam blessed the Israelites instead of cursing them (Num. 23.5). Balaam could not avoid pronouncing these blessings because Yahweh had put words of blessings into his mouth (cf. Jer. 1.7). Balaam was simply a spokesperson of Yahweh, speaking divine words which he could not restrain (Num. 23.7-11).

The similarities between African spirit mediums and early biblical prophets are striking. In 1 Sam. 10.5-13, Saul's sign that God had anointed him to be a *nāgîd*, a military leader, was that he would meet a band of prophets carrying musical instruments: a harp, tambourine, flute and lyre. Apparently they were playing them and dancing to the music. When Saul encountered these prophets, the *rwḥ yhwh*, 'the spirit of Yahweh', possessed him and he too prophesied to the amazement of those who had known him before as a normal person. They exclaimed, 'What has come of the son of Kish? Is Saul also among the prophets?' (1 Sam. 10.11b-12). This prophetic ecstatic behavior is reminiscent of the *svikiros* who went into a trance by the playing of drums, dancing and singing. The assertion that the *svikiros* were prophets is enhanced by the deuteronomistic admission that a *rō'eh*, a seer, that is, a clairvoyant, was, at a later time, referred to as a *nby'*,

9. Cf. Henri Frankfurt, *The Intellectual Adventure of Ancient Man* (Chicago: Chicago University Press, 1946), pp. 12-15.

'prophet' (1 Sam. 9.20; 10.2). What changed was the name, not the form and practice of the seers.

It is significant, therefore, that the African spirit medium and the biblical seer (*rō'eh*) were possessed by the spirit (*rwḥ*) during the singing and dancing accompanied with the playing of musical instruments. Textual evidence in 1 Samuel shows that it is when they were spirit possessed that clairvoyants became prophetic and predicted things. Some 'judges' like Deborah and Samuel were able to disclose hidden things exactly in the same way the *svikiro* used to do in Africa. Deborah foretold that the credit for killing Sisera would go to a woman, Jael, and not to Barak, Israel's army commander (Judg. 4.9). Similarly, Samuel disclosed to Saul that the donkeys he was seeking had been found and that his father was then worrying about him (1 Sam. 9.20). Although he is presented as an individual, Samuel was the leader of a prophetic guild (1 Sam. 19.20-24). At any rate, when the Israelites were about to attack the garrison of the Philistines at Aphek, Saul sought the oracle of Yahweh by dreams and prophets. Having failed to get an answer, he resorted to a woman spirit medium at Endor. She was able to bring Samuel up from the dead to answer his questions (1 Sam. 28.3-25).

The African spirit mediums functioned in a way similar to the role which Samuel and Deborah played in Israel. They declared the oracle of God when the land was confronted with disasters such as severe droughts and pestilence. They also determined whether the tribe should go to war and what strategies were to be employed to win it (cf. 1 Kgs 22.6). There are other functions in which the African spirit mediums were like the *šōpᵉṭîm*, the so-called biblical 'judges'. They settled disputes among the people by declaring to the evil doers what would befall them if they did not comply with the correct social norms. The *svikiro* could also impose a fine to settle the dispute, particularly in cases where one party suffered loss by the criminal behavior of another. The *svikiros* also disclosed where to find lost property and diagnosed the cause of an illness. They also directed the appropriate sacrifice to be performed to placate the ancestral spirits and God. Some spirit mediums were responsible for offering a sacrifice before the tribe could engage an enemy in battle (cf. 1 Sam. 13.8-12).

A more lucid similarity between the *svikiro* and the *šōpēṭ* is demonstrated by their roles in military matters. In 1883 the Shona spirit medium Chaminuka protected the Shonas by predicting the Ndebele military intrigue. He also predicted that Lobengula, the king of the

Ndebeles, would lose his land to the whites, a reality which came true soon afterwards.[10] In the 1980s, the spirit mediums played a decisive role in the liberation of Zimbabwe by rousing the Africans who had accepted colonialism and oppression as their unshakable lot in life to rise up and fight. Thus, after seventy years of oppression, the Africans of Zimbabwe, in their diverse ethnic groups—the Ndau, Manyika, Karanga, Ndebele, to name the major ones—united and ridded themselves of white oppression. Like the Israelites during the time of the 'judges', the Africans seriously believed that they were fighting a 'holy' war led by Mwari, God. Their assurance that this was a divine war was based on the fact that when the whites were ruling, Rhodesia experienced the worst drought in the Africans' memory. According to the spiritual mediums, the whites had neglected 'making peace with the land'.[11] For this reason, the spirit mediums told the Africans that it was the will of God that they drive out the whites but keep their property, which they would dedicate as an offering to Mwari.[12] The belief in God, inspired by the African spirit mediums, was instrumental in maintaining their military morale in spite of serious set backs which they initially faced during the wars of Zimbabwe's liberation.

The 'Judges': Their Status and Functions

The controversy posed by the enigmatic usage of the root *špt* and the title *šōpēṭ* in the book of Judges has been the focus of several scholars.[13]

10. T.O. Ranger, *Revolt in Southern Rhodesia 1896-7: A Study in African Residence* (London: Heinemann, 1967), p. 4.

11. T.O. Ranger, *Revolt in Southern Rhodesia*, p. 147. Cf. Amos's reference about why Israel was experiencing a drought and pests (Amos 4.4-10). Cf. also the Assyrians' complaint to their king about the danger of vicious lions which were encountered in Israel. They asked that priests should be sent with them to Israel who knew the *mišpāṭ 'elōhê hā'āreṣ*, 'the customs of the land' (2 Kgs 17.26; cf. 1 Kgs 18.18).

12. This brings to mind the answer Saul gave to Samuel, that he had saved some of the animals and the loot under the ban becuse he wanted to sacrifice them to Yahweh (1 Sam. 15.13-15).

13. E.A. Speiser, 'The Manner of the King', in *Judges: The World History of the Jewish People* (New Jersey: Rutgers University Press, 1971), p. 280; H. Fergusson, '*špt*', *JBL* 8 (1988), p. 131; P. Jensen, '*šāpiṭum, mišpāṭ und mišpāṭîm)*', *ZAW* 4 (1889), pp. 278-80; L.W. Batten, 'The use of *mišpāṭ*', *JBL* 11 (1892), 206-10; G.F. Moore, *Judges* (ICC, 7; Edinburgh: T. & T. Clark, 1895), pp. xi-xiii.

Using a contextual method of interpreting the root *špṭ* and with limited utilization of extrabiblical sources, the majority of scholars have been convinced by Grether's argument that the 'judges' function was that of delivering the Israelites from enemy oppression. He therefore suggested the title *môšîᵃ‘*, 'savior' or 'deliverer', as being more appropriate for the premonarchical leaders who commanded Israel's battles than the title *šōpēṭ*.[14] The substitution of *šōpēṭ* by *m ô šîᵃ‘*, however, raises more difficult questions than it answers. The immediate question which arises is, If the so-called judges of the book of Judges should be regarded as *môšᵉ‘îm*, who then were the people designated by the title *šōpᵉṭîm*? What was their particular function in Israel? How were they appointed, and by whom? Could two or more *šōpᵉṭîm* be in office at the same time? Could *šōpᵉṭîm* appoint members of their families to succeed them? The difficulty in answering these questions indicates that although the title *môšᵉ‘îm* is suitable for the military *šōpᵉṭîm* such as Othniel (Judg. 3.7-11), Ehud (3.12-30), Deborah (4.1–5.31), Jephthah[15] (10.6–12.7), and the legendary 'judge' Samson[16] (13.1–16.31), it does not include those *šōpᵉṭîm* who are simply mentioned but with no specific roles which they played. These *šōpᵉṭîm* are Tola (10.1-2), Jair (10.3-5), Ibzan (12.8-9), Elon (12.11-12), and Abdon (12.13-15).[17] Scholars have tried to reconcile the discrepancy regarding the status of these *šōpᵉṭîm* b y offering several hypotheses.

Alt suggested that a distinction should be made between two types of *šōpᵉṭîm*: 'the major' and 'minor judges'. He based this suggestion on the fact that the book of Judges presents two types of *šōpᵉṭîm*: the military

14. O. Grether, 'Richter', p. 120; cf. T. Ishida, '*Šôpᵉṭ, Šôpᵉṭîm*', *Rekishi-Jinrui* 5 (Annual of History-Anthropology Cluster of Tsukuba University, 1978), pp. 29-38 (Japanese).

15. Scholars like Noth see him as belonging to both the so-called 'major' and 'minor judges'.

16. His pursuits are more personal vendettas against the Philistines and not representative of the Israelites' own military campaigns against the Philistines and other enemies.

17. M. Noth in an article, 'Das Amt des Richters Israels', in *Festschrift Alfred Bertholet* (Tübingen: J.C.B. Mohr, 1950), p. 407; *Überlieferungsgeschichtliche Studien*, I (Tübingen: Niemeyer, 1943), pp. 47-50, postulated that the real 'judges' of Israel were the so-called 'minor judges'. The connection between the 'minor' and the 'major judges' was achieved by the deuteronomistic insertion of the story of Jephthah in the middle. Jephthah, Noth assumed, belonged to both categories of the *šōpᵉṭîm*.

hero-leaders and those leaders who were not associated with any military pursuits. On the basis of their functions, he categorized the military heroes as 'major judges' and the latter as 'minor judges'.[18] Since the 'major judges' played their military roles pursuant to their endowment with the spirit of Yahweh, Alt regarded them as charismatic leaders.[19] The thorny problem which he then confronted was to identify the office and function of the 'minor judges'. Basing his inquiry on an erroneous assumption that the root *špṭ* basically meant 'to judge' in the sense of conducting Israel's wars, Alt was puzzled to find that,

> The minor judges, on the other hand, have no connections with military functions or authority of this sort. In fact the only thing that is recorded of any of them, apart from his home and the site of his grave, is the stereotyped phrase 'He judged Israel'.[20]

Ergo, Alt assumed that the non-military *šōpᵉṭîm* were responsible for reciting and teaching the law to the people of Israel.

Noth agreed with Alt and pointed out that the book of Judges was made up of two complexes of traditions. The first tradition was about the charismatic or 'major judges' and the other complex was based on the traditional official records dealing with the 'minor judges'. The redactional means by which these two traditions were fused was devised by the deuteronomistic historian who used the story of Jephthah (Judg. 12.7), a *šōpēṭ* who appears as a 'minor judge', but one whose tradition is recorded separately.[21] Noth argued that the use of Jephthah as a bridge between the 'major' and 'minor judges' enabled the application of the title *šōpēṭ*, 'judge', on both groups. Otherwise, according to his hypothesis, there is no basis for the charismatic military heroes to be called *šōpᵉṭîm*. Moreover, according to the Alt-Noth school, the original function of the 'minor judges' was one of deciding cases. But the office of the 'minor judges' as administrators of justice was complicated by the fact that, *sensu stricto*, it was the *zᵉqēnîm* at the gate who functioned as legal administrators.[22] Noth therefore felt that it was far more likely that

18. Albrecht Alt, *Essays on Old Testament History and Religion* (Garden City, NY: Doubleday, 1966), p. 130.

19. Alt, *Essays*, pp. 231-32.

20. Alt, *Essays*, pp. 131-32.

21. M. Noth, 'Richters Israels', pp. 47-50.

22. Noth, *The History of Israel* (New York: Harper & Row, 1959), p. 102.

the central judicial office of Israel was related to the law that was valid in
the whole of Israel, the divine law to which Israel was subject and which
had to be regularly proclaimed anew...the 'judge' of Israel was the one
who had to know and interpret it and give information about it.[23]

The 'judge' had to see to it that the law was observed and perhaps had
himself to proclaim it in public. His duty was to apply the law to new
situations, thereby assuming responsibility for its development. He constantly instructed the tribes about the meaning and application of its
individual clauses.[24] The authenticity of the office of the 'minor judges',
Noth went on, is evident in the fact that their tenures in office are not
expressed in round figures, as are those of the 'major judges' which are
in multiples of ten.[25] Noth further speculated that during the period of
the tribal confederation there existed two legal administrative systems.
The first was the legal system which was concerned with the admin-
istration of justice. This was administered by the $z^e q \bar{e} n \hat{\imath} m$ at the gate. The
$\check{s} \bar{o} p^e \hat{\imath} m$, on the other hand, were responsible for reading and interpreting
the divine law. The forum at which they proclaimed the law was the
central Israelite shrine when annually, the Israelites, besides performing
some annual ceremonies, also came to hear the recitation of the divine
law. Because of the lack of biblical evidence attesting the performance of
sacrifices at the beginning of the Israelite national epic, Noth surmised
that the recitation of the law was of central importance. Since no
functionary was assigned to the recitation of this law, he assigned it to
the $\check{s} \bar{o} p^e \hat{\imath} m$. As he put it,

> From the very beginning then, Israel's speciality did not consist in a par-
> ticular and unique form of worship at the central shrine but in the fact that
> it was subject to a divine law which was recited at the tribal gatherings at
> regular intervals and to which Israel committed itself in constantly
> renewed acts of affirmation. This is consonant with the fact that the only
> office for all Israel explicitly mentioned in the oldest Old Testament tradi-
> tions was not a priestly but a judicial one.[26]

Noth added that, 'The older tradition knew only the minor judges as the
judges of Israel, and to them alone does the title judge properly apply, in
accordance with the traditional material.'[27] From the list of 'judges',

23. Noth, *History*, pp. 102-103.
24. Noth, *History*, p. 103.
25. Noth, *History*, p. 103.
26. Noth, *History*, p. 101.
27. Noth, *History*, p. 101.

Noth pointed out that there was conclusive evidence of an authentic list and chronology of the *šōpᵉṭîm*. He saw them as occupying the office of judge one man at a time.[28] He trusted the material because it seemed to be based on official records. He concluded his discussion of this subject by pointing out that if his reconstruction, based on records in the book of Judges, is correct, then the central shrine to which the twelve tribes came annually, played a decisive role in the association. Noth admitted, however, that his reconstruction of the period of the judges and the speculation on their function left more questions unanswered. For instance, he asked,

> Were the judges who came from quite different tribes in an apparently irregular succession, elected from time to time by the tribes?... Or was the choice left to a divine decision which was obtained by drawing lots at the central shrine?[29]

Alt and Noth's discussion of the 'judges', albeit brilliant, well-developed, and plausible, is problematic for several reasons. It is primarily based on a hypothetical premise. The moment the hypothesis is proved to be futile, then their whole structure of the Israelite premonarchical administration collapses, allowing the question of the *šōpᵉṭîm* to peak once again. The tenuous nature of Noth's evidence is clearly reflected throughout his discussion.[30] While he admitted that the whole book of Judges had been edited by the deuteronomist to reflect a theological perspective of a much later time, he maintained that it was still possible to retrieve those passages which reflected the *šōpᵉṭîm*'s administration of the divine law during the period of the amphictyony (*sic*).

In spite of the problems of, and the hypothetical nature of, the Alt-Noth reconstruction of the appointment and function of the *šōpᵉṭîm*, it is quite intriguing that several notable scholars have adopted it and have freely used the categorization of the *šōpᵉṭîm* into 'major' and 'minor judges'. They regard the 'major judges' as being those who engaged in

28. Noth, *History*, pp. 102-103.
29. Noth (*History*, p. 102) in a note compared this election by lot to the election of Saul by lots in 1 Sam. 10.19b-21. He admits that this reference is of a late date. He cited also Josh. 7.16-18. These references, according to Noth, proved that the practice of election by lots was known in Israel.
30. There is too much use of these terms 'apparently', 'seems', 'probably', and several others; terms which reveal that the writer was aware that his thesis was not based on biblical evidence. See especially Noth's discussion in *History*, pp. 100-102.

military campaigns and the 'minor judges' as those who were associated with no specific duties.[31] This hypothetical solution to a very complex biblical problem regarding the functions of the *šōpᵉṭîm* has only compounded the problem. Commenting on these so-called 'minor judges' in Judg. 10.1-5, the scholars who translated the RSV stated that, 'The role played by the so-called "minor judges"...is one of the puzzles of the book, since they were apparently not leaders in war.'[32] The assumption underlying this statement is that, basically, the *šōpᵉṭîm* were military leaders. The categorization of the *šōpᵉṭîm* into 'major' and 'minor judges' can no longer be sustained in the light of evidence derived from extrabiblical literature and from the biblical texts outside the book of Judges. The Mari documents attest that the function of the *šāpiṭūtu* of Mari were, in most cases, exactly the same as those of the *šōpᵉṭîm* of the Old Testament.

The usage of the root *špṭ* in Judges and in other biblical books like Samuel and Kings shows that the biblical title *šōpᵉṭîm* was not restricted to military commanders who delivered the Israelites from enemy oppression. The stories of Deborah (Judg. 4.4-5) and Samuel (1 Sam. 7.15) reveal that these two leaders were regarded as *šōpᵉṭîm* primarily because they both decided (*špṭ*) civil cases just like the *dayyānum*, 'professional court judges' did in Mesopotamia.[33] The Mari texts attest that there was no clear cut distinction between the *dayyānum* and the *šāpiṭum* in their performance of the role of administrating justice in civil cases.

In early Israel, however, the office of the *dayyān* does not seem to have existed. The reason for its apparent absence should be attributed to the fact that the office of the *šōpᵉṭîm* was more suitable for the time of the Israelites' semi-nomadic culture than it was for the time of the monarchy. In pre-monarchical Israel most of the legal functions were carried out by the *zᵉqēnîm*, and serious ones, perhaps, were referred to the *šōpēṭ*. That a *šōpēṭ* in Israel performed the same legal function as did a *dayyānûm* in Mari is demonstrated by the fact that the root *dyn* is rarely used in the Old Testament, especially in the earlier texts. Whenever it is employed elsewhere, it is often placed in synonymous

---

31. C.U. Wolf, 'Judge', IDB (New York: Abingdon), pp. 1012-13.

32. *The Oxford Annotated Bible*, RSV (1962). See note on p. 308. Although these scholars were familiar with the Alt-Noth hypothesis, they still returned to the traditionally held view that a *šōpēṭ* was a *môšîaᵃ*.

33. T.J. Mafico, 'Judge/Judging', ABD 3, pp. 1104; 1106.

parallelism with *špṭ*. This is the case in poetic texts where the usage supports the assertion that the *šōpᵉṭîm* were adjudicators in Israel.[34] Thus a *šōpēṭ* played many roles in Israel among which was the administration of justice to maintain or restore peace in the land.

In the book of Judges, the *šōpᵉṭîm* were viewed as the agents of Yahweh, the king of Israel (Judg. 8.22-23; 9.23; 1 Sam. 8.7; Isa. 33.32). Thus the *šōpᵉṭîm* in Judges were accountable to Yahweh for all the decisions they made and for the role they played. The Israelites were, therefore, expected to administer justice equitably because they were doing it on behalf of Yahweh (cf. Deut. 1.16-17). Besides their decisive roles in military and judiciary functions, the *šōpᵉṭîm* also functioned as religious leaders.[35] In Judg. 2.16-19 we read:

> And Yahweh raised *šōpᵉṭîm* and they saved them (the Israelites) from the hand of their oppressors. But to the *šōpᵉṭîm* they did not pay attention because they went whoring after other gods (*'elōhîm 'aḥērîm*) and worshipped them; they turned away from the way of their ancestors. As for the observance of the commandments of Yahweh, they did not do thus. But when Yahweh raised the *šōpᵉṭîm* for them, Yahweh was with the *šōpēṭ*, and he saved them from the hand of their enemies all the days of the *šōpēṭ*; because Yahweh became compassionate by their groaning on account of those who afflicted them and oppressed them. But when the *šōpēṭ* died, they turned back and behaved worse than their ancestors, going after other gods (*'elōhîm 'aḥērîm*) to serve them and to worship them; they did not drop from their usual practices nor from their stubborn ways.

Several points raised in this passage need to be highlighted in order to clarify the context in which the root *špṭ* is used. It is quite clear that the deuteronomistic historian is making a general summary of what Yahweh did to save Israel during the pre-monarchical period. In God's graciousness (*ynḥm Yhwh*), Yahweh appointed the *šōpᵉṭîm* to deliver Israel from enemy oppression (Judg. 2.19).[36] However, the Israelites did not always

---

34. Jer. 21.12; 22.15-16; cf. *Corpus des tablettes en cunéiformes alphabétiques decouvertes à Ras Shamra-Ugarit de 1929 à 1939* (A. Herdner [ed.]; Mission de Ras Shamra 10; 2 vols.; Paris: Imprimerie Nationale, 1963), 16.6.46; 17.5.8, etc.

35. In peace time, it is strongly implied that the military *šōpᵉṭîm*, perhaps due to the great prestige they had acquired by leading the Israelites to victory against their enemies, spent the rest of their lives administering justice among the people.

36. Judg 2.19; cf. CTA 5.6.11-14; 14.1.35-43, where *'il* is described as *ltpn 'il d p'id*, 'the kindly one', *'il* 'the Compassionate' (see F.M. Cross, *Canaanite Myth and Hebrew Epic* [Cambridge, MA: Harvard University Press, 1973], p. 19).

observe the commandments of Yahweh because they sinned more than their ancestors.[37] According to the deuteronomistic historian, the worst sin the Israelites committed was to worship the *'elōhîm 'aḥerîm*, 'the other gods.' Thus verse 19 reveals the stubbornness of the Israelites who persistently succumbed to the temptation of worshipping other gods instead of Yahweh, the *'elōhê hā'ābôt*.

To underscore the *šōpᵉṭîm*'s dependence on Yahweh's rulership, the deuteronomist presents them as commanding Israel's armies only after their endowment with the *rûaḥ yhwh*. It is not stated in Judges how the non-military *šōpᵉṭîm* were appointed, but it is clear in Exodus 18:13-23 that they were people of integrity, possessing some unusual gifts.[38]

Summary and Conclusion

There are several features of the *šōpᵉṭîm* and the African spirit mediums which are very similar. In the book of Judges the *šōpᵉṭîm* were leaders who were filled with the spirit of God. It is that spirit which enabled them to lead in military campaigns and also to predict victory. Apparently they also admonished the Israelites to observe the commandments of God, because, during their tenure in office, the Israelites refrained from following after the *'elōhîm 'aḥerîm*, 'the other gods'. It was following the death of a *šōpēṭ* that the Israelites did what was evil in the sight of God, by forgetting Yahweh and serving other gods (Judg. 2.11; 3.7).

Some *šōpᵉṭîm*, for example Deborah and Samuel, wielded much authority and influence among the Israelites. They rendered their services in permanent centers which were widely known to the Israelites. For their services, especially in matters of divination, the *šōpᵉṭîm* received small gifts (1 Sam. 9.7-8). Apparently, when kingship emerged in Israel, a power struggle seems to have developed between Saul and the mediums. This struggle for influence may account for the reason why Saul banned the mediums. It is not clear who these mediums were and what functions they performed. They are not mentioned in the book of Judges. We only hear about them when they are banned by king Saul

37. This is a deuteronomistic formula which is also used to summarize the reigns of several kings (e.g. 1 Kgs 14.22; 16.25; 2 Chron. 33.9, 23).

38. This point is clarified by Moses who was advised to choose people of integrity and religious conviction and appoint them as *śārîm* who would 'judge' the people (Exod. 18.13-27).

when the era of the *šōpᵉṭîm* comes to a charismatic end. It is, therefore, reasonable to assume that the mediums might have formerly been called *šōpᵉṭîm* or *rō'îm*, 'seers'. That they went underground when Saul banned them is manifested by the fact that when Saul wanted to consult one, the Israelites were able to inform him of the medium at Endor (1 Sam. 28.7).

The African spirit mediums (*svikiros*), like the biblical *šōpᵉṭîm*, arbitrated in civil cases. Many people walked very long distances to consult the most famous *svikiros* whose oracles were more trustworthy. Normally, the *svikiros* would receive a gift for their services. They did not charge a fee since they were rendering the decision of the spirits and of God.

The *svikiros* interpreted the signs and warned the people if there was a breach of the norms and customs by an individual or by the community. The *svikiros* could appropriately be regarded as guardians of justice in Africa just like the *šōpᵉṭîm* in Judges and later, the *nᵉbî'îm*, 'prophets' who succeeded them. When there was a crisis of tribal or national proportions in the land, the tribal chief would summon the people to congregate. The *svikiro* would be consulted to disclose what was displeasing the spirits and to declare what was to be done to placate them. The *svikiros* also encouraged the Africans to rise against the white governments for several reasons, one of which was that the whites disregarded the norms of the people and the customs of the land.

The leadership of the African spirit mediums so parallels that of the biblical *šōpᵉṭîm* that there is justification for the question, 'Were the biblical *šōpᵉṭîm* like the African spirit mediums?' This question will be the focus of intense study in the years ahead. Meanwhile, it is fascinating to realize that there are many allusions to African tradition in the Old Testament, a fact which explains why Africans find the Old Testament to be more appealing than the New Testament.

INDEXES

INDEX OF REFERENCES

OLD TESTAMENT

NEW TESTAMENT

INDEX OF AUTHORS

THE BIBLICAL SEMINAR

Supplement Series